Routledge Revivals

The Coventry Leet Book or Mayor's Register

The Coventry Leet Book or Mayor's Register

Containing the records of the city Court Leet or View of frankpledge, A.D. 1420-1555 with divers other matters

Mary Dormer Harris

Routledge
Taylor & Francis Group

First published in 1907 for The Early English Text Society by
Kegan Paul, Trench, Trübner & Co., Ltd.

This edition first published in 2018 by Routledge
2 Park Square, Milton Park, Abingdon, Oxon, OX14 4RN
and by Routledge
711 Third Avenue, New York, NY 10017

Routledge is an imprint of the Taylor & Francis Group, an informa business

© 1907 by Taylor & Francis

All rights reserved. No part of this book may be reprinted or reproduced or utilised in any form or by any electronic, mechanical, or other means, now known or hereafter invented, including photocopying and recording, or in any information storage or retrieval system, without permission in writing from the publishers.

Publisher's Note
The publisher has gone to great lengths to ensure the quality of this reprint but points out that some imperfections in the original copies may be apparent.

Disclaimer
The publisher has made every effort to trace copyright holders and welcomes correspondence from those they have been unable to contact.

A Library of Congress record exists under ISBN: 7029021

ISBN 13: 978-1-138-60483-4 (hbk)

ISBN 13: 978-1-138-60484-1 (pbk)

ISBN 13: 978-0-429-46273-3 (ebk)

Early English Text Society.

Original Series, 134.

The Coventry Leet Book:

OR

Mayor's Register,

CONTAINING THE RECORDS OF THE CITY

Court Leet

OR

View of Frankpledge,

A.D. 1420–1555,

WITH DIVERS OTHER MATTERS.

TRANSCRIBED AND EDITED BY

MARY DORMER HARRIS,

AUTHOR OF "LIFE IN AN OLD ENGLISH TOWN: A HISTORY OF COVENTRY COMPILED FROM OFFICIAL RECORDS."

PART I.

LONDON:

PUBLISHED FOR THE EARLY ENGLISH TEXT SOCIETY

BY KEGAN PAUL, TRENCH, TRÜBNER & CO., LIMITED,

DRYDEN HOUSE, 43, GERRARD STREET, SOHO, W.

1907.

Price Fifteen Shillings.

Early English Text Society.

Committee of Management:

Director: DR. FREDERICK J. FURNIVALL, M.A.

Treasurer: HENRY B. WHEATLEY, Esq.

Hon. Sec.: W. A. DALZIEL, Esq., 67 VICTORIA ROAD, FINSBURY PARK, N

Hon. Secs. for America: North & East: Prof. G. L. KITTREDGE, Harvard Coll., Cambr., Mass
South & West: Prof. J. W. BRIGHT, Johns Hopkins Univ., Baltimor

LORD ALDENHAM, M.A. | PROF. NAPIER, M.A., PH.D.
REV. DR. ANDREW CLARK, M.A. | EDWARD B. PEACOCK, Esq.
PROF. ISRAEL GOLLANCZ, D.LIT. | ALFRED W. POLLARD, M.A.
SIDNEY L. LEE, M.A., D.LIT. | REV. PROF. WALTER W. SKEAT, LITT.I
HENRY LITTLEHALES, Esq. | DR. HENRY SWEET, M.A.
REV. PROF. J. E. B. MAYOR, M.A. | DR. W. ALDIS WRIGHT, M.A.
DR. J. A. H. MURRAY, M.A.

(*With power to add Workers to their number.*)

Bankers:

THE UNION OF LONDON AND SMITH'S BANK, 2, PRINCES STREET, E.C

THE Early English Text Society was started by Dr. Furnivall in 1864 for tl purpose of bringing the mass of Old English Literature within the reach of tl ordinary student, and of wiping away the reproach under which England had lon rested, of having felt little interest in the monuments of her early language and life.

On the starting of the Society, so many Texts of importance were at once taken hand by its Editors, that it became necessary in 1867 to open, besides the *Origin Series* with which the Society began, an *Extra Series* which should be mainly devot to fresh editions of all that is most valuable in printed MSS. and Caxton's and otl black-letter books, though first editions of MSS. will not be excluded when the cc venience of issuing them demands their inclusion in the Extra Series.

During the forty-three years of the Society's existence, it has produced, wi whatever shortcomings, and at a cost of over £30,000, an amount of good solid wo for which all students of our Language, and some of our Literature, must be gratef and which has rendered possible the beginnings (at least) of proper Histories a: Dictionaries of that Language and Literature, and has illustrated the thoughts, t life, the manners and customs of our forefathers and foremothers.

But the Society's experience has shown the very small number of those inheritc of the speech of Cynewulf, Chaucer, and Shakspere, who care two guineas a year the records of that speech. 'Let the dead past bury its dead' is still the cry of Gre Britain and her Colonies, and of America, in the matter of language. The Society h never had money enough to produce the Texts that could easily have been got read for it; and many Editors are now anxious to send to press the work they have pre pared. The necessity has therefore arisen for trying to increase the number of th Society's members, and to induce its well-wishers to help it by gifts of money, eithe in one sum or by instalments. The Committee trust that every Member will brin before his or her friends and acquaintances the Society's claims for liberal suppor Until all Early English MSS. are printed, no proper History of our Language or Socia Life is possible.

The Subscription to the Society, which constitutes membership, is £1 1s. a yea for the ORIGINAL SERIES, and £1 1s. for the EXTRA SERIES, due in advance on the 1st c JANUARY, and should be paid by Cheque, Postal Order, or Money-Order, crost 'Unio of London and Smith's Bank,' to the Hon. Secretary, W. A. DALZIEL, Esq., 67, Victori Rd., Finsbury Park, London, N. Members who want their Texts posted to them must add to their prepaid Subscriptions 1s. for the Original Series, and 1s. for th Extra Series, yearly. The Society's Texts are also sold separately at the prices pu after them in the Lists; but Members can get back-Texts at one-third less than th List-prices by sending the cash for them in advance to the Hon. Secretary.

☞ The Society intends to complete, as soon as its funds will allow, the Reprints of its out-of-print Texts of the year 1866, and also of nos. 20, 26, and 33. Dr. Otto Glauning has undertaken *Seinte Marherete;* and Dr. Furnivall has *Hali Meidenhad* in type. As the cost of these Reprints, if they were not needed, would have been devoted to fresh Texts, the Reprints will be sent to all Members in lieu of such Texts. Though called 'Reprints,' these books are new editions, generally with valuable additions, a fact not noticed by a few careless receivers of them, who have complained that they already had the volumes.

June 1907. A gratifying gift is to be made to the Society. The American owner of the unique MS. of the Works of John Metham—whose Romance of Amoryus and Cleopar was sketcht by Dr. Furnivall in his new edition of *Political, Religious and Love Poems,* No. 15 in the Society's Original Series—has promist to give the Society an edition of his MS. prepared by Dr. Hardin Craig of Princeton, and it will be issued this year as No. 132 of the Original Series. The giver hopes that his example may be followed by other folk, as the support hitherto given to the Society is so far below that which it deserves.

The Original-Series Texts for 1906 were No. 130, Part II of the englishing, ab. 1450 A.D., of the Deeds in the *Register of Godstow Nunnery*, edited from the unique MSS. by the Rev. Andrew Clark, LL.D.; No. 131, *The Brut*, or *The Chronicles of England*, edited from the best MSS. by Dr. F. Brie, Part I.; No. 132, *John Metham's Works* mentiond above will probably be issued in 1907 for 1906.

The Original-Series Texts for 1907 will be, No. 133, Part I of the *English Register of Oseney Abbey, by Oxford*, edited by the Rev. Andrew Clark, LL.D., already issued, and No. 134, Part I of the *Coventry Leet Book*, copied and edited for the Society by Miss M. Dormer Harris—helpt by a contribution from the Common Council of the City:—it will be publisht by the Society as its contribution to our knowledge of the provincial city life of the 15th century.

Among the Texts for 1908 and 1909 will be Part II of *The Brut;* Part III of the *Alphabet of Tales*, edited by Mrs. M. M. Banks; Part III of the *English Register of Godstow Nunnery;* Part II of the *English Register of Oseney Abbey*, edited by the Rev. Dr. Andrew Clark, and Part II of the *Coventry Leet Book*, copied and edited by Miss M. Dormer Harris. Future Texts will be Part III of Robert of Brunne's *Handlyng Synne*, edited by Dr. Furnivall, with a Glossary of Wm. of Wadington's French words in his *Manuel des Pechez*, and comments on them, by Mr. Dickson-Brown; Part II of the *Exeter Book*—Anglo-Saxon Poems from the unique MS. in Exeter Cathedral—re-edited by Israel Gollancz, M.A.; Part II of Prof. Dr. Holthausen's *Vices and Virtues;* Part II of *Jacob's Well*, edited by Dr. Brandeis; the Alliterative *Siege of Jerusalem*, edited by the late Prof. Dr. E. Kölbing and Prof. Dr. Kaluza; an Introduction and Glossary to the *Minor Poems of the Vernon MS.* by H. Hartley, M.A.; Alain Chartier's *Quadrilogue*, edited from the unique MS. Univ. Coll. Oxford MS. No. 85, by Prof. J. W. H. Atkins. Canon Wordsworth of Marlborough has given the Society a copy of the Leofric Canonical Rule, Latin and Anglo-Saxon, Parker MS. 191, C. C. C. Cambridge, and Prof. Napier will edit it, with a fragment of the englisht Capitula of Bp. Theodulf: it is now at press.

The Extra-Series Texts for 1906 are to be No. XCVII, *Lydgate's Troy Book*, edited from the best MSS. by Dr. Hy. Bergen, Part I; No. XCVIII, *Skelton's Magnificence*, edited by Dr. R. L. Ramsay, with a special Introduction; No. XCIX, *The Romance of Emare*, re-edited by Miss Edith Rickert, Ph.D.

Further Extra-Series Texts for 1907, &c., will be *The Harrowing of Hell*, four parallel Texts, re-edited by Prof. Hulme, with an Introduction tracing the history of the Legend from the East; *Lydgate's Troy Book*, Parts II and III, edited by Dr. Hy. Bergen; *Ballads and Carols* from Jn. Hyde's Balliol MS., edited by Dr. R. Dyboski; *The Owl and Nightingale*, two parallel Texts, edited by Mr. G. F. H. Sykes; Dr. Erbe's re-edition of *Mirk's Festial*, Part II; Dr. M. Konrath's re-edition of *William of Shoreham's Poems*, Part II; Prof. Erdmann's re-edition of Lydgate's *Siege of Thebes* (issued also by the Chaucer Society); Prof. I. Gollancz's re-edition of two Alliterative Poems, *Winner and Waster*, &c., ab. 1360; Dr. Norman Moore's re-edition of *The Book of the Foundation of St. Bartholomew's Hospital, London*, from the unique MS. ab. 1425, which gives an account of the Founder, Rahere, and the miraculous cures wrought at the Hospital; *The Craft of Nombrynge*, with other of the earliest englisht Treatises on Arithmetic, edited by R. Steele, B.A.; and Miss Warren's two-text edition of *The Dance of Death* from the Ellesmere and other MSS.

These Extra-Series Texts ought to be completed by their Editors: the Second Part of the prose Romance of *Melusine*—Introduction, with ten facsimiles of the best woodblocks of the old foreign black-letter editions, Glossary, &c., by A. K. Donald, B.A. (now in India); and a new edition of the famous Early-English Dictionary (English and Latin), *Promptorium Parvulorum*, from the Winchester MS., ab. 1440 A.D.: in this, the Editor, the Rev. A. L. Mayhew, M.A., will follow and print his MS. not only in its arrangement of nouns first, and verbs second, under every letter of the Alphabet, but also in its giving of the flexions of the words. The Society's edition will thus be the first modern one that really represents its original, a point on which Mr. Mayhew's insistence will meet with the sympathy of all our Members.

Later Texts for the Extra Series will include *The Three Kings' Sons*, Part II, the Introduction, &c., by Prof. Dr. Leon Kellner; Part II of *The Chester Plays*, re-edited from the MSS., with a full collation of the formerly missing Devonshire MS., by Mr. G. England and Dr. Matthews; Prof. Jespersen's editions of John Hart's *Orthographie* (MS. 1551 A.D. blackletter 1569), and *Method to teach Reading*, 1570; Deguilleville's *Pilgrimage of th Sowle*, in English prose, edited by Prof. Dr. L. Kellner. (For the three prose version of *The Pilgrimage of the Life of Man*—two English, one French—an Editor is wanted. Members are askt to realise the fact that the Society has now 50 years' work on its Lists,—at its present rate of production,—and that there is from 100 to 200 more years' work t come after that. The year 2000 will not see finisht all the Texts that the Society ought t print. The need of more Members and money is pressing. Offers of help from willin Editors have continually to be declined because the Society has no funds to print their Text.

An urgent appeal is hereby made to Members to increase the list of Subscribers to th E. E. Text Society. It is nothing less than a scandal that the Hellenic Society should hav nearly 1000 members, while the Early English Text Society has not 300!

Before his death in 1895, Mr. G. N. Currie was preparing an edition of the 15th and 16th century Prose Versions of Guillaume de Deguilleville's *Pilgrimage of the Life of Man*, with the French prose version by Jean Gallopes, from Lord Aldenham's MS., he having generously promist to pay the extra cost of printing the French text, and engraving one or two of the illuminations in his MS. But Mr. Currie, when on his deathbed, charged a friend to burn *all* his MSS. which lay in a corner of his room, and unluckily all the E. E. T. S.'s copies of the Deguilleville prose versions were with them, and were burnt with them, so that the Society will be put to the cost of fresh copies, Mr. Currie having died in debt.

Guillaume de Deguilleville, monk of the Cistercian abbey of Chaalis, in the diocese o Senlis, wrote his first verse *Pèlerinaige de l'Homme* in 1330-1 when he was 36.[1] Twenty-fiv (or six) years after, in 1355, he revised his poem, and issued a second version of it,[2] a revisio of which was printed ab. 1500. Of the prose representative of the first version, 1330-1 a prose Englishing, about 1430 A.D., was edited by Mr. Aldis Wright for the Roxburghe Clu in 1869, from MS. Ff. 5. 30 in the Cambridge University Library. Other copies of this pro English are in the Hunterian Museum, Glasgow, Q. 2. 25; Sion College, London; and th Laud Collection in the Bodleian, no. 740.[3] A copy in the Northern dialect is MS. G. 21, St. John's Coll., Cambridge, and this is the MS. which will be edited for the E. E. Te Society. The Laud MS. 740 was somewhat condenst and modernised, in the 17th centur into MS. Ff. 6. 30, in the Cambridge University Library:[4] "The Pilgrime or the Pi grimage of Man in this World," copied by Will. Baspoole, whose copy "was verbati written by Walter Parker, 1645, and from thence transcribed by G. G. 1649; and from then by W. A. 1655." This last copy may have been read by, or its story reported to, Bunya and may have been the groundwork of his *Pilgrim's Progress.* It will be edited for the E. T. Soc., its text running under the earlier English, as in Mr. Herrtage's edition of t *Gesta Romanorum* for the Society. In February 1464,[5] Jean Gallopes—a clerk of Ange afterwards chaplain to John, Duke of Bedford, Regent of France—turned Deguilleville's fi verse *Pèlerinaige* into a prose *Pèlerinage de la vie humaine.*[6] By the kindness of Lord Ald ham, as above mentiond, Gallopes's French text will be printed opposite the early pro northern Englishing in the Society's edition.

The Second Version of Deguilleville's *Pèlerinaige de l'Homme*, A.D. 1355 or -6, was englisht in verse by Lydgate in 1426. Of Lydgate's poem, the larger part is in the Cotton MS Vitellius C. xiii (leaves 2-308). This MS. leaves out Chaucer's englishing of Deguilleville' *A B C* or *Prayer to the Virgin*, of which the successive stanzas start with A, B, C, and run al thro' the alphabet; and it has 2 main gaps, besides many small ones from the tops of leaves being burnt in the Cotton fire. All these gaps (save the A B C) have been fild up from the Stowe MS. 952 (which old John Stowe completed) and from the end of the other imperfect MS. Cotton, Tiberius A vii. Thanks to the diligence of the old Elizabethan tailor and manuscript-lover, a complete text of Lydgate's poem has been given. The British Museum French MSS. (Harleian 4399[7], and Additional 22,937[8] and 25,594[9]) are all of the First Version.

Besides his first *Pèlerinaige de l'homme* in its two versions, Deguilleville wrote a second "de l'ame separee du corps," and a third, "de nostre seigneur Iesus." Of the second, a prose

1 He was born about 1295. See Abbé GOUJET's *Bibliotheque française*, Vol. IX, p. 73-4.—P. M. The Roxburghe Club printed the 1st version in 1893.

2 The Roxburghe Club's copy of this 2nd version was lent to Mr. Currie, and unluckily burnt too with his other MSS.

3 These 3 MSS. have not yet been collated, but are believed to be all of the same version.

4 Another MS. is in the Pepys Library.

5 According to Lord Aldenham's MS.

6 These were printed in France, late in the 15th or early in the 16th century.

7 15th cent., containing only the *Vie humaine*.

8 15th cent., containing all the 3 Pilgrimages, the 3rd being Jesus Christ's.

9 14th cent., containing the *Vie humaine* and the 2nd Pilgrimage, *de l'Ame*: both incomplete.

ınglishing of 1413, *The Pilgrimage of the Sowle* (with poems by Hoccleve, already printed 'or the Society with that author's *Regement of Princes*), exists in the Egerton MS. 615,[1] at Hatfield, Cambridge (Univ. Kk. 1. 7, and Caius), Oxford (Univ. Coll. and Corpus), and in Caxon's edition of 1483. This version has 'somewhat of addicions' as Caxton says, and some hortenings too, as the maker of both, the first translater, tells us in the MSS. Caxton leaves ut the earlier englisher's interesting Epilog in the Egerton MS. This prose englishing of he *Sowle* will be edited for the Society by Prof. Dr. Leon Kellner after that of the *Man* is nisht, and will have Gallopes's French opposite it, from Lord Aldenham's MS., as his gift the Society. Of the Pilgrimage of Jesus, no englishing is known.

As to the MS. Anglo-Saxon Psalters, Dr. Hy. Sweet has edited the oldest MS., the əspasian, in his *Oldest English Texts* for the Society, and Mr. Harsley has edited the test, c. 1150, Eadwine's Canterbury Psalter. The other MSS., except the Paris one, being terlinear versions,—some of the Roman-Latin redaction, and some of the Gallican,—Prof. ɔgeman has prepared for press, a Parallel-Text edition of the first twelve Psalms, to start the ɔmplete work. He will do his best to get the Paris Psalter—tho' it is not an interlinear ıe—into this collective edition; but the additional matter, especially in the Verse-Psalms, very difficult to manage. If the Paris text cannot be parallelised, it will form a separate 'olume. The Early English Psalters are all independent versions, and will follow separately n due course.

Through the good offices of the Examiners, some of the books for the Early-English Exminations of the University of London will be chosen from the Society's publications, the ɔmmittee having undertaken to supply such books to students at a large reduction in price. ıe net profits from these sales will be applied to the Society's Reprints.

Members are reminded that *fresh Subscribers are always wanted,* and that the Committee an at any time, on short notice, send to press an additional Thousand Pounds' worth of work.

The Subscribers to the Original Series must be prepared for the issue of the whole of the 'arly English *Lives of Saints*, sooner or later. The Society cannot leave out any of them, 'en though some are dull. The Sinners would doubtless be much more interesting. But in any Saints' Lives will be found valuable incidental details of our forefathers' social state, d all are worthful for the history of our language. The Lives may be lookt on as the ligious romances or story-books of their period.

The Standard Collection of Saints' Lives in the Corpus and Ashmole MSS., the Harleian S. 2277, &c. will repeat the Laud set, our No. 87, with additions, and in right order. (The ındation MS. (Laud 108) had to be printed first, to prevent quite unwieldy collations.) The pplementary Lives from the Vernon and other MSS. will form one or two separate volumes.

Besides the Saints' Lives, Trevisa's englishing of *Bartholomæus de Proprietatibus Rerum*, e mediæval Cyclopædia of Science, &c., will be the Society's next big undertaking. Dr. von Fleischhacker will edit it. Prof. Napier of Oxford, wishing to have the whole of r MS. Anglo-Saxon in type, and accessible to students, will edit for the Society all the ıprinted and other Anglo-Saxon Homilies which are not included in Thorpe's edition of lfric's prose,[2] Dr. Morris's of the Blickling Homilies, and Prof. Skeat's of Ælfric's Metrical ɔmilies. The late Prof. Kölbing left complete his text, for the Society, of the *Ancren wle*, from the best MS., with collations of the other four, and this will be edited for the ociety by Dr. Thümmler. Mr. Harvey means to prepare an edition of the three MSS. of the *Earliest English Metrical Psalter*, one of which was edited by the late Mr. Stevenson for the Surtees Society.

Members of the Society will learn with pleasure that its example has been followed, not only by the Old French Text Society which has done such admirable work under its founders Profs. Paul Meyer and Gaston Paris, but also by the Early Russian Text Society, which was set on foot in 1877, and has since issued many excellent editions of old MS. Chronicles, &c.

Members will also note with pleasure the annexation of large tracts of our Early English territory by the important German contingent, the late Professors Zupitza and Kölbing, the living Hausknecht, Einenkel, Haenisch, Kaluza, Hupe, Adam, Holthausen, Schick, Herzfeld, Brandeis, Sieper, Konrath, Wülfing, &c. Scandinavia has also sent us Prof. Erdmann and Dr. E. A. Kock; Holland, Prof. H. Logeman, who is now working in Belgium; France, Prof. Paul Meyer—with Gaston Paris as adviser (alas, now dead);—Italy, Prof. Lattanzi; Austria, Dr. von Fleischhacker; while America is represented by the late Prof. Child, by Dr. Mary Noyes Colvin, Miss Rickert, Profs. Mead, McKnight, Triggs, Perrin, Craig, &c. The sympathy, the ready help, which the Society's work has cald forth from the Continent and the United States, have been among the pleasantest experiences of the Society's life, a real aid and cheer amid all troubles and discouragements. All our Members are grateful for it, and recognise that the bond their work has woven between them and the lovers of language and antiquity across the seas is one of the most welcome results of the Society's efforts.

1 Ab. 1430, 106 leaves (leaf 1 of text wanting), with illuminations of nice little devils—red, green, tawny, &c.—and damnd souls, fires, angels, &c.

2 Of these, Mr. Harsley is preparing a new edition, with collations of all the MSS. Many copies of Thorpe's book, not issued by the Ælfric Society, are still in stock.
Of the Vercelli Homilies, the Society has bought the copy made by Prof. G. Lattanzi.

ORIGINAL SERIES.

1. **Early English Alliterative Poems,** ab. 1360 A.D., ed. Rev. Dr. R. Morris. 16*s*. 186
2. **Arthur,** ab. 1440, ed. F. J. Furnivall, M.A. 4*s*. ,,
3. **Lauder on the Dewtie of Kyngis, &c.,** 1556, ed. F. Hall, D.C.L. 4*s*. ,,
4. **Sir Gawayne and the Green Knight,** ab. 1360, ed. Rev. Dr. R. Morris. 10*s*. ,,
5. **Hume's Orthographie and Congruitie of the Britan Tongue,** ab. 1617, ed. H. B. Wheatley. 4*s*. 186
6. **Lancelot of the Laik,** ab. 1500, ed. Rev. W. W. Skeat. 8*s*. ,,
7. **Genesis & Exodus,** ab. 1250, ed. Rev. Dr. R. Morris. 8*s*.
8. **Morte Arthure,** ab. 1440, ed. E. Brock. 7*s*. ,
9. **Thynne on Speght's ed. of Chaucer,** A.D. 1599, ed. Dr. G. Kingsley and Dr. F. J. Furnivall. 10*s*. ,
10. **Merlin,** ab. 1440, Part I., ed. H. B. Wheatley. 2*s*. 6*d*.
11. **Lyndesay's Monarche, &c.,** 1552, Part I., ed. J. Small, M.A. 3*s*. ,
12. **Wright's Chaste Wife,** ab. 1462, ed. F. J. Furnivall, M.A. 1*s*. ,
13. **Seinte Marherete,** 1200-1330, ed. Rev. O. Cockayne; re-edited by Dr. Otto Glauning. [*Out of print.* 18
14. **Kyng Horn, Floris and Blancheflour, &c.,** ed. Rev. J. R. Lumby, D.D., re-ed. Dr. G. H. McKnight. 5*s*. ,
15. **Political, Religious, and Love Poems,** ed. F. J. Furnivall. 7*s*. 6*d*. ,,
16. **The Book of Quinte Essence,** ab. 1460-70, ed. F. J. Furnivall. 1*s*. ,,
17. **Parallel Extracts from 45 MSS. of Piers the Plowman,** ed. Rev. W. W. Skeat. 1*s*. ,,
18. **Hali Meidenhad,** ab. 1200, ed. Rev. O. Cockayne, re-edited by Dr. F. J. Furnivall. [*At Press.* ,,
19. **Lyndesay's Monarche, &c.,** Part II., ed. J. Small, M.A. 3*s*. 6*d*. ,,
20. **Hampole's English Prose Treatises,** ed. Rev. G. G. Perry. 1*s*. [*At Press.* ,
21. **Merlin,** Part II., ed. H. B. Wheatley. 4*s*. ,
22. **Partenay** or **Lusignen,** ed. Rev. W. W. Skeat. 6*s*. ,
23. **Dan Michel's Ayenbite of Inwyt,** 1340, ed. Rev. Dr. R. Morris. 10*s*. 6*d*. ,,
24. **Hymns to the Virgin and Christ; the Parliament of Devils, &c.,** ab. 1430, ed. F. J. Furnivall. 3*s* 186
25. **The Stacions of Rome, the Pilgrims' Sea-voyage, with Clene Maydenhod,** ed. F. J. Furnivall. 1*s*. ,,
26. **Religious Pieces in Prose and Verse,** from R. Thornton's MS., ed. Rev. G. G. Perry. 2*s*. [*At Press.* ,,
27. **Levins's Manipulus Vocabulorum, a ryming Dictionary,** 1570, ed. H. B. Wheatley. 12*s*. ,,
28. **William's Vision of Piers the Plowman,** 1362 A.D.; Text A, Part I., ed. Rev. W. W. Skeat. 6*s*. ,
29. **Old English Homilies** (ab. 1220-30 A.D.). Series I, Part I. Edited by Rev. Dr. R. Morris. 7*s*. ,
30. **Pierce the Ploughmans Crede,** ed. Rev. W. W. Skeat. 2*s*. ,
31. **Myrc's Duties of a Parish Priest,** in Verse, ab. 1420 A.D., ed. E. Peacock. 4*s*. 18
32. **Early English Meals and Manners: the Boke of Norture of John Russell, the Bokes of Keruynge, Curtasye, and Demeanor, the Babees Book, Urbanitatis, &c.,** ed. F. J. Furnivall. 12*s*. ,
33. **The Knight de la Tour Landry,** ab. 1440 A.D. A Book for Daughters, ed. T. Wright, M.A. [*Reprinting.*
34. **Old English Homilies** (before 1300 A.D.). Series I, Part II., ed. R. Morris, LL.D. 8*s*.
35. **Lyndesay's Works,** Part III.: The Historie and Testament of Squyer Meldrum, ed. F. Hall. 2*s*.
36. **Merlin,** Part III. Ed. H. B. Wheatley. On Arthurian Localities, by J. S. Stuart Glennie. 12*s*. 1
37. **Sir David Lyndesay's Works,** Part IV., Ane Satyre of the Three Estaits. Ed. F. Hall, D.C.L. 4*s*.
38. **William's Vision of Piers the Plowman,** Part II. Text B. Ed. Rev. W. W. Skeat, M.A. 10*s*. 6*d*.
39. **Alliterative Romance of the Destruction of Troy.** Ed. D. Donaldson & G. A. Panton. Pt. I. 10*s*. 6*d*.
40. **English Gilds,** their Statutes and Customs, 1389 A.D. Edit. Toulmin Smith and Lucy T. Smith, with an Essay on Gilds and Trades-Unions, by Dr. L. Brentano. 21*s*. 1
41. **William Lauder's Minor Poems.** Ed. F J. Furnivall. 3*s*.
42. **Bernardus De Cura Rei Famuliaris,** Early Scottish Prophecies, &c. Ed. J. R. Lumby, M.A. 2*s*.
43. **Ratis Raving,** and other Moral and Religious Pieces. Ed. J. R Lumby, M.A. 3*s*. ,,
44. **The Alliterative Romance of Joseph of Arimathie, or The Holy Grail:** from the Vernon MS.; with W. de Worde's and Pynson's Lives of Joseph: ed. Rev. W. W. Skeat, M.A. 5*s*. 1871
45. **King Alfred's West-Saxon Version of Gregory's Pastoral Care,** edited from 2 MSS., with an English translation, by Henry Sweet, Esq., B.A., Balliol College, Oxford. Part I. 10*s*. ,,
46. **Legends of the Holy Rood, Symbols of the Passion and Cross Poems,** ed. Rev. Dr. R. Morris. 10*s*. ,,
47. **Sir David Lyndesay's Works,** Part V., ed. Dr. J. A. H. Murray. 3*s*.
48. **The Times' Whistle,** and other Poems, by R. C., 1616; ed. by J. M. Cowper, Esq. 6*s*.
49. **An Old English Miscellany,** containing a Bestiary, Kentish Sermons, Proverbs of Alfred, and Religious Poems of the 13th cent., ed. from the MSS. by the Rev. R. Morris, LL.D. 10*s*. 187
50. **King Alfred's West-Saxon Version of Gregory's Pastoral Care,** ed. H. Sweet, M.A. Part II. 10*s*. ,
51. **The Life of St Juliana,** 2 versions, A.D. 1230, with translations; ed. T. O. Cockayne & E. Brock. 2*s*. ,,
52. **Palladius on Husbondrie,** englisht (ab. 1420 A.D.), ed. Rev. Barton Lodge, M.A. Part I. 10*s*. ,,
53. **Old-English Homilies,** Series II., and three Hymns to the Virgin and God, 13th-century, with the music to two of them, in old and modern notation; ed. Rev. R. Morris, LL.D. 8*s*. 187
54. **The Vision of Piers Plowman,** Text C: **Richard the Redeles** (by William, the author of the *Vision*) and **The Crowned King;** Part III., ed. Rev. W. W. Skeat, M.A. 18*s*. ,,
55. **Generydes,** a Romance, ab. 1440 A.D., ed. W. Aldis Wright, M.A. Part I. 3*s*. ,,
56. **The Gest Hystoriale of the Destruction of Troy,** in alliterative verse; ed. by D. Donaldson, Esq., and the late Rev. G. A. Panton. Part II. 10*s*. 6*d*. 1874
57. **The Early English Version of the "Cursor Mundi";** in four Texts, edited by the Rev. R. Morris, M.A., LL.D. Part I, with 2 photolithographic facsimiles. 10*s*. 6*d*. ,,
58. **The Blickling Homilies,** 971 A.D., ed. Rev. R. Morris, LL.D. Part I. 8*s*. ,,
59. **The "Cursor Mundi,"** in four Texts, ed. Rev. Dr. R. Morris. Part II. 15*s*. 1875

). **Meditacyuns on the Soper of our Lorde** (by Robert of Brunne), edited by J. M. Cowper. 2*s.* 6*d.* 1875
1. **The Romance and Prophecies of Thomas of Erceldoune,** from 5 MSS. ; ed. Dr. J. A. H. Murray. 10*s.* 6*d.* ,,
2. **The "Cursor Mundi,"** in four Texts, ed. Rev. Dr. R. Morris. Part III. 15*s.* 1876
The Blickling Homilies, 971 A.D., ed. Rev. Dr. R. Morris. Part II. 7*s.* ,,
Francis Thynne's Embleames and Epigrams, A.D. 1600, ed. F. J. Furnivall. 7*s.* ,,
Be Domes Dæge (Bede's *De Die Judicii*), &c., ed. J. R. Lumby, B.D. 2*s.* ,,
The "Cursor Mundi," in four Texts, ed. Rev. Dr. R. Morris. Part IV., with 2 autotypes. 10*s.* 1877
Notes on Piers Plowman, by the Rev. W. W. Skeat, M.A. Part I. 21*s.* ,,
T .e "Cursor Mundi," in 4 Texts, ed. Rev. Dr. R. Morris Part V. 25*s.* 1878
Adam Davie's 5 Dreams about Edward II., &c., ed. F Furnivall, M.A. 5*s.* ,,
Generydes, a Romance, ed. W. Aldis Wright, M.A. Part II. 4*s.* ,,
The Lay Folks Mass-Book, four texts, ed. Rev. Canon Simmons. 25*s.* 1879
Palladius on Husbondrie, englisht (ab. 1420 A.D.). Part II. Ed. S. J. Herrtage, B.A. 15*s.* ,,
The Blickling Homilies, 971 A.D., ed. Rev. Dr. R. Morris. Part III. 10*s.* 1880
English Works of Wyclif, hitherto unprinted, ed. F. D. Matthew, Esq. 20*s.* ,,
Catholicon Anglicum, an early English Dictionary, from Lord Monson's MS. A.D. 1483, ed., with Introduction & Notes, by S. J. Herrtage, B.A. ; and with a Preface by H. B. Wheatley. 20*s.* 1881
Aelfric's Metrical Lives of Saints, in MS. Cott. Jul. E 7., ed. Rev. Prof. Skeat, M.A. Part I. 10*s.* ,,
Beowulf, the unique MS. autotyped and transliterated, edited by Prof. Zupitza, Ph.D. 25*s.* 1882
The Fifty Earliest English Wills, in the Court of Probate, 1387-1439, ed. by F. J. Furnivall, M.A. 7*s.* ,,
King Alfred's Orosius, from Lord Tollemache's 9th century MS., Part I, ed. H. Sweet, M.A. 13*s.* 1883
b. *Extra Volume.* **Facsimile of the Epinal Glossary,** ed. H. Sweet, M.A. 15*s.* ,,
The Early-English Life of St. Katherine and its Latin Original, ed. Dr. Einenkel. 12*s.* 1884
Piers Plowman : Notes, Glossary, &c. Part IV, completing the work, ed. Rev. Prof. Skeat, M.A. 18*s.* ,,
Aelfric's Metrical Lives of Saints, MS. Cott. Jul. E 7., ed. Rev. Prof. Skeat, M.A., LL.D. Part II. 12*s.* 1885
The Oldest English Texts, Charters, &c., ed. H. Sweet, M.A. 20*s.* ,,
Additional Analogs to 'The Wright's Chaste Wife,' No. 12, by W. A. Clouston. 1*s.* 1886
The Three Kings of Cologne. 2 English Texts, and 1 Latin, ed. Dr. C. Horstmann. 17*s.* ,,
Prose Lives of Women Saints, ab. 1610 A.D., ed. from the unique MS. by Dr. C. Horstmann. 12*s.* ,,
Early English Verse Lives of Saints (earliest version), Laud MS. 108, ed. Dr. C. Horstmann. 20*s.* 1887
Hy. Bradshaw's Life of St. Werburghe (Pynson, 1521), ed. Dr. C. Horstmann. 10*s.* ,,
Vices and Virtues, from the unique MS., ab. 1200 A.D., ed. Dr. F. Holthausen. Part I. 8*s.* 1888
Anglo-Saxon and Latin Rule of St. Benet, interlinear Glosses, ed. Dr. H. Logeman. 12*s.* ,,
Two Fifteenth-Century Cookery-Books, ab. 1430-1450, edited by Mr. T. Austin. 10*s.* ,,
Eadwine's Canterbury Psalter, from the Trin. Cambr. MS., ab. 1150 A.D., ed. F. Harsley, B.A. Pt. I. 12*s.* 1889
Defensor's Liber Scintillarum, edited from the MSS. by Ernest Rhodes, B.A. 12*s.* ,,
Aelfric's Metrical Lives of Saints, MS. Cott. Jul. E 7, Part III., ed. Prof. Skeat, Litt.D., LL.D. 12*s.* 1890
The Old-English version of Bede's Ecclesiastical History, re-ed. by Dr. Thomas Miller. Part I, § 1. 18*s.* ,,
The Old-English version of Bede's Ecclesiastical History, re-ed. by Dr. Thomas Miller. Pt. I, § 2. 15*s.* 1891
The Earliest English Prose Psalter, edited from its 2 MSS. by Dr. K. D. Buelbring. Part I. 15*s.* ,,
Minor Poems of the Vernon MS., Part I., ed. Dr. C. Horstmann. 20*s.* 1892
Cursor Mundi. Part VI. Preface, Notes, and Glossary, ed. Rev. Dr. R. Morris. 10*s.* ,,
Capgrave's Life of St. Katharine, ed. Dr. C. Horstmann, with Forewords by Dr. Furnivall. 20*s.* 1893
Cursor Mundi. Part VII. Essay on the MSS., their Dialects, &c., by Dr. H. Hupe. 10*s.* ,,
Lanfranc's Cirurgie, ab. 1400 A.D., ed. Dr. R. von Fleischhacker. Part I. 20*s.* 1894
The Legend of the Cross, from a 12th century MS., &c., ed. Prof. A. S. Napier, M.A., Ph.D. 7*s.* 6*d.* ,,
The Exeter Book (Anglo-Saxon Poems), re-edited from the unique MS. by I. Gollancz, M.A. Part I. 20*s.* 1895
The Prymer or Lay-Folks' Prayer-Book, Camb. Univ. MS., ab. 1420, ed. Henry Littlehales. Part I. 10*s.* ,,
R. Misyn's Fire of Love and Mending of Life (Hampole), 1434, 1435, ed. Rev. R. Harvey, M.A. 15*s.* 1896
The English Conquest of Ireland, A.D. 1166-1185, 2 Texts, 1425, 1440, Pt. I, ed. Dr. Furnivall. 15*s.* ,,
Child-Marriages and -Divorces, Trothplights, &c. Chester Depositions, 1561-6, ed. Dr. Furnivall. 15*s.* 1897
The Prymer or Lay-Folks Prayer-Book, ab. 1420, ed. Henry Littlehales. Part II. 10*s.* ,,
The Old-English Version of Bede's Ecclesiastical History, ed. Dr. T. Miller. Part II, § 1. 15*s.* 1898
The Old-English Version of Bede's Ecclesiastical History, ed. Dr. T. Miller. Part II, § 2. 15*s.* ,,
Merlin, Part IV : **Outlines of the Legend of Merlin,** by Prof. W. E. Mead, Ph.D. 15*s.* 1899
Queen Elizabeth's Englishings of Boethius, Plutarch &c. &c., ed. Miss C. Pemberton. 15*s.* ,,
Aelfric's Metrical Lives of Saints, Part IV and last, ed. Prof. Skeat, Litt.D., LL.D. 10*s.* 1900
Jacob's Well, edited from the unique Salisbury Cathedral MS. by Dr. A. Brandeis. Part I. 10*s.* ,,
An Old-English Martyrology, re-edited by Dr. G. Herzfeld. 10*s.* ,,
Minor Poems of the Vernon MS., edited by Dr. F. J. Furnivall. Part II. 15*s.* 1901
The Lay Folks' Catechism, ed. by Canon Simmons and Rev. H. E. Nolloth, M.A. 5*s.* ,,
Robert of Brunne's Handlyng Synne (1303), and its French original, re-ed. by Dr. Furnivall. Pt. I. 10*s.* ,,
The Rule of St. Benet, in Northern Prose and Verse, & Caxton's Summary, ed. Dr. E. A. Kock. 15*s.* 1902
The Laud MS. Troy-Book, ed. from the unique Laud MS. 595, by Dr. J. E. Wülfing. Part I. 15*s.* ,,
The Laud MS. Troy-Book, ed. from the unique Laud MS. 595, by Dr. J. E. Wülfing. Part II. 20*s.* 1903
Robert of Brunne's Handlyng Synne (1303), and its French original, re-ed. by Dr. Furnivall. Pt. II. 10*s.* ,,
Twenty-six Political and other Poems from Digby MS. 102 &c., ed. by Dr. J. Kail. Part I. 10*s.* 1904
Medieval Records of a London City Church, ed. Henry Littlehales. Part I. 10*s.* ,,
An Alphabet of Tales, in Northern English, from the Latin, ed. Mrs. M. M. Banks. Part I. 10*s.* ,,

127. **An Alphabet of Tales,** in Northern English, from the Latin, ed. Mrs. M. M. Banks. Part II. 10*s.* 19
128. **Medieval Records of a London City Church,** ed. Henry Littlehales. Part II. 10*s.*
129. **The English Register of Godstow Nunnery,** ed. from the MSS. by the Rev. Dr. Andrew Clark. Pt. I. 10*s.*
130. **The English Register of Godstow Nunnery,** ed. from the MSS. by the Rev. Dr. A. Clark. Pt. II. 15*s.* 19
131. **The Brut, or Chronicle of England,** edited from the best MSS. by Dr. F. Brie. Part I. 10*s.*
132. **John Metham's Works,** edited from the unique MS. by Dr. Hardin Craig.
133. **The English Register of Oseney Abbey, by Oxford,** ed. by the Rev. Dr. A. Clark. Part I. 15*s.*
134. **The Coventry Leet Book,** edited by Miss M. Dormer Harris. Part I. 15*s.*
135.
136.

EXTRA SERIES.

The Publications for 1867-1907 (*one guinea each year*) *are :—*

I. **William of Palerne; or, William and the Werwolf.** Re-edited by Rev. W. W. Skeat, M.A. 13*s.*

II. **Early English Pronunciation** with especial Reference to Shakspere and Chaucer, by A. J. Ellis, F.R.S. Part I. 10*s.*

III. **Caxton's Book of Curtesye,** in Three Versions. Ed. F. J. Furnivall. 5*s.*

IV. **Havelok the Dane.** Re-edited by the Rev. W. W. Skeat, M.A. 10*s.*

V. **Chaucer's Boethius.** Edited from the two best MSS. by Rev. Dr. R. Morris 12*s.*

VI. **Chevelere Assigne.** Re-edited from the unique MS. by Lord Aldenham, M.A. 3*s.*

VII. **Early English Pronunciation,** by A. J. Ellis, F.R.S. Part II. 10*s.* 18

VIII. **Queene Elizabethes Achademy, &c.** Ed. F. J. Furnivall. Essays on early Italian and German Books of Courtesy, by W. M. Rossetti and Dr. E. Oswald. 13*s.*

IX. **Awdeley's Fraternitye of Vacabondes, Harman's Caveat, &c.** Ed. E. Viles & F. J. Furnivall. 5*s.*

X. **Andrew Boorde's Introduction of Knowledge, 1547, Dyetary of Helth, 1542, Barnes in Defence of the Berde, 1542-3.** Ed. F. J. Furnivall. 18*s.*

XI. **Barbour's Bruce,** Part I. Ed. from MSS. and editions, by Rev. W. W. Skeat, M.A. 12*s.*

XII. **England in Henry VIII.'s Time:** a Dialogue between Cardinal Pole & Lupset, by Thom. Starkey, Chaplain to Henry VIII. Ed. J. M. Cowper. Part II. 12*s.* (Part I. is No. XXXII, 1878, 8*s.*)

XIII. **A Supplicacyon of the Beggers,** by Simon Fish, 1528-9 A.D., ed. F. J. Furnivall; with **A Supplication to our Moste Soueraigne Lorde; A Supplication of the Poore Commons;** and **The Decaye of England by the Great Multitude of Sheep,** ed. by J. M. Cowper, Esq. 6*s.*

XIV. **Early English Pronunciation,** by A. J. Ellis, Esq., F.R.S. Part III. 10*s.*

XV. **Robert Crowley's Thirty-One Epigrams, Voyce of the Last Trumpet, Way to Wealth, &c.,** A.D. 1550-1, edited by J. M. Cowper, Esq. 12*s.*

XVI. **Chaucer's Treatise on the Astrolabe.** Ed. Rev. W. W. Skeat, M.A. 6*s.*

XVII. **The Complaynt of Scotlande,** 1549 A.D., **with 4 Tracts** (1542-48), ed. Dr. Murray. Part I. 10*s.*

XVIII. **The Complaynt of Scotlande,** 1549 A.D., ed. Dr. Murray. Part II. 8*s.*

XIX. **Oure Ladyes Myroure,** A.D. 1530, ed. Rev. J. H. Blunt, M.A. 24*s.*

XX. **Lovelich's History of the Holy Grail** (ab. 1450 A.D.), ed. F. J. Furnivall, M.A., Ph.D. Part I. 8*s*

XXI. **Barbour's Bruce,** Part II., ed. Rev. W. W. Skeat, M.A. 4*s.*

XXII. **Henry Brinklow's Complaynt of Roderyck Mors** (ab. 1542): and **The Lamentacion of a Christian against the Citie of London,** made by Roderigo Mors, A.D. 1545. Ed. J. M. Cowper. 9*s.*

XXIII. **Early English Pronunciation,** by A. J. Ellis, F.R.S. Part IV. 10*s.*

XXIV. **Lovelich's History of the Holy Grail,** ed. F. J. Furnivall, M.A., Ph.D. Part II. 10*s.*

XXV. **Guy of Warwick,** 15th-century Version, ed. Prof. Zupitza. Part I. 20*s.*

XXVI. **Guy of Warwick,** 15th-century Version, ed. Prof. Zupitza. Part II. 14*s.*

XXVII. **Bp. Fisher's English Works** (died 1535), ed. by Prof. J. E. B. Mayor. Part I, the Text. 16*s.*

XXVIII. **Lovelich's Holy Grail,** ed. F. J. Furnivall, M.A., Ph.D. Part III. 10*s.*

XXIX. **Barbour's Bruce.** Part III., ed. Rev. W. W. Skeat, M.A. 21*s.*

XXX. **Lovelich's Holy Grail,** ed. F. J. Furnivall, M.A., Ph.D. Part IV. 15*s.*

XXXI. **The Alliterative Romance of Alexander and Dindimus,** ed. Rev. W. W. Skeat. 6*s.*

XXXII. **Starkey's "England in Henry VIII's time."** Pt. I. **Starkey's Life and Letters,** ed. S. J. Herrtage. 8*s.*

XXXIII. **Gesta Romanorum** (englisht ab. 1440), ed. S. J. Herrtage, B.A. 15*s.*

XXXIV. **The Charlemagne Romances :—1. Sir Ferumbras,** from Ashm. MS. 33, ed. S. J. Herrtage. 15*s.*

XXXV. **Charlemagne Romances :—2. The Sege off Melayne, Sir Otuell, &c.,** ed. S. J. Herrtage. 12*s.*

XXXVI. **Charlemagne Romances :—3. Lyf of Charles the Grete,** Pt. I., ed. S. J. Herrtage. 16*s.*

XXXVII. **Charlemagne Romances :—4. Lyf of Charles the Grete,** Pt. II., ed. S. J. Herrtage. 15*s.*

XXXVIII. **Charlemagne Romances :—5. The Sowdone of Babylone,** ed. Dr. Hausknecht. 15*s.*

XXXIX. **Charlemagne Romances :—6. Rauf Colyear, Roland, Otuel, &c.,** ed. S. J. Herrtage, B.A. 15*s.*

XL. **Charlemagne Romances :—7. Huon of Burdeux,** by Lord Berners, ed. S. L. Lee, B.A. Part I. 15*s.*

XLI. **Charlemagne Romances :—8. Huon of Burdeux,** by Lord Berners, ed. S. L. Lee, B.A. Pt. II. 15*s.*

XLII. **Guy of Warwick:** 2 texts (Auchinleck MS. and Caius MS.), ed. Prof. Zupitza. Part I. 15*s.*

XLIII. **Charlemagne Romances :—9. Huon of Burdeux,** by Lord Berners, ed. S. L. Lee, B.A. **Pt. III.** 15*s.*

XLIV. **Charlemagne Romances :—10. The Four Sons of Aymon,** ed. Miss Octavia Richardson. Pt. I. 15*s.*

XLV. **Charlemagne Romances :—11. The Four Sons of Aymon,** ed. Miss O. Richardson. Pt. II. 20*s.*

XLVI. **Sir Bevis of Hamton,** from the Auchinleck and other MSS., ed. Prof. E. Kölbing, Ph.D. Part I. 10*s.*

XLVII. **The Wars of Alexander,** ed. Rev. Prof. Skeat, Litt.D., LL.D. 20*s.*

XLVIII. **Sir Bevis of Hamton,** ed. Prof. E. Kölbing, Ph.D. Part II. 10*s.*

XLIX. **Guy of Warwick,** 2 texts (Auchinleck and Caius MSS.), Pt. II., ed. Prof. J. Zupitza, Ph.D. 15*s.*

arlemagne Romances:—12. Huon of Burdeux, by Lord Berners, ed. S. L. Lee, B.A. Part IV. 5*s.* 1887
orrent of Portyngale, from the unique MS. in the Chetham Library, ed. E. Adam, Ph.D. 10*s.* ,,
Bullein's Dialogue against the Feuer Pestilence, 1578 (ed. 1, 1564). Ed. M. & A. H. Bullen. 10*s.* 1888
Vicary's Anatomie of the Body of Man, 1548, ed. 1577, ed. F. J. & Percy Furnivall. Part I. 15*s.* ,,
Caxton's Englishing of Alain Chartier's Curial, ed. Dr. F. J. Furnivall & Prof. P. Meyer. 5*s.* ,,
Barbour's Bruce, ed. Rev. Prof. Skeat, Litt.D., LL.D. Part IV. 5*s.* 1889
Early English Pronunciation, by A. J. Ellis, Esq., F.R.S. Pt. V., the present English Dialects. 25*s.* ,,
Caxton's Eneydos, A.D. 1490, coll. with its French, ed. M. T. Culley, M.A. & Dr. F. J. Furnivall. 13*s.* 1890
I. **Caxton's Blanchardyn & Eglantine,** c. 1489, extracts from ed. 1595, & French, ed. Dr. L. Kellner. 17*s.* ,,
Guy of Warwick, 2 texts (Auchinleck and Caius MSS.), Part III., ed. Prof. J. Zupitza, Ph.D. 15*s.* 1891
ydgate's Temple of Glass, re-edited from the MSS. by Dr. J. Schick. 15*s.* ,,
Hoccleve's Minor Poems, I., from the Phillipps and Durham MSS., ed. F. J. Furnivall, Ph.D. 15*s.* 1892
The Chester Plays, re-edited from the MSS. by the late Dr. Hermann Deimling. Part I. 15*s.* ,,
I. **Thomas a Kempis's De Imitatione Christi,** englisht ab. 1440, & 1502, ed. Prof. J. K. Ingram. 15*s.* 1893
Caxton's Godfrey of Boloyne, or Last Siege of Jerusalem, 1481, ed. Dr. Mary N. Colvin. 15*s.* ,,
Sir Bevis of Hamton, ed. Prof. E. Kölbing, Ph.D. Part III. 15*s.* 1894
Lydgate's and Burgh's Secrees of Philisoffres. ab. 1445—50, ed. R. Steele, B.A. 15*s.* ,,
I. **The Three Kings' Sons,** a Romance, ab. 1500, Part I., the Text, ed. Dr. Furnivall. 10*s.* 1895
II. **Melusine,** the prose Romance, ab. 1500, Part I, the Text, ed. A. K. Donald. 20*s.* ,,
Lydgate's Assembly of the Gods, ed. Prof. Oscar L. Triggs, M.A., Ph.D. 15*s.* 1896
The Digby Plays, edited by Dr. F. J. Furnivall. 15*s.* ,,
The Towneley Plays, ed. Geo. England and A. W. Pollard, M.A. 15*s.* 1897
I. **Hoccleve's Regement of Princes,** 1411-12, **and 14 Poems,** edited by Dr. F. J. Furnivall. 15*s.* ,,
I. **Hoccleve's Minor Poems, II.,** from the Ashburnham MS., ed. I. Gollancz, M.A. [*At Press.* ,,
'. **Secreta Secretorum,** 3 prose Englishings, by Jas. Yonge, 1428, ed. R. Steele, B.A. Part I. 20*s.* 1898
Speculum Guidonis de Warwyk, edited by Miss G. L. Morrill, M.A., Ph.D. 10*s.* ,,
I. **George Ashby's Poems, &c.,** ed. Miss Mary Bateson. 15*s.* 1899
II. **Lydgate's DeGuilleville's Pilgrimage of the Life of Man,** 1426, ed. Dr. F. J. Furnivall. Part I. 10*s.* ,,
III. **The Life and Death of Mary Magdalene,** by T. Robinson, c. 1620, ed. Dr. H. O. Sommer. 5*s.* ,,
K. **Caxton's Dialogues, English and French,** c. 1483, ed. Henry Bradley, M.A. 10*s.* 1900
Lydgate's Two Nightingale Poems, ed. Dr. Otto Glauning. 5*s.* ,,
I. **Gower's Confessio Amantis,** edited by G. C. Macaulay, M.A. Vol. I. 15*s.* ,,
II. **Gower's Confessio Amantis,** edited by G. C. Macaulay, M.A. Vol. II. 15*s.* 1901
III. **Lydgate's DeGuilleville's Pilgrimage of the Life of Man,** 1426, ed. Dr. F. J. Furnivall. Pt. II. 10*s.* ,,
IV. **Lydgate's Reason and Sensuality,** edited by Dr. E. Sieper. Part I. 5*s.* ,,
7. **Alexander Scott's Poems,** 1568, from the unique Edinburgh MS., ed. A. K. Donald, B.A. 10*s.* 1902
7I. **William of Shoreham's Poems,** re-ed. from the unique MS. by Dr. M. Konrath. Part I. 10*s.* ,,
'II. **Two Coventry Corpus-Christi Plays,** re-edited by Hardin Craig, M.A. 10*s.* ,,
'III. **Le Morte Arthur,** re-edited from the Harleian MS. 2252 by Prof. Bruce, Ph.D. 15*s.* 1903
X. **Lydgate's Reason and Sensuality,** edited by Dr. E. Sieper. Part II. 15*s.* ,,
glish Fragments from Latin Medieval Service-Books, ed. by Hy. Littlehales. 5*s.* ,,
he Macro Plays, from Mr. Gurney's unique MS., ed. Dr. Furnivall and A. W. Pollard, M.A. 10*s.* 1904
ydgate's DeGuileville's Pilgrimage of the Life of Man, Part III., ed. Miss Locock. 10*s.* ,,
Lovelich's Romance of Merlin, from the unique MS., ed. Dr. E. A. Kock. Part I. 10*s.* ,,
Respublica, a Play on Social England, A.D. 1553, ed. L. A. Magnus, LL.B. 12*s.* 1905
ovelich's History of the Holy Grail, Pt. V.: **The Legend of the Holy Grail,** by Dorothy Kempe. 6*s.* ,,
Mirk's Festial, edited from the MSS. by Dr. Erbe. Part I. 12*s.* ,,
Lydgate's Troy Book, edited from the best MSS. by Dr. Hy. Bergen. Part I. 15*s.* 1906
Skelton's Magnificence, edited by Dr. R. L. Ramsay, with an Introduction. 7*s.* 6*d.* [*At Press.* ,,
The Romance of Emare, re-edited from the MS. by Miss Edith Rickert, Ph.D. 7*s.* 6*d.* [*At Press.* ,,
Harrowing of Hell, four parallel Texts, re-edited by Prof. Hulme, M.A., Ph.D. [*At Press.* 1907
llads and Carols from Jn. Hyde's Balliol MS., edited by Dr. R. Dyboski. ,,
lgate's Troy Book, edited from the best MSS. by Dr. Hy. Bergen. Part II. 1908
,,

RLY ENGLISH TEXT SOCIETY TEXTS PREPARING.

Besides the Texts named as at press on p. 12 of the Cover of the Early English Text ciety's last Books, the following Texts are also slowly preparing for the Society:—

ORIGINAL SERIES.

Earliest English Prose Psalter, ed. Dr. K. D. Buelbring. Part II.
Earliest English Verse Psalter, 3 texts, ed. Rev. R. Harvey, M.A.
glo-Saxon Poems, from the Vercelli MS., re-edited by Prof. I. Gollancz, M.A.
glo-Saxon Glosses to Latin Prayers and Hymns, edited by Dr. F. Holthausen.
l the **Anglo-Saxon Homilies and Lives of Saints** not accessible in English editions, including those of the Vercelli MS. &c., edited by Prof. Napier, M.A., Ph.D.

The Anglo-Saxon Psalms; all the MSS. in Parallel Texts, ed. Dr. H. Logeman and F. Harsley, B.A.
Beowulf, a critical Text, &c., edited by a Pupil of the late Prof. Zupitza, Ph.D.
Byrhtferth's Handboc, ed. by Prof. G. Hempl.
Early English Confessionals, ed. Dr. R. von Fleischhacker.
The Seven Sages, in the Northern Dialect, from a Cotton MS., edited by Dr. Squires.
The Master of the Game, a Book of Huntynge for Hen. V. when Prince of Wales. (*Editor wanted.*)
Ailred's Rule of Nuns, &c., edited from the Vernon MS., by the Rev. Canon H. R. Bramley, M.A.
Early English Verse Lives of Saints, Standard Collection, from the Harl. MS. (*Editor wanted.*)
A Lapidary, from Lord Tollemache's MS., &c., edited by Dr. R. von Fleischhacker.
Early English Deeds and Documents, from unique MSS., ed. Dr. Lorenz Morsbach.
Gilbert Banastre's Poems, and other **Boccaccio englishings**, ed. by Prof. Dr. Max Förster.
Lanfranc's Cirurgie, ab. 1400 A.D., ed. Dr. R. von Fleischhacker, Part II.
William of Nassington's Mirror of Life, from Jn. of Waldby, edited by J. A. Herbert, M.A.
More Early English Wills from the Probate Registry at Somerset House. (*Editor wanted.*)
Early Lincoln Wills and Documents from the Bishops' Registers, &c., edited by Dr. F. J. Furnivall.
Early Canterbury Wills, edited by William Cowper, B.A., and J. Meadows Cowper.
Early Norwich Wills, edited by Walter Rye and F. J. Furnivall.
Early Lyrical Poems from the Harl. MS. 2253, re-edited by Prof. Hall Griffin, M.A.
Alliterative Prophecies, edited from the MSS. by Prof. Brandl, Ph.D.
Miscellaneous Alliterative Poems, edited from the MSS. by Dr. L. Morsbach.
Bird and Beast Poems, a collection from MSS., edited by Dr. K. D. Buelbring.
Scire Mori, &c., from the Lichfield MS. 16, ed. Mrs. L. Grindon, LL.A., and Miss Florence Gilbert.
Nicholas Trivet's French Chronicle, from Sir A. Acland-Hood's unique MS. (*Editor wanted.*)
Early English Homilies in Harl. 2276 &c., c. 1400, ed. J. Friedländer.
Extracts from the Registers of Boughton, ed. Hy. Littlehales, Esq.
The Diary of Prior Moore of Worcester, A.D. 1518-35, from the unique MS., ed. Henry Littlehales, Esq.
The Pore Caitif, edited from its MSS., by Mr. Peake.
Trevisa's englisht Vegetius on the Art of War, MS. 30 Magd. Coll. Oxf., ed. L. C. Wharton, M.A.
Poems attributed to Richard Maydenstone, from MS. Rawl. A 389, edited by Dr. W. Heuser.
Knighthood and Battle, a verse-Vegetius from a Pembroke Coll. MS., Cambr., ed. Dr. R. Dyboski.

EXTRA SERIES.

Bp. Fisher's English Works, Pt. II., with his **Life and Letters**, ed. Rev. Ronald Bayne, B.A. [*At Press*
Sir Tristrem, from the unique Auchinleck MS., edited by George F. Black.
John of Arderne's Surgery, c. 1425, ed. J. F. Payne, M.D.
De Guilleville's Pilgrimage of the Sowle, edited by Prof. Dr. Leon Kellner.
Vicary's Anatomie, 1548, from the unique MS. copy by George Jeans, edited by F. J. & Percy Furnival
Vicary's Anatomie, 1548, ed. 1577, edited by F. J. & Percy Furnivall. Part II. [*At Press.*
A Compilacion of Surgerye, from H. de Mandeville and Lanfrank, A.D. 1392, ed. Dr. J. F. Payne.
William Staunton's St. Patrick's Purgatory, &c., ed. Mr. G. P. Krapp, U.S.A.
Trevisa's Bartholomæus de Proprietatibus Rerum, re-edited by Dr. R. von Fleischhacker.
Bullein's Dialogue against the Feuer Pestilence, 1564, 1573, 1578. Ed. A. H. and M. Bullen. Part II.
The Romance of Boctus and Sidrac, edited from the MSS. by Dr. K. D. Buelbring.
The Romance of Clariodus, and **Sir Amadas**, re-edited from the MSS. by Dr. K. D. Buelbring.
Sir Degrevant, edited from the MSS. by Dr. K. Luick.
Robert of Brunne's Chronicle of England, from the Inner Temple MS., ed. by Prof. W. E. Mead, Ph.]
Maundeville's Voiage and Travaile, re-edited from the Cotton MS. Titus C. 16, &c., by Miss M. Bate:
Avowynge of Arthur, re-edited from the unique Ireland MS. by Dr. K. D. Buelbring.
Guy of Warwick, Copland's version, edited by a pupil of the late Prof. Zupitza, Ph.D.
Awdelay's Poems, re-edited from the unique MS. Douce 302, by Prof. Dr. E. Wülfing.
The Wyse Chylde and other early Treatises on Education, Northwich School, Harl. 2099 &c., ed. G. Colla
Caxton's Dictes and Sayengis of Philosophirs, 1477, with Lord Tollemache's MS. version, ed. S. I. Butler,
Caxton's Book of the Ordre of Chyualry, collated with Loutfut's Scotch copy. (*Editor wanted.*)
Lydgate's Dance of Death, ed. Miss Florence Warren.
Lydgate's Lyfe of oure Lady, ed. by Prof. Georg Fiedler, Ph.D.
Lydgate's Life of St. Edmund, edited from the MSS. by Dr. Axel Erdmann.
Lydgate's Triumph Poems, edited by Dr. E. Sieper.
Lydgate's Minor Poems, edited by Dr. Otto Glauning.
Richard Coer de Lion, re-edited from Harl. MS. 4690, by Prof. Hausknecht, Ph.D.
The Romance of Athelstan, re-edited by a pupil of the late Prof. J. Zupitza, Ph.D.
The Romance of Sir Degare, re-edited by Dr. Breul.
The Gospel of Nichodemus, edited by Ernest Riedel.
Mulcaster's Positions 1581, and **Elementarie** 1582, ed. Dr. Th. Klaehr, Dresden.
Walton's verse Boethius de Consolatione, edited by Mark H. Liddell, U.S.A.
Sir Landeval and Sir Launfal, edited by Dr. Zimmermann.
Rolland's Seven Sages, the Scottish version of 1560, edited by George F. Black.
Partonope of Blois, edited from the complete MS., &c., by Dr. A. T. Bödtker.
Early English Fabliaux, a Collection, edited by Prof. George H. McKnight, Ph.D.
The Aunturs of Arthur, 2 texts from 3 MSS., edited by Wilhelm Wolff.

The Coventry Leet Book:

OR

Mayor's Register.

Early English Text Society.

Original Series, No. 134.

1907.

BERLIN: ASHER & CO., 13, UNTER DEN LINDEN.
NEW YORK: C. SCRIBNER & CO.; LEYPOLDT & HOLT.
PHILADELPHIA: J. B. LIPPINCOTT & CO.

The Coventry Leet Book:

OR

Mayor's Register,

CONTAINING THE RECORDS OF THE CITY

Court Leet

OR

View of Frankpledge,

A.D. 1420–1555,

WITH DIVERS OTHER MATTERS.

TRANSCRIBED AND EDITED BY

MARY DORMER HARRIS,

AUTHOR OF "LIFE IN AN OLD ENGLISH TOWN: A HISTORY OF COVENTRY COMPILED FROM OFFICIAL RECORDS."

PART I.

LONDON:

PUBLISHED FOR THE EARLY ENGLISH TEXT SOCIETY

BY KEGAN PAUL, TRENCH, TRÜBNER & CO., LIMITED,

DRYDEN HOUSE, 43, GERRARD STREET, SOHO, W.

1907.

Original Series, No. 134.

RICHARD CLAY & SONS, LIMITED, LONDON AND BUNGAY.

To the Mayor,

Aldermen and Citizens of the City of Coventry

are inscribed

These Records of the Court Leet

of their ancient

and renowned

City.

PREFACE.

SINCE the Introduction is to come when the whole volume is complete, here is place only for thanks. The Coventry Corporation by their readiness in lending the MS. for transcription, and the Chairman and Committee of the Leamington Free Library for housing the same so safely, and its transcriber so airily, sunnily and cheerfully, have great claims on my gratitude. I would crave the continuance of their forbearance if I seem long about my task. It is a heavy one, and the nature of the work necessitates such care that hurry could only spell disaster.

But it is the readers of the *Leet Book*, as well as myself, who should tender their acknowledgments to Mr. W. H. Stevenson and Mr. R. E. G. Kirk, who at Dr. Furnivall's request undertook to revise the proofs of an entire stranger. To all that the book has thereby gained in exactitude, in the elucidation of many a bewildering crux, and in occasional annotation, the transcriber can bear most grateful testimony. Their labours have not been light; the value of them has been inestimable. Miss Brocas Harris has been as unfailing in kindness in the revision of proofs as she has been quick-sighted in the detection of casual errors. And Dr. Furnivall has throughout lent me the aid of his kind help and encouragement.

Leamington, April 18, 1907.

ERRATA.

p. 41 note 1, p. 43, p. 62, p. 139, *for* Jorden *read* Jordan.

p. 70, *for* "Iklynton Collar" *read* Iklynton Collar.

p. 103 note 3, a suggested reading is epu*larum*, i. e. master of the banquets.

A NOTE ON COURTS LEET AND THE LEET BOOK.

A Leet is a court held by a lord of the manor or other liberty—or the lord's grantee—for the trial of petty offences. Concerning the meaning and derivation of the word itself scholars are divided, and where Professor Skeat and the late Professor Maitland only offer conjecture, it were best to suspend judgment. The derivation of the alternative to Court Leet, a word often occurring in these pages, view of frankpledge, is fairly assured; it is the Latinized—and mistaken—form of O.E. frithborh = peace-pledge, *i. e.* a tithing, or body of (normally) ten mutual sureties. The institution of the tithing tended to make every one his neighbour's policeman, and at a "view of frankpledge" every one amenable to the court's jurisdiction had to show himself properly included in an association of the kind.

With all this, however, we have here small concern. Justices-in-eyre and Justices of the Peace tended in time to diminish the importance of manorial jurisdiction, and the *Leet Book* reveals the court of fifteenth century Coventry less as a judicial than as a legislative body. It is the town parliament rather than the town tribunal of justice. The records show a series of ordinances or by-laws grounded on the petitions of aggrieved parties presented to the Leet, arranged year by year with fair regularity from 1420 to 1555. These touch mediæval urban life on every side, and are interwoven with a chronicle of the various happenings within the city. Of such is composed the great bulk of the matter of the *Leet Book*. A few leaves at the beginning and end of the volume, that would otherwise have been blank, were filled by Elizabethan and Stuart scribes with a miscellany that defies classification.

The value of the *Leet Book* from the social historian's point of view will be treated of in the Introduction in a subsequent part. Members of the E. E. T. S. may feel equally interested in the volume from the philological standpoint, as illustrating the Warwickshire dialect in the century before Shakespeare's birth.

One example of this, and I have done. In *Coriolanus*, II. i. 226, occurs the line, "Stalls, bulks and windows are smothered up." Dr. Murray gives no earlier example of the word *bulk* than the close of the 16th century, and Professor Skeat suggests as a derivation the O.N. *bálk-r* = beam, which should give M.E. *bolk*, hitherto not found. But in John Leeder's proclamation of 1421, p. 27, townspeople are enjoined to keep "no swyne in hur *bolkys*." Here is without doubt the connecting link between the Old Norse and the Shakespearian form.

[Note on the word *Leet* kindly communicated by Dr. Henry Bradley.] The difficult word *Leet* certainly represents 13th century Anglo-French *lete*. I think it possible that this may be adopted from O.E. *lǣþ*, which we have in the "lathes" of Kent (for a suggestion to account for the phonological anomaly see *N. E. D.*, article *Lathe* sb.[1]). *Lǣþ* seems to mean "landed property," and perhaps it may not be altogether too wild to suppose that it may have been used as a native synonym of "manor," and that either the simple word or some compound may have been employed to denote the meeting of the tenants of the manor, the manorial court. If such a use existed it would be natural that the Normans should adopt the term, pronouncing it as nearly as French phonetics would allow.

KEY TO ABBREVIATIONS, ETC.

a. r. r. = anno regni regis, the year of the king's reign.
b. = bailiff.
Burton MS. = Humphrey Burton's MS., Free Library, Coventry.
ch. = chamberlains.
cor. = coroner.
Corp. MSS. = MSS. in possession of the Coventry Corporation. Catalogued by J. C. Jeaffresson for Hist. MSS. Comm. 1896.
E. D. D. = English Dialect Dictionary (Clarendon Press).
m. = mayor.
mace = sergeant-at-mace, sub-bailiff.
M. E. = Middle English.
M. G. C. C. = Magister Gilde Corporis Christi, master of the Corpus Christi Gild.
M. G. S. T. = Magister Gilde Sancte Trinitatis, master of the Trinity Gild.
N. E. D. = New English Dictionary (Clarendon Press).
V. f. p. = Visum franci plegii, view of frankpledge, or leet.
w. = wardens.
" " in the margin denotes marginal annotations in MS.
(etc.) in the text denotes the omission from the transcription of some oft-repeated formula, *e. g.* maior (etc.) = maior civitatis Coventrie, the mayor of the city of Coventry, etc., without brackets, however, is a copy of the MS.
[ ] in the English text denotes an abbreviated rendering of a customary formula, *e. g.* [Ordained] = Hit was ordeyned by auctorite of this present lete.
[ ] also denotes a translation from the Latin. MS. abbreviations and contractions are represented in the transcript by italics.

§ 1. QUIT CLAIM OF GERARD DE ALSPATH TO THE FILLONGLEY MEN, 1251-2.

[Copy of deed shown in 1581 at Old Fillongley.]

[1]A true Coppie of a deide shewed forthe by Wm. Denton of ffyllingley at a Court holden at Old ffyllongley in the time of John Myles, maio*u*r.

[Because disputes had taken place between Sir Gerard of Alspath and all the freemen of Old Fillongley, about these men's liberties, before the Judges at Warwick in the 36th year of King Henry, King John's son (Oct. 28, 1251—Oct. 27, 1252), they finally came to an accord thus :

Cu*m* Lites et Contenc*i*ones moue*re*nt*ur* int*er* d*omin*um Gererdu*m* de Alespath ex vna p*ar*te, et om*n*es Lib*er*os homines de Olde Fillungl*ey* ex alt*er*o (*sic*) p*ar*te, sup*er* Lib*er*tatib*us* d*ictorum* hom*inum* Cora*m* Justic*iariis* apud Warwik a. r. r.[2] Henrici filii Joh*ann*is R*egis* tricesimo sexto in hunc modu*m* finalit*er* conquieu*er*unt :

[Let present and to come know that I, Gerard of Alspath, have granted and quitclaimed, and by this present charter confirmed to all men of Old Fillungley and their heirs for ever from me and my heirs all outside service, relief, ward and suit of court in free socage, freely and quietly without challenge, vexation or hindrance. Moreover I, Gerard, and my heirs, will warrant all liberties aforesaid to the men aforesaid of Old Fillungley and their heirs for ever. For this concession and quitclaim, warranty and recognition, the men aforesaid gave me for good of peace five marks and a half of silver. And that this my concession,

Sciant p*re*sentes et futuri q*uo*d ego, Gerardus de Alespath, concessi, et quiet*um* Clamavi, et hac p*rese*nti carta mea Confirmavi, o*mni*b*us* ho*mini*b*us* de Old Fillungl*ey* et hered*ibus* suis imp*er*petuu*m* de me et heredib*us* meis omne servic*ium* forinsecu*m* et om*n*e Releviu*m* et[3] om*n*em ward*am* et om*n*em sect*am* Cur*ie* in Lib*er*o Socagio, Lib*er*e et quiete, sine om*n*e (*sic*) calumpnia, vexac*i*one nec impediment*o*. Insup*er*, ego Gerard*us* et heredes mei, om*n*es Lib*er*tates p*redictas* p*redict*is ho*mini*b*us* de Old Fillungl*ey* et hered*ibus* suis imp*er*petuu*m* warrantizabim*us*. P*ro* hac autem Concessione et quiet*a* clam*acione* et warrant*acione* et Recognic*i*one dederu*n*t mihi p*redi*c*t*i viri p*ro* bono pac*is* quin*que* marcas et dimid*iam* argenti. Et vt hac (*sic*) mea concessio et quietu*m*

[1] leaf i a, Scribe Z, v. Introd. [2] anno regni regis. [3] MS. looks like 'pro.'

quitclaim, warranty & recognition may remain firm and established by me and by my heirs, in testimony of this thing I have affixed my seal to this present writing. These being witnesses, etc.]

Clamacio et warrantacio et Recognic*io* stabil*is* et rata p*ro* me et hered*ibus* meis p*er*maneant (*sic*), [1]In cuius rei testimoniu*m*[1] huic p*rese*nti Script*o* Sigillu*m* meu*m* apposui. Hiis testibus etc. [Scrawl possibly intended for monogram T. G. D. follows.]

§ 2. TRINITY GILD FIELDS.

[Mem. of a certain bill shown, as it appears, at the following leet, by the master, brethren and sisters of the Trinity gild, concerning £10, which they paid of their desire and will to the prior of S. Mary's Cathedral in exoneration of the community of the city of Coventry; which £10 the mayor and community are bound to yield every year to the prior and convent. For which £10 it is conceded, that the said master, brethren and sisters shall have and hold divers fields in severalty; and that the said master, brethren and sisters shall pay every year £10 to the said prior and convent in exoneration of the mayor and community, as it appears more plainly below.

[2]Mem. de quad*am* bulla (*sic*) p*er* magistru*m*, *frat*res et sorores Gilde S. T*r*initat*is* Couentr*ie* exhibit*a*, et ad letam sequent*em*, ut pat*et*, de decem libr*is*,[3] quas soluer*unt* ad eo*rum* libitum et ad eo*rum* volu*n*tat*em* p*r*iori eccl*esi*e Cath*edralis* B. Marie de Couentr*ia* in exon*eracion*em co*m*-*mun*itat*is* ciuitat*is* Couentr*ie*; quas quid*em* x li. maior et communitas Ciuitat*is* pre*d*icte singulis annis dict*is* p*r*iori et conventui reddere tenent*ur*. P*ro* quibus x li. concess*um*, concordat*um* et ordinat*um* est, q*uod* p*re*dict*i* magist*er*, *frat*res et sorores h*ab*eant et teneant diu*ersos* ca*m*pos in sep*arali*; Et q*uod* dict*i* magist*er*, *frat*res et sorores soluent sing*u*lis annis dict*is* p*r*iori et conuentui dict*as* x li. in exon*eracio*nem maior*is* et co*mmun*itatis ciuitat*is* p*r*edict*e* *pro*ut inferius pleni*us* liquet, etc.

[Michaelmas Leet, 1384.

[At the view of frank pledge held there Oct. 5, 1384, in the presence of J. de Marton, mayor, and the bailiffs of the

Ad visum francipleggi*i* tent*um* ib*idem* die Jouis p*roximo* post f*estu*m S. Michaelis arch*angeli* a. r. r. Ric*ard*i sec*un*di po*st* conq*uestu*m,

[1—1] Redundant. On the Alspath family of Fillongley and Meridon (Ailespede, in Domesday), v. Dugdale, 697, 725. [2] leaf 5 a. Scribe A of the *Leet Book* proper.
[3] By the Indenture tripartite between Queen Isabella, the prior and the corporation in 1355 the corporation agreed to pay the prior an annual ferm of £10 for the judicial rights he relinquished. v. Burton MS. ff. 98–105.

same town, by oath of

H. de Kele and others,

jurats.

[To which leet the master (etc.) of the gilds sent a certain bill of having allowance of £10, which the same master (etc.) annually paid and still pay to the prior and convent in the name of the community of the said town, of which bill the tenor followeth in these words :—

[To the mayor, bailiffs, chamberlains and other good people of the inquest sheweth the master of the gild of holy Trinity, S. Mary, S. John, S. Katherine of Coventry, that as the said master and his brethren bear from year to year a great charge for the town aforesaid, paying to the prior and convent of the same town £10 at the term of S. Michael. And besides that where they

octauo, coram Joh. de Marton, tunc maiore, Alex. Wright, & Joh. Smyth, hosier, tunc Balliuis eiusdem ville, per sacramentum Hen. de Kele, Will. Wolfe, Joh. de Maxtok, Joh. Botoner, Ric. de Teynton, Joh. de Crose, Hen. dell Hay, Gurdeler, Tho. de Nassyngton, Sim. de Langham, Tho. de Sutton, Joh. Inge, Joh. Tate, Rob. de Estelton, Joh. Gart, mercere, Hen. Draycote, Nich. de Dudlay, Rob. Bladdurwyk, Hen. dell Hay, mercere, Ric. Helony, Will. Welye, Will. Bondy, Ad. Deyster, Joh. de Wilye, & Will de Cayfeld, Juratorum :

Ad quam letam magister et confratres Gildarum S. Trinitatis, S. Marie, S. Johannis Baptiste et S. Katerine in Couentria miserunt quandam billam de habendo allocacionem decem librarum, quas iidem magister et confratres predicti annuatim soluerunt, et adhuc soluunt, priori et conventui de Couentria nomine communitatis euisdem ville, cuius bille tenor sequitur in hec uerba :—

As Maire, Ballyfs, Chamburlens, & autres bonez gentez del enquest moustre le mastre (*sic*) de la Gilde sanct Trinite, seynt Marie, seint Johan, seynt Katerine de Couentre, qe come lez ditz mastre & cez confreres portount de ane (*sic*) en ane vn graunt charge pur la vile auant dit, paiauntz a lez priour & Couent de mesme la vile x li. a la terme de seint Michell. Et outre icela, ou il solient (*sic*) auoir

are wont to have divers fields in severalty time out of mind, that is to say, Poddy-croft, Stivichallhurne, Long-croft, and Batemans-acre, now they are every year broken and laid open at the time of the Gule of August (Lammas), to the great impoverishing and ruin of the gild aforesaid, so that they cannot obtain more than half the rent according to the value of the said fields: That it may please the said mayor, bailiffs and chamberlains and good folk to ordain such a remedy that they may keep the said fields in severalty in peace; or otherwise for certain the said master and his brethren desire to be discharged of the payment of the said £10 in time to come.—And therefore by common assent of the honest and lawful men elected at that leet, it is thus agreed, that the master and brethren of the said gilds be discharged of the £10 which they were wont to pay to the prior and convent of Coventry, not by any compulsion but of their free will; so that the mayor, bailiffs and chamberlains of the town fix among themselves a certain day, at which day they shall cause to come before them from every street of the town six or four honest and lawful

diuersez chaumpez severals puis le temps de memorie, cest assauoir, Pody Croft, Stevechallhurne, le long Croft, & Batemansacre, Ore ils sount chescun ane acrauantz et mys ouertez a le temps de Goldaust, a graunt enpouerisment & anyentisment de la gilde auau*n*tdit, quare ne puissont auoir mez de la demy rent solonc la [1]valoue dez ditz Chaumpz: qe please as ditz maire, baillifs, chamburlens, & bones gents ordiner ent tiell remedie, quils puissount auer les ditz chaumps en seu*er*altie en peas; ou outrement pur certeine les ditz meistre & cez confreres voillent estre dischargez dell payment dez ditz x li. en temps a vener etc.—Et vnde p*er* co*mmun*em assensum p*r*obor*um* et legaliu*m* ho*min*u*m* ad hanc leta*m* elector*um*, ita concordat*um* est, q*uo*d magist*er* et conf*ra*tres gildar*um* p*re*dict*arum* exon*er*ent*ur* de x li. quas soluere consueueru*n*t p*r*iori et conventui de Coventr*ia*, non ex aliqua coherc*io*ne, set eor*um* spontanea voluntate; ita videl*icet* q*uo*d maior et Ball*iui* et cam*er*arii ville ordinent int*er* se vnu*m* cer*tum* diem, ad quem diem venire fac*iant* coram eis de quol*ibe*t vico ville sex u*e*l quatuor

[1] leaf 6.

men to try if they, for themselves as well as the whole community of the town of Coventry, will fully consent that the said fields, expressly named in the bill, be in future several, or not, without challenge of any one of the said community,

and that the said master and brethren pay the said £10 issuing from the said gilds to the same prior and convent and their successors while it shall please the said master and brethren. And now the mayor and bailiffs on Thursday after S. Denis' day in the 8th year abovesaid (Oct. 13, 1384), by the assent of [names following] for themselves and their neighbours in Gosford Street; and others for Mill Lane and New Street; and others for Jordenwell; others for Much Park Street; and others for Earl Street and Little Park Street;

probos et legales homines ad temptandum si ipsi, tam pro seipsis, quam pro tota communitate ville de Couentria, plenarie consentire voluerint quod predicti campi, in billa prescripta expresse nominati, sint de decetero separabiles, necne,[1] absque contradiccione vel perturbacione alicuius de communitate predicta, [et] quod predicti magister et confratres soluant dictas decem libras exeuntes de Gildis predictis eisdem priori et conventui et eorum successoribus dum eisdem magistro et confratribus placuerit. Et modo maior et Balliui & camerarii die Jouis proximo post festum S. Dionisii anno octauo supradicto & per assensum Ric. Luff, Ric. de Dodenale, Nic. de Frereby, Joh. de Molton, Joh. de Withibrook, Rob. de Cortenhall, pro se & vicinis suis in vico de Gosford; Joh. Twenge, Ric. Bobynhull, Will. Cowper, Joh. Benduyle, pro se et vicinis suis in le Mulnlone et New strette; Ad. Botoner, Joh. Toftes, Ric. Verdon, Dauid Corby pro (etc.)[2] apud Jordenwell; Ric. Clerk, Joh. Andrew, Joh. Lybard, Ric. Hatter, Hen. Dilcok, Joh. Northfolk, Sim. ffrebern, pro (etc.) in vico Parci Maioris; Joh. de Stow, Will. Gryme, Pet. de Charelton, Will. de Wodusbury, Joh. Crudworth, Joh. de Stafford, pro (etc.) in vico Comitis, & in vico Parci Minoris; Joh. Founder, Ric.

[1] MS. repeats after necne "consentire voluerint ut campi predicti sint in futuro separabiles."

[2] (etc.) between brackets denotes the omission of a repetition in the MS.; etc. without brackets is, on the contrary, found in the MS.

others in Bayly Lane and Hay Lane; others at Broad Gate and Friar Lane; others in Smithford Street; others in Spon Street; and others in Cross Cheaping; others within S. John's-bridge, it was ordained and conceded that the said master and brethren of the said gilds well, peacefully, freely and quietly may have and possess the said fields all times of the year for themselves and their successors, without hindrance or disturbance of any one of the community; paying yearly to the said prior and convent and their successors £10 while it shall please the said master and brethren.

[Another leet on this same matter following.]

Coteller, Sim. Sheffield, Joh. Bate, & Nic. Glasewright p*ro* (etc.) in Baylilane et Heylane; Rog. Dandy, Tho. M*ar*shall, Walt. Cull, Tho. Grene, Will. Cuttyler, Will. Okcam, Will. Peyntou*r* p*ro* (etc.) ad Latam Portam et Frere lane; Joh. Perry, Joh. Maxstock, Will. Craas, Ric. Dubber, Ric. Welton, Joh. Russell, Hug. Woleman, p*ro* (etc.) in vico de Smythford; Ric. de Duddeley, Joh. Pape, Ric. Helony, Tho. Godeale, Joh. de ffrereby, And. Napton, Joh. Haw, Joh. Raye, Joh. Wallsall, Tho. Flawndurs p*ro* (etc.) in vico de Sponna; Rob. Fureneaux, Joh. Moldriche, Rog. de Weedon, Rob. de Estelton, Ad. de Keresley, Tho. de Sutton p*ro* (etc.) in vico de Croschepyng; Will. Pakstaf, Joh. Meie, Rob. Ascheburne, Will. Cockes, Rob. Wolff, Rog. de Lodyngton, p*ro* (etc.) int*er* (*sic*) pontem S. Joh*ann*is, ordinat*um* et concess*um* fuit q*uo*d p*re*dict*i* magist*er* et conf*ra*tres dict*arum* Gildar*um* bene, pacifice, lib*er*e et quiete d*i*ctos campos omni temp*or*e anni h*ab*eant et p*er*cipiant p*ro* se et successorib*us* suis, absq*ue* aliq*uo* impedimento, vel p*ertur*bac*ion*e alicui*us* de co*mmun*itate ville p*re*dict*e*; soluend*o* annuatim p*re*fat*is* p*ri*ori et conventui et eor*um* successorib*us* p*re*dictas decem libr*as* dum eisdem m*agist*ro & conf*ra*trib*us* placu*er*it.

Alia leta sup*er* eade*m* mat*er*ia sequen*te*.[1]

[1] v. *infra*, p. 19, and *Life in an Old English Town*, 75–7.

§ 3. METES AND BOUNDS. RADFORD.

[12 H. IV. Sept. 30, 1410–Sept. 29, 1411.

[1] "Radford."

[Bounds begin at a stone cross in the highway between Coventry and Radford, thence by a lane under Cobelyng-croft to Batemans-acre, and thence to another lane between Batemans-acre and Myriholt leading to Schochers-lane including the pastures, Batemans-acre and Ashmore, thence to Hill-lane, thence to Shottes-lane or Boker-mill-lane, and thus through Whitmore-Park by the hedge and ditch below the said park between Thamley and Shottes-field, descending by the other ditch below the park to R. Beaufitz' tenement, including the whole

[2] 18° die Febuarii 1583.

A true Coppie of the metes, bond*es* and divisions of certen hamlett*es* neare vnto the Cittie of Coventre taken out of a boke written w*ith* old Gregories hand as followethe:

[3] A*nno* R. Henrici quarti post conquest*um* xii°.

Hec sunt mete, bunde et diuise totius hamlette de Radford. Im-p*ri*mis, incipit ad Crucem Lapide*am*, q*ue* stat in Regia via ducent*e* de Couentr*ia* u*er*sus Radford: Et a cruce p*er* vna*m* venella*m* subtus Croftu*m* Ric*ardi* Clarke, voc*atum* Le Cobelyng Crofte, q*ue* ducit ad[4] Botemans acre, et abinde ad alia*m* venella*m* int*er* le Batemansacre & magnu*m* campu*m*, vocatu*m* le Myriholt, ducent*em* ad al*iam* venella*m*, voca-t*am* Le Schocherslane, includend*o* pastur*as* de Batemansacre & Ashe-more, & abhinc ad venella*m* vocat*am* Lehullane int*er* Counduln & Chil-t*er*nsleys,[5] & abinde ad alia*m* venel-l*am*, vocat*am* Shotteslane,[6] sive Bokermillane,[7] & sic p*er* mediu*m* p*ar*ci de Whittemore p*er* cepem & fossat*um* infra p*ar*cu*m* p*re*d*ictum* int*er* Thamley & Shottesfield,[6] & sic descendendo p*er* aliud fossat*um* infra p*ar*cu*m* ad ten*ementum* Ric*ardi* Beaufitz, includend*o* semp*er* totu*m*

[1] The marginal notes between commas " " are in the MS.
[2] leaf ii, Scribe Z.
[3] See also Lansd. MS. 400, f. 3: Rentale fact*um* p*er* f*ra*trem Will*elmu*m Haloughton, monachu*m* Couentr*ie* . . . de redditibus pertinentibus Priori et Conventui . . . in Whytmore, Coundulne, Keruesley, Coreley, Ecclesale, Newlande, Wylnehale, ffolxhull, Stoke et Coventre. I refer to this as L. Unimportant variations are not noted. [4] p*er* L. [5] Chiternleys L. [6] Scottes- L.
[7] Bokermlane L.

manor of Whitmore, with fields and pastures on either side to Endemore water, and thus by that brook as far as Ounettes-forthe and from that ford through the middle of Shuckmore, and from Shuckmore to Sandipit-lane, and from that lane by the hedge between Hill-field above Radford and the field to the N. of S. Nicholas' Church, until the cross where it begins. Thus ends the vill of Radford, in Trinity parish, parcel of the half of Coventry in which the Cathedral was founded.

man*erium* de Whitemore cu*m* campis & pastur*is* ex vtrisq*ue* (*sic*)[1] p*ar*te annex*is*, & a ten*emento* d*icte* (*sic*) Ric*ardi*, vsqu*e* ad aqua*m* de Endemore,[2] et sic p*er* illud[3] Riuulu*m* vsq*ue* ad Ounett*es*forthe,[4] & ab illo vado p*er* mediu*m* Shuckmore,[5] excludend*o* le Steplefield, & a Schuckmore[5] ad Sandipitlane,[6] & ab illa venella p*er* sepem int*er* Hullfield sup*er* Radford & Campu*m* ex p*ar*te boreal*i*[7] eccl*es*ie S. Nich*olai* vsq*ue* ad crucem p*re*d*ictam* vbi incipit. Et sic t*er*minat*ur* villa de Radford, & est in p*ar*ochia S. Trinitat*is* in Couentr*ia*, ac p*ar*cell*a* mediet*atis* ville Couentr*ie* in qua fundata est eccl*es*ia Cath*edralis* Couentr*ie* cu*m* al*iis*.

"Counduln."

[Prior as lord of Coundon has view of frankpledge, gallows, pillory, assize of bread and beer, felons' and fugitives' goods, heriot, mortuary fee, waif and stray, and is rector; he has a pasture called Fowlesmore and Prior's-field.

¶ Prior de Couentr*ia* est d*ominus* de Coundulne, & h*ab*et ibi vis*um* f*ran*cipl*egii* o*mnium* tenen*tium* suor*um* ib*idem*, furc*as* & Collistrigiu*m*, assis*am* pan*is* & servis*ie*, et o*mn*ia q*ue* ad vis*um* [8]f*ranci*pl*egii*[8] [pertinent], Catall*a* felon*um* & fugitivor*um*, harriet*a* & principal*ia*, vay*vium* & extrah*uras*,[9] et est Rector eiusdem hamlet*i* et h*ab*et in manu sua vna*m* pastura*m*,[10] vocat*am* Le ffowlesmore & Priors feild, et om*nia* al*ia* terr*e* et ten*ementa* ib*idem* sunt in manib*us* tenent*ium*.

[The vill is part of the half of Coventry, in Trinity parish, and of the foundation of the mother church.

Ista villa est membru*m* mediet*atis* ville Couentr*ie*, et de p*ar*och*ia* S. Trinitat*is* Couentr*ie*, et de fundac*io*ne eccl*es*ie matric*is* Coventr*ie*.

[1] vtraque L.
[2] Corp. MSS. C. 95. Grant of a pasture called "Enedmere in t*er*ritorio de Radeforde." [3] *sic.* sup*er* illu*m* L. [4] f. 3 dorso. [5] Schuggemore L.
[6] Sandyput- L. [7] *sic.* boreali L. [8–8] omitted L.
[9] MS. here blotted and almost illegible. [10] grava*m* L.

[1] "Coundul*ne* dominii."

[Bounds of New Coundon. Begins in Hill-lane by Chiltern's land, and thus to the gate of Prior's-field, thence to Benitt hedge, including Benitte's-field, thence to Warensdam, and thence by Pokebrook as far as Northbrook by a boundary to an oak between two warrens, and thence by a mere to Brown's-lane, and thus by the lane to Brown's oak, thence to a ditch under Holynfast wood, and by the ditch to Thiefstake-field, thence by the highway which leads to Coundon gallows, and thence below Bushell-field to Shottes-lane, then across the highway to Hill-lane.]

[2] ¶ Mete, divise et bunde dominii noui Coundulne. Inp*r*imis incipit in introitu vocat*o* Le Hullane iux*t*a ter*ram* Rob*er*ti de Chilt*er*ne, et sic p*er* dic*tam* venell*am* vsq*ue* ad port*am* tocius[3] Campi, vocat*i* le Priors feild, deinde ad sepem voc*atam* Le Benitt hedge, includend*o* le Benitt*es* feild & Boyden grove, et ab illa hedge direct*o* ad Warensdam[4] illa*m* includend*o*, et abhinc direct*o* p*er* le Pokebroke usq*ue* ad Northebrocke, et ab illo riuo p*er* q*uamdam* meta*m*[5] vsq*ue* ad quarcu*m* (*sic*)[6] int*er* duos cunicular*ios*, includend*o* semp*er* vnu*m* cunicular*ium*, et abinde p*er* alia*m* mera*m* vsq*ue* ad Browneslane, & sic p*er* mediu*m* d*icte* venell*e* vsque ad Browneshack,[7] & tunc ab illa quercu vsq*ue* fossat*um* subtus boscu*m* de Holynfast, & sic direct*o* p*er* p*redictum* fossat*um* vsq*ue* le Theifestakefeild,[8] includend*o* dict*um* campu*m*, et deinde p*er* Regia*m* via*m*, que duc*it* ad furc*as* de Coundulne, et deinde p*er* regia*m* via*m* subtus Bushell feild vsque ad Shotteslane[9] et deinde direct*o* ex transv*er*so Regia*m* via*m* (*sic*)[10] vsq*ue* ad venella*m* de Hullane, vbi p*r*ius incipit.

"Coundul*ne* p*a*roch*ia*."

[Coundon parish begins at the oak called Brown's-oak, and thence to Brown's-lane, and

¶ Mete & bunde totius p*a*roch*ie* de Coundulne iux*ta* Couentr*iam*. Inp*r*imis incipit ad quarcu*m* (*sic*) voca*tam* Le Brounshacke, & deinde ad venella*m* vocata*m* Le Brounslane, & sic p*er* medium venelle, & ab hinc

[1] leaf ii a. [2] f. 9. [3] *sic.* illius L. [4] Warreynsdam L. [5] ? mera*m*. [6] quercum L, *et passim*. [7] Brounshoke L. [8] Thefetakefeld L. [9] Scottes L. [10] vie L.

turning by a boundary to the oak between two warrens, and thus direct to Frithbrook, and thence to Allesley mill, thence by the mill-water to Burton's mill on Spon bridge, and thus by the lane leading to Woodmilles-hey to Scocher-lane, and thence by the way leading to S. Chad's chapel below Batemans-acre to Hill-lane, and thence to the way that leads from Corley by Coundon gallows, and thence to Thiefstake, and by the ditch under Holifast, to the oak where it begins.]

diu*er*tend*o* p*er* quanda*m* meta*m*[1] vsq*ue* ad quarcu*m* int*er* duos cunicular*ios*, includend*o* semp*er* vnu*m* cunicular*ium*, et sic ab illa quarcu p*er* alia*m* mera*m* direct*o* vsq*ue* ffrith-broke, & sic p*er* illu*m* riuulu*m*[2] vsq*ue* ad molendinu*m* de Allesley, & abinde p*er* aqua*m* dict*i* molend*ini* p*er* mediu*m* Alshawe direct*o* p*er* aqua*m* pred*ictam* vsq*ue* ad molendinu*m* Ric*ardi* de Burton sup*er* pontem de Sponna, et sic ab illo molendino direc*to* p*er* p*ar*va*m* venella*m* ducente*m* u*er*sus Woodmilles[3] heye, vsq*ue* ad al*iam* venella*m*, vocat*am* Scocherlane, & sic p*er* regia*m* via*m* q*ue* ducit de Couentr*ia* u*er*sus Capella*m* S. Cedde subtus Botemansacre & Ashemore,[4] vsq*ue* ad venella*m* vocat*am* Le Hullane, & sic p*er* dicta*m* venella*m* vsq*ue* ad Regia*m* via*m* q*ue* ducit de Corley p*er* furcas de Coundulne, & sic abinde vsq*ue* ad Theefestake, & sic diu*er*tend*o* vsq*ue* ad fossatu*m* subtus Holifast, & sic p*er* fossat*um* pred*ictum* vsq*ue* ad quarcu*m* Brounshack vbi p*r*ius incipit.

"Counduln."

[5]Co*mmuni* (*sic*) fin*es*[6] de Counduln cu*m* operib*us* natiu*orum*[7] tenent*ium*.

[First from J. Northampton for the holding once R. Reynolds' of Coundon, 12*d.* a year. And he finds a cart for the carriage of hay from Fynford to Couentry, or pays annually 12*d.* for a cart.

¶ Inp*r*imis, de Joh. Northampton *pro* ten*emento* quonda*m* Ric. Reynold*es* de Coundulne p*er* ann : xij d. Et invenit Carect*am* *pro* Carriag*io* feni a Fynford vsq*ue* Couentr*iam*, vel sol*vit* annuat*im* xij d. *pro* carrect*a*.[8]

[From W. Odard for a common fine of that field in Coun-

Item de Will. Odard *pro* co*mmuni* fine illius campi in Conduln, que*m*

[1] mera*m* L. [2] rivu*m* L. [3] Woddemyll L. [4] f. 9 dorso. [5] leaf iii. [6] co*mmunis* finis L. [7] native L. [8] carecta L, *et passim*.

don, which he holds at the lord's will, called Bennettes field, 11*d.* a year.

tenet ad voluntat*em* d*omi*ni, vocat*i* le Bennettes feild, xjd. per ann:

[From the same William for his field which he holds by the king's highway, for the common fine of 8*d.* a year; half a cart at Fynford, 6*d.*

Item de eodem Will*elmo* p*ro* campo suo, quem tenet ib*ide*m iux*ta* regia*m* via*m* p*ro* co*mmun*i fine p*er* ann: viijd. Et p*ro* dimid*ia* carect*a* apud Fynford vjd.

[From R. Shipley for land in Coundon called Norman place common, fine 12*d.* a year, and for a cart at Fynford, 12*d.*

Item de Rob. Shipley p*ro* terra in campis de Counduln voc*ata* Norm*an* place, p*ro* co*mmun*i fine p*er* ann: xijd. & p*ro* carrect*a* apud Fynford xijd.

[From J. Hoore for his holding 7½*d.* a year, and for half a cart, 6*d.*

Item de Joh. Hoore p*ro* co*mmun*i fin*e* tene*men*ti sui p*er* ann. vijd. ob. et p*ro* dimidia carrect*a* vjd.

[From J. Boyden for common fine of S. Reynolds' land, 1½*d.* a year. And for a fork-load of hay at Fynford, 2*d.*

Item de Joh. Boyden p*ro* (etc.) de terr*a* Sim. Reynolds p*er* ann. jd. ob. Et vno furcatorio feni apud Fynford ijd.

[From J. Oneley for Gallows-tree-field, 7*d.* a year, and for a fork-load, 2*d.*

Item de Joh. Oneley p*ro* (etc.) de Gallowstrefeild[1] per ann. vijd., et p*ro* vno furcatorio ijd.

[From W. Collins for Hobcroft, 4*d.*

Item, de Will. Collyns p*ro* (etc.) de Hobcroft iiijd.

[T. Disher, Geffrey-field, 4*d.*

It*em* de Tho. Disher p*ro* (etc.) de Geffrey feild p*er* ann. iiijd.

[Keresley for J. Reynolds' holding, and for half a cart, 6*d.*]

Item de[2] Kerusley p*ro* (etc.) de ten*emento* Joh. Reynold*es* xijd., et p*ro* dimid*ia* carrect*a* vjd.

[Hasilwood within the liberties begins in Caludon lane, and contains all Stoke, much of Harnal, part of Whitmore, and Henley, and the wood of Lord Segrave in Hasilwood.

Boscus Intrinsecus de Hasilwood incipit in Calloudon Lane, & continet totu*m* Stoke, m*ultum* de Harehal, parte*m* de Whitemore & Henley, et bosc*um* d*omin*us (*sic*) Segrave in Hasilwood.

Segrave's deed;

[3]ij deid*es* of demises made by John

[1] Gallowtrefield L. [2] No other name in MS.

[3] These are probably notes of miscellaneous copies. For Ranulf's charter v. Dugd. 110; for Joh. de Segrave of Caludon *ib.* 88, and for Osbarte *ib.* 180.

dominus de Segrave.

[the Abbot's deed;] One deide of Osbarte, abbott of Stoneley.

[other deeds;] One deide of demyse made by R. of Stivechall, & Wm. of Pynley.

[Ranulf's deed.] One deide of Randle, Ear[l]e of Chester.

"Stychall."

[Stivichall parish, part of S. Michael's, from Dillotford by the river Sherborne to Heathe mill, and by the said watercourse to the Bagington fuller's mill, and thence to Alsorsaie meadow, and thence to Merdon-siche, and turning by the ditch to Grange-lane, thence by the ditch to Corks-lane, thence to Sandely-green, and athwart the green to K. de Shultern's close, the Cannocks or Canley yard, and thence to Hallane, and by that lane to the Ridings, and thence to the king's

[1] Mete, bunde et divise parochie de Stichall.

¶ Inprimis, parochia de Stichall, que est parcella ecclesie S. Michaelis Coventrie, incipit ad Dillotford in le Hale, illud croftum de le Hale includendo. Et sic per aquam de Sherbourn vsque ad Heathe milne, illud molendinum includendo, & sic per cursum aque [2] vsque ad molendinum ffullonis de Bakington, includendo le floodeyates dicte (*sic*) molendini et dimidium cursum aque decurrentis de predicto molendino. Et abinde per aquam predictam diuertendo ad pratum de Alsorsaie, illud pratum includendo. Et abhinc vsque Merdonsiche. Et sic per illam siche diuertendo vsque venellam vocatam Grange lane end, et abinde per fossatum quod ducit ad Corkslane. Et sic per illam venellam vsque Sandeley grene, et sic ex transverso dicti greene vsque ad fossatum Clausure Katerine de Shultern [*interlined* Kanox de Canley] vocate Canley yard, et [3] sic per illud fossatum vsque ad Hallane[3] [*interlined* Harnale] & sic per Litle wast [*interlined* ad Astull wast][4], et sic per illam venellam vsque le Ruydinges,

[1] leaf iii a. Not in L. [2] insert *predicte*.

[3–3] Repeated again except the word "illud" in MS. after 'Astull waste.'

[4] Margin reads: 'Mem. that the wordes that be enterlined are the wordes that be lately Corropted and Rased in the prior's boke in the Exchequer.'

highway that leads to the highway to Coventry.]	et abinde ad regiam Viam, qui (*sic*) ducit ad regiam viam uersus Couentriam.
	Rentale de Stychall.
[J. Francis, Joh. Marshall and T. Overton held a chief messuage in Stivichall	Item, Joh. ffraunces, Joh. Marshall & Tho. Overton tenent simul vnum Capitale messuagium in Styuchall, quondam Vitalis de Folxhull, quondam Johannis de Shultern, et quondam Johannis de Honington in campis
of the prior, and pay 8*s*. "viij s." to the treasurer, also heriot, ward, relief and other services.	eidem annexis, de priore et Conuentu de Coventria, pro quo soluunt per ann: officio Thesaurarii viij s. ad quatuor terminos [anni] et harriet (*sic*), ward, relivium, et omnia alia seruicia inde debita et Consueta.
[This service reserved in a fine between William, the prior, and R. de Mohaut, concerning land in Stivichall and Wyken.	Istud servicium reseruatur in fine levato inter Willelmum, priorem et Rogerum de Monte Alto et Ciciliam vxorem eius, de terra dicti Vitalis in Styuchall et Galfridi Langley in Wiken.[1]
[The same John and his joint holders hold Little-waste, paying 2*s*. "ij s." to the Treasurer; they inclosed this waste lately with the prior's licence.	Idem Johannes et parcenarii sui predicti tenent in feodo in eadem villa vnum vastum, vocatum Le Litle wast, pro quo soluunt per ann: officio Thesaurarii ij s. et alia omnia serviciia inde (etc.). Quod quidem vastum nouiter incluserunt licencia prioris et Conuentus etc.
[Joh. Clarke holds also a message and two pieces of land in Stivichall-fields, which messuage is at the Coventry end of Stivichall, and was once [? part of] the glebe, for which he pays 8*s*. "viij s."	Item, Joh. Clarke de Stychall tenet ad terminum vite vnam (*sic*) messuagium et duas magnas pecias terre in Campis de Stichall, quod quidem messuagium situatum est ad finem ville *de* Stychall uersus Couentriam, quod quondam fuit gleba rectorie de Stichall, pro quibus soluit per ann: officio Thesaurarii viij s., et

[1] For Roger de Mohaut see *Life in an Old English Town*, 59, 60, Dugdale, 94–5.

to the treasurer every year, and all other usual services.

[Dom. J. Hallome, chaplain, has a cottage,

and pays 6*d.*

"vj d."

a year,
and this cottage belongs to the Convent treasury.

[The prior has the reversion of three cottages

and ten acres of land,
after the said John's and A. Elcock's death.

[The prior as rector has tithes of sheaves, hay, lambs, fleeces, mortuary fee, and tithes of fish caught in the fuller's mill,

and of the meadow assigned to tithe.

[Prior finds a chaplain to celebrate Divine service three days a week, and buries the dead at Coventry.

[Tithe of sheaves worth 100*s.* and of hay, lambs and fleeces, 26*s.* 8*d.*]

[2] "Kerresley."

[Bounds of Keresley, demesne and parish.

[It begins at Coundon gallows under Gallows-tree-field, and thence by the king's high-

harriet et om*n*ia al*ia* se*r*uic*ia* inde (etc.).

Item, d*ominus* Joh. Hallome, Capell*anus*, ten*et* ad t*er*minu*m* vitè vnu*m* Cottag*ium* in eade*m* qui (*sic*) iacet int*er* terr*am* Will*elm*i Canley, et ter*ram* Joh*ann*is ffraunc*is* & socioru*m* suoru*m*, *pro* quo sol*uit* *per* ann. vj d. et heriet et om*n*ia al*ia* seruic*ia* inde (etc.). Istud Cottagi*um* p*er*tinet Cam*er*e Convent*us* Coventr*ie*. Et sciend*um* est q*uod* p*re*d*ictus* p*r*ior et Conventus habent reu*er*c*io*ne*m* triu*m* Cottag*iorum* simul situat*orum* in Styuchall, cu*m* decem acr*is* terr*e*, post decess*um* p*re*d*icti* Joh*ann*is et Agn*etis* Elcock.

Prior est rector eiusdem hamlett*i*, et h*ab*et dec*imas* garbar*um*, feni, agnello*rum*, velles (*sic*), principal*ia* et dec*imas* pisciu*m* capt*orum* in le flodyates molend*ini* ffulonis de Baginton. Et dec*imas* p*r*ati iac*entis* in p*a*rcell*is* assignat*is* *pro* dec*imatione*. Et p*r*ior invenit ib*ide*m Capellanu*m* di*vi*na ib*ide*m celebrat*urum* *per* tres dies in septimana, et sepeliet[1] Cadau*er*a mortuor*um* ap*u*d Coventr*iam*. Et valet (*sic*) decime garbar*um* ib*ide*m C s. et dec*ime* feni, agnell*orum*, et vellor*um* (*sic*) xxvj s. viij d.

¶ [3]Met*e*, diuis*e* et bunde tocius dominii de Kerresley ac p*a*roch*ie* eiusdem q*ue* est p*a*roch*ia* S. Mich*ael*is Coventr*ie*. Inp*r*imis incipit ad furcas de Counduln, q*ue* situat*ur* (*sic*) subtus le Gallowetrefeild, et sic directo a p*re*d*ictis* furc*is* *per* Regia*m* via*m*, q*ue* ducit de Coventr*ia* u*er*sus Corley

[1] MS. reads 'sepelieit.'

[2] leaf iv.

[3] L. f. 16.

way to Allesley gallows, thence to Thiefstake-field pits, and thus by a hedge by R. Priest's land to Hen-lane, which divides Keresley demesne from Corley and Keresley parishes; and thus to the highway toward Astley under Corley grove; and thus to the corner of the field of the Manor of Newland called the Bryches, and by the hedge to Ouerheye-field, and by the hedge towards Newland, and by a way as far as Whitmore park, and by a way below the park, and a hedge called Ledyat-lane, and a hedge under R. Sewall's meadow, to Coundon gallows.]

vsq*ue* ad furcas de [1]Allesley, uel[1] Corley, et abinde ad Campu*m* vocatum le Theiffestake feild pit*is*, ipsu*m* Campu*m* includend*o*, & sic p*er* sepem et fossat*um* int*er* *le* Theiffestakefeild pitt*is* et terr*am* Ric*ard*i Preist de Corley, vsq*ue* ad venell*am* vocat*am* Heyne lane, q*ue* diuidit int*er* domin*ium* et p*a*roch*ias* de Kerresley & Corley; & sic p*er* illa*m* venella*m* vsq*ue* ad regia*m* via*m* q*ue* ducit u*er*sus Astley subtus grova*m* prior*is* vocat*am* le Corley grove, & sic p*er* illa*m* Regia*m* via*m* ad corne*r*am campi man*er*ii de Nova terra, voc*atam* le Bryches; et sic p*er* ill*am* sep*em* ad campu*m* voc*atum* le Ouerheye, et sic direct*o* p*er* sepem et fossat*um* illius campi, q*ue* duc*unt* u*er*sus p*a*rcu*m* de Whitemore u*er*sus Nova*m* terr*am*; et sic p*er* illa*m* via*m* vsq*ue* ad p*a*rcu*m* de Whitemore, et abinde p*er* via*m* subtus p*a*rcu*m* u*er*sus austru*m* vsq*ue* ad venella*m* subtus p*a*rcu*m* voc*atam* Ledyatlane; & sic p*er* illa*m* venella*m* & p*er* sepem subtus p*a*rcu*m* voc*atum* le medowe Rob*er*ti Sewall, & sic direc*to* p*er* sepem terre d*ict*i Rob*er*ti vsq*ue* ad furc*as* de Counduln, vbi incipit.

'Ecclessall.'

[Boundaries of Exhall. It begins at Newland corner, stretching by the ditch of S. John's hospital called Corley-heye, and Meynerd's-field,

[2]¶ Iste sunt mete, bunde & diuise totius p*a*roch*ie* de Ecclessall. Inprimis, incipit ad cornera*m* [1]terre,[1] Nove terre, extendent (*sic*) p*er* quo*d*dam fossat*um* hospital*is* S. Joh*ann*is vocat*um* le Corley heye in p*a*roch*ia* de Corley, et campu*m* p*re*d*icti* hospital*is* vocat*um* Meynerdsfeild, illud

[1—1] omitted L.

[2] f. 28 dorso.

as far as Corley brook, and by the brook to Smercote water mill, and thence turning by the hedge and ditch called Row-ditch, as far as Lufay-green, and by the highway to Catcroft-lane, and thus to Little-heath, and thus to Bedworth rectory gate, and to Dounbroke, and to the Doun-gate, and How-gate, and by Weston-heye to Priest's-wood-end. And thence by the ditch between the Hey and Sydnall-wood, to Boyse-waste; and thence to Warche-lane, to Foleshill-gate. Sydnall-wood, the Breches, and Sidells are in both Exhall and Foleshill parishes.

And thence to Blackamore, and by the hedge to the pen which R. in le Close holds. And thence

campu*m* includend*o*, vsq*ue* ad cursu*m* aque ib*idem*, vocat*um* Corley broke; et sic p*er* illu*m* cursu*m* aque vsq*ue* ad portas aquatici molend*ini* de Smercote[1]; et deinde diu*er*tend*o* p*er* sepem et fossat*um* ib*idem*, vocat*um* le Rowdiche, vsq*ue* ad Lufay grene; & sic p*er* Regiam via*m* semp*er* p*er* *le* Rowdiche vsq*ue* ad Catcroft Lane; & sic p*er* ill*am* venell*am* vsq*ue* ad Litle heathe, & abhinc semp*er* p*er* le Rowdiche vsq*ue* ad porta*m* Rectorie[2] de Bedworthe, semp*er* p*er* le Rowdiche vsq*ue* ad Dounebroke, & abhinc diu*er*tend*o* p*er* le Rowdiche int*er* Exall & Bedworthe vsq*ue* ad le Dounȝate; & abinde semp*er* p*er* *l*e Rowdiche vsq*ue* ad Howyate, & abhinc semp*er* p*er* le Weston heye vsq*ue* ad Preiste*s* wood end. Et abinde p*er* fossat*um* int*er* le Hey & Sydnall wood,[3] (hic[4] int*er*mediant[5] p*a*roch*ie* de Ecclesall & Folleshill)[4] vsq*ue* ad Boyse wast, et abhinc vsq*ue* ad Warchelane,[6] & abinde p*er* fossat*um* vsq*ue* ad Folleshull yate. Et sic boscus de Sidenhall, le Breches, & Sidell*s* et quicquid continet*ur* int*er* Merston waye et ffolkushull yate sunt de p*a*roch*iis* de Exall et ffolleshull simul mixt*is*.[7] Et a ffolkeshull yate vsq*ue* ad Blackamore, & sic per fossat*um* & sepem de Blackamore, vsq*ue* ad le pene qua*m* Ric*ard*us in le Close modo tenet. Et tunc abinde p*er* meta*m* diu*er*tend*o*[8] transu*er*so regia

[1] Smertcote L. [2] Rectoris L. [3] wod L.
[4—4] This also repeated in margin. [5] int*er*mediante L. [6] Wright- L.
[7] mixte L. [8] ex L.

across the kings highway towards Eaton, as far as Madgeleys,
and by the hedge
and W. Bandy's gate
to Wyblyns brook,

thence to R. Sewall's land,

and thence to Gybe-lane.

[1]"ffolkeshull."
[Bounds of Foleshill.

[Parish begins at hedge of Boyswaste by "Stakecrosse,"[2] and goes down by "Hooe" to "the le broke," and along it to "Lady lane," and goes up by this lane

to the further corner of "Mordiffe," and thence

across the end of Wood-lane by the ditch to a way opposite W. Bagott's house, including the Ruydinges and the Wethersfield, to the cross before H. Ive's gates. [Here the three parishes of Sow, Foleshall, Wyken end.] And thence

to the hedge and ditch which divides between Wyken and

via (*sic*)[3] q*ue* ducit de Couentr*ia* u*er*sus Eaton vsq*ue* ad Madgeleys, & sic p*er* sepem int*er* Madgeleys et terr*am* qua*m* Will. Bowton quonda*m* tenuit, & abinde p*er* porta*m* Will*elm*i Bandy, vsq*ue* ad Wybylyns-broke, & sic assendend*o*[4] p*er* regia*m* via*m* vsq*ue* ad [5]terr*am* qua*m* Rob. Sewall de Counduln modo tenet, illam excludend*o*, quia in p*a*roch*ia* de ffolkeshull [est], & abhinc vsq*ue* ad Gybe-lane etc.

¶ Mete, bunde & diuise [6]p*er* p*re*cinct*us* toti*us* dominii et[6] p*a*roch*ie* de ffolkshull.

[7]Inp*ri*mis, p*a*roch*ia* incipit ad vlt*er*iore*m* sepem de Boyswast iux*ta* Stake Crosse, illud vastu*m* includend*o*; et sic desendend*o* (*sic*)[8] p*er* sepem de le Howe vsque ad the lebroke,[9] et sic p*er* le broke vsq*ue* ad Lady Lane, et abinde ascendend*o* p*er* dict*am* venell*am* u*er*sus orient*em*, vsq*ue* ad vlt*er*iorem corner*am* de Mordiffe,[10] illud includend*o*; & adhinc ex t*ra*nsu*er*so finis de Woodlane p*er* fossat*um* vsq*ue* ad via*m* exopposito tenement*i* quond*am* Will*h*el*m*i Bagott includend*o* Le Ruyding*es* & le Wethersfeild,[11] vsq*ue* ad crucem que stat ante hostiu*m* Henr*ici* Iue. [Hic terminat*ur* (*sic*) p*a*roch*ie* de Sowe, ffolkeshull & Wiken.[12]] Et ab illa cruce descendend*o* u*er*sus ffolleshill p*er* Regia*m* via*m* ad sepem et fossat*um* que diuidunt int*er* Wiken & Henley vsq*ue*

[1] leaf iv (dorso). [2] The names within inverted commas are in margin.
[3] regie vie L, *et passim*. [4] *sic*. ascendendo L, *et passim*. [5] L. f. 29.
[6–6] omitted L. [7] L. f. 36 (dorso). [8] descendend*o* L. [9] Telebroke L.
[10] Morcyf L. [11] Wenchesfeld L. [12] In margin also with "nota ubi."

Henley as far as Henley brook, and thence to Miles-meadow, as far at Deedmore corner, and thus by the watercourse coming from Caludon well,—and from the well to Waterifield, as far as Hasilwood, including all the Henley demesne; and thus by Hasilwood as far as Redeslowe, and by Harnal-waste ditch, to Brood-oak, and thence across the highway to the farther hedge of the Ridings of S. John's Hospital, and by the croft called the Stripe to Ounetsford, and thus by Endemer water to the Slowe in Lockhurst-lane, and thence to Whitmore park corner, as far as Walsiche-lane, and thus as far as the way leading to Newland, as far as Lullehurst-lane, including Corley waste and Farthing-heye, and thus by the sich (brook) to Hugland, and by the hedge to W. Holbroke's land, as far as R. Green's land,

Henley broke; et sic p*er* illa*m* semp*er* vsq*ue* ad[1] Miles medowe, illud pratu*m* includend*o*, vsq*ue* ad cornera*m* de Deedmore; et sic assendend*o* (*sic*) per cursu*m* riuuli venient*is* de fonte de Calloughdon, & ab illa fonte direct*o* ad Wattorisfeild, illud campu*m* includend*o*, vsq*ue* ad Haselwood, totu*m* dominiu*m* de Henley includend*o*; et sic p*er* Haselwood vsq*ue* ad Redeslowe; & sic riu*er*tend*o* p*er* fossat*um* de Harnalwast, illud vastu*m* excludend*o*, vsq*ue* ad Brodehocke; et abinde ex t*r*ansu*er*so re[g]ia via (*sic*) ibi*dem* vsq*ue* ad vlt*er*iorem sepem de le Ruydinge*s* hospital*is* S. Joha*nn*is; & sic p*er* fossat*um* duor*um* campor*um* p*re*d*ictorum*, que vocant*ur* le Ruydinges,[2] et p*er* croftu*m* vocat*um* le Stripe vsq*ue* ad Ounetsford; et sic assendend*o* p*er* acqua*m* de Endemer vsq*ue* ad le Slowe[3] in Locarde*s* lane; et abinde diu*er*tend*o* ad cornera*m* p*ar*ci de Whitmore; et sic p*er* fossat*um* p*ar*ci p*re*d*icti* vsq*ue* ad Walsichelane, et sic p*er* illa*m* venella*m* vsq*ue* ad regia*m* via*m*, que ducit u*er*sus Nova*m* terra*m*, et dividit int*er* Folleshull & Kerusley[4] vsq*ue* ad Lullehurst-lane,[5] includend*o* totu*m* Corley wast & le Farthing heye; & sic descendend*o* p*er* le Seche vsq*ue* ad cornera*m* de Hugland; & sic assendend*o* (*sic*) p*er* sepem & fossat*um* int*er* Hugland et terr*am* Will*elm*i Holbroke vsq*ue* ad terra*m* p*re*d*ict*i Will*elm*i, illa*m* includend*o*, vsq*ue* ad terr*am* quond*am* Rad*ul*fi

[1] ab illa semper ad L. [2] Rudyng*es* L. [3] Slade L.
[4] In margin, 'divisio int*er* ffolleshull & Kerusley.' [5] Hulhurst L.

and thus by the well to Gibe-lane, and across Gib-lane to Elias Mylleward's land, and as far as the highway leading to Wolpitlediat, and thus to Madgeleys, and by the bound to the Eaton way, and thus to Shittehurneway, and thence to Shitt-croft corner, thence to Sydnall-gate, and thus by Merstone-way to Priest's-wood-end, and by that to the Heye; and by the ditch to Boyswaste; and thus Sydnall-wood, the Breches, and the Sidoles, and what is contained between Merstone way, Foleshill-gate, Blackamore and W. in the Close's pen, are of the joint parishes of Foleshill and Exhall.]

Greene, et sic ad pute[u]m inter terr*as* Rad*ulfi* Grene et Thome Grene, et a puteo directo ad Gibelane, et sic ex t*r*ansu*er*so le Gib-lane vsq*ue* ad terr*am* quond*am* Elie Mylleward q*uam* Rob*er*tus S[e]wald nu*n*c tenet, illa*m* terr*am* includend*o*, vsq*ue* ad Regia*m* via*m* que ducit ad Wolpitlediat; et sic p*er* illa*m* via*m* directo vsq*ue* ad Madgeleys, et sic direct*o* p*er* meta*m* vsq*ue* ad via*m* que ducit de Coventr*i*a u*er*sus Eyton, [1]vbi int*er*mediant pa*r*ochi*e* de ffolkeshull & Exall,[1] & sic direct*o* p*er* illa*m* via*m* vsq*ue* ad Shittehurne waye, & abhinc vsq*ue* ad Shittcrofte corner; & abinde ad Sydenhall-yate veniend*o* de Exall; & sic sequend*o* p*er* M*er*stone waye, vsq*ue* ad Preist*es* wood end, & sic sequendo le Preist*es* wood vsq*ue* ad le heye; & sic p*er* fossat*um* de le heye vsq*ue* ad Boyswast; & sic boscus de Sydenhall, le Breches, & le Sidoles & quicquid continet*ur* inter M*er*stone waye & ffolkeshull yate & Blackamore vsque ad le penne que*m* Will*helm*us in the Close nu*n*c tenet, sunt de pa*r*och*iis* de [2]ffolkeshull & Exhall simul mixte.[2]

§ 4. TRINITY GILD FIELDS.

[Oct. 4, 1414, it was ordained by the 24 honest and legal men of the same leet; viz. J. Pres-

[3]Ad v. f. p. tent*um* apu*d* Couentr*iam* die Jouis p*roximo* post fest*um* S. Michaelis arch*angeli* a. r. r. Henrici qui*n*t*i* (etc.) secu*n*do, Ordinat*um* fuit p*er* xx[ti] iiij[or] p*r*obos et legales ho*min*es eiusdem lete, v*idelicet* p*er*

[1]—[1] Repeated in margin. [2]—[2] In margin.

[3] Scribe A. leaf 6, back. V. f. p. = Visum franci plegii, view of frankpledge.

ton, etc.,

Joh. Preston, Joh. Skarborgh, Rob. Schipley, Will. Attilborgh, Joh. Allesley, Will. Bedford, Will. Belgraue, Joh. Goote, Joh. Horneby, Laur. Cooke, Pet. Weston, Joh. Parker, draper, Rob. Brodde, Joh. Happeford, Tho. Marchall, Joh. Wymondeswold, Hen. Wentbrygg, Tho. Harries, Galf. ffloure, Joh. Clerk, Ric. Joy, Edw. Lichefield, Will. Prees, jun: et Joh. Normaton,

that whoever in future damages the enclosure of the Trinity Gild fields be taken and imprisoned, there to remain until he have made amends fully according to the view of the then gild-master and six of his brethren without any grace.]

quod quilibet in futuro delinquens circa clausuram camporum gilde S. Trinitatis de Couentria capiatur et imprisonetur, ibidem com[m]oraturus donec sufficienter fecerit emendacionem per visum magistri Gilde predicte qui pro tempore fuerit, & sex suorum fratrum gilde predicte absque alia gracia.

§ 5. [1]MICHAELMAS LEET, 1420.

[V. f. p. Wednesday after Michaelmas day 8 Henry V. (Oct. 2, 1420.)]

[Jury of 24,

Joh. Onley, Will. Attilburgh, Will. Bedford, Will. Dilcok, Ric Southam, Laur. Cook, Ad. Deyster, Joh. Leeder, Rad. Garton, Tho. Wildgryse, Egid. Allesley, Rob. Byfeld, Joh. Herdburgh, Gal. Floure, Tho. Grene, Ric. Poweyr, Joh. Coton, Joh. Braytoft, Joh. Braunston, Will. Frysley,[2] Joh. Egeston, Joh. Montgomery, Joh. Dilcok, Joh. Michell.

who elect H. Peyto and J. Golofre bailiffs. At which view it was ordained that if any one prosecutes his neighbour in a strange county "court" without the mayor's

Qui elegerunt Hen. Peytoo et Joh. Golofre Balliuos.

Ad quem visum ordinatum fuit quod si aliquis imposterum prosequutus fuit (*sic*) proximum suum in Comitatu extraneo absque licencia

[1] leaf 11.

[2] ? Frysby.

licence he shall lose at every offence 100*s*.

maioris, q*uo*d pe*r*dat ad quodl*ibe*t delictu*m* centum solid*os*.

Street cleaning.

Allso hit was then ordenyd þ*a*t Will*iam* Oteley, wich kept[1] a cart & horses for clensyng of the stretys, shuld haue quarte*r*ly of eue*r*y hall dorre j d., & eue*r*y schop ob.

[Ordained that the openings in "cunduits" at Bablake and at the house formerly John Patch's, and in West Orchard be destroyed and stopt up, so that for the future they may not be used.]

Item ordinatu*m* fuit q*uo*d les Suspirales ap*u*d Bablake[2] et ap*u*d domu*m* nupe*r* Joh*ann*is Patch ac in le Westorchard deleant*ur* et obstupant*ur* (*sic*), Ita q*uo*d de cete*r*o no*n* vtant*ur*.

Item, at the same lete was ordenyd by the Justic*es* of peas, w*ith* thassent of the same lete, what artyficers and laborers shuld take from Mich*aelmas* vnto Estur aftur the fourm of the Statute, ut seq*uitur*.

ffirst, the m*a*ster mason shuld tak be þe day v d. w*ith*-out mete, and iij d. w*ith* meit & drynk.

"Raites of wages" of labourers fixed according to Statute of Labourers.

Item, a-noþ*er* mason þen a m*aste*r should take iiij d. w*ith*out meite, & ij d. w*ith* meit & drynk.

Item, a m*a*ster Carpynt*er* be the day v d. w*ith*out mete, & iij d. w*ith* mete, and a-noþ*er* iiij d. w*ith*-oute mete, and ij d. w*ith* mete.

Item, thakker, laborer, dawber, and palyer be the day iiij d. w*ith*out mete, & ij d. w*ith* mete.

Item, m*a*ster Tiler bo þe day iiij d. w*ith*out mete, and w*ith* met ij d., and his man iij d. w*ith*out mete, & j d. ob. w*ith* mete.

---

§ 6. [3]ELECTION OF JOHN LEEDER, JAN. 25, 1421.

Elecc*io* Noui maioris, Noui Coronatoris, [nouorum] Cam*erariorum* & Custod*um* reddit*um*, coram Joh*anne* Goote, tunc maiore, Henric*o* Peytoo et Joh*anne* Golofre, balliu*is* lib*er*tat*is* ciuitat*is* Couentr*ie*, die Saboti (*sic*) in festo conue*r*sionis S. Pauli, a. r. r. Henrici qui*n*ti post conq*uest*-

[Election of new mayor, coroner, chamberlains, & wardens of rents, before the mayor and bailiffs on Saturday, the Conversion of S. Paul, 8 Henry

[1] keepeth. [2] At the west end of Coventry. [3] leaf 1.

V until the same feast next following.

um octauo usq*ue* ad idem [festum] p*roximo* sequ*ens*.[1]

The under-written elect the mayor, coroner, bailiffs, wardens.]

Isti subsc*r*ipti elegerunt Joh*annem* Leeder Maiorem Ciuitat*is* Couentr*ie* p*ro* anno futuro, & Joh*annem* Dilcok coronator*em*, Joh*annem* Braytoft & Joh*annem* Bristow Came*r*ari*os*, et Wil*le*lm*um* Byfeld cum Joh*anne* Michell, Custod*es* redd*itum* ciuitat*is* p*re*d*i*cte.

24 Electors.

Joh. Oneley, Will. Bellg*r*aue, Joh. Esterton, Will. Dilcok, Will. Bedford, Will. Attilborgh, Rad. Garton, Tho. Grene, Egid. Allysley, Tho. Wildegryse, Will. Crose, Ric. Joy, Joh. Harborgh, Ric. Power, Joh. Clerk, Joh. Bowȝer, Joh. Egeston, Tho. Harrys, Joh. Tate, Will. Wymondeswold, Will. Crose, passynger,[2] Joh. Pynchebeke, Joh. Allysley, Irmonge*r*, Will. Barton, hosyar.

[Ordained that the wardens make their accounts on Monday after Mid-Lent Sunday next to come.]

Item, ordinaueru*nt* q*uo*d p*re*dict*us* (*sic*) Will*el*m*us* Byfelde, Joh*annes* Michell, Custod*es* reddit*um*, etc. facient compot*um* suu*m* p*ro* anno p*re*te*r*ito die Lune p*roximo* post diem Do*mini*cam in medio xlme p*roximo* futur*e*.

[Keepers of the keys of the common chest, where the common seal is kept.]

Isti sunt electi pe*r* maiorem Custodes, q*uorum* quil*ibe*t eoru*m* h*ab*et in custodia sua claues co*mmun*is pixid*is*, vbi co*mmun*e sigillu*m* co*mm*unitat*is* custodit*ur*, vide*lice*t, Joh. Leder, maior, vnu*m* (*sic*) clauem, Ad. Hyton, magister Gilde S. Trinitatis, aliu*m* clauem, Will. Bellg*r*aue, si*mi*lite*r* vnu*m* claue*m*, Ric. Southam aliu*m* clauem, Laur. Cooke vnu*m* clave*m*.

*Ordinacio maior*is *& consilii* p*ro* h*onestate ciuitat*is p*redicte.*

Ordinance of the Mayor and Council for the honesty of the said city.

Hitt is ordenyd that noo man put tymb*ur* ne kydd*es* ne Carry none thourho the churchyard, vpon the peyne of forfature of the forsaid tymb*ur* and kydd*es*; and that

[1] 1419 added in later hand. [2] v. Gloss.

no mān lay noo dōnge therin, vpon the peyn̄ of xij d. at euery defaute; Allso that no mān pyse in the churchyard, ne defile hit in noo maner wise, vpon the peyn̄ of vj d. for euery defaut without any grace.[2] "Church-yarde."[1]

[3]Allso that euery man make clene the streyte befor hur place be-twen this and Thursday, and so every Saturne-day aftur, that is to say, from Saturday thurgh the yer, vpon the payn of xij d. at euery defalte without any grace; and that no man Raak ne swep in tyme of rayne fro one to a-nothur, vpon the peyn of xij d. at euery default without any grace, and his body to prison. "Streets clensed."[1]

Allso that hit be lefull to euery sergeant & Constable to rere the peyn abouesaid, or els to tak distres þerfor, and who þat lettyth hym or stryvyth with hem, or fallyth at debate with hem doyng þer office, he shall have xl[ti] [daies] emprisonment, and pay xx s. to the vse of the Cite, with-outten any grace. Sergeant and constable to raise the fine.

Allso that no man [put] no dong out of hur housis in-to the hiȝe streit, but hit be caryed a-way within a nyght and a day, vpon the payn of xij d. at euery defaut to the vse of the Cite withouten grace. "Dung."

Allso that no man haue no tymbur, nor Stoonys nor stokkys[4] lyyng be-for hur places, ne vndur hur bulkes, ne in the highȝ streit, a-pon the peyn of xl d. and of forfatur of the said tymbur abovesaid. "Tymber in street."

Proclamacio maioris Coventrie.

THE MAYOR'S PROCLAMATION.

[5]We commaunde ȝou, on the kynges behalf of Inglond and of the maiours behalf and the Balyffes of Couentre, þat euery Baxster that bakethe to sale, that he bake & sell iiij wastels for a peny, and ij for a peny, and iiij cokett louys for a peny, & ij for a peny and no less, so þat they ben of good bultre, and well bake & weyyng as the "Bakers." Price of loaf and weight;

[1—1] The marginal notes in inverted commas are those in MS., but in a later hand.

[2] This sentence shows the line over the n and m, a recurrent feature of this scribe's work. It is not reproduced in any further citations in print.

[3] leaf 1, back. [4] MS. stolkys.

[5] See the Victuallers' Statutes, 13 Ric. II, st. 1, c. 8, and 23 Ed. III, c. 6.

kynges marchallsy wull, vp the peyn at the fyrst trespas xiij s. iiij d., at þe second trespas vp the peyn to lese xx s., and at the iijde trespas to stond apon the pillary, and at the fourthe trespas to forswer the fredom of this Cite a twelmonyth & a day. Allso þat they bake & sell iiij whet loues for a penny, and ij for a peny, and no lesse, and that they be well bake, & that hit be noo dowhȝ with*h*in, vp the same peyn; and iiij horselouys for a penny, up the same peyn, so þat they be made of bene meele and peise mele with*h*out branne[1] or draff, up the same peyne. Allso leeful be hit to the Bakers of the contre to com hid*u*r and sell hur brede, so that hit haue the weight as the kynges marchallsy wull; And þat no man lett them, vp the peyn of vj s. viij d. at euery trespas. Allso þat noo Osteler bake no maner of bred in h*u*r houses, nod*u*r mannys bred ne horsebred, to sell, up the payne of vj s. vii jd. at every trespas; and that they sell no derre in h*u*r Innes, ned*u*r benes, ne pesez, ne ootys in encrease, but as the Statute wull, that is to witt, at euery schillyng a penny.

penalties; country bakers; ostlers.

Allso we comm*a*unde that no maner man house no wyne till the maio*u*r haue sene hit, vp the peyne of xx s., and þat no tauerner put his wyne to sell but if hit be well fyned, vp the peyn of xx s. be the ouersight of the maio*u*r and his peerys at euery trespas; and þat they [2]sell þer wyn wit*h* mesur ensealyd, and that thei sell no red wyne, ner whitt wyne of Gascoyne no derre then viij d. a galon, and white wyne of Rochell no derre then vj d. a galon, & maluesey & romeney for xvj d. a galon and no derre, vp the peyn of xx s. at euery trespas. Allso that thei sell noo Osey ne algarbe ne no bastard till the meyres (*sic*) and his peres haue seen hit, & set price theron, as hit is worthe, vp the peyn of xx s. at euery trespas. And that thei set no maner of wyne abrooche till the maio*u*r haue seen hit, up the same peyn. Allso for-asmoche as hit is do the maio*u*r to witt þat tauerners haue sold wyne to certen men of h*u*r alye, be Tailes maid bytwen them, derre than þe maio*u*r hathe ordenyd hit to be sold, hit is comm*a*undyd þat as well he þat byeth

"Wyne"; Mayor to inspect wines.

[1] MS. inserts 'of.' [2] leaf 2.

wyne soo, as wele as the tauerner that sellyth his wyne so, schall lese xl s. at eu*er*y trespas.

Allso we com*m*aund that no breuster sell no derre a galon of good ale will hit is new vnd*ur* the here syve, but for j d.[1] q^a. and when hit is good and stale for j d.[2] ob. & noo der*re*, and that they seale *with* measures insealyd, & not *with* Cuppis ne bollys, and *with* sygne set oute; and that þei sell it furthe out of h*ur* housez, as well as *with*-Inne, by measuris ensealyd, vpon the payn þat who-so will mak trew playnt to the maio*ur* therof, he schall haue iiij d. for his travayll and a galon of the best ale. And all the remena*un*t schal-be sold for a ob. (½*d.*), and no derr*e* at euery trespas. And the maio*ur* schall take distrese of eu*er*y breuster or hukster founden in defaut, & pay vj s. viij d. at eu*er*y defaut; and that no breuster sell no derr*e* a Cestron ale to noo hukster but for xviij d., up the peyn of xl d. at eu*er*y defaut of eche brethon.[3]

"Bruer"; ale 1¼*d.* and 1½*d.* a gallon; bribe to informers.

Also we com*m*aund that no fyscher of Town ner of Contrey by no man*er* of fysche on Thursday over-nyght by way of regratry, ne on Fryday aft*ur* till hit be nyne of the Cloke, but if hit be lordys of the contrey or men of estate for h*ur* houshold, up the peyn of xx s. at eu*er*y t*r*espas. Allso þ*at* no man be so hardy to by ne reseyue in-to h*ur* housez, panyes *with* fyshe by way of regratry, up the payne of xx s., & lesyng all the fysche at euery trespas þ*at* they may be found *with*, and that they sell noo stynkyng fysche for mannys meit, vpon the same peyn.

"Fysche not regrated" on Thursday. Paniers of fish to be forfeited.

Allso we com*m*aund þ*at* no vitaler, ffyschemong*er*, ne non oþ*er* p*er*son, passe out of the Cite of Couentre for to by fische, ne non othur vitayle comyng toward the Cite, ne bye non in the Cite, till hit be ix of the clocke, till the maio*ur* haue seen hit, that hit be able for mannys mett, *with* the oue*r*sight of them þ*at* the maio*ur* hath ordenyd for to oue*r*se suche man*er* of vitales, vp the peyn of xl d. at eu*er*y defaut.

"Victuals to be viewed by the maiour," before purchase.

Allso we com*m*aund þ*at* no bocher sell noo beestis of moren, ne no roten Schēp,[4] ne Sussemy flesche, ne non

"Murrain beastz, rotten sheep," tainted flesh,

[1] quadrans, farthing. [2] obolus, ha'penny. [3] v. Gloss.
[4] The line occurs sometimes over vowels, v. note p. 23.

not to be sold by butchers.

swyn of brym, vp the peyn of xx s. at euery trespas; and þat thei put no flesche to sale on the Sonday that is left on the Thursday, but if hit be saltyd, and abull for mannys mette, up the same peyne. Allso lefull be hit vnto euery bocher of the contre that will com hithur, and sell flesche þat he com hidur when his lykyng ys, any day of the weke, & allso to take a house in what streit he will, and that no man let hym, vpon the [1] peyn of xl s. and hur boodies to be prisoned xl^ti daies. Allso lefull be hit to euery bocher within this cite to sley of euery maner of kynd of flesche sesonable to mannys mette, as myche as hem lykythe, and as ofte, so þat no caue be made among them in contrary, vnder the peyn of C s., and up the peyn of xx s. of euery bocher þat obeyth to suche Caue, and his boody to prison as ofte as he may be founden in suche defaute.

Country butchers;

no ordinance to the contrary under pain of 100s. fine.

"Cookes";

Allso we command[2] that no Cook by noo vitalys but in the comyn markett, as it is ordenyd, be wey of regratry, þat is [to] witt to kepe hem at the townys end or in the way, vp the peyn of vj s. viij d. at euery defaut. Allso þat no cooke sell no maner rechaufid meit[3] up the peyn aforseyd at euery trespas. Allso þat no Cook cast no maner of fylth vndur hur bordys, ne in the hye stret, ne suffur hit þer to lye, that is to wit, fethurs, here, ne entrayls of pygges, ne of no othur bestes, up the peyn of xl d. at euery trespas. And þat they sell the best Goos for iiij d., & no derre, up the same peyn. Allso þat thei bye noo maner of deed pykes ne Elys for to bake ne dyght for mannys meit, vp the same peyn.

no rechaufe;

no filth to be cast about;

no dead pikes or eels to be cooked.

"Corn not in Inz";

Allso we comaund þat non Osteler, ne non odur man dwellyng in this Cite, Receyve ne harbrugh no maner of Corn fro one day to anodur withoute the comune chepyng, up the peyn of xx s. at euery trespas. Allso þat noo bagger, ner non othur man sett no corn in hur houses ne in hydles,[4] but þat they leden hit in to the Chepyng, & put hit þer to sale hooly to-gethur, vp the peyn of forfature of all the Corn; And whosoeuer will com to the

badgers not to hide corn.

[1] leaf 2, back. [2] MS. comamd.

[3] Compare Chaucer's 'Jak of Dover' pies that had been 'twies hot & twies cold.' See also Bateson, *Leicester*, II, 321.

[4] *N.E.D.* hidels = hiding places.

maio*ur*, be he of town or of contrey, & warn him þ*er*of wher hit is hyd[1] or sett, he schall haue a st*r*ik of corne for his labour. Allso þ*at* all mane*r* of baggers that com to this Cite, w*ith* corne to sell, þ*at* they sett her corn by hem-selff, that is to witt, at the West orchard end, vp the peyn of xij d. at eue*r*y trespas.

Corn to be sold in the West Orchard.

Allso we com*m*aund þ*at* no man haue no Swyne goyng in the hyȝe streit, up the peyn of iiij d. at the first trespas, & at the second trespas viij d., ne that no man hold no swyne in hur bolkys,[2] ne in h*ur* stallys by the hyȝ way, up the payn of xl d. at eue*r*y trespas; and þ*at* no man haue no swyne goyng in no gardens ne pastures on the payn of xl d. at eue*r*y trespas.

"Swyne in the street"; no swine in bulks, or 4*d*. fine.

Allso we command þ*at* no Bocher ne vitaler in tyme comyng mak non ordyna*u*nce ne constituc*io*n, but ȝif thei byn oue*r*seen be the maio*ur* and the Balyff*es*, up the peyn of xl d. at eue*r*y trespas. Allso þ*at* no cong*r*egac*io*n be made be-cause echone to maynten odurs quarell,[3] ne goo to noo bede-ale out of this cyte, ne no rydyng into the contrey, w*ith*out leue of the maio*ur* and balyff*es*, up the peyn of xl s. at eue*r*y t*r*espas. Allso þ*at* no man be so bold ne so hardy to goo in-to the contrey to brek noo lordys park*es* for to sley hur dere, ne hur Conyes, vnd*ur* peyn of a C s., and hur boodies to p*r*ison.

"Boucher, Vitaylo*ur*, make no ordin*a*unce w*ith*out the Maio*ur*"; no maintaining of mutual quarrels among crafts; no one to break into lords' parks to slay conies and deer. 100*s*. fine.

[4]Allso þ*at* no man haue no dokys goyng in þe streit, vp the peyn of forfatur of the same dokes, at eue*r*y defaut þ*at* they may be founden w*ith*all, to the vse of the Cite.

"Duckes in the street."

Also þ*at* no man hold no g*r*ett hound*es* no byches goyng in the hyȝe way, up the payn of xl d. at eue*r*y trespas.

"Grey-houndes." 40*d*. fine.

Allso that no man throw ne cast at noo st*r*aunge man, ne skorn hym, ne draw no straw, ne hay, nor wood from no cart ne hors, vp the payn of emp*r*esonment of xl[ti] daies, and to mak fyne for the trespas to the maio*ur*.

"no scorno*ur* of stra*u*ge*rs*."

Allso we com*m*aund, and hit is ordenyd, that the Swan of this Cite drive the Swyne of this Cite to wastes and marreys a-bout this cite, & into non odur plac*es*, as in-to medows or in-to feldys, ne no whethur els as they may do harme, up the peyn of xl d. at eue*r*y trespas that

"Swine"; the swine-herd to drive swine to waste places.

[1] A deleted "of" follows. [2] v. Gloss.
[3] Something omitted. [4] leaf 3.

he may be founden *with*all, ȝif any man will playn on hym.

"Deister." "Nota."

Allso we com*m*aund þ*at* eue*r*y deister of this Cite, that hath a waturlad oue*r* the comyn Ryver, schall pay to the Chamb*ur*layns of this Cite eue*r*y yer xij d. to the vse of this Cite.

"Fysher"; fisher's board in the Cross Cheaping.

Allso we com*m*aund that eue*r*y fyscher, or any othur man þ*at* hath any borde or Crache stondyng in the Crosechepyng in the hiȝe way, that thay byn don a-way eue*r*y Saturneday aft*ur* none, up the peyn of xij d. at eue*r*y trespas, but ȝif hit be in Lent tyme.

"Sworde drawen." "Strikers."

Allso we com*m*aund that no man of town ne of contrey draw no swerd, ne knyfe, to odur, ne non othur wepon, up the peyn of xl d. at eue*r*y trespas, but if hit be hym-self defendant; and if he smyte *with* a swerd or a knyfe drawyn he schall pay half a ma*r*ke at eue*r*y trespas to the Baylyff*es*, but if hit be hym-self defendant.

"Sute in this cyty." 100*s*. fine.

Allso we com*m*aund þ*at* no man of this Cite plead oþ*er* of this Cite of cont*r*actes þ*at* be done in this cite in othur courtes *with*out the Cite, but onely in the court of the maio*ur* and baillif*es* of this Cite, np the peyn of a C s., at eue*r*y trespas þ*at* they may be found *with*, to be paid to the vse of this Cite.

"mares."

Allso þ*at* no man haue marys goyng in the comyn pastur, vp the peyn of xx s. at eue*r*y t*r*espas to the vse of the Cite.

"Cartz on Fryday."

Allso we com*m*and þ*at* no man bryng no kyddes to this Cite, ne non odur wood in cartes on the Fryday to sell, up the peyn of xij d. at eue*r*y t*r*espas to the vse of this Cite.

"Billz"; weapons forbidden.

Allso we com*m*aund that no bocher, ne non othur man of Craft, ne no nygh neighborgh of contre, ber no billys, ne gysarnez,[1] ne no grett stauys *with*in the Cite, up the peyn of forfat*ur*e of the same wepons, and h*ur* boodyes to p*r*ison and pay xx s. at eue*r*y trespas. And if ther [2]is ony of them þ*at* will goo to h*ur* pastures, than leve her wepons at the townes hend & som mannys house. Saue leefull be hit to eue*r*y bocher and othur man of town and of contrey comyng to ma*r*ket to dryve hur beestis *with* smale stavys and non othur.

[1] Gisarme = a kind of battle-ax, bill or halberd.—*N.E.D.*
[2] leaf 3, back.

Allso we com*m*aund þat eue*r*y hosteler warn hur geestys that they leve hur wepons w*ith*in h*ur* Innes, but if he be a knyght or a Squyer that may haue a swerd born aft*ur* hym, up the peyn of a xl d. at eue*r*y trespas. Innkeepers to warn guests about their weapons.

Allso þat no man of any Crafte w*ith*in this Cite mak Caue ne oth*ur* ordyna*u*nce among hem but hit be ouerseen be the maio*ur* & his cownsell, and if hit be resonable ordyna*u*nce & lawfull hit schal-be affermyd, or els hit shal-be correctyd be the maio*ur* & his peres, up the peyn of xl s. at eue*r*y trespas to the vse of the Cite. "No crafts make bylaws but by Consent of the mayor"

Allso þat no mane*r* of hand-Crafte were any lyue*r*y, but of his owne Crafte þat he vsith, up the peyn of xx s. and forfatur of the same lyue*r*y, but if hit be of the gyldys of the Cite. no strange livery to be worn by craftsmen.

Allso that no Baxster sell no horsebred in-to any Ostree of more increase then ij d. at schillyng, up the peyn of vj s. viij d. at eue*r*y trespas to the vse of the Cite. "Bakers."

Allso þat no Straunger sell bred w*ith*in this Cite, but hit be furst brought to the Geylhall dore, & oue*r*seen by the maio*ur* that hit haue lawfull wyghtȝ & duo paaste, up the peyn of xij d. at eue*r*y trespas, and þat no man by suche bred till hit be oue*r*seen, up tho same peyn.

Allso we com*m*and that no mane*r* of Straunger vitaler þat bryngithe See fische, heryng or any othur vitall to this cite for to sell, that he sell no mane*r* of suche fische ne no vitales till hit be ix of the cloke, & that hit be oue*r*sen by the maio*ur*, þat hit be abull for mannys meite, w*ith* the oue*r*sight of them þat the maio*ur* hath ordenyd to oue*r*se all suche mane*r* of vitalyes, up the peyn of xl d. at eue*r*y trespas þat they may be founden w*ith*all and proved Gylty. "Fish to be viewed before it be sold."

Allso we com*m*aund þat no mane*r* of fresche fysher by, ne take up, no mane*r* of fresche fysche of men of the contrey by way of regratry; þat is to witt, for to by hit of men of the contrey, and aft*ur* to sell hit agayn to hur neyghbures, up the peyn of iij s. iiij d. at eue*r*y trespas. Regrators.

Allso we com*m*aund that no man by hym-self, ne by his *ser*vauntes, cast no dong of h*ur* stablez, ne non othur fylthe in the comune Ryver, up the peyn to pay at the fyrst trespas half a marke, at the second t*r*espas j "Purpestures in the River": filth not to be cast into the river.

marke, and at the thryd trespas xx s. Allso þ*a*t no man make noo p*ur*presture ne stoppyng w*ith* trees ne stones ne w*ith* no othur filthe in the forseid Ryver up the peyn aforsaid. Allso þ*a*t no man put noo dong to his neygh-

"Sweeping streets."

bour, ne Rake ne Swep in tyme of Rayne, up the peyn of xij d. at eue*r*y t*r*espas. Allso þ*a*t no man by hym ne be his se*r*va*u*nte*s* cast in-to the dyke of this Cite no mane*r* of filthe be day ne by nyght, up the peyn of vj s. viij d. at eue*r*y t*r*espas þ*a*t they may be founde w*ith*all.

No hedge to be made near the town ditch.

And þ*a*t no man do make ony hegge [1]be viij foote nyghe the foresaid diche w*ith*in ne w*ith*oute be vj fotte, ne that no man dig ne lede thens any cley, up the peyn of vj s. viij d. at eue*r*y trespas to the vse of the Cite, & allso up the peyn of imp*ri*sonment of xl^{ti} dayes w*ith*out ony g*r*ace.

Dong to be laid near the ash.

Allso that no man Carry ne ley no dong vpon the hiȝe pauement leedyng from the New ȝate toward the quarell but at the asche, up the peyn of ij s. at eue*r*y trespas. Ne þ*a*t no man by hym, ne by his neygborous lay no dong at the townsend in no placys, but w*ith*out the stake*s* that be þe*r* sett in the dyke beyond the Frer gate, and in the pytt be-yond the Lytull pa*r*ke streitt gate, and at Derne yate up the payn of ij s. at eue*r*y trespas. Allso

Every man make his pavement clean every Saturday.

þ*a*t eue*r*y man mak his pauement clen be-for his housz eue*r*y Sat*ur*neday in the yer, up the peyn of xij d. at eue*r*y trespas. Ne that no man Carry no dong out of h*ur* houses ne out of h*ur* stables in-to the strett, but if they haue Cartes redy to carry hit a-way, up the payn of xl d. at eue*r*y trespas w*ith*-Inne a day and a nyght to the vse of this Cite.

"Sand [and] Clay."

Allso we com*m*and no man do dig clay at Botesgrene, ne that no man dig sond vnd*ur* Saynt Nicolas churche-yard, up the peyn of vj s. viij d. at euery t*r*espas. Allso þ*a*t no man dig no sond in the Lytull pa*r*ke w*ith*outen leve, up the peyne of xl d. at eue*r*y t*r*espas. And that all thes peynyes abouesaid, when they be forfetid, be reryd to the vse of the comyn p*r*ofet of the cite of Couentre.

"Bills to be brought 4 daies before the lighte" (leet).

Allso hit is ordenyd þ*a*t all mane*r* men, þ*a*t will sew here aft*ur* remedy for to haue by ordyna*u*nce of the lete

[1] leaf 4.

gene*r*all or specyall, þ*at* they mak hur bylles, and delyue*r* hem to the maio*ur* iiij dayes be-fore eue*r*y lete, þ*at* the maio*ur* may tak afor the lete the gene*r*al councell of this cite, xxiiij to comyn of the maters conteynyd in h*ur* billes for the mor spede of the day of the lete, and that no byllez aft*ur* the forsaid iiij day be receuyd.

Allso þ*at* eue*r*y man that hath byn maio*ur* & Baliff, and eue*r*y comyner of this Cite, be attendant and com to þe maio*ur* up reasonable warnyng, up the peyn of eue*r*y man þ*at* hath byn maio*ur* of half a marke, and baliff*es* and Chamb*ur*layns of xl d., and comyners at xx d. at eue*r*y defaut, levey to be made to the vse of the Chambure. "Fines for not appering at the Leet."

Allso that þe Ryuer and the brokes þ*at* comyth and rennyth in to this Cyte, & allso the Red-dyche be enlargid of the breed he owithe to haue of ryght cours, þe wiche, be encrochment of dwellers of both sydes, be strayted and narrowid, & wi*th* filthe, dong and stonys the wat*ur* stoppyd of his cours; þ*at* eue*r*y man voide afor his ground thorugh the wat*ur*, and dyche and clense hym vnto his old ground, to thend the waturs in flod tyme may the lyghtlyer passe, eschewyng dyue*r*s perels had afortyme by floodys thurgh stoppyng and st*r*ayting of the same Ryvers & dyches, a this side mydsome*r* day, up the peyne of eue*r*y man founde in defaut xx s. And þ*at* all the p*r*evies vpon the same Red-dych[1] be remouyd, & done a-way by Whitsonday, wi*th*out makyng or releuyng of hem, up the peyn of xl s. of eue*r*y man þ*at* may be found in defaute. "For þe straiting of the Rivers." River to be cleansed, so as to avoid floods.

[2]Allso that the waturlades[3] after the same Ryvers and brokes set wi*th*in the streme be vtt*ur*ly remeuyd and done a-way a this side Whitsonday, up the peyn of xx s., Provided allwey that the maio*ur* haue power be the gene*r*all counsaill of the Cite to treitt wi*th* the dwellers aft*ur* the wat*ur*sydes for hur wat*ur*lades vnd*ur* this forme for the comyn p*r*ofett of this Cite. That is to witt, that whoso will haue ony esement a-pon the Ryver as by wat*ur*lades, þ*at* he sue vnto the maio*ur* suche esement to haue, bothe of lenght aftur the ryver and brookes, & brede in-to hem, yeldyng a ce*r*ten vnto the Chamb*ur* as he may accord wi*th* the maio*ur* & his councell aforsaid. And þ*at* the wat*ur*- "Diers and others to Agree with the mayor for water-lays."

[1] In Little Park Street. [2] leaf 4, back. [3] v. Gloss.

lades, suche trety and acord had *with* the maio*ur*, be drawyn up eu*ery* nyght eschewyng p*er*ell of ffloodes fallyng in nyghttyme, up the peyn of xx s. at eu*ery* defaute. And allso þ*at* no deister put no groundez of hur fattes, ne non othur fylthe, into the comyn Ryver, up the peyn of xij d. at eu*ery* defaut.

Cleansing of town ditch.

Allso þ*at* eu*ery* man, hauyng housz or land a-gaynst the town dyk *with*out the town wall Joynyng up the same dyke, void and clense the same dyke ayenst his house & lond, þe wich is throw down, streytid and stoppid in the defaut of the occupiers of the same housz & lond, a this side Whitsonday, up the peyn of eu*ery* man in defaut founden of xx s.

Craft rules.

Allso that the maio*ur*, Recorder & Balyff*es* takyng to the maio*ur* viij or xij of the gen*er*all councell [command] to com a-for hem the wardens of all the Craftes of the cite *with* hur ordyna*un*ce touchyng h*ur* craftys and h*ur* articles. And the poyntes þ*at* byn lawfull, good and honest for the Cite be alowyd hem, and all othur throw[n] asid, and had for none; and þ*at* they mak [no] new ordyna*un*ce a-yenst the law in opp*re*ssion of the people, up the peyn of imp*re*sonment, & to tak fyne at the kyng*es* wyll.

"Sellers of oatmeale to show at Jayle hall with bakers."

Allso þ*at* Sellers of Otemele of the contrey stond nyghȝ the Jeilhall dore *with* sellers of brede, and that they sell by mesures ensealid, aft*ur* the stondard for comyn p*ro*fett of the people up the peyn of xx s.

"Butchers kill no flesh within the wall."

Allso that no man*er* of bocher fro this tyme forward sle no man*er* of beest *with*in the wall of þis cite saue onely Swyne, up the peyn of xx s. at eu*ery* defaute. And allso-sone as the skaldyng-house ordenyd by this Cite be full fynyshid and redy that they skald þ*er* swyne in the same house, & in no othur house, up the peyn of xx s. at eu*ery* defaute. And þ*at* eu*ery* bocher fro this tyme forward haue flesch to sell, and sell a-pon the Saturnday to eu*ery* man þ*at* will bye hit, up the peyn of xl d. at eu*ery* defaut. And that all man*er* bochers sell all man*er* offall of beestys, the wiche is abull for mannys meite, to eu*ery* man & woman þ*at* will bye þ*er*of, up the peyn of ij s. at eu*ery* defaute þ*at* they be founden in. Allso lefall be hit to eue*r*y man of town and contrey to com and by flesche vpon the Saturday as well as any othur day in the weeke.

Allso fyschers þ*at* bryng See fysche in-to this cite be not Osted ne Inned at any fischers housz of this cite, but at othur Innes at lymytac*i*on of the maio*ur*; and to mak true relac*i*on to hym how many panyers and what mane*r* fysche the forsaid fischers bryng in-to h*ur* Innes ther hoost schal-be sworne to the maio*ur*. And allso þ*at* hur hoost haue in charge that they [1] bryng all hur fysche in-to the m*ar*kett, w*ith*out they sett up any fische in any othur fyschers houses, or that they conseyll hit in any mane*r*, up the peyn of eche of hem þ*at* may be found in defaut of xl d. "fish." "fish-mongers."

Allso that þe T*r*inite gilde haue h*ur* close feldis severell, þe wich haue be g*r*aunted a-fore tyme for the payment þ*at* they pay to the p*r*iour, that is to witt x li, the wiche all the comyns be bound for to the same p*r*iour. Trinity Gild closes.

Allso hit is ordenyd that the fraunches of this Cite be Ryden this yere w*ith*in the monyth of May, what day the maio*ur* will lymyt hit, be good aduyse and at his leysure. "Riding the bounds."

THE COUNCIL.

John Leder, maio*ur* of the Cite of Couentre w*ith* his councell the Thursday next aftur the feest of the Purificac*i*on of our Lady haue made a hall, and they haue made this ordyna*u*nce folowyng: Mayor's Council. Feb. 6, 1421.

In p*r*imis they haue ordenyd þ*at* the Chamburlans shull begyne to wurche at the New yate and the Cook strett yate. Chamberlains to repair gates.

Allso they haue chesyn Will*i*am Oteley comyn se*r*geaunt for this yer.

Allso þ*at* all good ordyna*u*nce of the leetys be sought up and wryton in a regestre, that they may be of record foreuermore, be oue*r*sight of the recorder, for worschip and honesty of this Cite. Register of Leet ordinances.

Allso thei haue ordenyd þ*at* John Golofre and Robe*r*t

[1] leaf 5.

Chamberlains' accounts.

Melburn ȝef h*ur* accompt for the yer that thei wer chamb*ur*leyns at Esture next comyng, up the peyn of a C s.

Allso þ*at* Henry Breux & John Cotton ȝef h*ur* accompt for the yere þat þei were chamb*ur*lens at mydsomer next comyng, up the peyn of C s.

Allso þ*at* Ric. Joy com and ȝef his accompt of offic*er* of chamb*ur*len at the fest of Saynt Michaell, up the peyn of C s.

Allso that John Golofre, & Rob*er*t Sklatier com & mak h*ur* accompt at the same fest of Saynt Mich*aell*, up the peyn of C s.

[1][Henry Breux & John Coton to give their accounts at All Hallows, and John Braytoft & John Bristow at the Circumcision under the same penalty.]

[[2]Mem. that on Mar. 15. 8 Hen. V.

John Leeder mayor (etc.) with his council gave the lord king at his coming from France £100 with a gold cup worth £10, and also to the queen on her coming from France to Coventry £100 with a gold cup worth £10.]

Mem. q*uo*d qui*n*todecimo die mens*is* Martii a. r. r. Henrici qui*n*ti (etc.) octauo Joh. Leeder, maior ciuitat*is* Couentr*ie*, cu*m* consilio suo dederu*nt* d*omi*no Regi in aduentu suo de Franc*ia* cent*um* libr*as* cu*m* vno Cipho de auro ad valenc*iam* decem libr*arum*. & etiam dederu*nt* regine in suo aduentu a Franc*ia* in Couentr*iam* Cent*um* libr*as* cum vno cipho de auro ad valenc*iam* x li.

EASTER LEET.

[[3]Leet held on Wednesday after close of Easter 9. Hen. V. (Ap. 2, 1421.)]

Coue*n*tre. V. f. p. tent*us* ib*ide*m die M*er*curii p*roxim*o post cl*ausu*m Pasche anno ix° Henrici qui*n*ti.

[for jury v. p. 36.]

"Court." concerning attorneys.

At wich lete was ordenyd þ*at* no attornay of the court of the Cite of Couentre, ne non othur p*er*son longyng to the court, be not a-bout for to adnule þ*at* is of Record in the court, & enrollyd in the court Rolles, that is to say somo*n* [of] any St*r*aungers, & conti*nu*ance of Capi*as* & Scire fac*ias*; and allso of his attorney and testament*es*, seyng to the Bayliff*es* or to the Clerk, hit is falsely entred

[1] leaf 5, back. [2] leaf 6, back. [3] leaf 11, back.

& falsly done, ne sklaundur not the court in no wise, vppon the peyn at euery defaut to lese vj s. viij d. to the vse of the Baliffes, & for to be put out of the courte for the tyme of the same maiour & bayliffes, as long as they byn in office. And allso that no attornay be attornay for no straunge person, but if he bryng the same person for to be receyvyd, or els þat he bryng a lawfull lettre attorney; and þat he bryng not one person for a-noþur, up the same peyn.

[[1]At the same Leet before John Leeder, mayor, Hen. Peyto & John Golofre, bailiffs, Ric. Crosby, prior of Coventry, Thomas [2]master of S. John's hospital, Mr John Bredon, doctor of theology, and many others, presented the following bill.]

To the reuerent and wurschipfull states that her byn, and to all wurthy men of this grett lete be this bill Schewid and Rad:—For-as-moche as þer be many good ordynauncez maid by the maiour and be his good counsell, God saue hem, the wiche with the grace of God shuld turne the town to grett worschip & prosperite: We wold desiren a thyng, the wiche was neuer ordenyd be no lete, nor be counsell of the maiour and his peerys, That hit myght by your hye and good discression be set in a-nothur kynd, and that is the grett multytude of peopull, the wich is gatherid to-gethur on mydsomer evyn, and apon Seynt Peturs, for we supposyn þat hit lyeth in no mannys power, thowȝe he ordeyn for hem as well as he can, for to plese hem all. And not onely for this cause, but allso of grett debate and man-slauȝghter and othure perels and synnes þat myght fall, and late haue fallen. And þerfor ȝif hit lyke yow, we wold shew you how us thynkyuth best hit myght be sett in bettur Gouernanse in Eschewyng of many peryls. If hit lyke your discression, vs thynkyth þat hit were good Gouernauns that euery ward kept hem within hur own ward in good and honest aray; and euery ward within hem-self chese hem ij wardens for to haue the gouernance of the ij nyghtes beforseid; and the maiour to walk with certen men, the wiche byn pleasyng vnto hym; and the Baylyffes the same wyse on the second

The prior and others present a bill concerning the riots on Midsummer Eve and S. Peter's Night.

[1] leaf 9, back. [2] Blank in MS.

nyght, for to walk thorow all the wardys of the town; and the maio*ur* to gyve a subsydye of money to the wardens of yche warde on the furst nyght, and the Bayliffes to doo the same on the second nyght; The wich subsidye must be ordenyd be the maio*ur* and his counsell what hit schal-be in this mayres tyme, and allso in tyme comyng. Now ȝe haue herd the entent of this bill wurche now by yo*ur* disc*re*ssion in the name of the Trinite.

[[1]At this leet before J. Leeder, mayor, J. Weston, A. Hiton, and his fellows, the lord king's Justices of Coventry, a certain Joh. Rook and Ric. Goddesley put up a bill, of which the tenor followeth in these words:]

Petition of two men for a reward.

To you worshipfull & Reue*re*nt masturs & soue*re*ns of this wurthy Cite, Besechith, ȝif hit lyke yow, John Rook & Ric. Goddesley, your *ser*uant*es*, þ*at* ȝe wull vouchesaufe be consideraci*on* of the good & greable *ser*uis þ*at* they haue done yow, and *pur*posen to contynew at your will with all hur myght and connyng, vpon h*ur* good beryng, to g*ra*unt hem a reward at yo*ur* good avyse, in supportyng of h*ur* honestye, to be takyn of the Chamburlens that tyme beyng or heraft*ur* for to be.

[And thereupon by common assent of the honest and lawful men elected to this leet, by assent of [24 names] they have answered thus: that the said John and Richard shall have 20*s.* a year on their good behaviour, viz. 10*s.* apiece, for the fame of the city, from the Chamberlains for the time being.]

& vnde p*er* co*mmun*em assensum p*ro*bor*um* et legaliu*m* ho*minum* ad hanc letam elect*orum*, vi*delice*t p*er* assensum Ad. Hiton, Will. Belgraue, Joh. Goote, Will. Dilcok, Will. Attylburgh, Ric. Southam, Laur. Cooke, Will. Bedford, Tho. Wyldgryse, Rad. Garton, Will. Crose, Ric. Joy, Ric. Power, Egid. Allesley, Tho. Grene, Joh. P*ar*ker, Gal. ffiore, Joh. Braytoft, Hen. Breux, Rob. Melburn, Joh. Bowyer, Joh. Coton, Joh. Michell & Will. Byfeld sic responsum dederu*nt*: q*uod* pre*d*icti Joh*annes* et Ric*ard*us sup*er* eor*um* bona gestura annuatim h*a*bebu*nt* viginti solid*os*, vi*delice*t quil*ibe*t eor*um* decem soli-

[1] leaf 10.

d*os*, p*ro* honestat*e* Ciuitat*is* p*re*dicte, de Cam*er*ariis qui p*ro* temp*or*e exist*unt* (*sic*) etc.

THE KING'S LOAN.

Loan of £100 to Henry V, May 3, 1421.

[1][The following lent (prestiterunt) £100 to the King at the feast of the Invention of the Holy Cross, 9 Henry V.]

From Gosford Street.

De Vicō de Gosforde.

		£	s.	d.
In primis	Laur. Cooke	4	0	0
	Joh. Golofre	2	0	0
	Will. Crose	2	0	0
	Joh. Wellford	1	0	0
	Joh. Ellford		6	8
	Bened. Marshall		6	8

From Jordenwell and Mill Lane.

De vico vocat*o* Jurdenwell & Millane.

	£	s.	d.
Tho. Wildegryse	4	0	0
Ric. Power	1	0	0
Joh. Coton	2	0	0
Will. Deyster, Cardmak*er*		6	8
Joh. Abram		6	8
Joh. Dilcok		6	8
Joh. Walley		6	8

Much Park Street.

Muche p*ar*ke streit.

	£	s.	d.
Joh. Esterton	5	0	0
Hen. Peyto	4	0	0
Joh. Braytofte	2	0	0
Will. Byfelde	1	0	0
Joh. Clerk	1	0	0
Will. Faseman	1	0	0
Will. Brydd		6	8
Tho. Crose		6	8

Bayly Lane.

Bayly lane.

	£	s.	d.
Will. Brooke		6	8
Hen. Brydde		6	8
Joh. Benet, wyrdrawer		6	8
Joh. Hurley		6	8
Leonardus Lyney		6	8

Little Park Street

Litull p*ar*ke streit.

	£	s.	d.
Will. Belgraue	5	0	0
Joh. Goote	5	0	0
Rad. Garton	2	0	0
Rob. Byfeld	2	0	0
Joh. Herdeborgh	1	0	0
Joh. Michell	1	0	0
Will. Frysby		6	8
Joh. Warrant		6	8

	£	s.	d.
Johanna Northwood	1	0	0
Will. Swanne		6	8
Will. Repyngton		13	4
Joh. Normanton		6	8
Joh. Launde		6	8
Rob. Cotoner		6	8
Will. Attylburgh	2	0	0
Joh. Eu*er*don	1	0	0

Broadgate.

Brodeyate.

	£	s.	d.
Egid. Allesley	2	0	0
Ric. Oneley	1	0	0
Ric. Bushebury, barbo*ur*		10	0
Rog. Cokkes		6	8

Smithford Street.

Smythford [Street].

	£	s.	d.
Joh. Oneley	3	0	0
Joh. Bowȝer	2	0	0
Joh. Brystow	2	0	0
Will. Wymswold		13	4
Gal. Flour	2	0	0
Will. Coppe		13	4
Will. Pewt*er*er		6	8
Joh. Bramston		13	4

Spon Street.

Sponstreit.

	£	s.	d.
[2]Joh. Deist*er*, wolman		6	8
Will. Pratte, deister		6	8

Cross Cheaping.

Crose Chepyng.

	£	s.	d.
Adam Hyton	5	0	0
Tho. Greno	3	0	0
Ric. Joy	2	0	0
Joh. P*ar*ker	1	0	0
Rob. Melburn	2	0	0
Hen. Breux	2	0	0
Joh. Cambryge		6	8
Joh. Egeston		6	8
Hen. Sircok		6	8
Will. Bettley		10	0
Ric. Botone*r*		13	4
Joh. Brydde, pewt*er*er		6	8

[1] leaf 8.
[2] leaf 8, back.

	£	s.	d.			£	s.	d.
Joh. Style, deyster		6	8	Bishop Street.	Bischopestreit.			
Ric. Dene		6	8		Ric. Southam	5	0	0
Agnes Weedon		6	8		Will. Staunton		6	8
Joh. Doughty		6	8		Joh. Montgomery		6	8
					Hen. Knott		6	8
					Joh. Walgraue		6	8
					Will. Crudworthe	1	0	0

THE GILD FIELDS.

[[1]On July 12, 1421, all underwritten were called to, and assembled in, S. Mary's Hall, by the mayor's requisition, to enquire about certain fields of the Trinity Gild, whether they are several or no, viz. Poddy-croft, Stivichall-Hiron, Long-croft and Bateman's-acre, who indeed say that on Thursday after Michaelmas 8 Ric. II, at a leet held at Coventry before J. Marton, mayor (etc.) it was ordained and granted that the Trinity gild master should have and hold those fields in severalty, and that the gild master should pay as long as he pleased £10 on the community's behalf, as appears more fully in the same leet. Therefore by these honest and legal men, chosen for this cause by the mayor, it was ordained and confirmed —that the said fields be held

Mem. quod duodecimo die Julii a. r. r. Henrici quinti post conquestum nono omnes subscripti conuocati fuerunt et congregati in aula S. Marie Couentrie, per requisicionem Johannis Leeder, tunc maioris ciuitatis Couentrie, ad inquirendum de quibusdam campis pertinentibus Gilde S. Trinitatis Couentrie etc.: Vtrum sunt separabiles vel non: Videlicet de campis vocatis Podycroft, Stycheall-hiron, le Long Croofte & Batemans-acre. Qui uero[2] dicunt quod die jouis proximo post festum S. Michaelis archangeli a. r. r. Ricardi secundi (etc.) octauo ad vnam letam apud Couentriam tentam coram Johanne Marton, tunc maiore predicte ciuitatis Couentrie, Ordinatum fuit et concessum quod magister Gilde S. Trinitatis (etc.) haberet et teneret campos illos in separali: & quod magister Gilde predicte solueret pro communitate ville predicte quolibet anno quamdiu sibi placuerit decem libras, prout in eadem leta plenius continetur etc. Ideo per istos probos et legales homines, ex parte maioris causa predicta electos, ordinatum est et confirmatum quod campi predicti teneantur in separali quamdiu

[1] leaf 6, back.

[2] MS. looks like "non."

several, as long as the master will pay the £10 for the community, to the prior of S. Mary's Cathedral, as appears etc.]

magister Gilde predicte decem libras predictas pro communitate (etc.) soluere voluerit priori ecclesie Cathedralis B. Marie de Couentria, prout in leta predicta plenius apparet.

[Names follow.]

sequuntur nomina.

[1]Joh. Oneley, Will. Belgraue, Joh. Goote, Ric. Southam, Laur. Cook, Ad. Deyster, Joh. Esterton, Hen. Peytoo, Joh. Golofre, Joh. Parker, Rad. Garton, Egid. Allesley, Tho. Grene, Tho. Wildegrise, Ric. Power, Gal. fflower, Joh. Harborgh, sen., Rob. Byfeld, Ric. Joy, Will. Crosse, Hen. Breux, Joh. Coton, Joh. Braytoft, Joh. Bristow, Joh. Welford, Bened. Marchall, Rad. Alot, Joh. Dilcok, Joh. Lysturley, Joh. Clerke, Will. Brydd, Joh. Euerdon, Will. ffrysby, Hen. Brydde, Joh. Sircok, Joh. Doughtye, Joh. Styll, deyster, Joh. Montgomery, Joh. Allesley, Iremonger, Joh. Boteler, Hen. Knott, Joh. Egeston, Rob. Lyrpole, Joh. Wallgraue, Joh. Deyster, wolman, Mat. White, Joh. Lychefeld, mercer, Will. Staunton, Sim. Deyster, Will. Deyster, cardmaker, Joh. Bryane, Joh. Stafford, wyrdrawer, Ric. Walkleyne, Rob. Pinnok, Joh. Lee, Nic. Gryve, Tho. Daw, Rob. Danyell, Will. Byfeld. Will. ȝate, cardemaker, Will. Bayly, mercer, Joh. Wilbye, Nic. Byfeld, Tho. Cokkes, Ad. Swete, Tho. Reyuer, Joh. Warront, Ric. Sharpe, Will. Swan, Rob. Cotoner, Joh. Chandeler, Ric. Benchis, Ric. Southam, jun., Joh. Michell, Tho. Bedford, Tho. Harrys, Joh. Normanton, Ric. Paunton, Joh. Harborgh, jun., Joh. Chubbok, Joh. Marston.

[2]Joh. Bramston, Joh. Crosse, Ad. Dyer, Will. Allesley, Joh. Whitley, Will. Brooke, Joh. Benett, wyrdrawer, Joh. Spencer, Will. fflekney, Rog. Cookes, Rob. Saxton, Will. Marchall, Joh. Archar, Ric. Bussheburry, barbour, Rob. Coteler, Will. Swetnam, Ric. Oneley, Will. Stoneley, Ric. Hiklyng, Joh. Tate, God. Barbour, Joh. Bowȝer, Tho. Carter, Joh. Blakman, Joh. Pynchebek, Tho. Ive, Rob. Melton, Hugo Rogeley, Will. Pratte, Joh. Marnam, Ric. Leysyngham, Joh. Menley, Tho. Russell, Joh. Caumbyrge, coteler, Ric. Melburn, Edw. Lychefeld, Joh. Brygtsmere, Joh. Ronten, Ric. Botoner, Joh. White, Bocher, Hen.

[1] leaf 7. [2] leaf 7, back.

Rondall, Joh. Edward, deister, Joh. Lychefeld, Ric. Marche, Hen. Walker, Will. Wilkyns, Joh. Auger, Will. Bate, Will. Crudworthe, Ric. Dean, Joh. Laund, Joh. Clyston, Walt. Assheby, mercer.

LAND GRANTS AND TOWN BUSINESS.

[1]Joh. Leeder, maior, Ad. Hyȝton, M. G. S. T.,[2] Joh. Esterton, M. G. C. Ch.,[3] Will. Belgraue,[4] Joh. Golofre,[4] Rad. Garton, Tho. Wildegryse, Egid. Allesley, Rob. Byfeld, Hen. Breux, Joh. Coton, Joh. Brystow, Joh. Braytoft, Will. Wymswolde, Joh. Ray, Joh. Warraunt.

Witnesses of sealing of grants of common property.

[The above-written worthy men were summoned to S. Mary's Hall to witness sealing of indentures conveying tenements (of common property) and to give good counsel.

It was seen to be more expedient and necessary that the mayor should call together the under-written and fellow citizens on this occasion. Therefore by the provision of the mayor the day fixed on the Thursday before S. James' day (Jul. 24), when the mayor summoned the under-written, who assembled for the sealing.]

[15 Jul. 9 Hen. V.] O*mn*es supr*a*-sc*r*ipti fidedigni convocati fueru*n*t et cong*r*egati in aula S. M*ar*ie de Couentr*ia* ad int*er*essend*um* sigilla-c*ioni* diu*er*sar*um* indentur*arum* fact-*arum* diu*ersis* p*er*sonis eiusd*em* ciui-tat*is* de ten*ementis* eis conces*sis*, et ad p*er*hibend*um* consiliu*m* suu*m* bonu*m* in hoc casu. & q*uia* videbat*ur* maiori et fidedignis sup*r*asc*r*ipt*is* ad tunc q*uo*d maius expediend*um*[5] foret et necesse q*uo*d p*r*edict*us* maior con-uocari fac*er*et et hab*er*i coram se in aula p*r*edict*a* p*er*sonas subsc*r*ipt*as* & plures conciues Ciuitat*is* p*r*ed*icte* occ*asion*e p*r*edict*a*. Ideo p*er* p*r*evi-dentia*m*[6] p*r*edict*i* maior*is* et sui consilii dies p*r*efixus est usq*ue* diem Jouis p*roximum* ante f*estu*m S. Jacobi ap*osto*li p*roxi*mo futur*um*, ad que*m* diem p*r*edict*us* maior venire fecit istos subsc*r*iptos, qui Sigillac*ion*e (*sic*) indenturar*um* p*re*-dict*arum* total*iter* se aggregaueru*n*t.

[1] leaf 9. [2] Magister gilde S. Trinitatis, Master of the Trinity Gild.
[3] Magister gilde Corporis Christi, Master of the Corpus Christi Gild.
[4] Bracketed as "ballivi." [5] *sic.* expediens.
[6] *sic.* ? providentiam.

De Vico Gosforde. Laur. Cooke, Will. Crose, Joh. Wellford, Bened. Marshall, Rad. Alott. More witnesses summoned by wards.

Erlestreit.[1] Will. Deyster, Joh. Dilcok, Ric. Power, Joh. Cressy, Joh. Bryan.

Muchepark. Will. Brydd, Rob. Pynnock, Will. Ȝate, cardmaker, Will. Bayly, mercer.

Brodyate. Will. Flekney, Rog. Cokkes, Will. Marchall, Ric. Bushebury, Ric. Oneley.

Erlstreit. Will. Attilburgh, Joh. Goote, Joh. Harborgh, sen., Tho. Bedford, Ric. Southam, jun., Joh. Euerdon, Tho. Harries, Will. Frysby, Tho. Cokkes, Nich. Byfeld.

Balylane. Joh. Harborgh, jun., Will. Brook, Joh. Runton,[2] Will. Allesley, Hen. Bryde, Ad. Dyer, Joh. Benett, wiredrawer.

Smythforde. Joh. Oneley, Galf. Flour, Will. Pewterer, Joh. Bowȝer, God. Barbour.

Spanstreit. Hugo Rogeley, Joh. Deyster, wolman, Joh. Pynchbek, Will. Pratte, Joh. Marnam, Will. Kerver.

Crosechepyng. Rob. Melburn, Joh. Cambrige, Joh. Egynton, Will. Bynley, Joh. Parker, Ric. Joy, Will. Dilcok, Rob. Lyrpoole, Joh. Pewterer, Tho. Grene, Hen. Sircok, Joh. Doughty, Will. Stylle, deyster.

Welstret. Ric. Southam, sen., Will. Staunton, Joh. Prentes, [3]Joh. Collyshull, Hen. Knott, Will. Porter, Joh. Allysley, Will. Crudworthe, Will. Bate, Joh. Lychefeld, bocher.

[4][V. f. p. before same[5] on Saturday after Michaelmas 9 Hen. V.] Michaelmas Leet, Oct. 4, 1421.

Ad. Deyster, Joh. Oneley, Will. Belgraue, Joh. Goote, Ric. Southam, Laur. Cooke, Joh. Esterton, Tho. Willgryse, Joh. Parker, draper, Rad. Garton, Gal. Floure, Rob. Byfeld, Ric. Power, Tho. Grene, Will. Crose, Ric. Joye, Joh. Herburgh, sen., Will. Byfeld, Joh. Michell, mercer, Joh. Northwod, Joh. Clerk, Tho. Bedford, Joh. Dilcok, sen., Joh. Euerdon. Jurors

[They elected Hen. Breux and Rob. Melburn bailiffs.]

[[6]Oct. 11. 9 Hen. V: Delivered by John Leeder, mayor 1421.

[1] An error for Jorden Well. [2] Ronton, Staffs.
[3] leaf 9, back. [4] leaf 11, back. [5] v. p. 35.
[6] leaf 8, back.

Bonds for £533 6s. 8d. and tallies for £100.

and his council to Ric. Acton in S. Mary's Hall the following bonds (obligaciones): a bond for £200 dating from John Goote's mayoralty; one for £100 from John Hornby's time; a bill of 200 marks upon a jewel (sup*er* vno jocali) from Laurence Cook's time; two of the king's Exchequer tallies for £100 from John Leeder's time.]

§ 7. JOHN ESTERTON, MAYOR.

"Couentre." Easter Leet, Ap. 22, 1422.

[1][V. f. p. held before John Esterton, mayor, Hen. Breux and Rob. Milburn, bailiffs, on Wednesday before S. George's day, 10 Hen. V.

Nothing ordained and enrolled.]

"Couentre." Michaelmas Leet, Oct. 3, 1422.

Jury of thirty names.

[2][V. f. p. before the same on Saturday after Michaelmas, 1 Henry VI.]

Ric. Southam,[3] Wil. Belg*r*aue,[3] Will. Dilcok,[3] Laur. Cook,[3] Ad. Deyster,[3] Joh. Leeder,[3] Tho. Wildgrise, Rad. Garton, Hen. Peyto, Will. Crose, Ric. Joye, Joh. Golofre, Joh. Herborugh, sen., Tho. Grene, Joh. P*ar*ker, Will. Byfeld, Ric. Oneley, Joh. Clerk de Mich[ael],[4] Joh. Michell, m*er*c*er*, Joh. Oneley, Will. Faseman, Tho. Paynell, Joh. Eu*er*don, Joh. Doughty, Joh. Bramston, Joh. Bryd, peynt*er*, Rob. Lirpole, Will. Crudworthe, Will. Wymondeswold, Rad. Alot.

[John Braytoft and John Bristow elected bailiffs.]

"þe choosinge of þe firste 48 men."

¶ At wiche lete hit was ordenyd þ*at* the maio*ur* shall chose xl[ti] viij p*er*sonez of the moost discreet co*m*in*er*s, oute of eu*er*y warde a c*er*tayn, to here the accompte of þe chamb*ur*lens from this tyme forward and iij yer before past.

The Forty-eight to witness grant under common seal.

¶ Allso hit is ordenyd þ*at* þ*er* schall no graunt be made vnd*ur* the Comyn Seale fro this tyme forward, but in the p*r*esens of xl[ti]viij Comyners by the maio*ur* to be takyn in eu*er*y ward a c*er*ten.

"Election of Constables."

¶ Allso hit is ordenyd þ*at* the g*r*ett enquest at Michaellmes shall chose Constabuls to þe nomb*ur* of xx[ti] iiij and no moo, and þ*at* they be sufficyent men and well gou*er*nyd and of good name.

"Bochers,"

Allso hit is ordenyd þ*at* notw*ith*standyng the ordyn-

1 leaf 11, back. 2 leaf 12.

3 All bracketed together. The Twenty-four proper begin with Wildgrise. 4 ? of S. Michael's parish.

a*u*nce made afor this tyme þ*a*t Bochers of þis Cite shuld slee þ*er* beestys *with*out the wallys, and not *with*in, and hit is g*r*aunted now at this lette þ*a*t for this yer*e* the Bochers schall slee Beefys, veell and moton *with*in thor own howsen, and Swyn at the comyn slaught*er* housz; and non to slee in the strett, vppon the peyn of forfatur; of þe beest*es* so slayn in the strett, to be reryd to the co*m*en p*r*ofett of this Cite. And that thei tye noo beestys at þ*er* dorr up the same peyn. Allso þ*a*t they Carry a-way þ*er* offall of ther beestys in-to the pitt vnd*ur* the Poody Crooft, up the peyn of iiij d. at eu*er*y def*aut*. And þ*a*t eu*er*y man kepe his durr*e* clen*e* fro bloode and oþ*er* fylthis, vppon the payn of xij d.

and the slaughter of beasts.

Offal in the pit in Poddy-croft.

Allso hit is ordenyd þ*a*t þ*er* schall noo beestys be pynnyd at the co*m*en pynfold by the co*m*ien s*er*iante, but chapmannys warr*e*, and the fyne & p*r*ofett þ*er*of to be to the Chamb*ur*.

Pinning of beasts.

[[1]Names of collectors, four in each ward, of a half fifteenth, collected at the feast of S. Martin "in yeme," 1 Henry VI.]

Half fifteenth, Nov. 11, 1422.

(Names omitted.)

[From Gosford Ward £2 18*s.*; from Earl Street £2 16*s.* 10*d.*; from Jorden Well £2 11*s.*; from Much Park Street £2 10*s.*; Baylly and Hay Lane £1 15*s.*; Broad Gate £1 3*s.* 4*d.*; Smithford Street £2 0*s.*; Cross Cheaping £3 12*s.* 6*d.*; Spon £2 16*s.* 10*d.*; Bishop £2 16*s.* 6*d.*]

§ 8. HENRY PEYTO, MAYOR, 1423.

[2][Election of a new mayor (etc.) before Joh. Esterton, mayor, Joh. Braytoft and Joh. Brystow, bailiffs, on Monday the Conversion of S. Paul, 1 Hen. VI.]

Election of Henry Peyto, Jan. 25, 1423.

Isti subsc*r*ipti eligeru*n*t (*sic*) Hen. Peytoo maiorem (etc.) Joh. Dilcok coronator*em*, Will. Faseman & Joh. Braunston Cam*erarios*, Joh. Michell & Joh. Eu*er*don Custod*es* (etc.) a festo P*u*rificac*io*nis B. Ma*r*ie virginis[3] a. r. r. Henrici sexti (etc.) p*r*imo vsq*ue* idem f*estu*m ex tu*n*c p*roximo* seque*ns*, & Will. Oxton co*mmun*em clauigerul*um* p*ro* eode*m* anno: videl*ice*t:

The underwritten elect the officers

to serve from the Purification (Feb. 2) to the same feast next following, and Will. Oxton sergeant-at-mace.

[1] leaf 10. [2] leaf 12, back.

[3] Although the election took place on S. Paul's day the mayoral year began at the Purification (Candlemas day).

Twenty-four electors.

Will. Belgraue, Will. Dilcok, Ad. Deyster, Joh. Leeder, Joh. Braytoft, Joh. Brystow, Rad. Garton, Joh. P*ar*ker, Egid. Allesley, Will. Crose, Ric. Joy, Joh. Golofer, Tho. Grene, Joh. Harborgh, Hen. Breux, Joh. Clerk, Joh. Franklen, Will. Bryde, Ric. Sharp, Joh. Warrant, Will. Frisbye, Joh. Montgom*er*y, Joh. Pynchebek, Hugo Rogeley.

J. P.s, and keepers of the keys.

[Hen. Peyto, mayor, John Weston, recorder, Laur. Cook, Will. Belgraue, Ric. Southam and John Leeder, justices and wardens of the keys of the common chest.]

[Ordinances of the mayor & his council.]

The mayor's council of Forty-eight.

In the fest of Conu*er*sion of seynt Pall the yer reynyng of kyng Herry the Sixt aft*ur* the Conquest the fyrst, at þe elecc*io*n of Herry Peyto, maio*ur* of the Cite of Couentre, hit was p*r*ouydyd by the same elecc*io*n, þ*at* the seid maio*ur* shuld call and tak to hym the same xx^{ti} iiij wurthy men þ*at* wer of his elecc*io*n *with* oth*ur* xxiiij wyse men & discrett chosen to them & namyd by the seid maio*ur*; and then þ*at* the said meir and thes xl^{ti} viij whurthy men shuld orden & put in good rule all man*er* of good ordynnaunc*es* þ*at* ar p*ro*fitable to the seid Cite of Couentre. Wich namys as well of tho þ*at* wern of the elecc*io*n, as tho þ*at* wern chosen by the meyre, heraft*ur* folowen :

"xlviijti men."

Eleven ? of the election.

[1]Will. Belg*r*aue, Laur. Cooke, Ric. Southam, Will. Dilcok, Adam Hyton, Joh. Leder, Joh. Esterton, Joh. ffranklen, Joh. Clerk, Will. Brydd, Ric. Sharp.

Isti subsequen*tes* electi fue*r*unt pe*r* maiore*m*.[2]

The following 36 were elected by the mayor.

Tho. Wildgryse, Joh. Braytoft [following ten down to Hen. Breux inclusive as above], Joh. Wellford, Bened, Marchall, Joh. Whalley, Joh. Cooton, Will. Byfeld, Will. Faseman, Joh. Michell, Joh. Eue*r*don, Joh. Warrant, Joh. Runton, Ric. Acton, Ric. Bussheburу, Ric. Oneley, Joh. Bowȝer, Joh. Onelcy, Tho. Paynell, Joh. Brown, drap*er*, Joh. Stylle, Deyster, Rob. Lirpole, Will. Crudworthe, Joh. Walgraue, Joh. Deyst*er*, woleman, Will. ffrysby, Hugo Rogeley.[2]

[1] leaf 13.

[2] Curious arrangement of 11 and 36. Not all the names in the company of the mayor's electors.

SURVEY OF THE COMMONS.

Disturbances about common lands.

[1]ffor-asmoche as dyssencions, stirrynges and mocions haue byn had a-fore tyme, and not long a-gone,[2] for certen comen, the wich hath not byn conuersantly knowen as for comyn, In escewyng of perell þat myght fall, the xvi^ten^ day of the moneth of February the yer of the reign of kyng Henry the sixte aftur the Conquest the first, The said maiour and his councell thus haue ordenyd & prouyded that þer schall of four parties of the Cite of Couentre, þat is to say, of þe Est, West, Northe & southe, a certen of aunceant and wise men be chargid for to enquere of the Comyn of the said Cite, and what felldys owyn as of old tyme & of comyn ryght to be comyn; and than to bryng hit Inne to þe said maiour in wrytyng, to þat end þat heraftur hit myght be regestred, & so the comyn openly knowen. Wheruppon tho þat wer Chargid to enquer for the Est parte of the said Cyte, þat is to say, from the hye way that is callyd Sewall Pauement, þe wiche ledyth from Couentre to Leycestre, vnto a noþer hie waye, þat ledythe from Couentre vnto a town þat is callyd Bynley, on the other syde, and to bring[3] hit in in wrytyng vnto þe said Maiour on Monday next a-for the fest of saynt Gregory the Papa next aftur sweyng.

"4 juries of 48 men to set out the Comens," Feb. 1423.

Wise and ancient men to survey the commons,

their verdict to be registered.

The survey of the East part; "*pur* le Est *partie*." Between Sewall pavement and Binley highway.

Mar. 8.

At the same day Comyn vnto þe said maiour, and say in the maner as heraftur folowen: And thies byn þe namys of thest syde:

Jury.

Joh. Wellford, Bened. Marchall, Rad. Alot, Ric. Walker, Joh. Stretton, tailour, Joh. Stafford, wirdrawer, Joh. Breton, Joh. Coton, Will. Deister, Joh. Abram. weuer, Rob. Defford, Rob. Rechford, Joh. Bryan. [4]Hamlettes þat long to þe same side: Wykyn, Stooke, Bygyng.[4]

Hamlets. Wyken, Stoke, Bigging.

Verdict.

The wiche John Wellford and his felows aboue-namyd at þe day to them lymyted Comyn & seyn, þat þer is a feld wich is callyd Byschops-hay, and hit lyeth in brode[5] fro Wallforlong on that one partie vnto a hie way in

[1] leaf 13, back. v. Corp. MSS. E. 7, for probable original of this Survey. Insignificant variations between the two versions not noted. The language of E. 7 is, of the two, the more archaic.

[2] In 1421 gardens at Cheylesmore were destroyed by the commons. Dugd. (1730), 1. 148.

[3] 'I' is here introduced in MS.

[4–4] Not in E. 7.

[5] brede E. 7, *et passim*.

Hasill-wood ledyng fro*m* Couentre to Leycestre, & in lenght from Cotes-wast vnto a hie way in Hasill-wood ledyng from Couentre toward Nunceton, and þat feld, þ*at* is to say Byschoppeshay, thay sayn is comyn at the fest of Lammas.

[1]Allso thei say þat Billyng*es* feld, þe wich lieth betwen le Long-Crofte & Swanneslane in brede, and lenght fro a noþ*er* feld, þat is callyd Swannys-Croofte, vnto a feld of Ric. Bellours þ*at* is callyd New-feld, and they seyn þat the same Billyng*es*-feld is Comyn from the fest of saynt Michaell tharchaungell vnto þe fest of the P*ur*ificac*io*n of our blessid Lady v*ir*gy*n*.

Michaelmas land.

Allso þei say þ*at* the P*r*ioure*s* wast in Hasillwod, þe wich strechit in bred fro*m* Sewall-pament vnto Swannys-lane & in Lenght from the land of Ric. Bellours vnto þe brod ooke in Hasill-wod, hit is comyn as thei haue herd of oold tyme, but þei say, as in[2] that as for as þei may thynke, hit hathe byn othur whylis holden as Comyn, and oþ*er*-while*s* as seue*r*all. [3]As for þe said wast in Hasillwod, þ*at* longeth to the p*r*iour, hit was made by a g*r*ett leett holden in the tyme of Will. Sawndurs then maio*ur*[4] for such Evidence then shewyd þ*at* hit shuld be seue*r*all all tymes of the yer to þe said p*r*iour of Coventr*e* & his successours for eu*er*.[3]

Allso they seyn that Ludlow-feld, wiche strechythe fro Danyell-grove vnto Gosford-grene in lenght, & in breide from Sow-lane to þe way þ*at* gothe toward Bynley, is comyn att Lammas.

The south side from Whitley water to Hearsall.

And tho þ*at* weren chargid for to enquer for the southe side, þ*at* is to say, from the wat*ur* of Schirburn, þ*at* rennyth to Whitley vnto Hethesale, com in and seyn in the man*er* as aft*ur* folowithe : And thies byn ther namys :

Jury.

Joh. Clerk, Will. Bryd, Rob. Pynnok, Will. Faseman, Joh. Chetwyn, Tho. Daw, Joh. Eu*er*don, Tho. Harrys, Will. Swan, Nic. Byfeld, Joh. Frankelen, Will. ffrysby, Will. Brook, Joh. Runton, Tho. Wyrley, Hen. Brydd, Ad. Dyer, Joh. Benett, wyrd*r*a*wer*, Ric. Bushbery, Will. Marchall, Rog. Cokk*es*, Tho. Sporyour, Joh. Archer,

[1] leaf 14. [2] in ther tyme and as fer as thei mow E. 7.
[3–3] An interpolation; v. Introduction. Not in E. 7.
[4] 1469, v. p. 47.

Sadeler, Joh. Janyns. [1]Hamelett*es* within the said side, Stycheall. Hamlets, Stivichall;

The names of the forens þ*at* thei [tak] to them to tak Euydence—Baron sen. Joh. Clark de Sticheall, Ric. Huett.[1] foreigners to give evidence.

The wiche John Clerk and his felows seyn þ*at* þ*er* is a Croofte wi*th*out the New-yate of John Clerk*es*, þ*at* lyeth be-hynd the Gardens of the same John Clerke, & hit conteynyth iij land*es* & di*midium*, is Comyn at Lammas, and all tho feldys, Croft*es* and medows, þ*at* lyne from the said Croft[2] and barn of John Michels vnto Whitley in lenght, and in brod fro the the hie way þ*at* ledithe to London vnto þe wat*ur* of Schyrburn, þe wiche rennyth to Whytley, be comyn at Lammas, Except a Grove þ*at* Tho. Wildgryse holdithe of the brethren and systren[3] of the T*r*inyte guylde of Couentre, & a Grove callyd Saynt Anne grove, & except allso a medow þ*at* is callyd Alltogedir medow, þe wich Laur. Cook now holdithe, for þei ar[4] seue*r*all. Verdict.

[5] [6]At a grett lette holden in the tyme of Will. Sawndurs, then beyng maio*ur*, hit was grauntyd þ*at* the tenement, su*m*tyme in the holdyng of Hochyn Possell[7] wi*th* a quarrell lyyng þ*er*to wi*th*oute the New yate on the ryght hand, schal-be seue*r*all to þe p*r*iour of Couent*r*e, and to his successors for eue*r* all tymes of the yer; wi*c*h g*r*aunt is registred in the yer of the said Wyll*i*am Sawndurs meraltie.[6] 1460.

Allso þei say þ*at* all the feldys, medows and Croftys[8] on the right side of the said wey, þ*at* ledithe from Couentre toward London, þ*at* is to say fro the tenement*es* quond*am* Thom*e* Libard, the wiche Hochyn Possell[7] [9]wi*th* a quarrell[9] modo tenet, vnto a wat*ur* Renny*n*g vnd*ur* Whitley in lenght,[10] and in brede, fro þe said hie way vnto a garden and quarrell, þ*at* is callyd Pa*r*adise, & so be the side of the Lytull-pa*r*ke & Michepa*r*ke vntill Pa*r*k-myll-foord ar Comyn at Lammas. "Lamas grounds."

Allso thay say þ*at* the feld, þ*at* is Crabtre-feld, wi*th*

[1–1] Not in E. 7. [2] of John Clerk and the bern E. 7.
[3] bredern & sistern E. 7. [4] arn E. 7, *et passim*.
[5] leaf 14, back. [6–6] Interpolation, v. p. 46. Not in E. 7.
[7] Written without caps in MS. [8] -ez is the usual plural, E. 7.
[9–9] omitted E. 7. [10] a lengethe E. 7.

oþer[1] iij Croftys annexid to þe same feld, and allso Penny-feld, þe wich lyen by-twen þe hiȝe[2] way þat ledyth from Coventre to Stycheall & Somerlesow in breed, and in lenght from Chelsmore-grene vnto Miryefeld and Alsden-feld, ar comyn at the fest of Mychellmas vnto Candyllmass.

Michaelmas land.

Allso þei say þat Somerlesow-feld with all þe Crooftys annext vnto þe same feld, wich lye from Somerlesow-lane vnto a feld callyd Parsonnys-feld of the Spanne[3] in breid, and in lenght fro a croft of Adam Huyȝtons vnto a lane þat ledyth fro Spanne vnto Hethsall, ar comyn.

Allso þei say þat Poody-Crofte, þe wich lieth from Crow-lane vnto a diche, þat is callyd the town diche in breid, and in lenght from the Gardens on Chelsmore-grene vnto the Spanne-broke, is comyn from the feest of Lammas vnto Candyllmass.

The survey of the west side, between Coundon-Lane and Hearsall. Jury.

And tho þat wer charged for to enquire of the west syde of the Cyte of Coventre, þat is to say fro Coundon-lane to Hethsall: Ric. Hikelyng, Joh. Tate, Will. Pewterer, Joh. Mowton, Joh. Bramston, Joh. Deister, Joh. Bowyer, Tho. Paynell, Joh. Brown, draper, Will. Pratte, Hugh Rogeley, Joh. Lesyngham. [4]Hamlettess within the said partie: Cowndull. Kersley, Whaburley.

Hamlets.

Names of those chosen to give evidence.

Nomina electorum ad dandam evidenciam prefate inquisicionis:[4] Godefrid. Barbour, Joh. Pynchbek, Will. Keruer, Ric. Style, Will. Stone, Will. Colyns, Rob. Sewall, Hen. Colyns.

Verdict.

"Lamas grounds."

[5]The wiche Ric. Hyckelyng & his felows aboue-namyd comyn in at hur day to hem lymyted and sayn, þat thes ffeldys vndurwryton owtȝ[6] to be comyn from Lammas vnto the Puriffıcacion of our Lady from yer to yer[7]; þat is to say, ffrythefeld, Hamondfeld, with a medow at þe end of the same feld, Braysfeld with a medow at the end, Bannefeld, Bowyerscroft, Skinnerscroft, Hulfeld, wich Hullfeld strechith hym-selff vnto Aschaw, wich feldys aboue-namyd longen to the place of the Spoone, the wich Tho. Bedfford holdyth, and thies feeldys lyne on the north side fro the hyȝ way fro Couentre to Allyslay.

[1] oder E. 7. [2] hye E. 7.
[3] Originally the field of the parson of Spon chapel. A pencilled note in Sharp's hand-writing says "Spon Causeway."
[4]—[4] Not in E. 7. [5] leaf 15. [6] own E. 7. [7] ȝer E. 7.

And also they say þat John Ray of Couentre, theldur, in his tyme made couennaunt with the maiour and chamburleyns of the same Cyte þat[1] if he shuld haue the said feldys seuerall during his lyffe and his wyues, þat than aftur þer decesse þe seyd feldys shuld remayn to þe vse and profuyt of the chambur of the said cyte foreuermore, for wyche graunte he and his wyffe wer[2] sufferd to hold þe said feldys as seuerall duryng þer lyues, but þe sayn þat anon aftur the said John Ray the couenaunt abouesayd brake,[3] and the feldys abouesayd sold to one Rob. Neuton off Couentre; wherfore the Cyte[4] seyng his disseite in-to þe seid feldys in tyme off comyn enterden, & for comyn occupyden,[5] as ryght was; and so þai seyn thay own to be comyn, as hit is abouesaid. Allsoo þei seyn þat [6] Goldy-crofte longyng to the house of the hospytall[7] of Saynt Johannys in Couentre, lyeng by a hiȝe way leedyng from the said Allysley way to Coundull, owth to be comyn at Lammas, as hit is aboue-sayd.

John Ray's deceit, and breaking of covenant concerning these fields;

he sells them to R. Newton.

The Commons enter and occupy the fields.

Allso they seyn that þe said hyȝe way þat leedyth from Allysley way to Coundull is stoppyd,[8] wher hit owȝte to be[9] open.

Highway stopt.

Allso they say þat on the west side of the said hyȝe way þat is stoppyd, thes Croftez and feldes þat folowen own to be comyn, as hit is abouesayd, þat is to say, Curweyns crofte of the tenure of the prior of Couentre, a Croft wich Joh. Pynchebeke holdyth of the Trinite ȝelde,[10] Cros-feld, and a felde I-called Lychefeldys-feld, the wich Rob. Lyrpole holdythe.

Certain fields should be common,

Allso þai seyn þat the Crofte, þat strechith hym-selffe vnto Blake Orchard & Marl-felde beȝond the seyd Blak-orchard, wiche Wylliam Stone holdythe of the prior & Covent of Coventre, own & ben comyn at þe fest of Lammas, as hit is aboue namyd.

Allso þei seyn that a hye way that is Called Blak-low,[11] the wich ledyth from Allesley-way vnto Hethsall is Comyn all tyme of the yere.

and a highway to Hethsall.

Allso þai sayn þat all the feldys of Joh. Parker, that

[1] ȝif E. 7. [2] wern E. 7. [3] breke E. 7.
[4] Comunalte E. 7. [5] -on E. 7. [6] Goldrich- E. 7.
[7] hospitalite E. 7. [8] E. 7 inserts "& enclosed."
[9] E. 7 inserts "ouert &." [10] yeld E. 7. [11] Blak-lane E. 7.

arn callyd Whaburley-feld*es*, þ*at* lyen on this halue Guphul-lane, ar and own to be comyn at Lammas, as hit is aboue-said, except the Hoomestall*es* & ij Croftez next Guphul-lane forseyd, w*i*ch arn seue*r*all.

Other fields common at Lammas.

Allso þei seyn þ*at* on the northe-side beȝond Bedfordes-feld*es* aboue-said, thes feld*es* folowyng be comyn at Lammas, as hit is aboue-sayd, þ*at* is to say, a feld of w*i*ch feld a pa*r*cell is[1] Joh. Clerk*es* of Couentre, and a-noþ*er* pa*r*cell longithe to ye Chauntry, I-callyd Percyes Chauntry, and a feld callyd Percies felde longyng to þe said chauntry, allso a feld callyd Shel-felde of the said chauntry and Dudmanneswell-felde.

Another way stopt.

Allso thei say þ*at* þ*er* is a way strechyng from Conndull wey thorought[2] þe Milhay vnto þe Spane Cross, wiche is stoppyd wrongfully, as hit comyth,[3] by heggyng*es* & pa*r*tyng*es* on eue*r*y-side.

[4]Allso þei seyn that on the oþ*er* pa*r*tie of the same way so stoppid, thez feld*es* vnd*ur*-wryton ar comyn from Lammas vnto the Pur*ificacion* of o*ur* Lady yerely, that is to say, Skorchers-feld, the Pere-tre-feld, and a feld of Wyll*iam* Wymeswold stretchyng hym-selff vnto a comyn hyȝe-way, þat is callyd the Deed-lane.

Allso Wyndmyl-feld, ii Croft*es* lyeng fro the said way, þat is callyd the Deed-lane, vnto a moore of Wyll*iam* Wymswoold; allso a-noþ*er* Crofte of Margett Hall stretchyng hym-selffe to þe Spane-broke. Allso þei say þ*at* þe said way, þ*at* is callyd Deed-lane, þat strechithe hym-selff fro the Span-brooke[5] toward the [6]Hill-Crosse, þe wiche oweth to be opyn all tymys of the yer.

Deed Lane should always be open.

Allso þei sayen þ*at* þez feld*es* next aftur folowyng lyeng on the oþ*er* side of the said Deede-Lane, own to be comyn at Lammas vnto þe Pury*ficacion* etc., þ*at* is to say, a Croft þ*at* is callyd the Hullȝarde[7] w*ith* certen gardens þ*er*in ordynyd, of wiche gardyns Ric. Southam[8] holdyth a pa*r*cell, the heir*es* of John Poope[9] holdythe a pa*r*cell, and Wyll*iam* Attylbourghȝ holdyth þe iij[d] pa*r*cell, and forasmoche as þe same pa*r*cels of gardens byn[10] honestly made,

Land appropriated for gardens;

[1] of Johnȝ Clerk E. 7. [2] thorgh E. 7. [3] apereth E. 7.
[4] leaf 15, back. [5] brigge E. 7. [6] Hul- E. 7.
[7] -yerd E. 7. [8] The mayoral families have got a little slice.
[9] There is a "nota" in margin here. [10] costly & E. 7.

and lytull harme to the Cyte, þai besechyn the mai*our* & h*is* counsaill þ*at* þe said holders of the for-namyd p*ar*cels of gardens may haue them[1] seue*r*all all tymez of þe yer payng[2] a C*er*ten to þe chamb*ur* yerly as thei may accorde.

matter compromised on payment of rent.

And tho that were*n* chargid for to enquyre for the Northe p*ar*te of the Cite of Couentr*e*, that is to say, fro*m* Leycestr*e*-way to Coundon-lane comyn in and say in the man*er* as here-aftur folowith: & these byn ther namys.

Rob. Lirpoole, Joh. Peut*er*er, Joh. Doughty, Joh. Style, deyster, Rad. Chaundeler, Joh. Lichefeld, m*er*cer, Joh. Allesley, Will. Crudworth, Will. Wymyswold, Joh. Mongom*er*y, Will. Kersley, Will. Staunton.

Survey of north side.

[3]Hamlett*es* w*ith*in þe said p*ar*tie: Radford, Ecclesall, Folkeshull.[3]

Hamlets.

The wich Rob. Lyrpoole & his felows a-boue-namyd comyn in & sayn þ*at* þ*er* ar ij Croftez þe wich lye fro a barn of Wyll*iam* Wymysswoold vnto a feld, þ*at* is callyd [4]Crampy-feld in brede, & lenght fro Coundon-lane vnto Hulmyll-medow, & þei ij Croftys ar comyn at Lammas vnto þe fest of þe Pur*ificacion*. Allso þei sayen þ*at* Crampy-feld, oþ*er*wyse callyd Miryhull-groue, lyeng fro þe said ij Croftez vnto Batemannys-acre in lenght, and bred fro Coundul-lane vnto Hullmyl-medow, is Comyn at Lammas and so vnto Candilmas.

Verdict.

"Lamas grounds."

Allso Batesmannys-acre, þe w*i*ch lyethe bytwen[5] and Ashemore-feld in lenght, and brede fro Coundul-lane vnto þe Childern leys, þei sayn is comyn at Lammas vnto þe Purific*acion* of o*ur* Lady.

Allso þei sayn þ*at* all Childern[6] leys arn comyn at Lammas etc.

Other fields

Allso þei sayn that thay ij Croftez, w*i*ch ar callyd Pakes-Croftez lyeng bytwen Batemannys-acre & ij parock*es* lyeng[7] by Radford-way in lenght, and in brede fro Childern-lays vnto a feld of Wyll*iam* Wymeswold, þe w*i*ch Rob. Weston now holdyth, ar comen at Lammas vnto þe Puryfic*acion* etc.

common at Lammas.

[8]Allso thei sayn that a Croofte of Wyll*iam* Wymonds-

[1] hem E. 7. [2] payeng E. 7. [3–3] Not in E. 7.
[4] Grampy- E. 7. [5] E. 7 inserts "Grampy-feld."
[6] Chiltern E. 7. [7] lyne E. 7. [8] leaf 16.

wod*es*, lyeng betwen the hyȝ-way þ*at* is callyd Radford-way & Pakes-croftez, is comyn at Lammas vnto the Pur*ificacion* of o*ur* Lady.

Allso þe say þ*at* Bell-orchard & Hullmyll-medow w*ith* all the feldys and Croftys lyeng bytwen Radford-wey and Crampy-feld in brede, and in lenght fro*m* ij Croftez & þe housez and gardyns longyng to Saynt Mary awt*ur*[1] in the Trinite churche, þe w*i*ch ij Croftez, housez and Gardyns ar seue*r*all, vnto a lane ledyng fro*m* Batemannysacre, ar comyn at Lammas vnto þe Purif*icacion* of o*ur* Lady; except a house w*ith* gardyne sumtyme off John Askemare of Kenelworthe,[2] & a barn w*ith* a Gardyn of John Walgraue, and a Crofte w*ith* a dufhous[3] of the tenur*e* of þe prio*ur* & Couent of Couentr*e*, þe w*i*ch ar seue*r*all.

Two crofts, houses and gardens are several.

Allso thei sayen that a quarell þe w*i*ch Edward Lichefeld holdithe, þe w*i*ch liethe a this halfe[4] the church of Saynt Nich*olas*, is comyn at Lammas vnto þe fest of þe P*u*rificac*i*on of o*ur* Lady.

Allso thei sayen þ*at* fro*m* the house and Gardyne of Henry Preston, & also from the Crofte off Will*iam* Wymyswolde, w*i*ch is seue*r*all, vnto a lane ledyng to Nuneeton-way toward Seynt pyt-lane[5] in lenght, and in brede fro þe way þ*at* ledythe to þe churche of Saynt Nich*olas* to Nuneeton-way, all Croftez and feldys ar Comyn at Lammas vnto þe P*u*rificac*i*on of o*ur* Lady.

Crofts and fields common at Lammas.

Allso þei say þ*at* all Croftez and feldys þ*a*t lyen fro the churche of Saynt Nich*olas* vnto Whitmore-hege in lenght, & in brede fro Seynt pit-lane & Sukers-Groue vnto Radford and Radford way, arn comyn at Lammas etc., except a Croofte of John Oneley, & a Croft callyd Radfordmyll-crofte, w*i*ch ar seue*r*all.

Other crofts also common.

Allso þei sayn þ*at* the ij Croft*es* of the tenur*e* of the p*r*io*ur* of Couentr*e*, þe w*i*ch lyen betwen Stapull-crofte & Bushefeld-lane [6]in lenght,[6] ar comyn at Lammas vnto þe P*u*rificac*i*on of our Lady.

Allso þei sayn þ*at* þer ar oþ*er* ij Croft*es*, þ*at* ar callyd Sugmore Croft*es*, lyeng betwen Stapullfeld and Whitmor-feld in brede, & in lenght fro Saynt-putlane vnto a hie

[1] v. Corp. MS. C. 158. [2] Kyllyngworth E. 7. [3] dove-house.
[4] halue E. 7. [5] Sandy-pit lane. [6–6] Not in E. 7.

way, þ*at* is callyd Eton way ; and þei ar comyn at Lammas vnto þe P*ur*ificacion of o*ur* Lady.

Allso þ*er* is a-noþ*er* Crofte, þ*at* is callyd Sweyns-crofte, & a Crofte of the p*r*ioure*s* of Couentre, w*i*ch John Bryghtmer now holdyth, þe w*i*ch lyeth bytwen a Crofte of the said p*r*ioure*s* þ*at* Rob. Lirpole holdythe, & a Crofte of the m*aster* of the hospit*al* of Saynt Johannys vnto Botgrene in brede, & in lenght from the way ledyng to Eton vnto a lane w*i*ch strechithe to Pykedpere-crose, ar comyn at Lammas, ut sup*r*a. **More crofts common at Lammas.**

Allso thei sayen þ*at* all the feldys & Croftez lyeng fro Pennymore vnto a hie way ledyng to Ouenettesford in le*n*ght, and in brede fro the hye way, þ*at* is callyd Eton way vnto a wat*ur* renny*ng* fro Ouenettesford to Swannes-well, ar comyn at the feest of Lammas vnto þe P*ur*ificac*i*on of o*ur* Lady.

Allso thei sayn þ*at* þ*er* is a Crofte in Hasillwode lyeng in lenght by Eton way, & in brede fro þe said way vnto þe lond of þe brethren & sistern of Saynt Johannys, and þ*at* Croft is comyn at Lammas vnto þe P*ur*ificac*i*on of o*ur* Lady.[1]

[2]*Memorandum*, that þe Thursday þe xx day of January the vj yer of kyng Henry þe viith, the verdit of Tho. Plant, Rob. Smyth, walker, Ric. Norys, Will. Fisher, Coruise*r*, Will. Goodlade, Wyll. Paynell, Will. Bamboro, Tho. Fleshehewer, Joh. Solsell, Will. Pootell, Ric. Sampson, Will. Wigston, tyler, Tho. Bredon, baker, and Tho. Oures, baker:—The w*i*ch xij pe*r*sonnys say apon þ*er* hoolydome the day & yere a-foresaid afore Ric. Lee, maio*ur* of the Cite of Couentre, S*ir* Rob. Oneley, knyght, m*aster* of the Trinite gilde, Joh. Gawge, Ric. Braytofte, Hen. Kebull, Ric. Cook and Tho. Bayly: That þe Hillmyllfeld, þ*at* the wyndmyll standyth in, wherof the fondac*i*on is of stoone, w*i*ch Nich. Randull late held, lyeth in bred betwene Bryghtmere feld on the one p*ar*tie, and ij Croftez, gardyns, and howsez of o*ur* lady awt*ur* of the T*r*inite church of the oþ*er* p*ar*tie, and in lenght from the hiȝe way þ*at* ledyth fro Couentre to Radford vnto Hillmyll [3]medow, as in the quadri-

"Ciuitas Couentre." Jan. 20, 1491.

A jury of 12

swear before the mayor

that Hill-mill field

[1] End of E. 7. [2] Interpolation ; v. p. 46, 47. [3] leaf 16, back.

is common, and declared open to commonalty.

p*ar*tite more playnly it appearith, is & hath byn comyn fro*m* Lammas to Candilmass of tyme þ*at* noo mannys mynd is; The wich verdite so herd by the said maio*ur* and his brethern, the day and yer abouesaid, [they] will þ*at* the comens Occupie the said feld as ther comens fro*m* Lammas to Candyllmas as of oold tyme it hathe byn used, Except þ*at* heraft*ur* bettur euydens can be shewid to the cont*r*ary.[1]

EASTER LEET.

"Couentr*e*." Ap. 13, 1423.

¶ [V. f. p. on Monday after the close of Easter 1 Hen. VI. before Hen. Peytoo, mayor, Joh. Braytofte and Joh. Brystowe, bailiffs.]

Jurors.

Laur. Cooke, Will. Belg*r*aue, Ric. Southam, Will. Dilcoke, Ad. Deister, Joh. Esterton, Tho. Wildgrise, Rad. Garton, Will. Crosse, Joh. P*ar*ker, drap*er*, Tho. Grene, Tho. Groue, Joh. Golofre, Hen. Breux, Joh. Harborough, sen., Tho. Paynell, Joh. Coton, Ric. Oneley, Will. Fasceman, Joh. Braunston, Joh. Bowyer, Joh. Clerke, Joh. Mychell, m*er*ce*r*, Joh. Eu*er*don.

The town ditch to be kept free from dung; no cattle to pasture by the banks, nor bridge to be made across it under a 20*s*. fine. Other rules appear in the files.

Ad qua*m* let*am* ord*inatum* fuit q*uo*d le towne diche p*er* totam villa*m* civitat*is* Couen*trie* sit bene custod*itus* & mu*n*de (*sic*), & vbi aliquod fimu*m* in illo p*r*ostrat*ur* (*sic*) q*uo*d cito emendat*ur* (*sic*). Et q*uo*d null*us* h*ab*eat aliq*uo*d a*nim*al pastur*ans* p*er* littor*a* ffossat*i* p*re*dict*i*, nec aliq*ua*lem pont*em* vlt*ra* fossat*um* p*re*dict*um*, s*ub* pe*n*a xx s.; & al*ie* ordinac*iones* tu*n*c ib*ide*m ordinat*e* fuer*unt*, pr*out* p*atet* in filaciis ips*ius* vis*us*.

OFFICIALS' ACCOUNTS AND ORDERS OF COUNCIL.

May 4, 1423. "Compot*us* Camar*er*iorum."

[Hen. Breux and Joh. Coton, render their accounts for the time they were chamberlains before Hen. Peyto, mayor, and the other Forty-Eight honest and lawful men chosen by the mayor to hear accounts.]

[Upon this account the amount of the charge (regular receipts) amounted to £99 16*s*. 1*d*.]	Sup*er* q*uo*quide*m* compot*o* su*m*ma on*er*is p*re*dict*orum* cam*er*ario*rum* extens*a* fuit ad iiij^{xx} xix li. xvj s. j d. su*m*ma sup*er* eor*um* disone*racion*is
[The sum of the discharge	(*sic*) extendit se, ut p*atet* p*er* libr*os*

[1] End of interpolation.

(regular expenses) to £95 17*s.* 3*d.*]

eorum disoneracionis, ad iiij^{xx} xv li. xvij s iij d., & summa que (*sic*) dicti camerarii onerantur, que vocatur le rest, extendit se ad iij li.[1] quas quidem iij li. predicti camerarii onerantur ad inducendum prefato maiore infra octo dies post compotum eorum camerariorum,[2] videlicet post iiij diem mensis Maii.

[Balance (le rest) £3, which the chamberlains are charged to pay up within 8 days of presenting the account on May 4.]

Quas quidem iij li. predictus Hen. Peytoo, maior, recepit de predictis camerariis, exceptis iiij^{or} solidis, qui eis allocantur pro stipendio Clerici eorum, videlicet in pecunia & districcione, prout plenius apparet per indenturam inter predictum maiorem et prefatos camerarios factam & instructam.

Balance received (except 4*d.* for the clerk's pay) in distress & in money as appears in the indenture.

Mem. quod die Jouis proximo post festum Petri & Pauli a. r. r. Henrici VI^{ti} (etc.) primo, ordinatum est per maiorem & consilium suum, quod omnia arreragia in manu Johannis Leder et Johannis Esterton existencia, si que fuerint, simul cum districcionibus in manubus (*sic*) Camerariorum, uel precium eorundem, erunt leuata & in possessione maioris, videlicet Henrici Peytoo, posita ad faciendam vnam nouam crucem in vico Crucis, & similiter ad mundanda fossata Ciuitatis Couentrie.

[[3]July 1, 1423. the mayor and council ordain that all arrears in late mayors' hands, with the chamberlains' distrained goods, be placed with the mayor to make a new cross, and clean the ditches.]

Item, eodem die ordinatum fuit quod indenture pro Communia ciuitatis Couentrie facte et ordinate erunt posite in iiij partes ciuitatis predicte, videlicet, vna indentura in vna parte, et alia in secunda, & sic tercia, et quarta etc.

["Ind*entur*e of common" to be placed in four parts of the city.]

[1] 18*s.* 10*d.* are ignored. [2] Word seems to be omitted here. [3] leaf 17.

[Late mayor's charges.]

[J. Leeder charged with £16 of money of defective weight worth £12 12*s.* 4*d.* and from Joh. Golofre with £15 15*s.* 2*d.* worth £11 15*s.* 4*d.*]

[From R. Joy £1 13*s.* 8*d.* worth £1 9*s.* 7½*d.*]

[Received of distraint £3 16*s.* 2*d.*]

[From J. Golofre £10 worth £8 8*s.*]

[Sum of receipts £38 1*s.* 4*d.*, whence he asks allowance for the following.]

Mem. quod Joh. Leeder oneratur de istis, que sequuntur, receptis de Johanne Golofre & Ricardo Joy. In primis xvj li. de pecunia minus (*sic*) ponderis, que valet xij li. xij s. iiij d. Item de Johanne Golofre et Johanne Bowȝer xv li. xv s. ij d. de pecunia minus ponderis, que valet xj li. xv s. iiij d. Item recepit de Ricardo Joy xxxiij s. viij d. de pecunia (etc.) que valet xxix s. vij d. ob. Item, Recepit de districcione iij li. xvj s. ij d. Item recepit de Johanne Golofre x li. de pecunia (etc.) que valet viij li. viij s. Summa Receptionis xxxviij li. xvj d.[1] vnde petit allocari de parcellis sequentibus :—

[2][Henry Peyto receives from John Leeder an account for a tower newly made without the New Gate.]

[lead £8 3*s.* 2*d.*]

In primis pro plumbo viij li. iij s. ij d.

[solder 4*s.* 2*d.*]

Item pur sowdur iiij s. ij d.

[timber, etc. £3.]

Item a Derby wright pur tymbur & workmanshyp iij li.

[boards & lathes 6*s.* 8*d.*]

Item pur bordes & lathis vj s. viij d.

[hooks, etc. 1*s.* 4*d.*]

Item pur hookes, hynges & j loke xvj d.

[to plumber £1 5*s.*]

Item pro labore vnius plumer xxv s.

[J. Leeder pays £5 of arrears from his chamberlaincy.]

Item predictus Joh. Leeder soluit Johanni Esterton v li. de vna parcella a retro existente de tempore quo fuit Camerarius.

[Simon Mason's reward £2.]

Item soluit Simoni Mason pur vne reward xl s.

[For an earthwork, etc. 5*s.* 3*d.*]

Item, pur Erthwark[3] & Whytyng v s. iij d.

[1] Really £38 1*s.* 5½*d.* [2] leaf 17, back.

[3] Earliest example in *N. E. D.* dated 1633.

[For this register 7*s.*]

Item, isto lib*ro*, voc*ato* le Registre, vij s.

[For a sum which he gave to the poor, when he collected £200 for the king & queen, viz. £2 18*s.* 3*d.*

Item petit allocari p*ro* ce*r*ta pecu*nia*, S*um*ma qua*m* dedit pauperib*us* quand*o* colleg*it* CC li. Regi et Regine, videl*icet* lviij s. iij d.

[17 Aug. the mayor receives arrears £6 2*s.* 6*d.* of sufficient weight;
and £10 worth £8 5*s.*]

[Mem. Henry Peytoo received from John Leeder £6 2*s.* 6*d.* "de poise;"
and on the same day from the same, £10 "de pecun*ia* min*us* pond*eris* ad valorem" £8 5*s.*]

[1][On the Thursday after S. Matthew's day[2] Henry Peyto "made a halle of tho xl^{ti}viii pe*r*sonys and wurthy men a-boue[3] namyd," when it was ordered that a cross should be built in Cross Cheaping.] Sep. 23. Ordinances of the Forty-eight. "xlviij." "A Cross set vp in Cros-cheapping."

Allso hit was ordenyd & g*r*auntyd that tho wurthy men þ*at* Rydon *with* the maio*ur* to London at Mich[aelmas] þe yer abouesaid be com*ma*undment of the duke of Gloucest*re*, leue-tena*unt* of Inglond, eue*r*y man schuld ber his own cost; and as touchyng thes othur pe*r*sonys, the wich ridon to London the same tyme, þ*at* is to say of eue*r*y Craft a ce*r*ten, hit is allso g*r*auntyd & ordenyd by the same xl^{ti}viij wise & wurthy men, þ*at* eue*r*y crafte schall bere the cost as for her men þ*at* rydon to London the same tyme. Cost of riding to London to be borne by crafts.

[The former chamberlains, Hen. Breux and John Coton, John Braytoft and John Brystow, ordered to make their accounts, the former couple within the month of April next "at the vtterest," and the latter within eight days after the next S. John Baptist's day.] Chamberlains' accounts.

[4]Allso be hit had in mynd þ*at* at the same tyme thies xlviij aboue-namyd p*ar*donyd Symon Mason of iiij perchis of the towne wall *with*oute the New-yate, wiche he shuld haue made, by couena*u*nt afore tyme by-twene the Chamburl*ens* of the said Cite and hym compoosid and fully made. Simon Mason's perches of wall.

[1] leaf 13.
[2] Probable error for S. Matthias, Feb. 23. St. Matthew's, Sept. 21, 1423, would not fall within the first regnal year of Henry VI. [3] p. 44. [4] leaf 13, back.

The gates of the city to be furnished with leaves and doors.

Allso hit is ordenyd that the Chamb*ur*lens schall make the Hill-streit yate new, & allso all the yat*es* of the said Cite, þ*at* be not leuyd ne dorryd, þ*at* they schall leue hem als sone as thei mow.

MICHAELMAS LEET.

"Couentre." Oct. 6, 1423.

[1][V. f. p. Wednesday after Michaelmas day, 2 Henry VI], Laur. Cooke, Will. Belg*r*aue, Will. Dilcoke, Ric. Southam, Ad. Hiton, Joh. Leeder, Joh. Esterton, Tho. Wildgrise, Joh. Herdborgh, Tho. Grene, Ric. Joy, Will. Crose, Joh. P*ar*ker, Joh. Golofre, Hen. Breux, Rob. Milb*ur*ne, Will. Byfeld, Will. Fasema*n*, Joh. Braunston, Joh. Egeston, Joh. Mychell, Joh. Oneley, Joh. Clarke, Joh. Warrant.

Jury.

[These elect Ric. Onley and Joh. Bowyer, bailiffs.]

[2]Allso thai orden þ*at* no bocher of the Cite of Couentr*e* sle no booll but ȝif he be baityd a-fore at a place consuet,[3] a-pon the payn of vj s. viij d., and allso of forfayture [of] the same booll at eu*er*y trespase.

Bulls and baiting.

Allso þ*at* no oþ*er* man or bocher kep w*ith*in the wallys of this Cite noo swyne in sties, ne bulkes,[4] ne w*ith*in þ*er* housez in þe Bochery, vpon þe payn of iij s. iiij d., and allso of forfait*ur* of the same swyne so I-founden.

No swine in the city.

Allso þ*at* þe maio*ur* and the baileffez shall enserche the bochery, and all oþ*er* Craftez of c*er*ten defaut*is* þ*at* they haue t*r*espassid in against ordyna*u*ncez of leet*is* a-fore this tyme; & þ*at* the paynez may be reryd, þ*er* as defaute is, aftur the ordyna*u*nce of the said lett*is*, and allso of ther own gra*u*nte.

Fines to be collected for trespasses.

Allso þ*at* the maio*ur* & þe bayliffez wit*h* þ*er* officers schall strenght the wardens of this Cyte to take distress for the rent of the town, þ*at* is to say of Wyll*iam* Keresley & all oþ*er*, ryghtȝ as þe Law wyll.

Wardens to take distress.

Allso it is ordenyd þ*at* noo Constable w*ith*in the Cite take no syluer for no rest þei make by way off þ*er* office, oþ*er*wais þen þe Law wyll.

Constables to take no money for arrests.

Allso þ*at* eu*er*y man repair*e* his pament afore his tene*mentes* bytwyxt this and the next leet, eu*er*y man a-pon

"Paving streets."

[1] leaf 17, back. [2] leaf 18. [3] accustomed. [4] v. Gloss.

the payn of iij s. iiij d., halfe to þe vse of the balyffes, & half to þe chambur, & þat by þe comen sergeant.

Allso þai orden þat the Reddyche be clansyd, & all þe pryves & swynesties þeron be done away. "Clensing Reddich."

Allso þei orden that Ric. Waite for his good seruice he hathe doone to þe Cite of Coventre, and for his long contynuanse in the same, shall haue of the Trinite gylde whill he lyuythe xiij s. iiij d., of Corpus *Christi* yeld vj s. viij d., & of the wardens of the said Cite xx s. Ric. Wait's pension.

[1]Allso thei haue ret*ained* Mathew Ellerton, Thomas Sendell, Will*iam* Howton & John Trumpere, Mynstrells as for the Cite of Couentre; and þat þei haue as oþer haue had a-fore them. Allso þat thai haue of euery hall place j d., of euery Cottage ob., euery quarter; & aftur þer beryng bettur to be rewardyd. And also þai orden þat thei shall haue ij men of euery ward euery quarter to help them to gathur þer Quarterage. Minstrels. 1*d*. from every hall-place, and ½*d*. from every cottage each quarter; 2 men to collect these fees.

Allso thai sayen þat Symon Mason shall haue xl s. in rewarde of þe chambur to his costis. Simon Mason's reward.

Allso þat all men of Contrey, that com to town to sell Otys, þat thei stond with them be-nethe þe peesen, þat is to say at þe West-orchard end. "Pease market; ote markett." Sellers of oats at West Orchard.

Allso þat John Cambirge be alowed for his costis þat he made agaynst the comyng of kyng Henre the Fifte, þat is to say xiij s. iiij d. ob.; and þat be þe chamburlens. Reward for preparation for Henry V's coming.

Allso þat Mold Lichefeld pay to þe murage of this cite aftur þe lond þat she holdithe, & no oþer wyse. Mauld Lichefeld's murage.

Allso þat John Sheynton haue a yerez rent to alowanse of his Costys þat he hathe made. Sheynton's costs.

Allso þat þer be a Cookestowle made apon Chelsmore-grene to punysche skolders and chidders as þe law wyll. "Cookstool" for scolds.

Allso þei orden þat John Moweton, Clerke, be examynyd by the maiour whethur he be Notary impereall, or he be not; and if so be he be a Notary sworen & admyttyd, & may nott refuse[2] hit, þat then the sayd John Mowton be put a-wey from the court of Couentre, þat is to say, the mairez court & bayliffes. Notary imperial.

[1] v. Sharp, *Cov. Mysteries*, 207 *sqq*. [2] refuse = deny.

TOWN BUSINESS.

Oct. 17, 1423. A hall of 69 men summoned by mayor.

[On the vigil of S. Luke Ev. 2 Hen. VI, Hen. Peyto made a hall (fecit aulam) of the following :]

Gosford [Street]. Laur. Cooke,[1] Will. Crose,[1] Joh. Welford, Joh. Stafford, Joh. Goloffre,[1] Rad. Alott, Bened. Marchall.

Jurden [Well]. Thos. Wildgryse,[2] Joh. Stretton, Will. Deist*er*, Joh. Leeder, Joh. Dilkok, Joh. Whalley, Joh. Bryan, Joh. Cotton.[1]

Muchp*ar*ke [Street]. Joh. Harbourgh, sen., Joh. Prentes, Will. Byrde, Joh. Esterton,[1] Joh. Clarke, Joh. Ray, Joh. Braytofte,[1] Will. Faseman,[1] Rob. Danyell, Will. Byfeld.

[3]Erlestre*et*. Ric. Sharp,[1] Joh. Warrant,[1] Tho. Wirley, Ad. Swette, Nich. Byfeld, Joh. Launde, Joh. Frankelen.

Lytull [Park Street]. Ric. Southam, Rad. Garton,[4] Joh. Mychell,[4] Joh. Eu*er*don, Gal. Willnale, Will. Tolas.

Byschop [Street]. Joh. Lychefeld, Ric. Southam,[1] Will. Wymyswold.

Baill[y Lane]. Will. Brooke, Joh. Ronton,[1] Ad. Dyer,[1] Joh. Benett,[1] Joh. Spence*r*, sadeler, Hen. Bryde.[1]

Frer[*e* Lane]. Ric. Bushebury,[1] Egid. Allesley, Ric. Oneley,[1] Rob. Praty.

Smythf[ord Street]. Joh. Tate, Ric. Hicklyng, Joh. Brystow,[1] Joh. Wymondswold, Joh. Bowyer,[1] Joh. Blakman, Joh. Braunston,[1] Joh. Egeston.

Span [Street]. Tho. Paynell,[1] Joh. Brown.

Crosche[ping]. Rob. Milb*u*rne,[1] Ric. Botone*r*, Hen. Breux,[1] Ad. Hyton, Joh. P*ar*ker, drap*er*,[1] Will. Dilkoke,[1] Ric. Joye,[5] Tho. Grene.

[Adam Hiton and John Leeder journey to London to negotiate about the royal debts.]

Qui ordinaueru*nt* q*uo*d Adam Hiton & Joh*ann*es Leeder irent London' ad p*ro*seque*ndum* p*ro* ce*rt*is debit*is* que deb*e*nt*ur* p*er* dom*inum* Rege*m* Henric*um* quart*um* et dom*inum* H[enricum] quint*um*, nup*er* Rege*s* Anglie, vi*delice*t, temp*or*e Will*elm*i Whitchurche d*omi*no H[enrico] quarto

[Henry IV owed £163;

(*sic*) CCC li., vn*de* reman*ent* Clxiij li.

[1] In list, p. 62–3. [2] In Gosford, p. 62–3. [3] leaf 18, back.
[4] Earl Street, p. 62–3. [5] Bishop Street, p. 62–3.

non solute per talliam: & tempore Johannis Goote, tunc maioris, domino H[enrico] V^to CCli. per obligacionem: & tempore Johannis Horneby, tunc maioris, domino H[enrico] V^to C li.: & tempore Laurencii Cooke (etc.) domino H[enrico] V^to CC marce.[1]

[... Henry V £200; and £100 and 200 marks.]

[John and Adam to obtain a licence to acquire in mortmain a tenement in Earl Street;

Item, ordinauerunt quod predictus Joh. Leeder et Adam prosequi debent pro le mortesment vnius tenementi nuper Willelmi Whitchurch, iacentis in le Erlestrett de Couentria meliore modo quo sciunt aut poterint (*sic*).

they are also to communicate with Sir R. Babthorp[2] and with the prior for buying the reversion of Wymondswold's houses and land to the use of the Chamber, if they consider it would be profitable.]

Item, ordinauerunt quod predicti Johannes et Adam communicare debent cum Roberto Bapthorp,[2] milite, et cum Ricardo Crosby, priore (etc.) ad emendam reuersionem terrarum et tenementorum Willelmi Wymondswold ad vsum Camere ciuitatis (etc.), si eis videtur expedire, & quod sit [ad] proficuum predicte ciuitatis.

[And the 69 persons put these matters entirely in their hands,

& qui lxix persone supranominati submiserunt omnia supradicta ad ? manus & disposicionem predictorum Johannis Leder & Adam (*sic*) Hiton, ut ipsi ordinant (*sic*) et disponent secundum eorum discressionem etc. ad proficuum ciuitatis predicte.

and John and Adam get 10 marks for their costs.]

Item, deliberatum est prefatis Johanni et Adam per manus Henrici Peytoo, maioris, ad eorum costagia decem marcas.

[[3]Oct. 17, 1423.]

[3]Mem. quod in vigilia S. Luce, Euaungeliste a. r. r. (etc.) secundo, ordinatum fuit per aulam antedictam:[4]

[1] These debts were contracted in the years 1399, 1411 or 1420, 1412 and 1415 respectively.

[2] Steward of the Duchy of Lancaster. For Crosby, Prior of S. Mary's, v. *supra*, p. 35. [3] leaf 19. [4] v. p. 60.

[Ordained by the aforesaid hall that G. Allesley go to London to save the citizens of Coventry from paying £382, which the sheriff would have levied because the bailiffs, though they paid the fee farm each year, have not got their receipt (quietus est).]

Quod Egid. Allesley iret Londonias ad saluandum homines Couentrie indempnes de CCClxxxij li. quas vicecomes Warrewici habuit in precepto ad leuandum de hominibus ville de Couentria, pro eo quod per longum tempus elapsum balliui ciuitatis predicte non habuerunt quietus est,[1] prout etc.; & non obstante quod quolibet anno ipsi soluerunt feodi firmam (etc.); & predictus Egid. Allesley habuit pro costagiis suis forma que sequitur, videlicet:—

[Allesley has his costs from the following persons: total £8 3*s.* 4*d.*]

[Will. Crosse, Joh. Goloffre, Joh. Braytoft, Hen. Peito, Joh. Esterton, Joh. Leder, Joh. Brystowe, Ric. Oneley, Joh. Bowyer, Rob. Milburne, Hen. Breux, Tho. Wildgrise, Giles Allesley, Joh. Hardborghe, Ric. Joye, contribute 10*s.* each, and Rad. Garton, Tho. Grene, 6*s.* 8*d.* each. Total £8 3*s.* 4*d.*]

[[2]Nov. 2. A hall of certain from each ward to inquire whether the people will consent to receive jewels now to the worth of half the debts owed by Henry IV and Henry V.]

[2]Mem. quod secundo die Novembris a. r. r. (etc.) secundo, Henricus Peitoo, maiour, fecit aulam, ad quam aulam ordinatum fuit quod certe persone cuiuslibet warde adquiri (*sic*) deberent inter se vtrum ipsi vellent consentire et consedere (*sic*)[3] ad accipienda debita que debentur eis per dominum H. quartum & dominum H. V^tum^, nuper Reges Anglie, in jocalibus nunc ad valorem dimidietatis debitorum predictorum; & super hoc ipsi adquisitores warde de Gosford veniunt & dicunt ut sequitur:

[The wards represented are Gosford Street, Much Park Street, Mill Lane and Jorden Well,[4] Bailly Lane, Earl Street, Broadgate and Friar Lane, Smithford and Spon

[1] MS. quiestus. [2] leaf 18, back. [3] condescendere. [4] Joh. Rochford not in p. 60.

Streets,[1] Cross Cheaping, Bishop and Well[2] Streets. The representatives number 33, from two to four of the principal men from each ward; and each set announces that all those who bore their share of the loan are willing to abide by the decision of John Leder and Adam Hyton.]

[[3]Nov. 5, 1423.

[A licence of mortmain and other muniments sent to John and Adam in a sealed box with £10 sterling.]

Item, alio temp*ore* miss*us* fuit eisdem Joha*nn*i et Adam, videl*icet* v^{to} die mens*is* Novembr*is* a*nno* secu*n*do R*egis* nunc, p*er* Joha*nn*em Prentes de Couentre, m*er*cer, le licens dell mortisment de cam*era* ciu*itatis* Couent*re* cum vna alia Cart*a*, & aliis ce*r*tis muniment*is* eidem p*er*tinen*tibus*, in vno Cofano (*sic*) sigillat*o*, & decem libr*is* st*er*lingor*um*.

[They have the Duke of Bedford's bond for £200.]

Item, p*re*dict*i* Joh. Leder et Adam h*ab*ue*runt* vna*m* obligac*ion*em i*n* q*ua* Joha*nn*es dux Bedford*ie* tenet*ur* et obligat*ur* in CC li.

[[4]Jan. 14, 1424.

[The mayor and others place in a chest in the tower in S. Mary's Hall, of which chest the mayor and gild master have a key each, a sealed box containing the Duke of Bedford's bond in £200, and another bond in £289 of the prior, which is owed for two jewels; of which a tally of equal weight remains in the box;

Mem. q*uo*d xiiij^{o} die Januar*ii* a. r. r. (etc.) *secun*do Hen. Peitoo, maior, Joh. Leeder, mayst*er* gilde S. Trinitat*is* etc., & Laur. Cooke posueru*nt* & ib*id*em dimiseru*nt* in vna*m* Cist*am* in t*ur*re [aule] B. Ma*ri*e exist*entem*, cui*us* Ciste maio*ur* h*abet* vna*m* clauem, & magist*er* Gilde p*re*dict*e* alia*m*, videl*ic*et vnu*m* box sigillat*um*, in q*uo* vna obligac*i*o in q*ua* Joha*nn*es dux Bedf*ordie* tenet*ur* in ducent*is* libr*is*; et alia*m* obligac*ion*em in q*ua* p*r*ior et [5]Conuent*us* eccl*esi*e cathed*ralis* B. Ma*ri*e de Coue*ntria* tenet*ur* in CCiiij^{xx} ix li., quas p*re*fat*us* p*r*ior deb*et* p*ro* ij^{obus} Jocalibus, cui*us* Jocale le Countre-poise[6] rema*net* i*n* p*re*fat*a* pixide. Item, vna*m* acquientanc*iam* x li. p*ro*

[1] Smithford and Spon Streets classed together. Will. Kerver, Hugo Rugeley not in p. 60. [2] Joh. Walgrave not in p. 60.

[3] leaf 18, back. [4] leaf 19. [5] leaf 19, back. [6] v. Gloss.

also a receipt for a £10 annuity owed by the mayor and community; also a covered silver gilt cup worth £10; and a tally of Henry IV for £163.

vna annuitate prefatis priori & conuentui per maiorem & communitatem debita, videlicet pro tempore Henrici Peito, maioris. Item, dimiserunt in Cistam predictam vnum Cowp de argento, Couered & deauratum, ad valenciam x li. Item, dimiserunt et ibidem posuerunt, videlicet in Cistam predictam, vnam talliam domini Henrici, nuper Regis Anglie quarti (etc.) de Clxiij li.

[The mayor and others give to the prior a bond in £289, and receive two jewels, which they place in the common chest, where they remain to be kept.

Mem. quod in vigilia S. Osburge,[1] virginis, anno predicto, predictus Hen. Peytoo, maior, Joh. Leder, Laur. Cooke & Ric. Southam et alii deliberauerunt obligacionem predictam in qua prior et conuentus ecclesie cathedralis beate Marie de Couentria tenentur in CCiiij^{xx}ix li. prefatis priori et conuentui etc.; & iidem Henricus, Johannes & Ricardus receperunt duo Jocalia predicta etc. & imposuerunt in Cistam predictam, & ibidem remanent ad Custodiendum.

[See concerning this same matter in T. Wildgrise's time.]

Vide de eadem materia tempore Thome Wildgrise maioris ij° folio.[2]

[[3]Jan. 17, 1424, 10 marks from the late mayor.

[Henry Peytoo received from John Esterton ten marks of a certain sum remaining in his hands from the time of his mayoralty.]

[Late chamberlains give for complete settlement in distraint and money by tale £6 2*s*.

Mem. quod Hen. Peitoo recepit de Johanne Golofre, Roberto Milburn & Johanne Bowyer de tempore quo fuerunt camerarii (etc.) pro plena solucione eorum in districcionibus et pecuniis numeratis vj li. ij s.; & eodem tempore ex assensu et consensu H.

[1] Date unknown. It was determined on Oct. 13, 1410, that the saint's birthday should be celebrated through the archidiaconate. v. Dugdale, 110.

[2] In margin, v. p. 69, 70. [3] leaf 17, back.

[With assent of the "discreets," a great pan given to J. Golofre for being chamberlain for two years in his turn.

Peitoo, tu*n*c maior*is*, Joh*annes* (*sic*) Leeder, & alior*um* viror*um* discret*orum* ib*id*em int*er*essent*ium*, dat*a* & delib*er*at*a* fuit Joh*ann*i Golofre vna patella magua in remun*er*ac*io*ne q*uo*d fuit cam*er*ar*ius* p*er* duos annos ad invicem.

[The mayor receives £2 16*s*. from former chamberlains;

Item, Hen. Peitoo recep*it* de Henric*o* Breux & Joh*anne* Coton de temp*ore* quo fu*er*int (*sic*) cam*er*arii etc. in pecun*iis* num*er*at*is* & in dist*r*iccion*i*b*us* lvj s. p*ro* plena soluc*io*ne eor*um*.

and £5 4*s*. 10*d*. from J. Leeder, which the wardens received.

It*em*, Hen. Peito recep*it* de Joh*anne* Leeder v li. iiij s. x d. de temp*ore* q*uo* fuit maior & in manu sua vsq*ue* ad tu*n*c existenc*ia*, & p*r*ius p*er* custodes (etc.) recept*os* etc. p*r*out etc.

[See elsewhere.

Vide de ist*is* recep*tis* & aliis in t*er*cio folio ab isto folio in principio.[1]

[[2]Jan. 18, ? 1424.

Mem. q*uo*d xviij° die mens*is* Januarii a. r. r. (etc.) p*r*imo[3] [? secundo] Joh. Braytoft et Joh. Bristowe[4]

[J. Braytoft and J. Bristowe, late chamberlains' account before the mayor and the 48;

computauer*un*t coram Henr*ico* Peytoo, maiore (etc.) & xlviij hom*in*ib*us* etc. de temp*ore* quo fueru*n*t cam*er*arii (etc.) v*idelicet* :—

they are charged for murage with £84 3*s*. 2*d*., for goods valued at £15 16*s*. 1*d*. Total £99 19*s*. 3*d*.

[5]In p*r*imis on*er*ant*ur* p*ur* le murage ciuitat*is* p*re*d*i*cte iiij^{xx} iiij li. iij s. ij d. Item p*ur* Catell' extens*is* xv li. xvj s. j d. Su*m*ma to*talis* iiij^{xx}xix li. xix s. iij d.

[Discharge, or expenses as appear by items in the mayor's bag, and the chamberlains' books £99 2*s*. 11½*d*.

S*um*ma disone*r*ac*io*nis p*re*dicte cam*er*e eodem *anno*, ut p*atet* p*er* parcell*as* in baga Henr*ici* Peytoo, tu*n*c maior*is* exist*entis*, & p*er* libros dict*orum* cam-

[1] In margin, v. 66–7. [2] leaf 16, back.
[3] Or else an error for February. Henry Peytoo was not yet mayor on Jan. 18 of the first regnal year of Henry VI (1423), as his mayoral year began on Feb. 2.
[4] Chamberlains, 1421. [5] leaf 17.

balance for which they are "in debt" 16*s.*; which they ask to be allowed.

*er*ari*orum*, iiij^{xx}xix li. ij s. xj d. ob. & sic remane*nt* in debit*o* xvj s.[1] Vnde petu*nt* allocari de *predictis* xvj s.

[On the same day John Michell and John Egeston, wardens of the Chamber (custodes camere), render their accounts for the preceding year before the mayor and the Forty-eight.]

["Al*ia* compota." Wardens' charge £76 14*s.* 1*d.*, allowance for reduction of rents £3 10*s.* 6*d.*, for poor tenants £1 3*s.* 1*d.*, for Rothe 20*s.*, for repairs and chief rents £55 1*s.* 7½*d.*, for vacant houses £3 2*s.* 4*d.* and £2 15*s.* 1½*d.*

In p*ri*mis on*er*ant*ur* dict*i* custodes cum lxxvj li. xiiij s. j d. Vnde petu*nt* allocari p*ro* abatemente*s* de Rente*s* iij li. x s. vj d. Item, petu*nt* allocari p*ro* tenentib*us* pauper*ibus*[2] xxiij. j d. Item, allocar*i* petu*nt* p*ro* Rothe, wev*er*, de Gosford, xx s. Item, petu*nt* allocari p*ro* rep*aracion*ib*us* & Capitalib*us* reddit*ibus* lv li. xix d. ob.; & petu*nt* allocari p*ro* vacac*ioni*b*us* eodem anno iij li. ij s. iiij d. Item p*ro* eodem anno p*r*edict*o* lv s. j d. ob.

[Sum of allowance £66 12*s.* 7*d.* They owe the balance £10 1*s.* 6*d.*

S*um*ma to*talis* allocaci*onis*, lxvj li. xij s. vij d.

& sic dict*i* custodes clare debent et on*er*ant*ur* etc. x li. xviij d.

[[3]Jan. 1424.

[The mayor receives £33 2*s.* granted by a hall of discreet persons in Corpus Christi (S. Nicholas) Hall; which sum of £33 2*s.* was granted to be raised like a fifteenth, except that a sum of 20*s.* in every ward was forgiven; which sum should have been £40, but more than £33 2*s.* could not be levied.

Hen. Peytoo, maior (etc.) p*er* qua*n*d*am* aulam ex c*er*t*is* p*er*sonis discret*is* in aula Corp*or*is *Christi* (etc.) conces*sam*, videl*icet*[4] mens*is* Januar*ii* a. r. r. (etc.) secu*n*do, rec*epit* xxxiij li. ij s.; quas (? que summa) u*er*o xxxiij li. ij s. concess*a* fuit m*od*o et forma quib*us* xv^{ma}[5] leuari solebat, exce*pto* q*uo*d in q*uo*libet wardo xx s. eru*nt* p*er*donati; que s*um*ma ess*et* xl li., sed plus q*uam* p*r*edict*is* xxxiij li. ij s. mult*is* caus*is* levari no*n* potuit.

[The mayor received from

Item, p*r*edict*us* maiou*r* recep*it* de Joh*anne* Michell & Joh*ann*e Eu*er*don

[1] 3½*d.* omitted. [2] MS. paup*erum*. [3] leaf 19, back.
[4] Day omitted. [5] MS. xvme.

the warden £2 for J. Crosse of Gosford Street,

£10 for J. Happeford's soul;

£4 0*s.* 6*d.*

£1 12*s.* 2*d.*

£2 0*s.* 0*d.*
£3 0*s.* 0*d.*
£2 0*s.* 0*d.*

£8 0*s.* 0*d.*

[This parcel of money delivered by J. Michel, warden.

Of which moneys, as well as of other receipts,

he asks to be exonerated in these items:

for the acquisition of Whitchurch Place in Earl Street;

paid by the mayor £40;
for the amortization of this messuage, and for following up

certain debts owed by Henry V, to Leder and Hiton £24 13*s.* 4*d.*

[To W. Babynton, chief

gardian*is* (etc.) p*ro* Johanne Crosse de vico de Gosford xl s.

It*em*, predictus maio*ur* recep*i*t de Ric*ardo* Southam p*ro* an*im*a Joh*ann*is Happeford x li.[1]

It*em*, p*ro* an*im*a Joh*ann*is Garton sen. de Rad*ulf*o Garton iiij li. vj d.

[from Joh. Wellford for Alice Cortnale's soul £1. 12*s.* 2*d.*; from Hen. Breux for Ric. Marchall's soul £2; from Ric. Sharp for Tho. Pinkston's soul £3; from Will. Cross for Joh. Crosse's soul £2; from Joh. Esterton for Rob. Esterton's soul £8.]

Ista p*a*rcell*a* de pecun*ia* delib*erat*a fuit Henr*ico* Peito maiore p*er* Joh*an*-*n*em Michell, tu*n*c custod*em* (etc.)

De quib*us* pecun*iis* sup*ra*script*is*, videl*icet* de Recept*is* tam in isto folio q*u*am in viij° folio p*recedent*i,[2] p*re*dict*us* Henr*icus* petit exon*er*ari de ist*is* p*a*rcell*is* subsequen*tibus*, videl*icet*:—

In p*ri*mis p*ro* adquicic*io*ne vni*us* ten*ementi* in Coventr*ia*, vocat*i* Whitchurch-place, iacent*is* in vico Com*itis* etc., solut*e* p*er* man*us* p*re*dict*i* Henr*ici* (etc.) Will*elm*i Bowyer, Thome Wildgrise & Joh*ann*is Warrant, xl li.[3]

It*em* p*ur* le mortesment eiusd*em* messuag*ii*; et ad p*ro*sequend*um* et ad inducend*um* c*er*tas (*sic*) debit*a* q*ue* debent*ur* p*er* d*omin*um Henr*icum* nup*er* R*egem* Angl*ie* qui*n*tu*m*, Joh*ann*i Leder et Ade Hiton, ad hoc assignat*is*, Solut*i* xxiiij li. xiij s. iiij d.

It*em* Will*elm*o Babynton,[4] tu*n*c

[1] All the sums following are included in the "parcel of money."
[2] v. p. 64. [3] v. p. 61. [4] Chief justice of the common bench 1420.

Justice of the common bench,	capit*ali* Justic*iario* d*omi*ni R*egis* de co*mmu*ni banco, ad essend*um* de
for his counsel £3 6*s.* 8*d.*	consilio p*redict*o faciend*o* iij li. vj s. viij d.
paid to G. Allesley, besides the former sum,	Item, solut*i* Eg*id*io Allesley ult*r*a S*um*mam viij li. iij s. iiij d. conces*sam* et solut*am*, p*er* cert*os* ball*iuos*[1] ciuit*atis* Couen*trie*, p*r*out in decimo fol*io* temp*or*e Henr*ici* Peito plen*ius*
£3 6*s.* 8*d.*	apparett (*sic*), iij li. vj s. viij d.
[For the new cross in the Cheaping £50.	It*em*, factura nove cruc*is* in vico de Crosechepyng, solut*e* p*er* man*us* eiusd*em* Henr*ici* l li.
[Allesley's business of the bailiffs' "quietus est," as appears in certain	Mem. q*uo*d Hen. Peitoo recep*it* de Egidio Allesley tres Rotul*os*, in quib*us* comp*re*hendit*ur* labor de le quietus est de temp*or*e decem ball*ivorum*,[2] p*r*out in p*redict*is Rot*u*lis plen*ius* ap-
rolls, which remain in the	paret. & que quidem Rot*u*le (*sic*) remanent in vna baga p*redict*i Hen-
mayor's bags in S. Mary's Hall.]	*rici* Peito in aula B. Mar*ie* virginis existent*e* etc., que vocat*ur* le meyr*es* bagges.

[3]THO. WYLDGRISE, MAYOR, 1424.

[Election of officers.] [Jan. 25. ["N*omina* elect*orum*." [27 names.	Joh. Leeder, Will. Dilcok, Ad. Hyton, Joh. Esterton, Egid. Alesley, Rad. Garton, Tho. Grene, Will. Crose, Ric. Joy, Joh. Golofre, Hen. Breux, Joh. Braytofte, Joh. Bristow, Will. Byfeld, Joh. Clerke, Ric. Sharp, Ric. Deen, Joh. Franklen, Will. Fryssby, Joh. Egeston, Will. Crosse, passynger,[4] Mat. White, Nic. Byfeld,

[1] v. p. 62. [2] v. *ib.*

[3] leaf 20. See for the formula, p. 21. The names of the outgoing mayor and of the bailiffs before whom the transaction took place will henceforth be omitted for brevity's sake. The election always took place on the Conversion of S. Paul, though the mayor did not take up office till Candlemas. The bailiffs, elected at the Michaelmas leet, served till the following Michaelmas.

[4] v. Gloss.

THE COUNCIL.

Joh. Pynchebeke, Will. Bryde, Ric. Hicklyng, Joh. Warrrant.

[Officers.

[[1] m. Tho. Wildegrise; cor. Joh. Dylcok; ch. Will. Crudworthe, Will. Kerver; w. Joh. Michell, Joh. Euerdon; mace (clavigerilus), Will. Oxton.

[J. Ps.

Tho. Wyldgryse,[2] m., Joh. Weston, rec., Joh. Leeder,[2] Laur. Cooke,[2] Ric. Southam,[2] Ad. Hiton.[2]]

[Names of those chosen by the mayor to be of his council, with the other 24 being present at his election.

24 names.

Isti subscript*i* electi su*n*t p*er* Thom*am* Wildgryse maior*em* etc. ad int*er*essend*um* consilio eiusd*em* maior*is* cu*m* ill*is* xx[ti] iiij discret*is* et honorabil*ibus* vir*is*, de elect*ione* pre-dict*i* maior*is* essent*ibus* (*sic*) etc., vide*licet*: Ric. Southam, Laur. Cooke, Hen. Peito, Ric. Oneley, Joh. Bowe yer, Joh. Dilcoke, Joh. Whalley, Joh. Coton, Will. Faseman, Joh. Ray, Joh. Mychell, Joh. Eu*er*don, Joh. Oneley, Joh. Egeston, Tho. Harres, Tho. Paynell, Joh. Stille, deist*er*, Joh. Runton, Joh. Braunston, Will. Wymondeswold, Will. Crudworthe, Will. Keru*er*, Ric. Bushebury, Joh. Harbourghe.

PAYMENT OF ROYAL LOANS.

[Feb. 17. 1424.

[An agreement between the prior, Ric. Croseby, and the chief men of the corporation about the jewels in which the

Mem. q*uo*d die Ven*er*is p*ro*x*imo* ant*e* fest*u*m S. Math*ie*[3] ap*osto*li a. r. r. H*enrici* vj[ti] (etc.) sec*un*do, Sup*er* tractat*u* h*abi*to int*er* Ric*ardu*m Croseby, p*r*iorem eccles*ie* cathedral*is* B. Mar*ie* de Couent*ria* (etc.), ex par*te* vna, ac Thom*am* Wildegrise,

[1] m. = mayor, cor. = coroner, w. = warden, ch. = chamberlain, mace = sergeant-at-mace or sub-bailiff, rec. = recorder. [2] All keepers of the common-chest keys.
[3] S. Matthias falls on Feb. 24; S. Matthew on Sep. 21.

maiorem, Joh*anne*m Leeder, M.G.S.T.[1] Couentrie, Laur*encium* Cooke, Ric*ar*d*u*m Southam, Joh*anne*m Esterton, Henric*um* Peitoo & alios ex p*ar*te alt*er*a, p*ro* etc. de & sup*er* diu*ers*is iocalib*us* eisd*em* maiori & diu*ersis* aliis p*er*sonis i*n* ill*is* iocalib*us* int*eresse* h*abe*ntib*us* de denar*iis* de p*r*estit*is* d*omi*no H*enrico*, nup*er* R*egi* Anglie qui*n*to, fact*is*: videl*ice*t, de vno jocal*i*, vocat*o* Iklynton Coller,[2] & alio jocal*i* vocat*o* Cournall, et q*uo*dam Nowche, p*ro* satisfact*ione* denar*iorum* predict*orum* liber*atis*. Sup*er* q*uo* talit*er* e*st* concordat*um* q*uo*d p*re*dict*us* prior h*abe*bit dict*a* Jocalia p*ro* V[c]l marc*is*,[3] soluend*o* a*nn*uat*im* C marc*as*, q*uo*usq*ue* V[c] marc*e* plene p*er*soluant*ur*, videl*ice*t in f*est*o Pasche, a*nn*uat*im*, et in f*est*o S. Michael*is* pr*o* dat*a* (*sic* ? post datam) sexti obligac*ionis* & vltimi (*sic*) l m*ar*c*as*, p*r*out p*er* diu*ers*as sex obligac*io*nes, p*er* p*re*d*i*ct*um* p*r*io*rem* et conuent*um* Thome Wildgryse, maiori, & successorib*us* fact*as* etc., & sub custodia dict*i* Thome Wildgrise & Joh*anni*s Leeder existent*es* in quad*am* Cista sub duob*us* (*sic*) Clauib*us* eor*um* remanent*e* in aula B. Mar*ie* Couentr*ie*, pleni*us* apparet. & q*uorum* jocaliu*m* id*em* p*r*ior sub forma p*r*edict*a* h*abe*t delib*er*ac*io*nem. Que o*mn*ia et sing*u*la acta sunt et fuer*unt* [4] ex assensu et concensu

mayor and others have interest on account of the loans made to Henry V;

the jewels are the "Iklynton Collar," a coronal, and an owche, delivered in satisfaction of the loans. It is agreed that the prior shall have the jewels for 550 marks, paying annually 100 marks at Easter until 500 are paid, and 50 marks at Michaelmas after the date of the sixth and last bond, as appears by six bonds made between them remaining in a chest in S. Mary's Hall, of which Wildgrise and Leeder have keys. The prior has delivery of the jewels. All which is done with the consent

[1] Magister Gilde Sancte Trinitatis.

[2] Issue Rolls of Exchequer, H. III—VI. 402. The money was lent in the years 1399 and 1415, v. *supra*, pp. 60, 61. In 1422 Parliament ordered large sums in money and jewels to be transferred to the executors of Henry V and Henry IV in payment of debts, Ramsey, I. 328.

[3] £366 13*s*. 4*d*. [4] leaf 20, back.

of the mayor, the gild-masters, and others.]	subscriptor*um* : videl*icet*, Thome Wildgrise tu*n*c maior*is*, Joh*annis* Weston, Recordator*is*, Joh*annis* Leder, M. G. S. T., Will*elmi* Dilcoke, Ric*ardi* Southam, Laur*encii* Cooke, Ade Hiton, Joh*annis* Esterton Henr*ici* Peito, Egid*ii* Allesley, maior*is* (*sic*) [gilde] Corp*or*is Ch*risti*, Ric*ardi* Oneley & Joh*annis* Bowyer, ball*ivorum* (etc.), Will*elmi* Crose, Ric*ardi* Joy, Joh*annis* Golofre, Henr*ici* Breux, Rob*erti* Melb*urne*,[1] Joh*annis* Braytofte, Joh*annis* Bristow, & Joh*annis* Mychell, cu*m* aliis.

THE KING'S COUNCIL.

[2] Thes byn c*er*ten p*ro*uisions for the good gou*er*na*u*nce of this land, þ*at* the lord*es*, þe w*i*ch byn of the counsell, desiron at a p*ar*liament holden at Westmynst*er* in the yere of o*ur* kyng Henry the VI[te] the second.

The Duke of Gloucester to show no favour.

ffirst for þ*at* my lord of Glocestre, ne noo oþ*er* man of the counsell, in noo suete þ*at* shal-be made unto them, shall no fauo*ur* g*r*aunte, neithur in billes of ryght ne of office ne of benefice þ*at* longithe to þe counsell, but only to answer þ*at* the bill shal-be seen by all the councell, and the p*ar*tie sueyng so to haue answer.

Bills.

Item, þ*at* all þe bill*es* þ*at* shal-be put vnto þe councell shul-be oonys in the weke att leste, þ*at* is to sai, on þe Wennysday, red before þe counsell, and þ*er* answers endosid[3] by the same counsell, and on þe Friday next folowyng declaryd vnto þe p*ar*tie sueyng.

Matters terminable at common law not within the Council's province.

Allso þ*at* all the billys þ*at* comp*re*hend mat*er*s termi*n*able at þe co*m*en law, þ*at* semyth not feyned, be remytted þ*er* to be t*er*myned, but ȝif hit so be þ*at* disc*re*ssion of the counsell fele to grette myght on þ*at* one side and onmyght[4] on þ*at* oþ*er* side.

[1] ? From Milburn in Stoneleigh parish.

[2] Almost verbatim version in Rot. Parl. iv. 201, referred to below as R. P.

[3] Earlier form of endorse, v. *N.E.D.* endoss.

[4] unmight = weakness.

In case of diversity of opinion, nothing shall be enacted unless there is a majority.

Item, ȝif hit so be þat any mattur sued in the counsaill fall in any dyuers opynions, þat onlesse þen þat the moore partie of the counsell ben[1] present in tyme of discorde, fall to þat one partie, þat hit be not enact and assentyd, and the namys of the bothe parties enacted by the Clerk of the counsell with þer assent or dissent.

Item, þat in all suetes þat shal-be made to þe counsell in matturs whose determynacion longithe vnto þe counsell, but ȝif hit so be þat thei touche the well of the kyng our souerayng lorde or hies realme, hastely to be sped, ellys þat thei be [noght][2] enact doon by the counsell, onless then by the nombur of vj or iiij at þe leste of the counsell, with the officers that byn present, be of oon assent; and at þat tyme the namys of the sueters to be wryton of þer own hand in the same byll.

Unanimity of council's pronouncements.

Item, for-alsomoche [as][2] hit is to grette a shame þat in straunge contres our souerayne lorde shall wryte his letteres be the advyse of his counsell for such matters & the personez as the counsell wrytith in his name, & singler personez of the counsell to write þe contrary, þat hit be ordenyd þat no man of the counsell presume to do hit on payne of shame & repreffe.

The poorest suitor's bill to be taken first, and assistance given to poor suitors without fee.

Item, þat þe Clerk of the counsell be sworn þat euery day þat the counsaill syttythe on any byllys by-twyxt partie and partie, þat he shall, as ferr as he can, esspie which is the pooryst sueters byll, & that first to be redd and answeryd, & the kynges serieant to be sworn truely and playnly to ȝyue the pore man, þat for suche is accepte to the counsell, assistens & true counsaill in his mattur so to be sueyd without [eny][2] good takyng, on payn of discharge of þer officez.

The justices to be consulted in matters touching the king's prerogative.

Item, for-alsomoche as hit is likly þat many matters shal-be treatyd afore the counsell, þe which touchithe þe kynges prerogatyue & frehoold, [o][2] that oo partie, & oþer sogettes of that oþer, in the which maturs the counsaill is nott lernyd to kep the kynges [ryghtes][2] and þe parties bothe, withoute the aduyce of the kynges Justicez, which be lernyd in his prerogatyffe, & in his comen law, þat in all suche matturs his Juggez be callyd þerto, and þer

[1] beyng R. P. [2] Supplied from R. P.

aduyse *with* ther namys allso be entryd of record what & how they det*er*myne, & þe aduyse þ*er*in.

Members of the Council.

Le duke[1] de Gloucestre, leuek de Cantelbers,[2] leuek de Loundres,[3] leuek de Wynchestre,[4] leuek de Norwyche,[5] leuek de Worcestre,[6] leuek de Duresme,[7] cha*u*ncelle*r*, le duk dExcestre,[8] le Counte de Marche,[9] le Counte de Warwyck,[10] le Counte de Northumb*erland*,[11] le Counte de Westmorl*and*,[12] le *sieur* de Fitz Hugh, le *sieur* de Crumwell, le *sieur* de Lescrop,[13] Mounts*ieur* Wat*ur* Hongerford, mon-*sieur* John Typtoft,[14] Thom*as* Chausers,[15] Wilh*el*m*us* Halyngton.[16]

THE COMMON SEAL AFFIXED TO INDENTURES.

[The following men seal the bag, in which the common seal is kept.

M*emorandum*, quod isti subseque*ntes* sigillaueru*nt* bagam in qua co*mmune* sigillu*m* existit: videl*icet*, Ric. Oneley, Joh. Bowyer, Will. Crudworthe, Will. Keru*er*.

[Apr. 5, 1424.

[The following witness the sealing of divers indentures, sealed with the common seal, made to W. Bynley (etc.).

& isti subsequente*s* inte*r*fu*erunt* sigillac*ioni* diu*ersarum* indent*urarum* sigillat*arum* sigillo co*mmuni*: videl*icet*, die Me*r*curii p*roximo* po*st* fes*tum* S. Ambrosii a. r. r. H*enrici* vj[ti] *secundo*, & fact*arum* Will*el*mo Bynley, bocher, Will*el*mo Saw, Tail*our*, Joh*anni* *seruiente*[17] Ric*ardi* Southam.

[Sixteen witnesses.

Tho. Wildgryse, mai*our*, Joh. Leeder, M. G. S. T., Ric. Southam, Laur. Cooke, Ad. Hiton, Joh. Esterton, Ric. Oneley, Joh. Bowyer, Ric. Joye, Joh. Braytofte, Will. Crosse, Joh. Mychell, Will. Crudworthe, Will. Keru*er*, Joh. Euerdon, Rob. Melb*urne*.

[1] leaf 21. "Duke" repeated in MS. [2] Henry Chicheley. [3] Tho. Kemp.
[4] Cardinal Beaufort. [5] John Wakering. [6] Phillip Morgan.
[7] Thomas Langley. [8] Thomas Beaufort, son of John of Gaunt.
[9] Edmund Mortimer. [10] Richard Beauchamp. [11] Henry Percy.
[12] Ralph Neville. [13] John, Lord le Scrope of Masham.
[14] Later, Earl of Worcester. [15] Twice Speaker.
[16] Added to the Council in 1423. Lord Bourchier's name is omitted.
[17] A servant or a sergeant.

A ROYAL LOAN.

March 29. [1]*Memorandum*, that in the tyme of Tho. Wildegrise, then beyng maio*u*r of the Cite of Couentr*e*, C li. was lant vnto kyng Henr*y* the vj[t] by a *lett*re of the p*ri*vye seale (**The king's letter.**) direct vnto [the] maio*u*r and the co*min*alte of the said Cite, of the w*i*ch *lett*re the tenour folowith in thes woord*es* :—

Treschiers & bien amez, come p*u*r lexploit de le p*re*sent guerre en n*ost*re Realm de Fraunce, et p*u*r mett*er* oue laid de Dieu brieff fin & conclusion a memse[2] (*sic*) le guerre, ainsi come souereig*n*ment le desirons, nous couiendra necessarement auoir cheua*u*nce & p*ro*uision dun gra*nte*[3] & notable sum*m*e de dyners, si come pluis au plein de par nous & n*ost*re counsaill vous exposeront li reu*er*ent pier en Dieu, leveq*e* de Wircestur, & n*ost*re tresch*ier* & foiall cosyn, le Counte de Warr[ewyk]; lesqueux ioientment auoms assignez de lauis de n*ost*re dit counsaill par nous letterez de co*m*mission de souz n*ost*re p*r*iuie seale, en absenc*e* de g*r*aunt, pur comun*i*qer & traitter ouec vous de & sur la chevance daucune somme notable par vous p*re*ster a nous en cest graunt necessetie, & pour vous p*ro*metter pour & en n*ost*re nomz sufficeant suertie de repayment de tiell summe, come nous vous vuillez en ce cas app*re*ster. Si vous prions treschere*m*ent Iqueu[4] avauncem*en*t de cest besoigne, quel a laid de n*ost*re creatour tournira au b*ie*n & tranquillite de nous [et] de vous & dont[5] (*sic*) cristianite, priendre vous voilez le

[In order to put an end to this present war, as is earnestly desired, it is necessary for the king to have provision of a notable sum of money, as the reverent father in God, the Bishop of Worcester, and the Earl of Warwick will lay before them; being jointly assigned in letters under the privy seal, in the absence of the great seal, to communicate with them about the business of lending a notable sum in this great necessity, and to promise sufficient security in the case of a loan.

[The king and council desire that in the advancement of this business, which will profit Christendom generally,

[1] leaf 22. [2] mesme le. [3] MS. looks like grame.
[4] *sic.* ? quen = que en. [5] de toute.

they will as quickly as they can, lend a notable sum, such as the bishop and earl will inform them of, putting faith in them, and belief in their account of what the council desire should be done in this matter.

[Given under our privy seal at Westminster.]

pluis pr*est* qe vous purres en vois[1] aidant a ceo foitz p*ar* voie dap*re*stre dune notable sum*m*e, tiell com p*ar* les susditz Eueqe & countte vous serra lemitre[2] (*sic*) et designe, en adioustant nientmains a exu[3] (*sic*) ferm foy & c*r*edance en sa relac*io*n a vous a faire de par nous & n*ost*re dit counsaill en cell p*ar*tie. Doné souz n*ost*re priuie seale a Westm-[oustre], le xxix iour de Marce.

And for-asmoche as the said Erle of Warr[ewyk],[4] the w*i*ch was assigned Jointely w*ith* the said bischop of Worcest*ur* for to treet of this notable su*m*me aboue namyd, myght not p*er*sonally com vnto the said Cite for to treate as the lett*ur* of þe p*r*ivy ceale aboue-namyd openly specifiethe, the said Erle vnto þe said maio*ur* & burges of the said Cite in Confirmac*io*n of this said matt*ur* his *lett*re vnd*ur* his signet sendythe, of þe w*i*ch the tono*ur* folow*i*th in thes word*es* :—Dere and wel-belouyd, we grett you well ofte-sythis. And for-as-moche as now late þ*er* is comyn a com*m*yssion vnd*ur* the kyng*es* greate seale, our soue*r*yan lorde, direct vnto the ryght reue*r*ent fathur in God, the bischop of Worcest*ur*, and to vs to comune w*ith* you & w*ith* oþ*er* of the moost notabull & sufficiant Burgesses of the Cite of Couentre, þ*at* ye wold vpon sufficyant & couenable[5] suertie make cheua*u*nce of a c*er*ten sum*m*e of gold vnto o*ur* soue*r*ayne lord in the supportac*io*n of the highe and notable astatez of his Realme of Ingland and of Fraunce, & of the wellfare & good spede of my lord of Bedford, his vncle, the w*i*ch and all Englysche-men þ*at* byn ther stonde in grett Jeop*ar*die, but prouysyon and remedy be ordenyd from hennez w*ith* all possible delib*er*ac*io*n & hast. And for dyue*r*s matt*er*s, þe w*i*ch þ*at* touchen o*ur* estate & he*r*ettaunce we may not com p*er*sonally to you for the said cause at this tyme, but haue buesied us here at Brystow w*ith* the maio*ur* and Burgessez of that town by the com*m*aundment of the kyng, o*ur* said soue*r*ayne lorde, in the

The Earl of Warwick unable to come,

so he sends a letter;

praying for loan of a sum of gold for the king's necessities;

as Englishmen in France stand in great jeopardy unless speedy provision made.

The earl remains at Bristol, where the burgesses

[1] ? nous. [2] ? limite, v. Gloss. [3] eux. Text corrupt.
[4] Richard de Beauchamp, 1382–1439. [5] = fit, proper.

have been very compliant,

same & lyke case; the wich town hathe ryght Notabully and kyndly acquyt them, soo þat the same reuerent fathur in God comyth vnto you in his propre person in the name of the kyng, our said souerayng lord, be vertue of the commaundment direct vnto vs bothe for the said cheuysaunce; prayng you als hertly as We can, þat all this mattur a-fore considred, wich schal-be moore effectually & expressly notified vnto you by the reuerent fader in God than we can do wryte to you at this tyme, Ye woll goodly enclyne you & consent vppon his certificacion for to do make by your good, kynd & wyse discression a conable prouysion and Cheuaunce of good[1] vnto our said souerayng lorde, now in his tendur age & his grettyst nede, and as ȝe haue full kyndly and notably doon to his wurthy auncestres tofore thies tyme, to his ease and your good worship als effectually and kyndly as we wer with you in propre persone for our loue and for the hiȝe trust we haue in you. Dere & Wel-belouyd, the Trinite haue you allway in his kepyng. Wryton in our manor of Wotton vndur Egge,[2] the xiiij day of Aprill. Shirley.[3]

and he hopes the Coventry burgesses will goodly incline them to make the provision of money needed by the king in his tender age and greatest need.

From Wootton under Edge.

The king's loan.

[[4]The mayor and his council order that £100 shall be collected through the wards in the following manner.]

Gosford Street.

Collectores de Gosforde.

Joh. Stafforde, Bened. Marchall, Rad. Alott, Sim. Baker, deister, Joh. Melton, deister.

£11 12*s*. 0*d*.

Summa xj li. xij s.

Jorden Well.

Jurdenwell.

Joh. Recheford, Joh. Prentes, Will. Deyster, Rob. Defforde, Joh. Cooton.[5]

£10 4*s*. 0*d*.

Summa x li. iiij s.

Much Park Street.

Michparke.

Joh. Lee, smythe, Rob. Danyell, Rob. Pynnok, Joh. Yate.

£10 0*s*. 0*d*.

Summa x li.

[1] *sic.* ? gold.

[2] Beauchamp held this manor in right of his wife Elizabeth, daughter of Thomas, Lord Berkeley. Of the lawsuits between the Berkeleys and the Beauchamps, v. Smyth, *Lives of the Berkeleys*, II. passim. [3] The scribe. [4] leaf 22, back. [5] ? Cootoner.

Erle. — Earl Street.

Will. Swane, Joh. Frankelen, Nich. Palmer, Tho. Harres, Joh. Euerdon, Will. ffrysbye.

S*um*ma xj li. vij s. iiij d.; rec*epti* inde xj li. viij d.; & sic remanet p*ro* Nich*olao* Metley vj s. viij d. — £11 7*s.* 4*d.*

Baill[y]. — Bayly Lane.

Joh. Rounton, Joh. Benett, Ad. Dyer, Joh. Sircoke, Will. Brook.

S*um*ma vij li.; rec*epte* inde vij li. — £7 0*s.* 0*d.*

Brodeyate. — Broadgate.

Ric. Bushebury, Rog.[1] Cook*es*, Rob. Praty, Rob. Saxston, Tho. Lyones.

S*um*ma iiij li. xiij s. iiij d., rec*epti* iiij li. xiij s. iiij d. — £4 13*s.* 4*d.*

Smythf[ord]. — Smithford Street.

Ric. Hickeleng, Joh. Egeston, Joh. Blakman, Wal. Ashebye.

S*um*ma viij li. — £8 0*s.* 0*d.*

Spoon. — Spon Street.

Will. Pratte, Hugo Rigeley, Joh. Deister, whittaw*er*, Joh. Broun, Joh. Essex.

S*um*ma xj li. vij s. iiij d. — £11 7*s.* 4*d.*

Crosche[pyng]. — Crosscheaping.

Joh. Lichfeld, m*ercer*, Rob. Lyrpoole, Joh. Style, deist*er*, Ric. Boton*er*.

S*um*ma xiiij li. x s. — £14 10*s.* 0*d.*

Byschop. — Bishop Street.

Joh. Lichfeld, bocher, Will. Wymondeswold, Joh. Mongomery, Hen. Knott, Joh. Walg*r*aue.

S*um*ma xj li. vj s. — £11 6*s.* 0*d.*

S*um*ma tot*alis* C li. — Total £100 0*s.* 0*d.*

Vide ult*er*ius in folio sequent*e* q*uo*mo*do* s*um*ma pre- — See further in the following leaf how

[1] MS. Rong*er*us.

the sum of £100 was lent, and by what persons and how. The following contributed £100, lent to the king.

dict*a* de C li. p*re*stit*a* fuit, & de q*ui*b*us* p*er*sonis & q*uomodo*, etc.

[1]Mem. q*uo*d o*mn*es isti subsequent*es* soluerunt ad C li. d*omi*no R*egi* p*re*stit*as* modo et forma quib*us* subsc*ri*bu*ntur*. & similit*er* ut p*atet* folio p*re*cedente,[2] vbi collect*ores* sc*ri*pti sunt.

49 names.

[Gosford Street.]

	£	s.	d.		£	s.	d.		£	s.	d.
Tho. Wildegryse	1	6	8	Hen. Abram[3]		2	0	Will. Inge		1	8
Laur. Cooke	1	6	8	Rob. Tylor		1	8	Ric. Skott		1	8
Will. Crose		15	0	Joh. Baker		3	4	Rad. Alett		6	8
Joh. Wellford		6	8	Will. Bagott		3	4	Bened. M*ar*chall		6	8
Joh. Style		6	8	Rog. Deist*er*		2	0	Simon Deister		6	8
Nich. Heywood		2	4	Joh. Knyght		1	8	Joh. Stafford		3	4
Joh. Wylde		2	0	Ric. Nicole		5	0	Joh. Melton		3	4
Juliana Twyng		2	0	Will. Cook*es*		2	6	Ric. Walker		1	8
Joh. Newby		2	0	Isabella Elford		3	4	Joh. David		1	6
Tho. Smyth		2	0	Joh. Solyhull		1	6	Tho. Draught*on*		1	8
Joh. Sheldon		3	0	Hugh Spenc*er*		1	8	Walt. Bonde		1	4
Joh. Breton		6	8	Marg. Hall		2	0	Will. Colas		1	0
Tho. Mason		3	4	Ad. Baxster		6	8	Will. Horner			10
Joh. Stretton		6	8	And. Evesham		6	8	Su*m*ma xj li. xii s. £11 12s.			
Tho. Stoone		2	0	Ric. Beller		1	6	Ista su*m*ma sup*ra*scrip*ta* solut*a* est collectori*bus* eiusd*em* warde.[4]			
Joh. Evysham		5	0	Hen. Skyll		2	4				
Wyll. Abram[3]		2	0	Joh. Luff		2	6				
Ric. Kyng		5	0	Joh. Creke		3	4				

53 names.

Jurden-well.

	£	s.	d.		£	s.	d.		£	s.	d.
Ric. Hampt*on*, plum*er*		3	4	Joh. Bryant		6	8	Alex. Milner		1	0
Joh. Cressy, m*er*cer		6	8	Joh. Prentes		4	2	Pet. Tiler		1	8
Joh. Gale, Card-*maker*		2	0	Joh. Dilcok		10	0	Egid. Weu*er*		1	0
Joh. Sutton		3	4	Agnes Stanniforde		3	4	Joh. Folkeshull		1	0
Joh. Shaw		3	4	Joh. Coton		13	4	Ric. Plumer		2	0
Will. Leycester		3	4	Joh. Lee		3	4	Pet. Glasier		3	4
Ric. Boise		3	4	Ric. Mildenhall		1	0	Tho. Dykons		3	4
Rob. Grene		3	4	Rob. Defford		6	8	Will. Stoneley		2	0
Will. Gale		1	8	Tho. Steynour		1	0	Thrustans[5] Walker		2	0
Will. Cleybrok		3	4	J. Hawkyns, car-*penter*		1	8	Will. Shurley		2	6
Will. Warwyke		2	0	Joh. Morley		1	8	Joh. Plumer		3	4
Joh. Freman		1	8	Joh. Recheford		3	4	Joh. Lusterley		4	0
Tho. T*u*rnor		3	4	Tho. Grene		3	4	Joh. Abram		6	8
Ric. Rochford		1	0	Joh. Baxster		1	0	Will. Deister		3	4
Walt. Tyrrel		2	0	Rob. Clarke		3	0	Will. Wylde, molde-maker		1	8
Joh. Chandeler		1	8	Joh. Wade		1	8	Nich. Goor		3	4
Joh. Whalley		10	0	Joh. Gryme		3	4	Su*m*ma x li. iiij s. £10 4s.			
Joh. Leeder	1	13	4	Joh. Maidford		2	0	solut*a* est collect*oribus* eiusd*em* warde.			
				Walt. Eton		3	4				

[1] leaf 24, back. [2] v. *supra*, p. 77. [3] A Jew?

[4] This above-written sum was paid to the collectors of the same ward.

[5] ? Thurstan.

2 names.

Muche-parke-strett.

	£	s.	d.
Will. Southam		3	4
Will. Bridde		3	4
Ric. Dene		6	8
Joh. Esterton	1	6	8
Joh. Clerke		13	4
Hen. Peito	1	6	8
Will. Freman		3	4
Agnes Brodde		6	8
Will. Bifeld		13	4
W. Broune, draper		3	4
Hen. Hobbes		6	8
Emmott Chaundeler		1	8

	£	s.	d.
John Lee, smyth		3	4
Tho. Wallsall		1	8
Tho. Crose		5	0
Joh. Darby, coruis*er*		1	8
Tho. Daw		3	4
[1] Will. Lyberd		3	4
Ric. Staffordshyr		1	8
Joh. Young, baxster		1	8
Tho. Peyntour		3	4
Will. Charlton		3	4
Rob. Pynnok		1	8
Rob. Danyell		3	4

	£	s.	d.
Will. Yate, card-maker		3	4
Will. Faseman		13	4
Joh. Braitofte	1	0	0
Joh. Atwall, coruis*er*		1	8
Joh. Ray		3	4
Ric. Hobbys		3	4
Nich. Gryve		5	0
Tho. Elderbeke		1	8

Su*m*ma x li. £10 0*s*. 0*d*.

55 names.

Erle-strett.

	£	s.	d.
Joh. Harburgh		7	0
Rob. Chapman		2	0
Joh. Launde		3	4
Nich. Grene		3	4
Joh. Clifton		1	8
Joh. Cambrig		6	8
Johanna Goote		1	8
Marg. Cotener		1	8
Joh. Rivell		1	8
Joh. Vnd*ur*woode		1	8
Rog. Wales		1	8
Joh. Brabson		1	8
Ric. Sharman		1	8
Will. Repynton		6	8
Rob. Thed		1	8
Will. Swan		3	4
Ric. Cologne		1	8
Ric. Sharp		6	8
Will. Dawe		1	8
Thos. Reyuer		3	0

	£	s.	d.
Will. Frysby		3	4
Ad. Suett		3	4
Tho. Cock*es*		1	8
Joh. Warrant		5	0
Nich. Bifeld		1	8
Joh. Cart*er*		1	8
Joh. Frankelen		3	4
Rob. Bifeld		10	0
Joh. Wilowby		3	4
Ric. Cardemaker		1	8
Thos. Swan		1	8
Rob. Wildegrise		1	8
Johanna Northwode		10	0
Joh. Norres		1	8
Joh. Norma*n*ton		4	0
Tho. Harres		1	8
Galf. Wilnale		1	8
Joh. Eu*er*don		5	0
Joh. Burton		6	8

	£	s.	d.
Tho. Swette*n*ham		3	0
Will. Wellis, mason		1	8
Will. Belg*r*aue		10	0
Will. Donyngton		10	0
Will. Crose		3	4
Joh. Mychell		6	8
Will. Colas		1	8
Joh. Raymond		1	8
Nic. Palmer		3	4
Rad. Garton		10	0
Tho. Whirley		3	4
Ric. Southam		1	8
Joh. Shotteswell		1	8
Joh. Chacombe		1	8
Tho. Warmyngton		3	4
Will. Attilbourgh		6	8

Su*m*ma xj li. vj s. viij d. £11 6*s*. 8*d*.
solut*a* collect*oribus* eiusde*m* warde.

72 names.

Bayly-lane.

	£	s.	d.
Tho. Lock, thymeler[2]		1	0
Joh. M*ar*ston		2	4
Rob. Hert		1	8
Christiana Allesley		1	4
Joh. Skyle		1	4
Joh. Harborgh		2	4
Hen. Brydde		3	4
Joh. Sircoke		2	8
Tho. Shaw		2	0
Hen. Watstyd		1	4
Joh. Crose		3	0
Thos. Thorpe[3]		3	0
Joh. Chamb*ur*		2	4
Pat*r*icius Ray		3	4

	£	s.	d.
Will. Clerke		3	4
Tho. Dyvett		1	4
Joh. Whettley		1	0
Will. Ottley		1	4
Ric. Holte		2	0
Hen. Horneby		1	4
Hen. Walton		1	4
Joh. Bordall		2	8
Hen. Abram		2	0
Rob. Glouceste*r*		1	0
Rob. Herdwyk		1	4
Ad. Dyer		3	4
Tho. Tokeby		2	0
Ric. Dyvett		2	4
Will. Allesley		2	0

	£	s.	d.
Tho. Loke		2	0
Ric. Whithede		1	0
Ric. Deyst*er*		2	0
Joh. Burbage		3	0
Isabella Seward		1	0
Joh. Power		1	4
Joh. Chubboke		1	8
Nich. Edward		1	0
Hen. Upton		2	0
Johanna Wedon		1	0
Joh. Gamil		1	0
Joh. Hethull, coten*er*[4]		2	0
Hen. Brynklow		1	0
Will. Raynold		1	8

[1] leaf 25. [2] v. Gloss. [3] 3*s*. 4*d*. MS., the 4*d*. deleted.
[4] Earliest example in *N.E.D.* 1557: One who puts a nap on cloth.

Bayly-lane (*continued*).

	£	s.	d.
Hen. Bate		4	0
Tho. Warn*er*		1	0
Joh. Coten*er*		1	0
Ric. Leuer		1	0
Ric. Coup*er*		2	6
Will. Steynton		1	0
Eliz. Ookeam		2	0
Joh. Hull		1	4
Joh. Rounton		2	0
Will. Colvyll		1	8
Joh. Louthe		2	0

	£	s.	d.
Will. Brooke		4	6
Tho. Goldsmyth		1	0
Joh. Bechampe		2	6
Rad. Coten*er*[1]		1	8
Joh. Drasse		1	0
Tho. Peuterer		2	6
[2]Joh. Milette		2	0
Joh. Spencer		3	4
Joh. Braban, pate*n*-maker,[3]		1	2
Joh. Wiche		1	8

	£	s.	d.
Ric. Croseby		1	0
Joh. Joyner		1	8
Joh. Benett		4	0
Walt. Clarke		1	0
Joh. Patenmaker		1	0
Tho. Bayly		1	8
Joh. Freman		1	8
Tho. Gryme			6

S*um*ma vij li. soluta collect*oribus* eius*dem* warde. £7 0s.

40 names.

Brode-yate.

	£	s.	d.
Pet. de l*a* Mare		1	8
Will. Spenc*er*		1	4
Ric. Trenth*am*		2	0
Will. Flekney		3	4
Joh. Barnard		3	4
Edm. Collshull		2	0
Tho. Sporyar		1	8
Joh. Ballsall		2	0
Rog. Cook*es*		3	4
Ric. Bushebury		3	4
Joh. Capp*er*		1	8
Joh. Hosier		1	8
Tho. Barb*our*		3	4
Joh. Barrett		1	4
Joh. Huntley		2	0

	£	s.	d.
Tho. Cooke		1	8
Will. Prentes		2	0
Joh. George		1	8
Ric. Fyllipes		2	0
Will. M*ar*chall		1	8
Joh. Archar		1	8
Joh. Malory		1	4
Rob. Sporyar		1	0
Will. Dawbney		1	8
Rob. Saxton		2	0
Tho. Prentes		1	0
Ric. Sethe		1	0
Will. Sethe		1	0
Joh. Darby		1	8
Will. Okyn		1	4

	£	s.	d.
Joh. Janyns		3	4
Will. Broun		1	0
Will. Foster		1	8
Joh. Fysher		1	8
Ric. Grasier		1	0
Tho. Lyones		1	8
Egid. Allesley		13	4
Ric. Oneley		10	0
Rob. Praty		2	0
Joh. Harewood		1	0

S*um*ma iiij li. xiij s. iiij d. soluta est collector*ibus* eiusd*em* warde. £4 13s

36 names.

Smytheforde-strett.

	£	s.	d.
Joh. Maynard		1	8
Will. Flore		1	0
Joh. Yate		3	4
Will. Peut*er*er		10	0
Rob. Holme		6	8
Joh. Bristow		13	4
God. Barbeur		5	0
Will. Bredon, skyn-*ner*		1	0
Joh. Wymondes-wold		5	0
Tho. Broune		5	0
Magott Chaundeler		3	4
Tho. Cart*er*		6	8

	£	s.	d.
Hen. Preston		5	0
Joh. Ooneley		13	4
Joh. Lirpoole		3	4
Joh. Outered		1	8
Rad. Bredon		1	8
Tho. Colman		1	8
Nich. Smyth		5	0
Will. Happeford		3	4
Joh. Peer, coup*er*		1	8
Tho. Baxster		3	4
Joh. Bramston		10	0
Tho. Joy		3	4
Joh. Olyve		3	4
Joh. Multon, Clerk		3	4

	£	s.	d.
Joh. Goodwryght		1	0
Joh. Bower		10	0
Tho. Ive		5	0
Will. Jones, weu*er*		1	8
Ric. Burton, sad-eler		6	8
Joh. Egeston		4	0
Ric. Hicklyng		3	0
Wal. Asheby		2	8
Jos. Tate		2	0
Joh. Blakeman		2	0

S*um*ma viij li. & solut*a* est collect*ori*-*bus* eiusd*em* warde. £8 0s.

[1] or Coton. [2] leaf 25, back. [3] From Brabant; cf. Flawnders, p. 6.

Croschepyng.

71 names.

	£	s.	d.
Joh. Rooke		2	0
Joh. Symond*es*, coruis*er*		1	0
Hen. S*ir*coke, coruis*er*,		6	8
Rob. Myl*bu*rne		13	4
Rob. Grubber		5	0
Hen. Colyns		5	0
Joh. Doughty		5	0
Hen. Breux		13	4
Joh. Fryche		3	4
Joh. Harbourghȝ		1	8
Will. Huett		1	8
Sym. Payn		1	8
Wyll. Radclyff		1	8
Rad. Chaundeler		4	0
Joh. Burne		5	0
Joh. Parker, drap*er*,		13	4
Alic*ia* P*ar*ker		1	8
Joh. Bryghtmer		2	0
Rob. Mason		1	0
Agn*es* Dalby		3	4
Joh. Appulby		2	0
Ric. Joy	1	0	0
Pet. Sheffeld		1	8
Ric. Hendy		1	7
Edw. Lychefeld		3	4
Will. Benet, Cook,		1	0
Will. Dilcok	1	0	0
Will. Dey		2	0
Rob. Hardwyke		2	0
Agn*es* Wedon		6	8
Joh. Barbour		1	8
Will. Bynley		5	0
Hen. Rondull		4	0
Joh. Northampton		1	8
Joh. Rouley		1	0
Ric. Weuer		4	0
Joh. Carmaker		1	0
Rob. Lirpoole		4	0
Joh. White		3	4
Ric. Brykstook		2	0
Will. Potyng*er*		3	4
Tho. Lylynto[1]		4	0
Moricius Bocher		1	0
Joh. Huet, mason,		1	11
Ric. Bere		1	8
Joh. Peut*er*er		3	4
Tho. Norwiche		1	8
Ric. Boton*er*		4	0
Tho. Bassyngburn		3	4
Nich. Fysche		1	0
[2] Will. Bromyche		1	0
Joh. Lychefeld		3	4
Joh. Moole, coruis*er*		1	0
Joh. Gascoyn		3	4
Will. Chapman		3	4
Joh. Wall		3	4
Joh. Bandy, barbour		2	0
Tho. Grene		13	4
Tho. Lokyer		1	0
Joh. Holland		1	0
Reg. Rede		1	4
Nich. Hull		3	4
Ad. Deist*er*	1	6	8
Rob. Danyell, deist*er*		1	8
Joh. Style, deist*er*		6	8
Will. Darsett		3	4
Hen. Cooke		2	0
Joh. Stockton, coruis*er*		1	0
Joh. Haydon, Jun.			8
Rob. Stockton, coruis*er*,		1	0
Joh. Dyrham, goldsmyth		1	0

S*um*ma xiiij li. x s. ij d. solut*a* collect*oribus*. £14 10*s.* 2*d.*

Spon-strete.

73 names.

	£	s.	d.
Joh. Mershe		1	8
Joh. Club		1	8
Joh. Hastlyff		3	4
Joh. Nele		2	0
Joh. Essex		7	6
Tho. Paynell		10	0
Ric. Shustock		2	0
Joh. Sissetur		2	0
Ric. Waryn		3	4
Will. Pratte		17	6
Johanna Dudley		13	4
Joh. Menley		5	0
Nich. Barre		1	0
Joh. Ward		5	0
Nich. Pryse		3	4
Joh. Brere		1	8
Joh. Broun		7	6
Hugo Rugeley		7	6
et *pro* Simon*e* Busteler		1	8
Joh. Pynchebeke		6	8
Joh. Brettby		1	0
Joh. Sewyne		2	0
Will. Keru*er*		6	8
Joh. Deist*er*		15	4
Ric. Neuton		2	0
Joh. Chest*er*		1	8
Joh. Marnam		6	8
Tho. Skott		1	0
Joh. Eyre		3	4
Math. Wryght		1	0
Ric. Wellford		3	4
Joh. Wellynton		2	0
Joh. Miln*er*		1	0
Agnes Harries		1	0
Will. Stoone		1	0
Simon Est		3	4
Joh. Birde		1	0
Joh. Harres		1	0
Ric. Style		1	8
Hen. Holt		5	0
Hen. Mason		2	0
Will. Withybroke		1	8
Will. Stockton		1	4
Tho. Lenton		1	8
Joh. Baker		1	0
Will. Wellys		2	0
Will. Welsche		1	0
Rob. Balle[3]		1	8
Johanna Bondy		1	8
Will. Yerdeley		1	0
Joh. Rydale		3	4
Will. Iryshe		1	0
Joh. Loote		3	4
Rob. Myles		1	8
Tho. Smyth		1	0
Tho. Straunge		1	0
Steph. Couche		2	0
Joh. Plasterer		3	4
Isabell Walker		3	0
Tho. Poole		1	0
Math. White		6	8
Ric. Capper		2	0
Edm. Brogreue		3	4
Joh. Westley		1	0
Geo. Weu*er*		1	0
Rob. Baker		1	0
Joh. Ball		1	8
Tho. Skott		1	0
Tho. Pratte		1	8
Tho. Goldsmyth		1	8
Will. Walker		1	0
Tho. Brounale		1	8
Ric. Walforde		3	4

S*um*ma xj li. vij s. iiij d. solut*a* collectori*bus*. £11 7*s.* 4*d.*

[1] ? Lylyngton. [2] leaf 26.

[3] ? Related to John Ball, the priest, captured in Coventry 1381.

83 names.

Bysshop-strett.

	£	s.	d.
Joh. Lyncoln			8
Joh. Grynder		5	0
Alex. Barker		1	0
Joh. Attwoode		3	4
Ric. M*ar*che		5	0
Joh. Stockton		1	0
Ric. Stanlake		1	8
Joh. Woodmer		2	6
Joh. Stafford, mylner		2	0
Will. Kemp		2	0
Hen. Hull		1	0
Ric. Southam	2	0	0
Rog. Bylston		5	0
Tho. Chacombe		2	0
Rog. Taylour		2	0
Joh. Staunton			6
Joh. Folvile		1	8
Joh*anna* Palm*er*		1	0
Tho. Illage		1	8
Joh. Gilbert		3	4
Hen. Walker		2	6
Will. Barrett		1	0
Ric. Pisfort			8
Will. Staunton		5	0
Will. Pere		1	0
Edm. Dro*uer*		3	4
Ric. Byddell		1	8
Hugo Beu*er*		1	0
Joh. Kebull		2	0

	£	s.	d.
Will. Leche		1	0
Joh. Chacombe		1	0
Ric. Bylston		1	0
Joh. London		1	0
Joh. Cooke		1	8
Joh. Maunston			8
Rob. Bandy		1	8
Joh. Edward		1	0
Tho. Fyshe			8
Tho. Kerdyff		1	0
Joh. Pratte			8
Rob. Trueman		1	0
Joh. Gold		3	4
Will. Newton		1	8
Will. Bate		2	6
Will. Bayly		1	0
Ric. Wryght		1	8
Ric. Felypps		3	0
Joh. Baxster		1	0
Hugo Shaw		4	0
Joh. Belston		3	4
Wyll. Allesley		1	0
[1]Rob. Wryght			8
Will. Crudworthe		10	0
Reignald P*ro*phet		3	0
Joh. Benet		3	4
Rob. Harwarde		3	4
Will. Thornton		3	4
Joh. Wodcoke		1	8
Tho. Broun		1	8

	£	s.	d.
Joh. Schulton		1	0
Bareboche		1	0
Joh. Weston		1	0
Wal. Tryg		3	0
Hen. Hethe		4	0
Gal. Cole		1	8
Joh. Hayly			10
Joh. Fraiter			8
Simon More		1	8
Tho. Wryght		2	0
Rob. Weston		3	4
Rog. Lesyngham		3	4
Joh. Nele		1	8
Rob. Barbour		1	0
Joh. Couper		1	0
Tho. Smythe		1	0
Will. Wilkyns		6	8
Tho. Dovy		1	0
Rog. Goose		1	0
Will. Vmbem		3	4
Joh. Mathew		1	4
Will. Gamill[2]		1	0
Joh. Flecher		1	0
Joh. Augur		3	4
Joh. Allesley		2	0
de Collect*oribus* ibid*em*		13	4

Summa xj li. vj s. soluta collectoribus eiusdem warde. £11 6s.

[[3]Security for the aforesaid £100: 5 bonds and delivery of the same.] Securitas p*ro* p*re*dict*is* C li., v obligac*io*nes & delib*er*acio ear*um*.

"A C li. lent." Five bonds for £101 2s. 11¾d., of which 22s. 11¾d. Joh. Leder paid.

ffor the w*i*ch C li. and for the suertie þ*er*off v obligac*io*ns wer delyu*er*ed vnto the said Tho. Wildegryse, maio*ur*, the w*i*ch v obligac*io*ns the *sum*ma of hem is Cj li. ij s. xj d. ob. qa, the w*i*ch xxij s. xj d. ob. qa John Leder paid & ought to have hit agayn; & þe w*i*ch v obligac*io*ns the said maio*ur* hath delyu*er*ed to his successour, John Braytoft, oone w*ith* xxxij li. viij s. ij d. & iiij li. xiij s. iij d. qa, as moore plainly in endenturs betwen the saýd Thomas Wildgryse and John Braytofte made is specified; of the w*i*ch endent*ur* þat one[4] p*ar*te abydithe in the bag of the meraltie of the said Thomas in Saynt Mary Hall in the kepyng of Ric. Goddesley.

One bond together with £32 8s. 2d., and £4 13s. 3¼d., is delivered to John Braytoft.

And for as the sue[r]te of the C li. myght not be gotton

[1] leaf 26, back. [2] v. Sharp, *Antiq.* 75. [3] leaf 23.
[4] = the one. O.E. *þæt an*, neuter.

with*th*out grett labour & cost, hit was ordenyd by the hoole councell þ*at* John Leeder shuld ryde to London for the said suerty, and he had delyu*er*ed vnto hym by thand*es* of the said Tho. Wyldgryse xl s., þe w*i*ch xl s. com oute of the wardenship and thei owen to haue hit agayn.

John Leeder rides to London for the security; £2 for his costs.

EASTER LEET.

[[1]V. f. p. before Tho. Wildegrise m., Ric. Oneley and Joh. Bowyer b., on Thursday after the close of Easter.[2] 2, Hen. VI.

Couentre. May 4, 1424.

Joh. Leder, Laur. Cooke, Will. Dilcok, Ad. Hiton, Joh. Esterton, Hen. Peitoo, Rad. Garton, Will. Crosse, Ric. Joye, Joh. Harbourghe, Joh. Bristowe, Joh. P*ar*ker, drap*er*, Hen. Breux, Will. Byfeld, Will. Crudworth, Will. Keru*er*, Joh. Coton, Joh. Oneley, Joh. Clerke, Joh. Whalley, Joh. Eu*er*don, Will. Birde, g*ur*deler, Will. ffrysby, Joh. Tate.

Jury of 24.

At the wich lete was ordenyd þ*at* the chamb*ur*lens schullen let make a co*m*en mase for the-office of the co*m*en s*er*geaunt, or els to pay the money þ*at* he paith yerly for his mase.

"The Chamberleyns make the comon sergens mase."

Allso hit is ordenyd þ*at* the wardens schall make[3] the Cost*is* that John Leeder spendithe at London abought c*er*ten occupac*i*ons for the Cite of Couentr*e*, þ*at* is to say in getyng Suertie of C li. þ*at* was lent vnto kyng Henry the vj[te] in the tyme of Thom*as* Wildegrise, maio*ur* of the said Cite. And allso thei shall make good the cost*is* þ*at* was made unto þe buschop of Worcet*ur* in getyng his lordschip in furtheryng this said matt*ur*.

Leeder's expenses about the loan of £100 to Henry VI, paid by wardens.

Allso þ*at* the chamburlayns schall make a ryng at the Bullryng, to thend þ*at* bullez may be baytyd as they haue byn hertofore.

A ring at th Bull-ring.

And oþ*er* ordyna*u*nc*es* & g*ra*unt*es* arn ordyned & made at this said leett, as in the endosement*is* of c*er*ten byllys at þ*at* tyme put-to þe leet moore specyally doo appere.

Other ordinances transcribed.

LOAN TO THE DUKE OF GLOUCESTER.

[4]Mem. þ*at* by a l*ett*re directe vnto þe maio*ur*, baileffez, and Cetyzens of the Cite of Couentr*e* fro the duke of

"C marks" lent to the Duke of

[1] leaf 21, back. [2] Clausum Pasche, the Sunday after Easter.
[3] ? insert "good." [4] leaf 23.

Gloucester, June 27, 1424,

Gloucettur C marke was lent vnto þe said duke; of the wich lettre the tenour folowith in thies wordes:—Rightȝ trusty and wel-belouyd, we grett you well. And forasmoche as we haue takyn full purpos to pase ouer the see with Goddes myght in our own persone for to receyue in our handes our land and lordeships ther with due obeisaunce of our subiectes: We pray you hertly þat ye will do so moche for us at this tyme as for to ease us with CC li. vpon sufficiant suertie, Consideryng that the well of us and of this our viage is lyke to turne to ryght great ese of the people, & specially of thies merchauntis of this Realme; and þat ye will certifie us agayn of your entent & good will in this behalffe by the brynger of this and by your letturs; hauyng you so toward us in this mattur, þat we may feele your good affection, and haue cause for to show you in tyme to come contynuaunce of our good lordship. Right trusty and wel-belouyd, our Lorde haue you in his kepyng. Yeven vndur our pryvy signett at London, the xxvij day of Juyn.

in response to his appeal in this letter.

"Suprascripcio littere in principio."[1]

By the duke of Gloucestur, Erle of Haynnau, Holland, Yelland (*sic*), and Penbrok, lord of Friseland, highȝ chamburlen, protectour and defensor of Ingland.[2]

Worthy men

Wherupon the meir lett make of thies wurthy men folowyng, John Leeder, Ric. Southam, Will. Dilcoke, Ad. Hiton, Gil. Allesley, Ric. Joy, Rad. Garton, Joh. Braitofte, Joh. Bristowe, Joh. Golofre, Joh. Harborugh, sen., Will. Faseman, Joh. Mychell, Rob. Melburne, Joh. Parker, Will. Crose, Hen. Breux, Will. Byfeld, Joh. Coton, Joh. Bowyer, Joh. Egynton, Joh. Euerdon, Tho. Paynell, Joh. Dilcok, Joh. Clerk, Will. Frisby, Ric. Sharpe, Ric. Dene, Tho. Wirley, Will. Swane, Joh. Warrant, Joh. Welford, Joh. Whalley, Joh. Doughty, Joh. Tate, Joh. Broun, draper, Tho. Reyuer,[3] Joh. Style, Deyster, Joh. Frankelen, Joh. Deyster, woleman, and oþer, by wose avyse and many oþer was ordenyd þat the said duke shuld haue C marke

decide to lend the duke 100 marks,

[1] Superscription of the letter at the beginning.

[2] Humphrey, Duke of Gloucester (1391–1447), married Jacqueline, daughter of William IV, Count of Hainault, Holland and Zealand, and lord of Friesland, in 1422. In October 1424 Gloucester and Jacqueline invaded Hainault with an army of 5,000 soldiers, and Gloucester was recognised as Count of Hainault.

[3] or Reyner.

of lone vnd*ur* sufficiant suertie, & þ*at* þe said C marke shal-be leuyd and rerd in the man*er* as heraft*ur* folew*ith*. And allso thei orden þ*at* þ*er* shuld be in eu*er*y warde one or ij sufficiante men to ou*er*se the Collectours and to help them, þ*er* as nede is. under sufficient security.

[1]Warde de Gosforde.

Sup*er*uis*ores*,[2] Laur. Cooke, Joh. Golofre. Collector*es*, Joh. Stafford, wird*rawer*, Joh. Stretton, Bened. Marchall. £7. 14s. 8d. Collection made for the duke's 100 marks.

Jurdenwell.

Joh. Leeder,[3] Joh. Bray-Tofte,[3] Joh. Dilcoke, Joh. Whalley, Joh. Prentes, Joh. Rocheforde. £6. 16s. 0d.

Muchep*ar*ke.

Hen. Peitoo,[3] Joh. Bray-Tofte,[3] Joh. Clerke, Will. Brydde, Ric. Deene, Rob. Danyell. £6. 13s. 4d.

Erlo & Litulp*ar*k.

Rad. Garton,[3] Joh. Harbourgȝ,[3] Will. ffrisbye, Nic. Grene, Joh. Launde, Joh. Mychell, Nic. Palmer. £7. 11s. 8d.

Baill[y].

Joh. Rounton,[3] Will. Brooke,[3] Ad. Dier, Joh. Berett, wyrd*rawer*, Joh. Bechamp, Joh. Sircoke. £4. 13s. 4d.

Brodeyate.

Egid. Allesley,[3] Ric. Oneley,[3] Ric. Bussheburу, Rog. Cookes, Edm. Collshull, Will. M*ar*chall, Rob. Saxton. £3. 2s. 4d.

Smyth[ford].

Joh. Bowyer,[3] Joh. Brystowe,[3] Ric. Hicklyng, Joh. Braunston, Tho. Cart*er*, Joh. Blakeman. £5. 6s. 8d.

Spon.

Tho. Paynell,[3] Will. Keru*er*,[3] Will. Prate, Hugo Rugeley, Joh. Broun, drap*er*, Joh. Meenley. £7. 11s. 8d.

[1] leaf 23, back. [2] Overseers.
[3] Bracketed together as overseers.

Crosch[-epyng].

Will. Dilcoke,[1] Ric. Joye,[1] Joh. Brydde, peuterer, Joh. Style, deister, Rad. Chaundeler, Will. Darsett. £9. 13s. 4d.

Byschop.

Will. Crudworthe,[1] Will. Wymondeswold, Joh. Walgraue, Hen. Knott, Joh. Golde, Hen. Walker. £7. 10s. 8d. Total £66. 13s. 8d.]

Three obligations for security of the duke's debt.

[2]ffor the w*i*ch C mark*es*, & for suertie of the same, iij obligac*i*ons were delyu*er*ed to the maio*ur*. The w*i*ch iij obligac*i*ons the said Thom*as* Wildgrise hathe delyu*er*ed vnto his successour, Joh*annem* Braitoft, meir of the said Cite, as in endent*u*rus betwen the said Thom*as* & John made mor openly is conteynyd. The w*i*ch endent*u*rs þ*a*t one p*ar*te abydith in the kepyng of Ric. Goddesley in a bag in Saynt Mary Hall abydyng.

R. Joy goes to London,

ffor-asmoche as the suertie of the said C marke myght not be gotten w*i*t*h*out grett cost and labour, by thaduyse of the hoole counsell Ric. Joy was sent to London, & he spent xl s.

and spends 40*s*.

L. Cook to Boston, 13*s*. 4*d*.

And Laurens Cooke went to Boston to spek w*i*t*h* the customers þ*er*, & he spent xiij s. iiij d.

To London and Sandwich,

£6 1*s*. 10½*d*.

Total £8 15*s*. 2½*d*.

And the same Laurenc*e*, when he went to London and to Sondwiche & so hoome agayn, hauy*ng* suerty for the said C. marke, spendid vj li. xxij d. ob. S*um*ma tot*al*is, viij li. xv s. ij d. ob., the wiche viij li. xv s. ij d. ob. was receuyd of the wardens sauyng xx s., w*i*ch was receuyd of the chamburlens, and ow*i*th to be payd agayne.

The following paid towards 100 marks lent to the duke of Gloucester, which money was paid in the manner following as it was lent.

[3]M*emorandum* q*uo*d isti subsequente*s* soluer*unt* ad Centu*m* marcas duci Gloucestr*ie* p*re*stit*as* temp*or*e Thome Wildgrise tu*n*c maior*is*. & p*re*di*c*te cent*um* marc*e* solut*e* su*n*t subsequen*ti* modo & forma p*ro*ut p*re*stite fu*erunt*, videl*icet*:—

[1] Bracketed together as overseers.
[2] leaf 24. [3] leaf 29, back.

54 names.

Gosforte-stret.

	£	*s.*	*d.*
Tho. Wyldegrise		13	4
Laur. Cooke	1	0	0
Will. Crosse		10	0
Joh. Golofre		10	0
Joh. Wellford		5	0
Joh. Style		5	0
Hen. Abraham		18	0
Joh. Dau[i]d		1	0
Tho. Mason		2	6
Andreas Evysham		5	0
Ric. Skott		1	6
Joh. Sheldon		2	0
Ric. Walker		1	3
Joh. Solyhull		1	6
Will. Yonge		1	2
Will. Dagett		2	6
Nic. Heywood		1	8
Joh. Nueby et mat*er* ei*us*[1]		3	4
Joh. Baker, deyst*er*,		2	6
Joh. Knyghte		1	3
Joh. Wright			8
Joh. Euesham		3	4
Rob. Tyler		1	3
Ric. Som*er*		1	6
Tho. Stoone		1	6
Will. Cooke		1	6
Joh. Lee		3	4
Ad. Baxster		5	0
Tho. Draughton		1	2
Tho. Reve			8
Ric. Beller		1	0
Joh. Wellys			8
Will. Abrah*am*		1	6
Tho. Barker			8
Joh. Wilde		1	4
Ric. Moole		3	4
Joh. Breux			8
Tho. Smythe		1	6
Sim. Deist*er*		2	6
Margaret Hall		1	4
Wal. Bond		1	0
Hen. Skylle		1	6
Rog. Deister		1	6
Joh. Buyton		1	4
Joh. Luff		1	8
Ric. Kyng		3	4
Randolf Hauenell			8
Will. Colas			8
Joh. Streyte			8
Rad. Alott		3	4
Bened. Marchall		3	4
Joh. Stretton		3	4
Joh. Stafford		3	4
Joh. Mollton		3	4

£7 13*s.* 4*d.*

S*umm*a vij li. xiij s. iiij d. solut*a* collect*oribus*.

53 names.

Jurdenwell.

	£	*s.*	*d.*
Ric. Hampton		1	8
Joh. Cressy		1	8
Joh. Gale		1	4
Joh. Sutton		2	0
Joh. Shade		2	8
Will. Leicest*ur*		2	0
Ric. Boys		2	4
Rob. Grene		1	8
Will. Bale			8
Will. Cleybrook		2	3
Joh. Freman			8
Tho. T*ur*nor		1	8
Ric. Rocheford		1	0
Wal. Tirrell		1	4
Joh. Chaundeler			8
Joh. Whalley		3	4
Joh. Leeder	1	6	8
Joh. Bryan		4	0
Joh. Prentes		3	0
Joh. Dilcoke		6	8
Agn*es* Stamford		2	0
Joh. Cooton		10	0
Ric. Mildnale		1	0
Rob. Welford		4	0
Will. Warr[wyk]		1	8
Hen. Abram		2	4
Joh. Crooke		2	4
[2]			8
Joh. Hawkyn		1	0
Joh. Rocheforde		3	4
Tho. Groome		2	0
Rob. Clerke		2	0
Joh. Wade		1	0
Joh. Gryme		2	4
Joh. Maidforde		1	4
Walt. Etone		2	0
Alex. Mylner			4
Perkyn Tyler[3]		1	0
Ric. Plumer		1	0
Pet. Glasier		1	10
Tho. Dicons		2	0
Will. Stoneley		1	4
Thrustanus Walker[4]		1	0
Will. Shurley		1	4
Joh. Plumer		2	4
Joh. Listerley		3	4
Joh. Abram		3	4
Will. Deister		4	0
Joh. Wilde		1	4
Nic. Goore		2	4
Joh. Manton		1	0
Joh. Morley		1	0
Tho. Coryer			8
Tho. Kyrton			8

[Total £6 16*s.* 0*d.* paid etc.]

30 names.

Muche-[park-street].

	£	*s.*	*d.*
Hen. Peitoo	1	0	0
Joh. Esterton	1	0	0
Joh. Braitofte		13	4
Will. Faseman		13	4
Will. Bifeld		10	0
Joh. Clerk		6	8
Will. Glasier		1	8
Will. Southam		2	6
Will. Yate		1	8
Joh. Ray		2	4
Will. Freman		2	4
Tho. Walsall, weu*er*		1	0
Ric. Dene		1	8
Agn. Broode		3	4
Will. Broune		1	8
Hen. Hobbys		3	4
Joh. Lee		2	6
Tho. Crose		3	4
Joh. Darby		1	0
Tho. Dawe		4	0
[5]Staffordshire		1	0
Will. Libard		1	4
Joh. Yong, baxst*er*		1	0
Tho. Yorke		2	4
Will. Charlton		2	4
Tho. Eldurbek		1	2
Nic. Gryve		3	4
Hobbes, hosteler		2	6
Will. Bryde		1	4
Rob. Danyell		1	4

[Total £6 13*s.* 4*d.* paid to the collectors.]

[1] and his mother. [2] Blank in MS. [3] ? Name or trade.
[4] ? Thurstan. Walker = a fuller. [5] leaf 30.

58 names.

Bailly-lane.

	£	s.	d.		£	s.	d.		£	s.	d.
Joh. M*ar*ston[1]		1	7	Rob. Gloucestre			8	Will. Reynold		1	0
*Chris*tian Allesley			8	Rob. Herdwike		1	0	Hen. Bate		3	0
Joh. Skyll		1	0	Ad. Dyer		2	2	Tho. Warn*er*			8
Joh. Harbourgh		1	4	Tho. Tokeby		1	5	Ric. Beu*er*			8
Hen. Birde		2	4	Ric. Dyvett		1	7	Joh. Duale			6
Joh. Sircoke		1	9	Will. Allesley		1	4	Tho. Gryme			6
Tho. Shaw		1	5	Tho. Loke		1	6	Ric. Coup*er*		1	8
Hen. Watford			10½	Ric. Whithede			8	Will. Steynton			8
Joh. Crose		1	10	Ric. Deist*er*		1	6	Joh. Hull, baxst*er*		1	0
Tho. Thorp		2	0	Joh. Burbage		2	2	Joh. Runton		3	4
Joh. Chamb*ur*		1	6	Isabell Sewarde			8	Will. Colvyll		1	0
Patric. Kay		2	4	Joh. Power		1	0	Joh. Louth		1	4
Will. Clerk		1	7	Joh. Chubboke		1	2	Will. Broke		3	4
Tho. Dyvett		1	0	Nic. Edwarde			6	Tho. Goldsmyth			8
Joh. Whitley			8	Hen. Upton			8	Joh. Bechamp		1	8
Will. Otteley		1	0	Ric. Braitofte		1	9	Rad. Cotener		1	3
Ric. Holte		1	2	Johanna Wedon			8	Joh. Brase			8
Hen. Horneby			10	Joh. Upton		1	6	Tho. Peuterer		1	10
Hen. Walton		1	0	Joh. Gamil			8	[Total £4 13*s.* 4*d.* paid (etc.).]			
Joh. Bordale		1	10	Hen. Brinklow			8				

55 names.

Erle-strett.

	£	s.	d.		£	s.	d.		£	s.	d.
Joh. Wyloughby, drap*er*		2	6	Joh. Vnd*ur*wod		1	8	Will. Belgraue		5	0
Rob. Wildgrise		1	8	Joh. Ryvell		1	8	Will. Donyngton		5	0
Tho. Swan		1	0	Joh. Malory		1	0	Will. Crosse, passeng*er*		1	8
Ric. Cardmaker		1	0	Johanna Goote		6	8	Joh. Mychell		6	8
Rob. Bifeld		6	8	Joh. Cambryge		5	0	Joh. Raymond		1	8
Joh. Frankelen		2	6	Joh. Carter, hosier		1	8	Nic. Palm*er*		1	8
Nic. Bifeld		1	8	Joh. Clifton		1	8	Rad. Garton		6	8
Tho. Cook*es*		2	0	Nic. Grene		1	8	Tho. Wirley		2	6
Joh. Warrant		3	4	Joh. Launde		1	8	Ric. Ryvell		1	0
Ad. Suett		2	6	Joh. Harbourgh		6	8	Tho. Warmyngton		2	6
Will. Frysby		3	4	Rob. Laughton		3	0	Johanna Attil-boroughȝ		3	4
Tho. Reyu*er*		1	8	Will. Dey		1	0	Joh. Wellys, mason		1	8
Will. Dawe		1	0	Johanna Norwoode		6	8	Joh. Chacombe		1	4
Ric. Sharpe		5	0	Joh. Norwode		6	8	Joh. Schotteswell		1	0
Ric. Colgraue		1	8	Joh. Norres		1	8	Joh. Forest, tail*our*		1	0
Will. Swan		1	8	Joh. Normanton		3	0	Hen. Glasyer		1	0
Rob. Thede		1	0	Galf. Willnale		1	8	[Total £7 11*s.* 8*d.* paid (etc.).]			
Joh. Brabson		1	8	Joh. Eu*er*don		4	0				
Rog. Walles		1	8	Joh. Burton		5	0				
				Tho. Suetham		2	6				

42 names.

Broode-yate.

	£	s.	d.		£	s.	d.		£	s.	d.
[2]Rob. Melton, sadeler			8	Joh. Ballsall		1	6	Joh. Huntley		1	4
Alic*ia* Illage		1	0	Rog. Starky			8	Rob. Bradley		1	0
Pet. de l*a* Mare		1	4	Joh. Starky			6	Ric. Morell, sporyer		1	4
Will. Spenc*er*		1	0	Joh. Bredon		1	4	Will. Prentes		1	6
Ric. Trentham		1	4	Tho. Power		1	0	Joh. George		1	0
Will. Fleknay		2	6	Ric. Busshebury		2	0	Ric. Phelips		1	6
Joh. Barnard		2	6	Joh. Capp*er*		1	4	Joh. Archer		1	4
Tho. Barb*our*		1	0	Joh. Hosier		1	0	Rob. Sporiour[3]		1	0
Rad. Duffield			8	Tho. Barbour		2	0	Will. Dawbney		1	4
Tho. Sporiour		1	0	Joh. Barrett		1	0	Joh. Rodley			8

[1] (?) Ancestor of the Elizabethan dramatist. [2] leaf 30, back. [3] A spurmaker.

Broode-yate.

Name	£	*s.*	*d.*
Ric. Schether[1]			6
Joh. Darby, wryght		1	0
Rob. Flecher			8
Rob. Mannyng			8
Joh. Jamys		2	0
Egid. Allesley		10	0
Will. Foster			8
[2] Brasier extra portam			8
Ric. Oneley		6	8
Joh. Harewoode			6
Tho. Riconjay			4
Will. Olyue			6

[Total £3 2*s.* 4*d.* paid (etc.).]

37 names.

Smythefford-[street].

Name	£	*s.*	*d.*
Joh. Maynarde		1	0
Dauid Burton		1	0
Joh. Yate		1	8
Will. Peuterer			8
Rob. Holme		4	0
Joh. Bristowe		10	0
Godefrid Barbour		3	4
Tho. Broune		4	0
Matill. Chaundeler		2	0
Hen. Preston		3	0
Joh. Oneley		10	0
Wal. Asheby		2	0
Joh. Wymondeswold, hosier		1	8
Joh. Lirpole		2	6
Joh. Outerede		1	0
Rad. Bredon		1	0
Joh. Egeston		3	4
Tho. Colam		1	0
Nic. Smythe		3	4
Will. Happeforde		2	0
Joh. Peer, Couper		1	0
Tho. Baxster		2	0
Joh. Braunston		6	8
Ric. Osbern		1	0
Tho. Joy		2	0
Joh. Olyve		2	0
Joh. Bowyer		6	8
Tho. Ive		3	4
Will. Jonys		1	0
Ric. Sadeler		3	4
Joh. Wymondeswold		3	4
Joh. Goode			8
Joh. Bredon			8
Tho. Carter		2	2
Joh. Blakeman		1	8
Ric. Hickelyng		1	8
Joh. Tate		1	8

[Total £5 6*s.* 8*d.* paid (etc.).]

79 names.

Span-[street].

Name	£	*s.*	*d.*
[3]Tho. Brownall		1	2
Joh. Eire		2	4
Sim. Busteler		1	2
Mat. White			8
Tho. Skott			9
Rob. Baxster			9
Ric. Wallford		2	4
Ed. Brogreve		2	3
Lesyngham		3	4
Will. Withibroke		1	4
Joh. Baxster			8
Joh. Marnarme		5	0
Joh. Loote		2	4
Will. Kerver		5	0
Joh. Deisterer		5	0
Rog. Balle		1	2
Joh. Chestur		1	2
Hen. Holt		3	4
Rob. Withibroke[4]			9
Joh. Westley			9
Ric. Waren		3	4
Joh. Broun		4	6
Tho. Paynell		6	8
Joh. Clubb		1	2
Tho. Pratte		1	2
Ric. Capper		1	4
Tho. Barbour			8
Johanna Dudley		10	0
Ric. Shustoke		1	4
Joh. Syssettur		1	4
Joh. Plasterer		2	4
Joh. Balle		1	2
Joh. Nele		1	4
Joh. Mershe		1	4
Nic. Barre			9
Joh. Ridale		2	4
Hugo Stone[5]		1	4
Will. Wellys		1	4
Will. Welshe			8
Will. Stockton		1	0
Hugo Rugeley		5	0
Joh. Kelow			9
Steph. Couche		1	4
Joh. Wellynton		1	4
Rad. Honyman			8
Joh. Seywyn		1	4
Johanna Bondy		1	0
Joh. Saburton			8
Will. Keruer, carpynter			8
Joh. Pynchebeke		5	0
Sim. Est		2	4
Ric. Style		1	2
Joh. Bett			9
Tho. Goldsmyth		1	0
Tho. Standiche			8
Will. Yardeley			9
Ric. Neuton		1	4
Joh. Brettby			8
Ric. Wellforde		2	4
Isabell Walker		2	0
Will. George, weuer			9
Math. White		4	6
Joh. Menley		3	4
Hen. Mason		1	4
Joh. Ward		3	4
Will. Stoone			9
Joh. Broune, weuer			8
Raignald Whitacre		1	2
Burbage			8
Rob. Wattes			8
Joh. Brere		1	0
Will. Baxster			6
Joh. Hasclyffe		2	4
Agn. Harres		1	0
Will. Irysshe			9
Tho. Straunge			9
Joh. Essex		4	6
Tho. Lenton		1	0
Will. Pratte		4	6

[Total £7 11*s.* 8*d.*]

[1] ? Name or trade. [2] Blank. extra portam = outside the gate.
[3] leaf 31. [4] A village 8 miles N.E. of Coventry. [5] or Stene.

47 names.

Croschep[ing].

Name	£	s.	d.
[1] Hen. Sircoke		5	0
Rob. Melburne		10	0
Rob. Grubber		4	0
Hen. Colyns		3	4
Joh. Doughty		4	0
Joh. Atwalle		3	0
Hen. Breux		11	8
Ric. Ho [2]			
Will. Huett		1	8
Hen. Cooke		1	0
Nic. Hull		2	8
Ad. Huyton	1	0	0
Joh. Stile, deist*er*		3	0
Will. Darsett		2	0
Will. Radclyf		1	4
Rad. Chaundeler		2	0
Joh. Burne		4	0
Joh. Parker		10	0
Joh. Frithe		2	4
Joh. Bryghtmere		1	4
Rob. Mason		1	0
Agu. Dalby		2	0
Joh. Appulby		1	4
Ric. Joy		16	8
Edw. Lichefeld		2	0
Will. Dilcok	1	0	0
Will. Dey		1	4
Will. Byneley		3	4
Hen. Randull		3	4
Ric. Weu*er*		3	4
Rob. Lirpoole		5	0
Tho. Lylynton		2	8
Will. Deister		1	4
Joh. White		3	4
Joh. Hall		3	0
Joh. Northman		1	0
Will. Potager		3	0
Joh. Huett, mason,		1	8
Joh. Peut*er*er		3	0
Tho. Grene		6	8
Ric.Boton*er*		4	0
Joh. Lychefeld		2	8
Tho. Norwiche		1	0
Will. Chapman		2	8
Tho. Bassyngburne		2	8
Joh. Gasquyne		2	8
Joh. Northampt*on*		1	0

[Total £9. 8*s*. 4*d*.]

78 names.

Byschopstrette.

Name	£	s.	d.
Joh. Kebull		1	4
Joh. Golde		1	8
Joh. Edwarde		1	0
Middelham			8
Will. Leche			6
Joh. Manston			6
Joh. Pratte			6
Joh. Mongom*ery*		6	8
Ric. Bilston			8
Rob. Bandy		1	2
Tho. Kerdiffe			8
Will. Keresley		1	2
Will. Whithiford		1	8
Rog. Bilston		3	4
Johanna Palmer			8
Joh. Walg*ra*ue		3	4
Joh. Lyncoln			6
Tho. Chacombe		1	2
Ric. Marche		3	4
Houlott			8
Hen. Knott		1	8
Will. Staunton		3	4
Ric. Southam	1	6	8
Will. Barrett			8
Joh. Grynder		3	4
Will. Bett			6
Tho. Ilage		1	4
Joh. Lychfeld		6	8
Joh. Stockton			8
Joh. Atwoode		2	4
Rob. Horwarde		2	4
Hen. Walker		1	8
Joh. Staunton			4
Joh. Wadmore		1	8
Hen. Hull			8
Joh. Folvyle		1	2
[3] Joh. Reynold		1	4
Will. Kemp		1	4
Ric. Stanlake		1	2
Alex. Barker			6
Joh. Stafforde		1	4
Rog. Tailour		1	2
Edm. Drouer		2	6
Joh. Wodcoke		1	2
Tho. Broun		1	2
Hen. Hethe		2	8
Will. Vnbem		2	4
Will. Wilkyns		4	6
Rog. Gose			8
Joh. Allesley		1	0
Tho. Dovy			8
Tho. Smyth			8
Joh. Freman			8
Will. Gamill			8
Sim. Moore		1	2
Joh. Nele		1	2
Joh. Coup*er*			8
Barre			8
Rob. Trueman			8
Joh. Auger		2	4
Joh. Mathew		1	0
Joh. Hayly			8
Joh. Frayter			6
Wall. Trygg		2	0
Joh. Weston			8
Rob. Weston		2	4
Rob. Barbour			8
Ric. Wryghte		1	2
Rob. Wright			6
Rob. Baxster			8
Will. Crudworth		13	4
Ric. Phelips		2	0
Joh. Jacombe			8
Will. Nueton		1	0
Will. Allesley			8
Joh. Bels[t]on		2	4
Joh. Baxster			8
Will. Bate		1	8

[Total £7. 10*s*. 8*d*.] [4]

[1] leaf 31, back. [2] Blank in MS. [3] leaf 32.

[4] The arithmetic in these lists seems often faulty.

MICHAELMAS LEET.

[1][V. f. p. held on Tuesday after Michaelmas, 3. Hen. VI][2] Ric. Southam, Will. Dilcoke, Laur. Cooke, Will. Crosse, Joh. Warrant, Will. Swan, Joh. Golofre, Joh. Braytoofte, Hen. Breux, Rob. Milburne, Joh. Brown, Will. Brydde, Joh. H*ar*burgh, sen., Joh. P*ar*ker, drap*er*, Will. Kerver, Wyll. Byfelde, Joh. ffrankelen, Nic. Byfeld, Joh. Clerke, Joh. Walley, Ric. Sharpe, Tho. Paynell, Ric. Dene, Nic. Palmeer. "Couentre." Oct. 3, 1424. Jury.

[Will. Faseman, Joh. Michell.] Bailiffs.

& ordinat*um* est þ*at* noo man shall cast dust ne oþ*er* filth in the co*m*en Ryver on the payn of xx s. w*ith*oute*n* any g*r*ace at eue*r*y tresspase, and þ*at* the co*m*en s*er*geant goo aboute & serche eue*r*y weke þe forsaid Ryuer & make relac*i*on to þe maio*ur* of eue*r*y man þ*at* is fond giltye, to þe vse of the chamb*ur* to be rec*eived*,[3] and þ*at* hit be p*ro*clamyd. The river.

SETTLEMENT OF A DISPUTE AMONG THE WEAVERS.

[4][Oct. 24, 1424.	*Pro* le weu*er*s.
[Indenture between the master weavors and journeymen.	Hec indentura testat*ur* q*uo*d cum lites et discordie mote et exorte fu*er*int int*er* m*agist*ros & artificiar*ios* de weu*er*s Crafte ciuit*atis* Couen*trie* ex p*ar*te vna, & le Jornemen d*i*cte art*is*
By reason of the grievances between them both parties, through mediation of friends, and the mayor's desire,	ex p*ar*te alt*er*a, et sup*er* c*er*t*is* articulis et grauaminib*us* int*er* eos mot*is* et pendent*ibus*, tand*em* p*ar*tes p*re*dicte tam m*agist*ri quam lez Jorneymen, amicor*um* suor*um* mediantiu*m* (*sic*), ac de mandato et desiderio vene*r*abil*is* viri, Thome Wyldegryse,
and in order that for God's praise, peace, tranquillity and final concord should continue, voluntarily submit themselves,	maior*is* ciuit*atis* p*re*d*i*cte, vt ad laudem Dei, pax, t*r*anquillitas et finalis concordia reformaret*ur* et continuaret*ur*, se posueru*n*t sua spontanea

[1] leaf 21, back.

[2] The names of the mayor and bailiffs before whom the leet was held being identical in both leets, they will not be repeated henceforth at the Michaelmas one for brevity's sake.

[3] or "ret*ained*."

[4] leaf 27.

after each side had taken oath, to the judgment of arbitrators, namely the reverend Sir John Comber, perpetual vicar of S. Michael's, and Will. Wymondswold, chosen by the masters, and Thos. Euerdon, master of S. John's hospital, and Will. Porter, fisher, chosen by the journeymen, to arbitrate upon the business.

[The arbitrators having called before them the parties and heard their account, and evidence having been given, arbitrated in the following terms: that all good customs observed between the parties should remain permanent, if they are not inconsistent with the arbitration lately made by the arbitrators:

and every master of the craft may freely use as many looms for cloth and linen as he will:

and he may have as many apprentices as he will, without challenge;

and that John Grynder, weaver, may use as many looms for cloth and linen as he will:

vol*un*tat*e* et assensu, fide media inde affirmata, in p*rese*ntia arbit*r*ato*rum* subsc*r*ipto*rum* & alio*rum* fide digno*rum*, in arbit*r*io & ordinac*i*one Reue*ren*do*rum* viro*rum*, d*omi*ni Joh*ann*es (*sic*) Comber, pe*r*petui vica*rii* eccl*esi*e S. Michael*is* Couen*trie*, et Will*el*mi Wymondeswold, arbitrat*orum* pe*r* p*redi*ctos m*agist*ro*s* ex p*ar*te sua elect*orum*, et Thome Eu*er*don, m*a*g*ist*ri hospitalis S. Joh*ann*is Bap*tis*te Couen*trie*, et Will*el*mi Porter, fisher, arbitrat*orum* p*er* p*r*edict*os* Jornemen ex p*ar*te sua elect*orum*, ad arbit*r*and*um* inte*r* eos de p*r*emiss*is*. Qui quidem arbit*r*atores, conuocat*is* cora*m* eis p*ar*tibu*s* p*r*edict*is*, audit*is* et intellect*is* amba*rum* illa*rum* relac*i*o*n*ibu*s*, mate*r*iis, g*r*auaminibu*s* et euidenc*iis* hu*cus*q*ue* inde delibe*r*at*is*, arbit*r*ati su*n*t et concordat*i* in hunc modum: In p*r*imis q*uo*d o*mn*es bone ordinac*i*o*n*es et consuetudi*n*es inte*r* p*ar*tes p*redi*ctas antea fact*as* & usitat*as*, q*ue* hic no*n* specificant*ur* [in] robore*m* permaneant et effectu*m*, Ita q*uo*d no*n* sint in p*r*eiudiciu*m* uel subue*r*c*i*one*m* [arbitrii] inte*r* p*ar*tes p*r*edictas pe*r* p*redi*ct*os* arbit*r*atore*s* nupe*r* inde fact*i*. It*e*m q*uo*d quil*ib*et etia*m* m*a*g*iste*r d*i*cte art*is* libe*r*e de cete*r*o vti valeat tot wollenloomes & lynnenlomes quot volu*er*it h*ab*ere et occupare. & q*uo*d quil*ib*et etia*m* m*agist*er h*ab*eat tot apprentices quot volu*er*it h*ab*ere, sine cont*r*adicc*i*o*n*e alicuiu*s*. Item, arbit*r*ati su*n*t et ordinar*unt* p*er* p*r*esentes q*uo*d Joh*ann*es Grynder, weue*r*, libe*r*e vtatu*r* et h*ab*eat tot & q*uo*t de wollenlomes & lynnen-

and for better ensuring Grynder's liberty in this matter,

he shall pledge 100*s.*, part of which he shall pay to the masters according to the arbitrators' decision :

and whoever wishes as a master to employ journeymen or strangers shall pay the principal master 20*s.*, by which he may use the livery [or liberty] of the craft

with all its counsels and discussions :

and that the journeymen's wardens pay 12*d.* to the chief master for every brother admitted into their fraternity :

and that the chief master of the weavers shall pay to the journeymen's lamp[2] the third part of the damages for mutual trespasses agreed on :
and that each of the journeymen

shall yearly pay 4*d.* towards

lomes sicut voluerit habere et occupare. Item, arbitrati sunt (etc.) quod pro huiusmodi libertate ipsius Johannis Grynder in hac parte, & pro bona pace & amore inter magistros predicte artis & dictum Johannem Grynder de cetero habendis et continuandis, quod Idem Johannes Grynder vadiabit magistris artis predicte centum solidos de quibus soluere [debeat] eisdem magistris secundum arbitrium & reward predictorum arbitratorum. Item, arbitrati sunt (etc.) quod quicumque de cetero qui exigere voluerit ut magister artis predicte tam de Jornemen quam de extraneis in ciuitate predicta, quod soluet principali magistro eiusdem artis viginti solidos, pro quibus vti valeat liberacione[1] dicte artis cum omnibus conciliis et tractatibus inter eos habitis & habendis. Item, arbitrati sunt (etc.) quod custodes de le Jorneymen soluant duodecim denarios principali magistro eiusdem artis pro quolibet confratre in fraternitatem dictorum jorneymen admisso et recepto. Item, arbitrati sunt (etc.) quod magister principalis de Weuers Crafte, seu magistri eiusdem, soluat vel soluant ad luminare dictorum jorneymen de qualibet concordia pro transgressionibus inter eos factis terciam partem emendarum. Item arbitrati sunt (etc.) quod dicti Jorneymen et eorum quilibet soluet dictis magistris annuatim in futuro quatuor denarios ad

[1] or "libertate."

[2] A lamp the journeymen maintained most likely in S. George's chapel on Gosford gate. For the suppression of the S. George's (journeymen) Gild by the Trinity and Corpus Christi Gilds in Feb. 1425 v. Corp. MS. B. 43 and the Introduction.

the masters' pagent; and that the journeymen have their drinking and feast with their masters as of old:
and that all the good customs practised between masters may be had in future and continued:

and that the journeymen pay 3*d.* to the masters for any contumacy done in the future:

and that no master, by reason of this ordinance, hinder any of the journeymen

from working freely with the masters
as they were of old accustomed, preferring the journeymen of the city before strangers, and especially those of the livery;
and the journeymen shall work with their masters in preference to strangers:
and none of the journeymen shall hinder any of his fellows from working with his masters:

and the journeymen
may have the third part of the payment for weaving cloth, as well less as larger,
which they weave with their masters, as they used to have:

and every one, as well of the

opus de le pagent eorundem, & quod ipsi le jorneymen habeant cum magistris suis potacionem siue collacionem sicut antea consueverunt. Item, arbitrati [sunt] (etc.) quod omnes bone consuetudines vsitate inter magistros & lez Jorneymen artis predicte de cetero habeantur et continuantur. Item, arbitrati sunt (etc.) quod predicti Jorneymen soluet (*sic*) prefatis magistris tres denarios de qualibet contumacia dictorum Jornemen in futuro facienda. Item, arbitrati sunt (etc.) quod nullus magister artis predicte occasione ordinacionis predicte aliquem de lez Jorneymen impediat uel expellat, seu impediri uel expelli faciat quominus libere operarentur (*sic*) cum magistris illius artis, sicut ex antiquo ante litem motam consueverunt, preferendo lez Jorneymen dicte ciuitatis pre aliis extraneis, et specialiter illis de liberacione[1]; & etiam quod dicti Jorneymen operabuntur cum prefatis magistris suis pre aliis extraneis. & quod nullus de lez Jorneymen procurabit uel impediet opere, concilio uel ordinacione aliquem de sociis suis operari cum suis magistris. Item, arbitrati sunt (etc.) quod dicti lez Jorneymen, operantes de cetero cum dictis magistris, habeant terciam partem solucionis percipiende pro textura & operacione singularum telarum, tam minorum quam maiorum, quos (*sic*) dicti lez Jorneymen operantur & telant cum suis magistris, sicut solebant habere illam terciam partem. Item, arbitrati sunt (etc.)

[1] or "deliberatis."

masters as of the journeymen, in the matter of offences committed in the craft, be obedient to the chief master in reforming the same, as they were of old accustomed:

and that R. Marche shall restore to the wardens of the journeymen's lamp eight shillings of the debt delivered to him in exchange, for the journeymen's use:

and that W. Martyn shall restore *3s. 4d.* of the debt lent to him for his use:

and that all debts owed by masters and men to the said masters,

by reason of the custom of the craft hitherto observed, be entirely remitted:

and that every master, who disobeys these rules, shall pay a fine at the mayor's mercy of *40s.*

and for the like offence a journeymen shall pay *20s.*

[Lastly they ordain that the tenour of this indenture be

quod quilibet, tam de magistris quam de le Jorneymen artis predicte, pro quibuscumque transgressionibus seu delictis in arte predicta commissis, sint obedientes principali magistro dicte artis pro huiusmodi transgressionibus seu delictis reformandis, sicut ex antiquo consueverunt.

Item, arbitrati sunt (etc.) quod Ric. Marche, weuer, soluet & restituet custodibus luminaris de lez Jornemen dicte artis octo solidos de lez debitis sibi traditis ad excambium, ad opus dictorum Jorneymen. Item, arbitrati sunt (etc.) quod Will. Martyn, weuer, soluet et restituet custodibus de lez Jorneymen tres solidos et quatuor denarios de lez debitis sibi prestitis ad vsum ipsius Willelmi. Item, arbitrati sunt (etc.) quod omnia debita hinc inde per magistros dicte artis & lez Journeymen predictis magistris debita, racione consuetudinis artis predicte inter eos habite & consuete, remittant[ur] omnino et extinguantur. Item, arbitrati sunt (etc.) quod quicumque magistrorum, qui contra istas conuenciones uel aliquam[2] earum in futuro contrairet *(sic)*, quod soluat nomine pene ad muragium ciuitatis predicte in misericordia maioris eiusdem pro tempore existentis xl solidos. & similiter quod quicumque de lez Journemen qui contra istas ordinaciones vel earum aliquam contrairet *(sic)* in futuro, quod soluet nomine pene ad muragium ciuitatis predicte xx^{ti} solidorum in misericordia maioris. Nouissime uero arbitrati sunt (etc.)

[1] leaf 27, back.

[2] MS. *aliquem*.

written in the paper of the mayor's mayoralty; and that the mayor and his successors have power to levy the said money penalties, when they may happen to be due.]

[The seal of the mayor is attached to the document as well as that of the arbitrators.]

[Oct. 24, 1424.]

quod tenour huius scripti indentati de uerbo ad uerbum scribatur in papiro maioratus predicti maioris ad perpetuam rei memoriam. & quod Idem maior et successores sui habeant liberam potestatem & auctoritatem leuandi predictas penas pecuniarias de tempore in tempus cum acciderint. In Cuius Rei testimonium hiis indenturis sigillum maioratus predicti venerabilis maioris ad predictorum arbitratorum requisicionem et sigilla predictorum arbitratorum sunt appensa. Datum apud Couentriam, xxiiij^{to} die Octobris a. r. r. Hen. vj^{ti} (etc.) tercio.

A ?LOLLARD PREACHER.

Nov. 30, 1424.

[1] [2]At the feest of saynt Andrew theapostull, þe yer of our liege lorde our kyng Henry the vj^{te} aftur the conquest the iij^{d}, com [3]John Grace, þe wich at that tyme was callyd John Grace, heremyte, and sithen men said he was a moonke, aftur þat a frere, and sithen a recluse, com to this cite, and prechid v daies to-gethur in the Lytull-parke, seyng þat he was lyceuciate & licens had to preche of the bischops minysters of this diocese, and he had prechid at Lichfeld ther in the Close among the Canons iij dayes to-gethur, and aftur he prechid at Brynmyngham, and aftur at Wallsall, and aftur at Collyshull and so com doun hithur. The wich John Grace was at that tyme a famous man among the peopull þer, as he had prechid seyng that he was a gracyous man in sayng, and a hooly lyuer, and many marvelous made and shewed; for the wich sayng many men trowen that it had byn so as hit was said apon hym a-fore tyme, and that causyd the people the more & tenderer to her his prechyng. But neuer-the-later apon

John Grace, hermit,

preaches in the Little Park;

he is a famous man among the people;

shows many marvels,

[1] Coventry was a Lollard centre. Swinderby preached, and heretical books were published there, v. *Eng. Hist. Rev.*, xx. 447.

[2] leaf 24. Printed, Sharp, *Antiquities of Coventry* (ed. Fretton), p. 205. [3] ? oone.

the said saynt Andrew day, when the said John Grace had prechid, hit was said he was not licentiate, nor noo lycens had to preche, notwithstandyng he hym-selffe said in euery sermon þat he made þat he was licienciate and lycens had to preche. And at the same day at afturnone when Evensong was doon, Ric. Croseby, priour of saynt Mary church in Couentre, was in purpose to haue gone in-to þe pulpit in the Trinite churche, as the comen voise was then, to haue denouncyd acursyd all tho þat herd the sermon of the said John Grace; and so, what thurgh þe gouernance of the priour, and the sayng of oone Master John Bredon,[1] frere of the Gray frers in Couentre, castyng ouerthwart wordes amonges the people, grett seyng was a-mong the people þat þe priour and frer Bredon wold haue cursid all tho þat herdon the said John Grace preche; ffor the wich sayng þe priour nor þe said frere Bredon wold nott goo oute of the church vnto þe tyme þat the maiour com to hem, notwithstandyng they myght haue goone well I-noughȝe whethur thei wold, & þat wott Allmyghty God. And apon this matur a-boue-namyd grett noise rose in the Contre þat the comens of Couentre wer rysen, and wold haue distroyd the priour and the said frer, wher God wott hit was not so, nor non suche thyng wrought nor purposid; the wich noise com to the counsell of the said our leige lorde, for the wich the counsell at þat tyme beyng in London leten make a lettre to þe maiour & bayleffes and comens of this Cite of the wich the tenour folowith in thes wordes:—Trusty and wel-belouyd, we grett you well; and for-asmoche þat now late hit hathe byn reportyd vnto us, & sum of our councell, þat a certen person, sumtyme a monke aftur

[cætera desunt.]

but it is said he was not licentiate.

There is a great saying that the prior and Friar John Bredon will curse the audience of John Grace.

On account of the fuss made by the clergy,

erroneous reports arise.

So there is trouble made by the king's Council about the supposed riot,

and a letter written by them.

WARDENS' ACCOUNTS.

[[2]In this year Joh. Mychell and Joh. Everdon gave their accounts. The wardens are charged with £66. 12s.

[1] On Friar John's later escapade and dispute with the Convent about the funeral candles v. Leland, *Collectanea*, v. 304; Sharp, *Antiq.* 207; and *Life in an Old English Town*, p. 326–8.

[2] leaf 26, back.

2d. They ask allowance of £55. 15s. 5d. thus they remain in arrears £10. 16s. 11d.,[1] as it appears in their accounts in the mayor's bag; with which arrears they are charged in their accounts in the time of John Braytoft's mayorality.[2]]

JOHN BRAYTOFT, MAYOR, 1425.

1425. Election of John Braytoft.

[3]Elecc*io* noui maior*is* (etc.) temp*ore* & decessu Thome Wyldgryse, tunc maior*is*, Will. Faseman and Joh. Michell ball*iuorum* ciuitat*is* predict*e* a. r. r. H. vj[ti] (etc.) te*r*cio.

Electors.

Joh. Leeder, Joh. Dilcok, Ad. Hiton, Egid. Allesley, Will. Faseman, Rad. Garton, Will. Crosse, Hen. Breux, Rob. Melburn, Joh. Bowyer, Will. Byfeld, Joh. Onely, Joh. Pynchebeke, Joh. Egeston, Ric. Sharpe, Joh. Tate, Joh. Warrant, Will. Bryde, Joh. Frankelen, Joh. Whalley, Will. Cross, passynge*r*, Tho. Dawe, Ad. Suette, Joh. Runton.

Officers to serve from the Purification for one whole year.

[m. Joh. Braitoft; cor. Joh. Dilcok; ch. Tho. Paynell and Joh. Deist*er*, woleman; w. Will. Frissby and Joh. Eu*er*don; mace. Will. Oxton, "A festo Pu*rificacionis* a. r. r. H. vj[ti] p*ost* conq*uestu*m te*r*cio usq*ue* idem f*estu*m extu*nc* p*roxi*m*e* seq*uens*, etc."]

The wardens are not to be elected henceforth as chamberlains. This ordinance affirmed by the leet.

P*rouisum* est tu*nc* & ib*id*em q*uo*d custodes ciuit*atis* Couen*trie* no*n* eru*nt* amodo positi neq*ue* electi in off*iciu*m cam*erariorum* etc. Que quide*m* ordinaci*o* affirmat*ur* p*er* letam Pas[c]he temp*ore* Joh*anni*s Braytoft tu*nc* maior*is*.

J. Ps. within the city and suburbs.

[Joh. Braytoft, Joh. Weston, rec., Joh. Leeder, Laur. Cooke, Ric. Southam, Ad. Hiton.

Key-keepers.

The same except the recorder.]

THE SPECIAL COMMISSION.

Mayor's expenses in connection with the special Commissions during the Lent of 1425.

[4]Mem. q*uo*d Joh. Braitofte maior (etc.) soluit de suis p*ropri*is denar*iis*, videl*ice*t temp*or*e quo Ric*ard*us, Comes de Warr[ewyk] et alii Justiciarii p*er* co*m*missione*m* fueru*nt* hic ap*u*d Couen*triam* temp*or*e q*ua*dragesimali.[5] [For the justices' horses, and for rewards to their clerks and men

[1] It should be 9*d.* (ix*d.*). [2] v. p. 101.
[3] leaf 28. [4] leaf 28, back.
[5] In connection with the late riot. Warwick came "to seize upon the franchises." Grace was arrested by the mayor and taken to Coventry gaol. Sharp, 205.

with their dinner (*pr*andio) £11. 5s. 9d. To W. Oxton for riding three times to London £1. 1s. 4d. To John Breton at the same time for his advice £1. 0. 0. To [1] Mettley for the same 13s. 4d. To Will. Donnyngton for the same 13s. 4d. To Edm. Collyshull for the enrollment of presentations of indictments before the justices of the peace in Esterton's mayoralty £1. 0. 0.[2] Sum total £15. 13. 9d. Total £15 13*s*. 9*d*.

In this year £50 was granted by 48 discreet men to be levied and collected for certain business necessary for the city. It was delivered to John Braytoft, and used thus :— £50 granted for these necessities.

In expenses at the time of the special commission (*com*missione*m* specialem ad inq*ui*rend*um*) £11. 13s. 9d.[3] Expenses £11 13*s*. 9*d*.

To Breton, Donnyngton, Mettley, Collishull & Oxton as above £4. 8s. 0d. £4 8*s*. 0*d*.

To Laur. Cook and Ad. Hiton for riding to London about certain business, and for the men being in prison there (p*ro* ho*min*ib*us* ib*ide*m in prisona existent*ibus*) £20. 0. 0. To the men in prison, etc., £20 0. 0.

To Joh. Weston, recorder, for his labour and advice, and the necessary advice of others there £20. 0. 0. Total £55. 13s. 9d. Thus £5. 13. 9d. are owing to John Braytofte.] £20 0. 0. Total £55 13*s*. 9*d*.

CHAMBERLAINS' ACCOUNTS.

[On the vigil of the Assumption, Ric. Oneley and Will. Bifeld, chamberlains in Esterton's time, render accounts. Charged with £98. 6s. 0d. Allowance £96. 6s. 6d. So they remain in clear debt £1 19s. 4d.[4] Which sum they are enjoined to bring in before (citra) Michaelmas; they pay it to the mayor, and are discharged.] "Compot*us* Cam*er*ari*orum*," Aug. 14; accounts for 1422; balance £1 19*s*. 4*d*. quit.

MICHAELMAS LEET.

[5][V. f. p. on Monday after Michaelmas 4 Hen. VI.] "Couentre," Oct. 1, 1425.

Will. Dilcok, Ric. Southam, Joh. Leder, Ad. Hyton, Hen. Peyto, Tho. Wyldegrys, Egid. Allesley, Rad. Garton, Ric. Joy, Joh. Golofre, Joh. Parker, Hen. Breux, Rob. Melburn, Joh. Bower, Tho. Paynell, Will. Kerver, Joh. Jury.

[1] Blank.
[2] A probable reference to enclosure riots. See p. 50.
[3] ? £11. 5*s*. 9*d*.
[4] It should be £1 19*s*. 6*d*.
[5] leaf 38, back. Scribe of B type.

Deister, wolman, Joh. Clerk, Joh. Onley, Joh. Egiston, Will. Wymondeswold, Joh. Dilcok, Ric. Sharp, Ric. Dene.
Bailiffs. [Joh. Braunston, merchant, and Joh. Coton.]

Orders of Leet. Drapery. £10 fine.

Hit is ordeyned that all mane*r* men that sellen Cloth on ffrydays, that they sellen hit in the drapery, & nowhere elles, but if it be a woman that bereth on dosse*n* in her armes, vpon the peyne ordeyned by the Charter,[1] that is x li.

"River" 20*s*. fine.

[A fine of 20s. levied upon every man who does not cleanse the common river before his dwelling; the work to begin "a Monday next comyng" and be ended "be that day Sennyht," upon the same penalty.]

"Houses against the drapery."

Also all the bordes of the houell anenst the drapery dore be taken a-wey after that charter be cryed & p*ro*-claymed, and a wall there made in enclosyng the Chirche-yard.

John Montgomery fined 20*s*. for stopping the river.

Also is ordeyned that the peyne forfet by John Mon-gome*r*y, because of his stoppyng the Co*m*en Ryue*r* a-fore is tenement, þ*at* is to sey, xx s. be rered to the vse of the chaumbr*e*.

And also oþ*er* peynez forfeted be rered at eue*r*y defalt w*ith*outen redempcion.

[Any one within the liberties who surcharges the common with cattle shall pay 1*d*. for four sheep, 1*d*. for an ox, 1*d*. for a cow, and for every beast 1*d*.

Item, ord*inatum* e*st* q*uo*d si quis infra libe*r*tate*m* (etc.) co*mmu*nam pastur*e* supe*r*one*r*at cu*m* aue*r*iis soluat p*ro* quatuor bident*ibus* j d., & p*ro* vno boue 1 d., vna vacca j d. Et sic p*ro* quol*ibet* a*nim*ali j d. Hoc intelligit*ur* de pinguis (*sic*) a*nima*lib*us*.

[The chamberlains to farm out the grass and garth of Gosford Green chapel.

Item, volu*nt* q*uo*d Came*r*ar*ii* ordinant & ad firma*m* pona*nt* gramen & gardum de le Chapell de Goseford-grene.

[As for the common river they wish all ordinances, made aforetime, to be kept,

Et quoad le co*m*en Ryue*r* volu*nt* q*uo*d ordi*nacio*nes ante hec temp*ora* ordinat*e* amodo custodiant*ur*, sub

[1] The Drapery belonged to the Trinity Gild, v. Corp. MS. C. 194. It was let out in stalls among the drapers. No charter I know of mentions this fine; v. *infra*, p. 104.

and the penalty is to be levied by the chamberlains.

pena *prius* data[1] de & in *premissis*; & *quod* pena leuat*ur per* Cam*er*arios.

[John Barton to come to Coventry, if he will, and keep a grammar school, if he knows well how to teach children, and keep school.]

Item, volunt & ordinat[um est] q*uod* Joh*annes* Barton veniat ad ciuitate*m* Couentr*ie* scolam gramaticale*m* tenend*am*, si velit, & si cognoscit[2] abile (*sic*) pu*er*os informar*e* et scola*m* tener*e*.

OFFICIALS' ACCOUNTS.

[3][Will. Faseman and Joh. Braunston[4] render accounts before the mayor and the Forty-Eight. Charge £84. 3s. 2d. Allowance £74. 0s. 2½d. — Chamberlains' accounts Oct. 25, 1425.

So they remain in clear debt £9. 16s. 5½d.,[5] which sum they are enjoined to bring in on a day on this side of Christmas; on which day they bring £1. 6s. 8d. A later date, the Saturday before the Conversion of S. Paul, is given them, on which day they pay £8. 10s. 0d. of the £9. 16s. 6½.[6] and are discharged.] — Balance £9 16*s*. 5½*d*. quit, Jan. 19, 1426.

[Will. Crudworth and Will. Kerver render accounts before the same. Charge £84. 3s. 2d. Allowance for costs of murage £70. 14s. 9d., and for the Little Park (p*ar*vo p*ar*co) £2. 14s. 0d. They remain in arrears in clear debt £11. 4s. 5d.[7] The mayor gives them £4. 0. 0. Sum £15. 4s. 5d. They have a day on this side Pentecost. On which day they ask allowance for expenses at Cook-street gate £14. 11s. 11d. Hence arrears 12s. 6d.] — Chamberlains' accounts for 1424. Jan. 4, 1426. Balance £11 4*s*. 5*d*. Further augmented to £15 4*s*. 5*d*. Further expenses £14 11*s*. 11*d*. Balance in arrears 12*s*. 6*d*.

[Joh. Michell and Joh. Euerdon render accounts for Wildegrise's mayoralty. — Wardens' accounts for 1424. Jan. 19, 1426.

Charge £78. 8s. 9d. Allowance £53. 15s. 6½d. Balance in arrears £24. 13s. 2½d., whereof they remain in arrears as appears in their account in Joh. Braytofte's bag.] — Balance £24 13*s*. 2½*d*.

[8][Joh. Braytofte delivered to Ric. Joy, mayor, 100 marks in part payment of 500 marks from Ric. Crosby, prior, for the first year, by the first bond as appears in the second folio of Wildgrise's time.] — Prior pays 100 marks.

1 MS. repeats 'd*a*ta.' 2 *Sic.*
3 leaf 29. 4 Chamberlains 1423.
5 Something wrong. £10 2*s*. 11½*d*. would be correct.
6 *Sic.* They don't even stick to their own wrong calculations.
7 *Sic.* Correct £10. 14*s*. 5*d*. 8 leaf 32. v. p. 63.

RIC. JOY, MAYOR, 1426.

[Election of officers.]

Jan. 25, 1426. Electors. [1]Hen. Peyto, Will. Dilcok, Joh. Leder, Laur. Cook, Tho. Wildegryse, Joh. Braunston, Joh. Coton, Hen. Breux, Joh. Parker, Joh. Michell, Rad. Garton, Rob. Melburn, Joh. Onley, Joh. Clerk, Will. Byfeld, Will. Crudworthe, Will. Keruer, Joh. Egynton, Ric. Dene, Joh. Warant, Joh. Whalley, Will. Bird, Joh. Broun, drap*er*, Will. Crosse, passenger.[2]

Officers. [m. Ric. Joy; cor. Joh. Dilcok; ch. Ric. Busshebury, and Ric. Boton*er*; w. Joh. Euerdon and Will. ffrysby; mace, Will. Oxton.

J. Ps. Justices of the peace associated with the mayor, Joh. Weston, recorder, Hen. Peyto, Laur. Cook, Ric. Southam, Joh. Leder.

Custodians of the keys. The mayor, the master of the Trinity Gild,[3] Cook, Southam, and Leder.]

ACCOUNTS AND EXPENSES IN CONNECTION WITH THE DUKE OF BEDFORD'S VISIT.

Feb. 11. Present to Bedford. [[4]On the Monday before S. Valentine, it was granted by the following 48 discreet men that 50 marks and a gilt cup (cipho deaurato) should be presented to the Duke of Bedford.]

The "Forty-eight." Ric. Joy, mayor, Hen. P[e]yto, Will. Dilcok, Ric. Southam, Joh. Leder, Tho. Wildegrise, Joh. Braytoft, Joh. Brystow, Joh. Braunston, Joh. Coton,[5] Egid. Allesley, Rad. Garton, Will. Crosse, Joh. Golofre, Joh. Parker, Rob. Melburn, Hen. Breux, Joh. Bowyer, Ric. Busshebury, Ric. Boton*er*, Joh. Euerdon, Will. ffrisby, Will. Byfeld, Will. Crudworthe, Will. Keruer, Tho. Paynell, Joh. Deyster, Joh. Dilcok, Ric. Sharp, Joh. Whalley, Joh. Warant, Joh. Egeston, Joh. Clerk, Ric. Dene, Joh. Prentes, Joh. Stille, deister, Will. Swane, Joh. Welford, Joh. Blakeman, Rob. Lirpole, Joh. F*r*ankelen, Joh.

[1] leaf 39. Scribe of B type.
[2] *N. E. D.* ferry-man or ford-keeper. This is earlier than the first example given there, viz. 1533.
[3] Henry Peyto. [4] leaf 39. [5] or Coton*er*.

Runton,[1] Joh. Onley,[1] Joh. Broun,[1] draper, Joh. Launde,[1] Will. Brid, Joh. Walgraue, Bened. Marshall.

Expenses in the matter of the Duke of Bedford at the time of the presentation of the 50 marks and cup; master ? Sparver had 20*s*., the messenger and porter 3*s*. 4*d*. apiece; so had one who gave the mayor and others a stag; in expenses at a dinner at Warwick and for the horses 11*s*. Total £2. 1*s*.

Mem. q*uo*d iste fueru*n*t expense (?) expend*ite*[2] *versus* duce*m* Bedfordie, temp*or*e p*re*sentac*ionis* p*re*dict*orum* l marc*arum* et Ciphi.

In p*r*imis magister (?) Ep*er*u*er*[3] apud ffulbrooke[4] h*ab*uit xx s.; le messenger xl d.; le porter xl d.; ac ipse qui p*re*sentavit maiori ac aliis viris cum vno Ceruo xl d. Item, in expensis apud Warre*wyk*, du*m* fuerunt in p*r*andio ib*ide*m, et expens*is* equ*or*um xj s. S*um*ma totalis xlj s.

Mem. q*uo*d isti subseq*uentes* p*re*sentaueru*n*t duce (*sic*) Bedd*fordie* cu*m* predict*is* l marc*is* ac Cipho, videl*icet*:— Ric. Joy, maior, Hen. Peyto, Joh. Leder, Tho. Wildegrise, Will. Dilcok, Joh. Braytoft, Joh. Braunston, Rob. Melburn.[5] **The following presented the duke with 50 marks and a cup.**

[6]Hit is to haue in mynde that Ric. Joy, meire, reseyned of Joh. Braytoft l marc' & a cuppe ou*er*-gilte. The whiche l marc' & the Cuppe the seyd meir with oder wurthymen p*re*sented the duches[7] of Bedford at Fulbrok apon Gudtydmonday.[8] **The present to the duchess upon Good-tide Monday, Feb. 11.**

Also the seyd meire reseyved of the seyd John Braytoft son after the seyd tym od*er* l marc'. Also the seyd Ric. Joy reseyved in the secund weke of Lenton of **Mayor's accounts. 50 marks.**

[1] These names are bracketed together with the words, "non fuere p*re*sent*es*." [2] An inadmissible form.

[3] Quite plainly written epu. ? Sperviter = a keeper of sparrow-hawks (Halliwell).

[4] For Fulbrook Castle v. Dugdale, 470. The gatehouse was built by Joan, Lady Bergavenny (v. *infra passim*), and when the property came into Bedford's hand he enclosed a park and built this castle. It became ruinous before the end of the century, and Sir William Compton took the materials to build Compton Winyates.

[5] The last two paragraphs are bracketed together with "vacat q*uia* alibi, videl*ice*t folio subsequent*e*" (omitted because elsewhere, viz. on the leaf following) in the margin.

[6] leaf 40. ? Another scribe of type B.

[7] Anne, sister to Philip the Good, Duke of Burgundy. Married 1423; remembered for her protection of Joan of Arc.

[8] The day before Shrove Tuesday, v. E. E. D. Gooddit. It is likely the duke was not present, as a council was summoned to be held at Northampton on Feb. 13. Ramsey, I. 365.

£116 4*s.* 4*d.*

John Michell & John Breton[1] C li. xvj li. iiij s. iiij d. Also the seyd Ric. Joy reseyved the moyse of Ester of Ric. Crosseby, priour of seynt Mary hous in Couentre, C marc'. The whiche CC marc' receyued of John Braytoft & of the seyd priour, how hit is payed & deliuered more playnly aperithe in the lef next after followeng.

and 100 marks from the prior for the monies or payment of Easter.[2]

Mayor asks allowance for divers expenses in entertainment of the duke and duchess, Lord Talbot and others.

Of the whiche summes the seyd Ric. Joy askythe alowance for certen expenses made to the duke of Bedford, the duches of Bedford, the duk of Gloucestre, my lady of Bergeveney,[3] my lord Talbote,[4] & oder, the whiche expences the sume extendithe, as hit aperithe in a paper in the seyd meires bag beyng, to[5]

EASTER LEET.

"Couentr*e*." Apr. 6. Jury.

[[6]V. f. p. held before Ric. Joy m., Joh. Braunston and Joh. Coten b., on Saturday after Easter 4 Hen. VI.] Hen. Peyto, Ric. Southam, Will. Dilcok, Laur. Coke, Joh. Leder, Tho. Wilgrise, Joh. Braytoft, Joh. Bristowe, Rad. Garton, Will. Crosse, Joh. Golofer, Joh. Michell, Hen. Breux, Joh. Bowyer, Ric. Busshebury, Ric. Botoner, Will. Byfeld, Joh. Euerdon, Will. ffrisby, Joh. Deister, wolman, Joh. Clerk, Joh. Onley, Ric. Dene, Joh. Egeston.]

Orders of Leet. 'Selling cloth in drapery'; only 'dozens' to be sold by women on market days outside drapery or 6*s.* 8*d.* fine.

Hit is ordeyned þat no persone sell no cloth vppon þe ffriday but in the drapery, & in no place elles, except women sellyng dosens in hir armes, uppon the peyn at euery time of vj s. viij d. to be rered to the wardens of þe Cite.[7]

Chamberlains to enclose Barons Lane.

Also hit is ordeyned that a lane, called Barons-lane, be enclosed, so þat no man haue no harme in their gardens, ne hir closes, be no evell doers, and þat hit be inclosed be the Chamberleyns.

At which ther was put vp a bill be þe comens of the Croschepyng warde, the tenour wherof heraftur ensueth:—

[1] Michell was warden 1421 and 1423.
[2] v. *supra*, p. 63.
[3] Joan, Lady Bergavenny, daughter of the Earl of Arundel. Her husband owned Fillongley and Fullbrook in Warwickshire. See Dugdale, *Warw.* 470, 730, for an account of this lady, whose portrait was in a stained-glass window in S. Mary's Hall.
[4] John Talbot, Earl of Shrewsbury. He married Margaret, daughter of Richard Beauchamp, Earl of Warwick.
[5] Blank in MS. [6] leaf 38. Scribe B.
[7] v. p. 100, where the fine is the extraordinarily large one of £10.

To the worshipfull astat*es*, mair & his peres of the Cite of Couentr*e*, besecheth mekely yo*ur* por*e* neyghbo*urs* of þe Croschepyng: ffor-asmoch as a full nedefull & worshipfull thyng to þe Co*m*en p*ro*fet was made with gret coste of goode of þe worshipfull mens, Laur. Cooke, Tho. Wilgrise, Rog. Benet, Tho. Grene, Joh. Egeston & other, to come into þe Croschepyng to ease of all people, the co*m*e*n* Cundyte, and at diu*ers* letes billes han ben endosed and ordena*u*nc*es* made full worthely th*a*t þe Chamb*er*leyns shuld ordeyn the pypes to be kept of the seid condite withoute þe barres, & iche warde aftur as the cundyte cometh to, be ij kepers in eu*er*y warde to kepe & ou*er*see that no welles nor suspiralles, other then ben ordeyned, shuld be had to let the co*m*en Cours of the seid Cundyte; ayenst þe which John Stafford in þe West-orchard, & at þe place late of John Lirpole, both welles & sprynge*s* oute of þe same cundyte, su*m* made with lyme & ston[1]; & in other place also the cours of the Cundyte is letted, to gret hyndryng of þe co*m*e*n* people. Wherfore please yowe to ou*er*se these defalt*es* and amend he*m* as reason asketh, & assigne c*er*ten kepers in ich warde aftur your discrescion to take charge of kepyng of þe same.

'Conduit': Petition about its course, which against all good rules is letted by John Stafford and others with wells and springs; the petitioners request the leet to assign keepers in each ward to take charge of it.

Which bill is indosid as foloweth: Hit is ordeyned the mat*er* comp*re*hended in this bill be holden aft*ur* þe ordina*u*nc*es* made before tyme be lete; and ou*er* þ*a*t they ordeyn þ*a*t no man*er* man ne woman make no issue ne breke the Cundyte fro this tyme forward, vppon þe peyn of xl s.; and þ*a*t þe seid John make hit ayen within viij dayes, vppon xl s., & for his offens they am*er*cy hym at xl d.

The petition is endorsed with a confirmation of existing orders; a 40*s*. fine fixed against offenders; Stafford is fined 40*d*. and ordered to repair mischief within 8 days.

NIC. ASSHEBURN AND THE TRUST.

[2]Mem. that the sixt day of Jun the yer of kyng Henre the sixt after the conquest the fourthe at Couentre, Nich*ol*as Assheburn frely & of his own p*ro*fre afore Ric. Joy, that tyme meir, Joh. Braunston & Joh. Coton bayll*ifs* (etc.), Hen. Peyto, Will. Dilcok, Ric. Southam, Laur. Cook, Ad. Huyton, Joh. Leder, Tho. Wildegrise, Joh. Bristowe, Joh.

June 6, 1426. Nich. Assheburn

[1] ? Omission here.

[2] leaf 40. The same scribe as above, p. 103.

Michell, Rob. Melburn & Joh. Bowyer, preyed he myght be sworne to yif true enformac*i*on of a mater that folouthe, vpon the whiche he at that tyme afore the seyd persons sworne seyd:—that the feffement that the seyd Nich. made to Ric. Joy, Tho. Burton, grocer, of London & to John Swetton of Couentre was apon trist, & the relas that the [seyd] Richard Joy made afterward to the seyde John Swetton was made apon trist, at the preyer of the same Nich., & to refef the seyd Nich. when he were requyred, that is to sey, of a mece lyeng atte Brodyate in Couentre in the whiche Edmund Colshull now dwellethe, that is called the Belle.

is sworn to give true information

concerning a messuage called The Bell.

Hugh Rogeley

Also the same day of Jun Hugh Rogeley of Couentre cam afore the seyd meire, & all the seyd Wurthymen & p*ro*fered hym to yif enformac*i*on of the seyd mater; & he ther sworne seyd:—that wher Thomas Grene of Couentre enfeffed hym & Nich. Assheburn in the seyd mec*e* to haue to hem & to the Eyres of the seid Nich., that afterward the seyd Nich. confermede the astate of the seyd Hugh to hym & to his heires be a ded there shued. "And wher hit is seyd that I, the seyd Hugh, shuld be my dede rel[e]ce to the seyd Nich. all my right that I hadde in the seyd mece, I neuer relesed ne made dede except oon shued afore all the seyd wurthy men, the which abydethe stille in myn own kepyng & neu*er* was delyu*er*ed be-cause of diu*ers* condic*io*nes broken."

denies that he has released his right in the messuage to Hugh.

And hit is to be had in mynde that the seyd meire, baill*ifs*, & all oder wurthy men aboue named, haue grauntede yif the seyd Hugh dye to record this same mater, yif it be desyred, vnder the sele of the meyralte.

DECREES BY THE COUNCIL.

Sep. 7. 1426. 50 of the Council

[1]Hit is to haue in mynd that in vigill of the Natiuite of our lady thes p*er*sones folowyng, that is to sey, Ric. Joy, Laur. Cook, Joh. Braytoft, Joh. Braunston, Joh. Michell, Hen. Breux, Will. Dilcok, Tho. Wildegryse, Rad. Garton, Joh. Coton, Will. Crosse, Rob. Melburn, Will. Keruer, Will. Wymondeswold, Joh. Bowyer, Joh. Whalley, Ric. Sharp, Joh. Onley, Joh. Clerke, Joh. Warant, Joh.

[1] leaf 40, back.

Egeston, Ric. Botoner, Ric. Bussheburу, Joh. Walgraue, Hugo Rogeley, Joh. Euerdon, Will. Swane, Will. Belgraue, Joh. Ray, Will. Brid, Mat. White, Joh. Frankelen, Benet. Marchall, Joh. Mongomery, Tho. Reyner,[1] Rob. Lirpole, Will. Darset, Joh. Broun, draper, Joh. Runton, Will. Pratte, Will. Byfeld, Joh. Stille, Ad. Suette, Joh. Normanton, Nich. Palmer, Ric. Hykelyng, Joh. Prentes, mercer, Will. Broun, draper, Joh. Grynder, weuer, Joh. Lychefeld, bocher, Rob. Grubber, Will. Peuterer, Joh. Bryd, Joh. Deister, Hen. Sircok, Joh. Sircock, Joh. Bryd, peuterer, Tho. Illage, Nich. Hull, deyster, han ordeyned that the knyghtes[2] expences for this yere shall be payd be the wardens of this Cite, & not be the Chamburlens.

ordain that the knights' expenses be paid by the wardens,

Also they ordeyne that the seyd knyghtes expences, the x li. that the mere hathe yerely, the fee of the Clok, shall heraftur be payd be the wardens, & not be the Chamburlens.

and the same for the mayor's fee of the cloak.

Also they ordeyn, & hit is conformed be the lete, that ther be made a new extent of the murage thorough this Cite be-twene this and Cristmasse.

A new valuation for murage.

MICHAELMAS LEET.

[3]¶ [V. f. p. held on the Wednesday after Michaelmas 5 Hen. VI.] Will. Dilcok, Laur. Coke, Joh. Leder, Tho. Wilgrise, Joh. Braytoft, Rafe Garton, Joh. Parker, draper, Joh. Golofer, Will. Crosse, Hen. Breux, Rob. Milburn, Joh. Bowyer, Joh. Michell, Ric. Bussheburу, Ric. Botoner, Joh. Clerk, Will. Kerver, Joh. Deister, Will. ffrisby, Will. Wymondeswold, Ric. Sharp, Joh. Walgraue, Joh. Runton, Will. Belgraue.

"Couentre." Oct. 2, 1426. Jury.

[Will. Byfeld, Will. Crudworth.]

Bailiffs.

Hit is ordeyned þat no maner man cast no muke nor wede, ne no maner of filth in the watir cald Shirburn; and þat all maner of swyncote, stables & houses for bestes that ben ouer the watir be do awaye, and that all maner of lowpes[4] of stables & of other howeses be stopped vp, on þe peyn of xx s., and of euery defalt aboue-sed xij d.;

Orders of leet. "River Shirbourn," no filth to be cast in it; pigstyes etc. to be done away.

[1] or Reyuer. [2] ? Knights of the shire. [3] leaf 41, back. Scribe B.
[4] A loop-hole, probably a house drain communicating with the water. Not in *N. E. D.* in this sense.

and that þe comen seriant do execucion and rere hit to the vse of þe Citie. And all þe worthymen of the lete beseche the maire that hit be duely kept at her Instaunce; and þat Laur. Coke, Tho. Wilgrise & Joh. Golofre haue þe ouersight fro þe Erlesmill to Laur. Coke mylne; & Will. Dilcok, Hen. Breux, Rob. Milburn, & Ric. Botoner haue þe ouer-sight from þe corner of Adam house[1] Deister to the Erlesmyll; Will. Wymondeswold, Joh. Walgraue, Ric. Phelippes haue þe ouersight of þe water of Welstrete, Bishopstrete & Cokestrete to þe priours mylne, and þat Joh. Bowyer, Joh. Braunston, Rad. Bredon, Tho. Paynell, Tho. Goldesmyth & Joh. Blakeman from the Brodeȝate vnto Bablake-ȝate, & þe watir a both sides þe Brige of Smythford vnto Ad. Deister.

Overseers of the river nominated.

"Butchers' filth."

Also þat no Bochour cary no entrelles of bestes vppon þe ffriday [or 40 d. fine at every default.]

"None te impound Cattel at Chelesmore." "Pinffolds made."

[No man to "pynne" beast at Cheylesmore, or 40 s. fine to the use of the city at every default.]

[Four pinfolds to be made by the wardens in four parts of the city.]

Murage money to be applied only to the town wall.

Also they ordeyn and pray þe mair to extent of new þe murage or Cristmasse next comyng, and þat hit be apployed to þe Towne wall and no otherwyse, nor to non other vse.

"Cunduits Repaired"; no pipe more than a swan pen allowed to run from the conduit.

Also they ordeyn vppon a bill put to theym for þe Condyte that fro þe hedur-ende of þe Brige to þe hed of Cundyte that þe wardeyns haue þe ouersight & þe mendyng of hit, and þe wardes þe other parte, and þat warde þat woll not make þe coste and be founde fauty þat hit be stopped, and þat ther be no pype more then a swan penne.[2]

Ironmongers' horses to be led to water on pain of 4*d.* fine.

Also hit is ordeyned that Iremongers & other resortyng to this Cite with their horsez that they frohensfurth lede their horses to þe water, & not to drive theym for dyuers Incon[uen]iencez þat þeruppon myght fall; and þat þe comen seriant arest euery such horse, & take for a hors iiij d., at euery tyme they do contrarie to þis ordnaunce, to þe vse of þe Chambre.

[1] Correct M.-E. construction; dialectal omission of gen. sing. (Mr. Stevenson).

[2] pen = a quill-like pipe, a tube. v. *N. E. D.*

[Swine going on the common to be impounded in the common pinfold, and not at Cheylesmore.] "Swine to be impounded."

OFFICIALS' ACCOUNTS.

[[1]Tho. Paynell, & Joh. Deyster, 'wolleman,' render accounts before Ric. Joy, & other honest men being present, of their chamberlaincy. The said chamberlains are charged with £84. 3s. 2d., and with £4. 0s. 0d., which John Braytoft delivered them in money by tale (in pecun*iis* num*eratis*), total £88. 3s. 2d. They ask allowance for divers expenses connected with the wall etc. £87. 4s. 0d., and it is allowed them, as appears by the papers in the mayor's bag. And they remain in arrears 19s. 2d.] Jan. 16, 1427. Chamberlains' accounts for 1425. Charge £88. 3*s*. 2*d*. Expenses £87 4*s*. Balance 19*s*. 2*d*.

[On the Monday after the conversion of S. Paul, Ric. Joy, mayor, renders his account before Tho. Wildegryse, Will. Dilcok, Joh. Braytoft, Joh. Golofre, Joh. Bristow, Will. Byfeld, Rad. Garton, Will. Crosse, John Michell, Joh. Coton, Hen. Breux, Rob. Melburn, Joh. Braunston, Joh. Bowyer and Joh. Parker. He is charged with 200 marks, received from John Braytoft & the prior,[2] of which he asks allowance of £103. 0s. 8d.; and is in arrears £30. 6s. 0d. as appears by a paper in the mayor's bag.] Jan. 27, 1427. Mayor accounts before 15 worthy men; charge £133. 6*s*. 8*d*., allowance £103. 0*s*. 8*d*.; balance £30. 6*s*. 0*d*.

GILES ALLESLEY, MAYOR, 1427.

[3]Tempore Egidii Allesley, maioris. Jan. 25.

[Election of new officers.]

Tho. Wildegryse, Will. Dylcok, Ric. Southam, Joh. Leder, Hen. Peyto, Joh. Braytoft, Joh. Golofre, Will. Crosse, Hen. Breux, Joh. Parker, Joh. Michell, Joh. Braunston, Rob. Melburn, Joh. Bowyor, Tho. Paynell, Joh. Deyster, Joh. Onley, Ric. Sharp, Joh. Warant, Joh. Egynton, Joh. Whalley, Ric. Dene, Will. Wymondeswold, Will. Bryd. 24 electors.

[m. Giles Allesley; cor. Joh. Dylcok; ch. Joh. Prentes, Joh. Runton; w. Will. ffrysby, Joh. Doughty; mace, Will. Oxton. Officers.

The following justices of the peace were chosen (electi J. Ps.

[1] leaf 41. [2] v. pp. 103–4. [3] leaf 42.

sunt) by the new mayor, Joh. Weston, rec., Tho. Wyldgrise, Will. Dylcok, Laur. Cook, Hen. Peyto.

Key-keepers. Mar. 1. [The mayor, Tho. Wyldegryse, M. G. S. T., Laur. Cook, Hen. Peyto, Joh. Braytoft.]

ACCOUNTS AND ROYAL DEBTS.

Mar. 1, 1427. Henry IV's debts. Mayor's accounts. [1][Giles Allesley received from Ric. Joy £113. 4s. 4d. of a certain loan made to King Henry IV when Will. Whitchurch was mayor[2]; also £30. 6s. 0d. of the 200 marks received by Joh. Braytoft and Ric. Joy from the prior, as appears in the second leaf preceding.[3]]

3 Jan. ?1428.[5] [4]Mem. þat þe iij day of Januer the forseid Mair did come afore him c*er*tein p*er*sones in sancte Marie Hall, þ*er* beyng þe chirche Reves of senct Mighels of Couentre, and asked of þaym þe dettes þ*at* were owyng of þe tyme of kyng Henri þe iiij to go to þe vse of þe vestiments of þe forseid chirche. And so þei ȝiving good wille g*r*aunted, as a Rolle wole make menc*io*n; the whiche is in þe maires bagge, of þe whiche he askeþ alowance of his charge. S*um*ma[6]

King Henry's debt goes to church vestments in S. Michael's

Also the vj day of ffeuerer[7] þe forseid mair dud calle before hi*m* in senct Nicholas halle men þ*at* were owing of þe T*ri*nite parisshe dyu*er*s somes of time of king Henry þe fourthe to go to þe vce of vestments of þe T*ri*nite chirche. And so þei ȝiving good wille graunted þ*er*to, as a Rolle makeþ menc*io*n, þe whiche is in þe maires bagge, and an oþ*er* þ*at* Si*r* John Heydon haþ in his warde, of the which þe forseid mair askeþ alowance of his charge. S*um*ma xxxv li. v s. j d.

and Trinity churches.

EASTER LEET.

Couentre. May 1, 1427. [8][V. f. p. held before Giles Allesley m., Will. Byfeld and Will. Crudworthe b., on SS. Philip and James 5 Hen. VI.]

Jury. Will. Dilcok, Laur. Coke, Joh. Braytoft, Ric. Joye, Joh.

[1] leaf 42, back. [2] 1399. [3] v. p. 109.
[4] leaf 43. Another scribe, variant of B type.
[5] Year uncertain, v. next entry. [6] Blank in MS.
[7] It could not have been the same mayor in both cases, as the feast of the Purification and beginning of new mayoralty intervenes between this and the last entry. ? read Januer.
[8] leaf 43, back. Scribe B.

Golofer, Joh. Bristowe, Rafe Garton, Will. Crosse, Joh. Michell, Joh. Braunston, Joh. Coton, Joh. Bowyer, Joh. Euerdon, Tho. Paynell, Will. ffrisby, Joh. Runton, Joh. Prentes, Joh. Onley, Joh. Clerk, Joh. Burton, Joh. Doughty, Ric. Sharpe, Will. Birde, Joh. Warant.

Hit is ordeyned that þe Cokes frohensfurth make halpeny pyes as other Townes doth, vppon peyn to lese di*midiam* marc*am*[1] at euery def*alt*. 'Cookes' half a mark, 6*s*. 8*d*. fine.

Also that all man*er* Brewers, Tapsters & hueksters sell goode ale & sufficient, like as the mair ordeyneth, as well withoute house as within, vppon þe peyn of xl d. at eu*er*y def*alt*. 'victualers' 3*s*. 4*d*. fine.

THE DUKE OF GLOUCESTER.

[2]Hit is to haue in mynde that the Thursday next after the Ep*iph*an*ie*,[3] þe yer aboueseyd, the seyd meir, be avise of his Counsell, made com afore hym thes wurthymen foloweng:—Joh. Braytoft, Will. Dylcok, Ric. Southam, Laur. Cook, Hen. Peyto, Tho. Wyldegryse, Ric. Joy, Ric. Sharp, Tho. Paynell, Will. Crosse, Joh. Brystowe, Joh. Mychell, Rad. Garton, Joh. Launde, Nich. Palmer, Joh. Burton, Will. Belg*r*aue, Will. Broke, Hen. Bryd, Joh. Benet, Tho. Wirley, Rob. Praty, Joh. Onley, Joh. Egynton, Joh. Dylcok, Will. Bryd, Will. Swane, Joh. Clerk, Ric. Dene, Will. Cortenhale, Joh. Willowby, Joh. Revell, Ad. Swette, Tho. Reyner, Tho.(?) Glene, Joh. ffrankelen, Joh. Prentes, Joh. Runton, Will. ffrysby, Joh. Doughty, Joh. Warant, Joh. Whalley, Joh. Deyster, Will. Keruer, Mat. White, Will. Pratte, Joh. Broun, Joh. Esex. ? Jan. 9, 1427.[3] ? Aug. 1427. Council of forty-eight.

And then shewed & rad afore hem a letter directed be the duke of Gloucester, Erle of Haynnau etc. p*ro*tector & defensor of Englond, to the meire, Recordour & Bayllies of the Cite of Couentre. The whiche letter folouth in thes word*es*: The Duke of Gloucester's letter.

By the duk of Gloucestre, Erl of Haynnau, & p*ro*tectour & defensour of England.

Trusty and welbeloued, we wol, and in my lordes name and ouris, we charge you that ye shape you that ye be

[1] xl d. deleted. [2] leaf 42, back.
[3] Wrong date. Aug. 10 is date of letter.

Most peremptory! withe vs a Fryday next comyng atte firthist, wher-sumeuer we be, for certayne causes whiche we shull declare vnto you at your comyng. And that ye fayle not hereof in no wyse. Yeven vnder our signet at Leycestre, the x day of August.

To our tristy & welbeloued meire, Bayles, Recordour of the Cite of Couentre.

Mayor and others to go to London the quindene of Michaelmas, and peace to be kept with the Earl of Stafford.

And so the meir, Baylys, Recordour, & many oder wurthy Rydon to Leycestre to his wurthy presence to knowen the entent of his wille. And ther he comaunded the seyd meire, Bayles and Recordour to be at London afore hym the xv of Mich[aelmas] & the mene tyme to kepe the pese ageynest the Erle of Stafford & his.[1] Wherapon thes xlviij wurthy above named ordeyned the seyd meire, Baylis, Recordour, Laur. Cook, Henre Peyto, John Michell shuld ryde to London the seyd xv to the seyd wurthy lorde, and they ordeyned the Costes to be borne to Leycester & to London of the Tresour of this Cite, the whiche is in the seyd meires hondes. The whiche Costes apereth more pleyneley in a paper beyng in the seyd meires bag, beyng in seynt Mary halle.

They go, and the cost is borne by the treasury.

PRIOR'S DEBT.

[(Sept. 29.) The mayor received from Ric. Crosby, prior, 100 marks, and delivered to him his written bond of the same sum.]

MICHAELMAS LEET.

Couentre. Oct. 2, 1427.

[2][V. f. p. held on Thursday after Michaelmas 6 Hen. VI.] Tho. Wylgrise, Will. Dilcok, Ric. Southam, Joh. Braytoft, Ric. Joye, Will. Crosse, Rafe Garton, Hen. Breux, Joh. Michell, Joh. Bowyer, Joh. Coton, Joh. Braunston, Joh. Parker, Joh. Euerdon, Ric. Busshebury, Ric. Botoner, Will. ffrisby, Joh. Onley, Joh. Warant, Joh. Doughty, Joh. Egeston, Joh. Peuterer, Joh. Runton, Joh. Ray.

Bailiffs. [Ric. Sharpe, Tho. Paynell.]

[1] Humphrey, afterwards Duke of Buckingham, and owner of Maxstoke Castle, Warwick; killed at Northampton 1460.

[2] leaf 44.

Hit was ordeyned þ*at* noman ley no more muke at þe cross beyonde the Newe-ȝate, but vppon þe mukhill besid*is* þe crosse vppon the right hande, vppon þe peyn of xij d., and þ*at* hit be rered be þe co*m*en se*r*iant, or els þ*at* hit be stopped vppon the hire of þe seid co*m*en se*r*iant. **Orders of leet. "muck" on the muck-hill.**

Also hit is ordeyned that the Recorder haue his lyu*er*e of þe Trinite Gilde at þe coste of þe Baillifs as hit hath ben aforetyme, and also his lyu*er*e [? hyre] of the Baillifs as hit was before. **The recorder's livery.**

WARDENS' ACCOUNTS.

[1][Joh. Euerdon and Will. ffrisby account before Giles Allesley for the years 1425 and 1426, and are charged with the foot of the account (cum pede compoti) of Joh. Michell and Joh. Euerdon £24. 13s. 2½d.[2] and with £123. 17*s.* 0*d.* Total £148. 10s. 2½d.

They ask allowance for repair of houses, chief rents,[3] and other divers expenses, for the first year £38. 18s. 4d. The same for the second £72. 15s. 5d. And for vacancies (vac*ancionibus*) the first year £4. 7s. 3d.; and the second year for the same £2. 12s. 0d. And for arrears of rent the first year £1. 9s. 3d., and for the second year £1. 10s. 4d.; and for money given to the tenants for two years 7s. 7d., and for a certain breakfast (quodam iantac*ulo*) 6s. 6d., and for the clerk 3s. 4d. Also they ask allowance of £4. 2s. 7d. of the foot of the account of the said John Michell and John Euerdon because it could not be levied. Sum total £126. 12s. 7d. And so they remain in arrears £21. 17s. 6½d.[4]] **Expenses which appear in their book in the mayor's bag.** **Sum of allowances £126. 12*s*. 7*d*. Balance £21 17*s*. 6½*d*.**

JOHN BRISTOWE, MAYOR, 1428.

[5][Election of officers.] **Jan. 25, 1428. 24 electors.**

Joh. Braytoft, Will. Dilcok, Ric. Southam, Hen. Peyto, Tho. Wyldegryse, Ric. Joy, Will. Crosse, Joh. Parker, Rad. Garton, Hen. Breux, Joh. Bowyer, Ric. Sharp, Tho. Peynell, Will. Byfeld, Ric. Busshebury, Ric. Boton*er*, Joh. Euerdon, Joh. Onley, Joh. Clerk, Will.

[1] leaf 43. [2] v. p. 101. [3] Quit-rents.
[4] It should be £21. 17s. 7½d. [5] leaf 45.

Keru*er*, Joh. Deyster, Will. Belgraue, Joh. Coton,[1] Joh. Warant.

Officers. [m. Joh. Brystowe; cor. Joh. Doughty; ch. Joh. Lychefeld, grazier, and Joh. Stille, deyster; w. Will. ffrysby and Joh. Doughty; mace, Will. Oxton.

J. P.s elected by the mayor. [2]Joh. Weston, rec., Laur. Cook, Will. Dilcok, Hen. Peyto, Joh. Braytoft, Tho. Wildegrise.

Key-keepers. The same, except the recorder.]

WARDENS' ACCOUNTS.

? Jan. 28, 1428, or Jan. 26, 1429. [3]Mem. that Will. ffrysby & John Doughty, wardenes of this Cite,[4] haue acounted be-fore John[5] Brystowe, meire, & oder worthi on the Wednesday next after seynt Poule day of the tyme of Giles Allesley beeng meire.

Charge £83 16*s*. 1½*d*. Atte whiche accounte thei were charged withe iiij^{xx} iij li. xvj s. j d. ob. S*um*ma on*er*aci*on*is iiij^{xx} iij li. xvj s. j d. ob.

allowance £56 4*s*. 2*d*. Wherof thei aske alowans of lvj li. iiij s. ij d. of bates[6] & oder discharges, as hit aperithe in a boke beeng in John Bristowes bag in seynt Mary halle.

£2 6*s*. 2*d*. for poverty, etc. Also they aske alowance of xlvj s. ij d. that myght not be leued for pou*er*te & oder causes. S*um*ma allocaci*on*is

£58 10*s*. 4*d*. lviij li. x s. iiij d.

And so thei abyden in arrerage & clere dete xxv li. v s.

balance owed £25 5*s*. 9½*d*. ix d. ob. S*um*ma arrerag*ii* xxv li. v s. ix d. ob.

EASTER AND MICHAELMAS LEETS.

"Couentre" Apr. 15, 1428. [7][V. f. p. held before Joh. Bristowe m., Ric. Sharp, and Tho. Paynell b., on Thursday after the close of Easter.]

Jury. Joh. Braytoft, Will. Dilcok, Tho. Wilgrise, Ric. Joye, Rad. Garton, Will. Crosse, Hen. Breux, Rob. Milburn, Joh. Michell, Joh. Coton, Will. Byfeld, Joh. Bowyer, Joh. Onley, Will. ffrisby, Joh. Clerk, Joh. Doughty, Will. Keruer, Joh. Stylle, Joh. Warant, Joh. Whalley, Ric. Boton*er*, Joh. Lichefeld, Joh. Ronton, Joh. Prentes.

[1] or Coton*er*.
[2] The mayor's name should be included.
[3] leaf 46. [4] In 1427. [5] repeated.
[6] *N. E. D.* deduction, diminution, abatement. This example is earlier than the one there given.
[7] leaf 45, back.

Hit is ordeyned that Will. Wymondeswold fey[1] & clense his diches betwen Mich-graunpesfeld and Litel-graunpesfeld betwixt þis & þe Crossedayes,[2] vppon þe peyn of xx s. to þe vse of the Towne.

[3][V. f. p. held on Monday after Michaelmas 7 Hen. VI.] Joh. Braytoft, Will. Dilcok, Laur. Coke, Hen. Peyto, Tho. Wilgrise, Will. Crosse, Hen. Breux, Rob. Melburn, Joh. Michell, Joh. Braunston, Rad. Garton, Joh. Warant, Will. Byfeld, Joh. Bowyer, Joh. Parker, draper, Ric. Bottoner, Ric. Busshebury, Joh. Ronton, Joh. Egeston, Joh. Stille, Joh. Lychefeld, Will. ffrysby, Joh. Onley, Joh. Doughty. "Couentre" Oct. 4, 1428.

[Joh. Clerk, Joh. Euerdon.] Bailiffs.

Hit is ordeyned þat no maner huxster by no maner of vitaill þat cometh to þe Cite till hit be xj of þe Clok, vppon þe peyn at euery defalt to lose xl d. Orders of leet. Hucksters; 40d. fine.

Also þe ordeyn þat John Bretayn shall haue yerely whils he is Clerk of the Wardeyns xxvj s. viij d., with that he be abidyng & dwellyng within þis Cite. The wardens' clerk's fee.

Also they ordeyn þat no wiredrawer within þis Cite make no caue ne ordynaunce, but þat all journeymen of þe seid Crafte shall worch in their owne housez at their owne lust, vppon þe peyn þat who-so doth þe contrarie forfet Cs. at euery defalt, & that caue so made be theym be dampned, & had for nought. "Wier-drawers"; journeymen to work in their own houses.

At which lete þer was a bill put vp be þe priour to haue had seuerall Sacherscroft, Cristes-crofte,[4] alia pastura iuxta Blaklane, alia pastura iuxta Quetesforde, Swannes-crofte, Spitelcrofte, & le Conynger[5] in Hasilwode. Que peticio respectuatur. "Comons or Lamas Ground." The prior's petition is respited.

[6]Hit is to haue in mynde that at [this leet] the smythes of Couentre put vp a bille foloweng in thes wordes :— "Smiths pageant";[7]

To you fullwurshipfull Meir, Recordour, bayles, & to all your discrete counsell, shewen to you the craft of Smythes how thei were discharged of the Cotelers pachand be a lete in the tyme of John Gote than meire,[8] & The smiths complain

[1] To clean out.
[2] *N. E. D.* Rogation days; or the three days before Ascension day.
[3] leaf 46, back. [4] v. Corp. MS. C 62.
[5] *N. E. D.* a rabbit-warren. [6] leaf 45, back.
[7] On this pageant v. Sharp, *Mysteries,* and Hardin Craig, *Corpus Christi Plays* (E. E. T. S.), 82–91. [8] 1420.

quytances made be-twene the forseid craftes oder to oder, lik as hit is well knowen & redy for to shewe. And now late Giles Allesley in his office of meyralte preyed the forseid craft of smythes to take the gouernaunce of the seid pachand as for his tyme & no forther. And the seid craft did hit wilfully[1] to his plesaunce; for the whiche cause the forseid pachand is yete put to the forseid craft, & thei han no maner of dute to tak hit to hem. Wyche thei beseche that ye of your grete goodnes discharge the forseid craft of smythes of the pachand atte reuerence of God & of Truthe, and orden hit elles where ye ben better avised be your good discression.

that they are forced to produce a pageant, from which burden they had previously been discharged;

The whiche bull (*sic*) be the avise of all the wurthy of the seid lete, and all oder apon the same lete beeng, was onsuered & endosed in this wise:—Hit is ordeyned that the smythes shull ocupie the seid pachand forthe euery yere, apon the payne of x li. to be payd at euery defaute to the vse of the chambur.

the leet insist upon their continuing the practice.

OFFICIALS' ACCOUNTS.

[2][Ric. Botoner & Ric. Busshebury, late chamberlains, render accounts before the mayor.] And the Cite is founden in arrerage to the seid Chamburlenes xj li. xvij s. ix d., as hit aperith in a paper beeng in the seid meires bag. Summa xj li. xvij s. ix d.

The city owes the chamberlains for the year 1426 £11 17*s*. 9*d*.

Hit is to haue in mynd that John Brystowe hathe reseyued of Giles Allesley xxxviij li. of the money of the Cite, of the whiche summa xx li. he payd to the makyng of the hed of the condite, for the whiche xx li. John Onley is bonden be obligacion to pay x li. at Michelmas, the vii yere of the kyng that nowe is, & x li. at Michelmas then next foloweng, and the remenaunt is xviij li.

The mayor's money; £38 0*s*. 0*d*.

£20 paid for the work at the conduit;

balance £18 0*s*. 0*d*.

Also the seid John Brystowe hathe reseyued of the priour of Couentre at Ester the vij yere of the kyng that now is C. marc'.[3]

Prior's debt: 100 marks.

[1] Willingly, voluntarily.

[2] leaf 46.

[3] v. *supra*, p. 104.

LAURENCE COOK, MAYOR, 1429.

[1][Election of Officers.] 1429.[2]

Will. Dilcok,[3] Tho. Wildegrise,[3] Joh. Braytoft,[3] Ric. Joy, Egid. Allesley, Ric. Sharp, Joh. Clerk, Joh. Euerdon, Tho. Paynell, Joh. Coton, Hen. Breux, Joh. Braunston, Rob. Melburn, Joh. Bowyer, Will. Crosse, Rad. Garton, Joh. Egeston, Joh. Prentes, Joh. Ronton, Ric. Botoner, Ric. Dene, Joh. Onley, Will. Bryd, Joh. Warant. 24 electors.

[m. Laur. Cook ;[3] cor. Joh. Whalley ; ch. Joh. Launde and Tho. Crosse ; w. Will. ffrysby and Ric. Dene ; mace, Will. Oxton. Officers.

Joh. Weston, rec., Hen. Peyto, and see note.[3] J. Ps.

The same without rec.] Key-keepers.

MAYOR'S ACCOUNTS.

[4][In the presence of the following 48 worthy persons, Joh. Brystowe delivered to Laur. Cook, mayor, the prior's Easter payment for the sixth year of Henry VI, 100 marks ; also he delivered to him £18. 0*s*. 0*d*.[5]] Jan. 24, 1429.

Tho. Wildegryse, Hen. Peyto, Joh. Braytoft, Will. Crosse,[6] Joh. Golofre,[6] Joh. Dilcok, Joh. Whalley, Joh. Coton,[6] Joh. Prentes, mercer, Will. Bryd, Joh. Clerk, Will. Byfeld, Ric. Dene, Bened. Marchall, Joh. Welford, Ric. Sharp, Joh. Warant, Will. Swanne, Rad. Garton, Joh. Michell, Joh. Euerdon, Will. Belgraue, Joh. Willowby, Tho. Reyner, Joh. ffrankelen, Joh. Ronton, Ric. Busshebury, Joh. Bristowe, Joh. Onley, Joh. Bowyer, Joh. Braunston, Joh. Egeston, Tho. Paynell,[6] Joh. Broun, draper, Will. Keruer, Joh. Deyster, Joh. Benet, wirdrawer, Ric. Botoner, Hen. Breux, Rob. Melburn, Ric. Joy, Will. Dilcok, Joh. Stille, Joh. Doughty, Ric. Southam, Will. Wymondeswold, Joh. Lychefeld, bocher, Joh. Walgraue, Will. Staunton, Ric. Phelippes. The Forty-eight ; really 50 names.

EASTER LEET.

[[7]V. f. p. on Tuesday after the close of Easter 7. H. VI, before the mayor.[8]] Apr. 5, 1429.

[1] leaf 47. [2] No day given. [3] J. Ps.
[4] leaf 47, back. [5] v. p. 116. [6] A cross by these names.
[7] leaf 48. Another scribe of B. type.
[8] Names of jury and bailiffs omitted in MS.

Orders of leet. "Shirbourn." Mayor to oversee the brook.

Atte whiche lete among oder was ordeyned that the meyre shuld go be all the brooke, & se where hit is narowed, mysruled, or stopped, or encroched, & that hit be amended be his discression.

Actions at law to be brought in the city courts only.

Also they ordeyne that no man of this Cite sue non oder of the same Cite that is sufficiant withe-Inne this Cite, but only atte co*m*en lawe at Westm[ynstre], or elles withe-Inne this Cite [or 100 s. fine to go to the town-wall from any one "foundon fawty."]

Master Pynchard, schoolmaster.

Also they ordeyne that mayster John Pynchard, skolemayster of Grammer, shall haue the place that he duelleth Inne for xl s. ye yere, whyles that he duellithe In hit & holdythe gramer skole hym-self ther-Inne.

New assessment of murage.

[1] Also the murage be nowe extent be avyse of the mair, and that they þ*at* haue lande pay for their lande; and they that haue non that they be extent be advyse of þe mair*e* & hir agrement afor*e* their good*es*; and yf they woll not agree therto, that then they be extent be þe mair & his Counceill.[1]

MICHAELMAS LEET.

Oct. 3, 1429.

[V. f. p. before the same on Monday after Michaelmas 8. H. VI.[2]]

Orders of leet.

Town-ditch.

Atte whiche lete was ordeyned that no man cast non erthe ne oder fylthe in the town dyche [or 40 d. fine] to be rered to the vse of the town walle[3] be the co*m*en se*r*iaunt, be ouer-syght of the meyre & chamburlenes.

Sergeaunt taken in adultery.

Also they ordeyne that no se*r*iaunt ne oder officer taken in avowtery be no more officer, but that he be put out of her office at what tyme they or ony of hem ben founden in suche defaute.

Hermitage at Gosford-gate.

Also they ordeyne that the Ermytage withe-out the Gosford-yat be vsed as an hermytage, & that the meyre for the tyme beyng put in that place what Ermyte he wille, so that he be of honest conue*r*saci*o*n & vertues man.

Swearing at the leet.

[4]Also they orden that eue*r*y man at eue*r*y lete be

1–1 Scribe B. 2 MS. omits names.

3 The town-wall seems to have required much repair about this time. Perhaps it had been badly damaged during the quarrel with the Earl of Stafford.

4 leaf 48, back.

sworn that comyth vpon the grete enquest, except meyrez & baylyves that shullen [? be] charged after the old custome.

Also they orden that al-maner men of this Cite that may bere pay to the murage for ther godes as oder men don for her lond, as hit is graunted be the kynges patent[1]; and that the meyre take in eue*r*y warde iiij pe*r*sones suche as hym thynkethe best for to extent & assesse al-tho that han no lond in eue*r*y warde be tho iiij pe*r*sones, that the meyre takethe of the warde that they duell Inne.

The mayor to take four persons in every ward to assess the murage.

Also they ordeyne that the meyre serche the brooke, & lat cast down all mane*r* stakes and oder that letten the cours of the water, & that no man cast no muk ne weede ne non oder fylthe in to the co*m*en water, apon the peyne of di*m*. mark at eue*r*y defaut to be rered be the co*m*en se*r*iaunt to the vse of town walle, be oue*r*sight of the meyre. And that the co*m*en se*r*iaunt eue*r*y Saturday do serche eue*r*y mannes house be the broke, & certyfye the meyre as he fyndythe, apon the peyne of losyng of his office; & that the meyre execute hit in all haste witheouten ony grace.

No filth in the water or "River Shirbourn." 6s. 8d. fine.

[Privies and purprestures in or upon the Red-ditch to be done away with by certain persons assigned by the mayor. No more to be made there on pain of half a mark to the town wall. The common sergeant ordered to search it every week.]

"Red-dich."

TALBOT'S RANSOM.

Hit is to haue in mynde that for the Rawunsome of the lorde Talbote[2] thez gode men of the Cite of Couentre folowyng han ȝyvon to his Rawnsom wyth ale her gode hertes.

Gift towards Talbot's ransom.

[Joh. Bristowe, Joh. Leder, Tho. Wildegrise, Joh. Braytoft, Hen. Peyto, Ric. Southam, Will. Byfeld, 20 s. each; Ric. Joy, Joh. Braunston, Ric. Sharp, 13s. 4d. each; Rad. Garton, Joh. Eue*r*ton, Rob. Melburn, Joh. Mychell, Will. Carver, Hen. Syrcok, Joh. Cater, Thom. Dawe, Will.

[1] 38. Ed. III, p. 2, m. 32 (Dugdale 98).
[2] John Talbot, Earl of Shrewsbury, taken prisoner at Patay, June 18, 1429; killed at Castillon 1453.

Swanne, 6s. 8d. each; Joh. Bowyer, Will. Crudworth, Joh. Shadd, Joh. Ronten, Joh. Alen, Ric. Busshebury, Joh. Revell, Mat. White, 3s. 4d. each. Tho. Paynell 40s.
£15 6*s*. 8*d*. Total 23 marks.]

COLLECTION OF A FIFTEENTH.

[1]xv peny payd in tyme of Laurence Cooke beeng meyre, graunted at a p*ar*lyment holden in the terme of Mich[aelmas], the yere of kyng Henry the vj the viij.[2]

Collectors. Gosford-strete.

Will. Bryddesmere, Bened. Marshall, Joh. Stafford,
£5 16*s*. 0*d*. Joh. Baker, deyst*er*. S*um*ma v li. xvj s.

Jurden-well.

Joh. Cressy, Joh. ffreman, Joh. Lee, Rob. Derford.
£5 2*s*. 0*d*. S*um*ma v li. ij s.

Muche-park-stre*te*.

Will. Bryd, Will. Cortenhale, Will. Charlton, Joh. Lee,
£5 0*s*. 0*d*. Smyth. S*um*ma v li.

Bayly-lane.

Joh. Harborgh, Joh. Merston, Joh. Spenser, Tho.
£3 10*s*. 0*d*. Peuterer. S*um*ma iij li x s.

Erl-strete.

Ad. Suette, Tho. Reyner, Will. Belg*r*aue, Nich. Palmer.
£5 13*s*. 8*d*. S*um*ma v li. xiij s. viij d.

Brod-yate.

Tho. Draper, Rog. Wales, Rob. Saxton, Rob. Praty.
£2 6*s*. 8*d*. S*um*ma xlvj s. viij d.

Smyth-[ford-strete.]

Joh. Tate, Joh. Blakemon, Ad. Dyer, Ric. Hykelyng.
£4 0*s*. 0*d*. S*um*ma iiij li.

Spon-strete.

Ric. Walford, Joh. Broun, Mat. Whyte, Joh. Sysseter.
£5 13*s*. 8*d*. S*um*ma v li. xiij s. viij d.

[1] leaf 50, back. [2] Rot. Parl. IV. 336.

Cros-ch[eaping].

Will. Darsette, Joh. Halle, Ric. Chapman, Will. Bromwyche. S*um*ma vij li. v s. £7 5s. 0d.

Bysshop[-strete].

Will. Wymondeswold, Joh. Grynder, Hen. Knot, Ric. ffylyppes. S*um*ma v li. xiij s. £5 13s. 0d.

MAYOR'S ACCOUNTS.

[1][Laur. Cook paid away the prior's 100 marks, received from his predecessor Jan. 24] vnto certen p*er*sones that lant the seyd C. marc' to the sege of Harflete in the tyme of the seyd Laurence fyrst beyng meyre.[2]

Jan. 24, 1429.

100 marks lent to the siege of Harfleur, 1415, repaid.

Also the seyd Laurence hathe reseyued of John Bristow xviij li. [and] thus is spended: & first delyv*er*ed to John Clerk & John Euerdon, then bayles, iij li. for poor men that weren endited in the kynges benche & might not pay her fynes.[3] Also to Will*iam* Repynton 10 mark for brynge*r* of an C. li. fro the duke of Bedford, tho whiche was oweng to the Cite of Couentre. Also gyven to a messenger of the seyd duke of Bedford for bryngyng *lett*res to the seyd meyre & oder wurthy out of ffraunce, xxvj s. viij d. Also to iij mynstrelles of the kynges xx s. And to iij Trumpettes of the kynges xx s. Also to iij mynstrelles of the quenes x s. And the residu of the money spended apon the makyng of the Town dyche, & the spey[r][4] atte Gosford yate.

Mayor's further expenses; £3 to poor men endited at the King's Bench: to the duke's messenger £6 13s. 4d.; to another £1 6s. 8d.; the king's and queen's minstrels.

Hit is to haue in mynde that the seyd Lauraunce, meyre, in the fest of seynt Thom*as* of Caunte*r*bury last past, hathe reseyued of Will*iam* Repynton, auditur of the duke of Bedford, C li. of the su*m*me of the CC li., the whiche was lante to seyd Duke the tyme of Adam Deyste*r* beyng meyre.[5] The whyche C li. the seyd Laurance hathe payd to hem that lant hit withe-Inne iij wekes after that he reseyued hyt.[6]

July 7 or Dec. 29. The Duke of Bedford pays up £100.

[1] leaf 50.

[2] Cook was mayor 1415. Harfleur surrendered to Henry V Sept. 22, 1415.

[3] Probably on occasion of the Lollard rising under Grace the hermit, v. *supra*, p. 97.

[4] ? Spar = a bar or beam to fasten a door. *v.* E. D. D.

[5] Adam Huyton or Deyster mayor 1419.

[6] Some erasures here.

A further payment of the prior—100 marks—returned to Henry V.'s creditors. Siege of Harfleur 1415.

Hit is to haue in mynd that the seyd Laurance, meyre, hathe reseyved of the priour of Coventre C marc' for the payment of Ester the vij yere of kyng Herry the syxt; the whyche was lant to the sege of Harflete in the tyme of the seyd Laurence fyrst beyng meyre. And the seyd C marc' the seyd Lauraunce, meyre, hathe payd & delyu*er*ed at the fest of Cristmas last past vnto hem that lant hit; and the cause why hit was so long vnpayd was for the seyd meyre cowd not gete hit payd of the p*r*iour but at iij paymentes, & the last payment was a litell afore the seyd Crystmas.

The dilatory prior.

THO. PAYNELL, MAYOR, 1430.

Jan. 25.

[1][Election of officers.]

Electors.

Joh. Bristowe, Joh. Leder, Tho. Wildgr*i*se, Joh. Braitofte, Ric. Joy, Egid. Allesley, Ric. Sharp, Joh. Prentes, Ric. Boton*er*, Rad. Garton, Joh. P*ar*ker, Joh. Braunston, Joh. Clerke, Joh. Eu*er*don, Joh. Bowyer, Joh. Ronton, Joh. Egynton, Joh. Doughty, Joh. Warrant, Joh. Dilcoke, Will. Belgraue, Will. Bryde, Joh. Tate, Joh. Frankelen.

Officers.

[m. Tho. Paynell; cor. Joh. Whalley; ch. Will. Swane and Hen. Sircoke; w. Ric. Dene and Joh. Warrant; mace, Will. Oxton.

J. Ps.

Tho. Paynell, Joh. Weston, rec., Laur. Coke, Will. Dilcoke, Tho. Wyldegryse.

Key-keepers.

Tho. Paynell, Laur. Cooke, Tho. Wildegrise, Joh. Braytofte, Will. Dilcoke, Hen. Peytoo.]

[A letter was sent to the mayor and community about lending the king a notable sum; whereof the tenor is as follows:—

[2]Memorand*um* q*uo*d ista subsc*r*ipt*a* *lit*era miss*a* fuit maior*i* & co*mm*unibus ciuit*atis* Couen*trie* ad p*r*estand*um* do*min*o Reg*i* quand*am* notabil*em* su*m*ma*m*; cuiu*s* *lit*ere tenor sequit*ur* in hec u*er*ba:—

REQUEST FOR LOAN.

[Mar. 1, 1430.

[The king who, with the aid of our Blessed Creator, pro-

Chiers & b*ie*nz amez, come p*u*r lexploite de la viage, quell a laide de n*ost*re benoit c*r*eature no*us* p*u*rpos-

[1] leaf 52. Scribe A. [2] leaf 55.

poses to go over to France the next April,
to put short end to the war, as he earnestly desires,

wishes to be provided in all haste with a notable sum of money,
as will be shown to them by the reverent father in God, the Bishop of Chester, the Earl of Warwick, the Lady of Abergavenny,
Ferrers of Groby, the Prior of Coventry, Will. Mountforde, Barth. Brokesby, Joh. Weston, and the Sheriff of Warwick and Leicester, who by the Council's advice have been

jointly and severally assigned by letters and commissions under the Great Seal
to treat about this loan of a notable sum,
to be lent to the king in this great necessity. The commissioners have authority to promise repayment in the king's name,
to come from the fifteenth

granted by parliament,

to be paid in the following

ames far*e* en n*ostre* p*er*sone en le mois davrell[1] p*ro*chein venaunt, viers n*ost*re realme de Fraunce, p*ur* y metter breffe fyn et conclusionz a nous g*u*errez, ainsi come souer*eig*n*e*ment le desirons, nous couiendra necessarement estre p*u*ruoux a tout bon haste dun notable sume de money, sicome plus au plein vous exposeront de par nous le reuer*e*nt pier en Dieu, leuesq*e* de Cestre, & nos tr*e*schi*er*es & foiaxl (*sic*) cosenes, le counte de Warwik et le (*sic*) dame de Be[r]geuenny, & nous treschi*er*es & foialx le S*ieur* sire (*sic*) de Ferrers de Groby, le p*r*ioure de Couentre[2] & Will*iam* Mountforte, Chiualer,[3] Bartholemew Brokesby,[4] John Weston,[5] & nostre vicounte de nos countes de Warr[ewik] & Leic[estre], lesquex de lauis & assent de nostre counsell auo*m*z assignez iointment & seu*er*almen*t* p*ar* nous l*et*trez & co*m*missionez desouz n*ost*re graund seale p*ur* co*mmun*iquier & treter ouesq*e* vous de & sur le cheua*u*nce dune Notable[6] sume de money a nous ap*r*estre en cest n*ost*re g*r*aunte neccessite, & p*ur* vous p*ro*mitter p*ur* & en no*str*e noun sufficiant suertie & repaiment de l*e* dit sume de lez deners p*r*ouena*u*ntz de la quinzeisme de n*os*tre darrein p*a*rlement, p*ar* lez co*mmun*es de cest n*ost*re Realme a nous graunte, & a nous a paye[r] a le fest de seint Marten en Iuerne p*r*ochein venant, solonc

[1] MS. looks like darrell. [2] Ric. Croseby. [3] Of Coleshill, *v.* Dugd. 717.
[4] *ib.* 732. He was in 1419 Sheriff of Warwickshire, and one of the executors of Lady Bergavenny's will.
[5] Serjeant-at-law; he held lands in Wolston and Weston: *ib.* 25, 209, 541.
[6] *i. e.* a sum to be noted and repaid.

Martinmas.

[The recipients of the letter are urgently requested that for the advancement of this, the king's first, journey which, with the Creator's aid, will turn to the good and tranquillity of all the king's loyal subjects, they will quickly provide a notable sum and that avowrey, and send it by a trusty messenger to the treasurer at London, between then and Easter following. The treasurer, by authority of parliament, will give them such security of repayment as will content them withal.

[They are entreated not to fail the king in this great necessity, as they desire his honour and welfare, and the final salvation of his realms, giving credence to what the commissioner or commissioners will expound to them on the king's behalf. Given under the privy seal at Westminster on March 1.

[The letter having been heard and understood, the mayor, bailiffs and community consented to lend £100;

leffett & contenue dun ait (*sic*) pur money a nous aprestre en mesme *nostre* par*leament sur ce faite. Si vous p*ri*omez trescheirment quen avauncement de cest n*ostr*e p*r*imer viage, que ia a leid de n*ostr*e benoit creature turnera au bien & t*r*anquillite de nous & de vous & de toutz nos autrez bonez & loialx subiectz, Prendre vois voilez le pluis p*rest* q*e* bonement fair le purres en nous eidant a cest foitz *par* voie dapprestre dun somme notable, & icelle auourey,[1] de qui vous vous confies enueier & delyu*erer* a n*ostr*e Tresorer dengleter a Loundrez p*ar*entre cy & le fest de Paschq*e* p*ro*cheine vena*unt*; lui quel n*ostr*e t*re*sorer p*ar* autorite de n*ostr*e dit p*ar*lement vous ferra tiell & sufficiaunt suertie de Repayment de le dit somme q*e* de reason vous en *ser*rez contens. & cest chose p*ren*dre voilez t*re*sp*re*s a coer saunz nous en failer en cest n*ostr*e graund necessite, come vous desires lonneur et b*ie*n de nous & la finall soluc*io*n ?[saluacion] de nous Realmez: En adioustant meintenains foy et c*r*edens a nous ditz co*m*missarez & a ch*a*cun de eux, en ce quels vous exposeront ou aucum de eux vous exposera en cest matier de par nous. Done sus n*ostr*e priue seale a Westm[oustre], le prim*our* Jour de Mars.

Visuq*ue*[2] (*sic*) l*itt*era p*re*dict*a* & intellect*a*, Tho. Paynell, m., ball*ivi* & co*mmun*it*as* concesseru*n*t p*re*stare d*omi*no Reg*i* centum libras, ut p*atet*

[1] Word uncertain. *v.* Gloss.
[2] Error for visaque.

and the money was delivered to W. Hungerford, the treasurer, by L. Cooke, who had £3 for his expenses.]

foliis p*re*cedent*ibus*[1]; & p*ost*ea p*re*dict*e* cent*um* libre delib*er*at*e* fuer*unt* Walt*er*o Hung*ur*forde, Thes*aurario* d*omi*ni Reg*is*, p*er* man*us* Laure*ncii* Cooke; & iidem (*sic*) Laure*ncius* h*ab*uit p*ro* suo costag*io* inde ad tu*n*c fact*o* iij li. Su*mm*a iij li.

[[2]The following lent £100 to the king, Mar. 15.]

Mar. 15, 1430. 48 names.

Gosforde-[strete].

	£	s.	d.		£	s.	d.		£	s.	d.
Laur. Cooke	1	6	8	Sim. Deyster		5	0	Joh. Stafford		10	0
Tho. Wildegrise	1	6	0	Joh. Euesham		6	0	Ric. Molle		1	8
Joh. Breten		13	4	Will. Abram		1	8	Hugo Spenc*er*		1	8
Joh. Stille		6	8	Rob. Kyng		3	4	Joh. Sheldon		6	8
Nic. Heywood		3	4	Wal. Bond		1	8	Ad. Baxster		10	0
Tho. Smyth		3	0	Rob. Thomas		3	4	Will. Bagett		3	4
Joh. Straunge		1	8	Joh. Melton		1	8	Rob. Danyell		1	8
Bened. Marshall		6	8	Joh. Baker		6	8	Tho. Weue			
Will. Mason		1	0[3]	Ric. Skott		6	8	[?Weu*er*]		1	8
Joh. Stretton		6	8	Joh. Langton		1	8	Joh. Castell		3	0
Tho. Mason		5	0	Joh. Braban		6	8	Ric. Beller		1	8
And. Evesham		6	8	Joh. Wright		1	8	Hen. Coton*er*		3	4
Rob. Wildegrise		3	4	*Christ*ian Crosse		5	0	Hen. Skyll		5	0
Ric. Somur		4	0	Will. Ing		2	0	Tho. Dawe		6	8
Joh. Manton		1	8	Will. Cocke		3	4	Joh. Breust*er* de			
Ric. Cook*es*		2	0	Will. Rothewell		1	8	Priorat*u*		1	8
*Christ*ian Golofre		5	0	Tho. Stoone		4	0	Su*mm*a £12 3*s.* 8*d.*			

57 names.

Jurden-well.

	£	s.	d.		£	s.	d.		£	s.	d.
Ric. Hampton		4	0	Truston[4]		2	0	Rob. Clerke		3	4
Joh. Cressy		5	0	Tho. Dykons		4	0	Rob. Baxster		1	8
Joh. Shade		5	0	Ric. Adam		1	8	M*ar*geria Godfray		1	8
Joh. Symiond		4	0	Joh. Gamill		1	8	Joh. Lee		0	8
Joh. Sutton		4	0	Will. Coope		7	0	Tho. Grome		2	0
Rob. Grene		3	4	Nic. Gore		6	8	Joh. Rocheford		6	8
Tho. Illage		3	4	Tho. Gamill		2	0	Joh. Hawkyns		2	6
Will. Gale		2	6	Will. Bett		4	0	Joh. Wyllnale		1	8
Joh. ffreman		1	8	Joh. Heywoode		1	8	Joh. Whalley		7	6
Ric. Rocheford		2	0	Tho. Thruston[4]		4	0	Will. Harborugh		2	6
Joh. Croke		5	0	Joh. Ashewell		7	0	Joh. Car*t*er		7	0
Ric. Mildenall		3	0	Joh. Wilde		4	0	Joh. Bryan		6	8
Hugo Cowp*er*		1	8	Ric. Plumer		4	0	Joh. Prentes		10	0
Will. Deist*er*		6	8	Will. Eue		2	0	Joh. Dilcocke		7	6
Joh. Abram		6	8	Wal. Eton			10	Tho. Elderbek		3	4
Will. Wright		2	0	Joh. Egull		1	8	Rob. Defford		4	0
Tho. Maideford		5	0	Joh. Maidford		2	0	Joh. Freman		2	6
Joh. Plumer			10	Joh. Franklen		5	0	Su*mm*a £10 14*s.* 4*d.*			
Joh. Lacy		1	8	Joh. Woode		1	8				
Joh. Par*k*yn		2	0	Will. Shurley		5	0				

[1] See the list of names that follows. [2] leaf 52, back. [3] or 1*s.* 8*d.*

[4] *v.* p. 87, Thrustanus Walker.

44 names. **Much-pa*r*ke-strett.**

	£	*s.*	*d.*		£	*s.*	*d.*		£	*s.*	*d.*
Will. Bryde		5	0	Joh. Attwell		1	8	Ric. Hobbes		1	8
Ed. Sharman		1	8	Joh. Le, smythe		4	0	Joh. Braytoft		13	4
Tho. T*u*rnor		1	8	Tho. Crose		6	8	Will. Cortnale		3	4
Ric. Dene		6	8	Ric. Smythe		1	8	Will. Osburn		1	8
Will. Grene		1	8	Joh. Darby		3	4	Tho. Tyler		1	8
Joh. Ray		1	8	Tho. Warmynton		4	0	Johanna Coton*er*		6	8
Joh. Follipoot		3	4	Will. Libard		2	0	Ric. Knightley		2	0
Joh. Clerke		13	4	Ric. Staffordshire		2	0	Rog. Shipston		1	8
Hen. Peitoo	1	3	4	Wal. Neuton		2	0	Gossnore, passynger		3	4
Vx*or* Freman		1	8	Tho. Yorke, peynt*er*		3	4	Hen. Bug		2	0
Tho. Walsall, weu*er*		1	8	[1] Will. Charlton		3	4	Will. Southam		5	0
Joh. Leder	1	3	4	Joh. Cale[2]		1	8	Will. Warde		1	8
Will. Bifelde		16	8	Will. Cleibrooke		3	4	S*um*ma £10 10*s*. 0*d*.			
Joh. North[a]mpton		1	8	Will. Heys		3	0				
Hen. Hobbys		3	4	Nic. Gryve		5	0				
Rob. Hendman		1	8	Will. Glasier		2	0				

66 names. **Erle-street.**

	£	*s.*	*d.*		£	*s.*	*d.*		£	*s.*	*d.*
Tho. Swane		3	4	Will. Crose		1	8	Tho. Slonne[3]		3	4
Will. Waren		2	6	Joh. Chacombe		1	8	Joh. Radeley		1	8
Joh. Holy		1	8	Ed. Brogreve		1	8	Joh. Chaundeler		4	0
Joh. Wilowby		1	8	Joh. Eu*er*don		8	0	Joh. Revell		1	8
Ric. Bifeld		1	8	Joh. Burton		10	0	Joh. Malory		3	4
Joh. Warrant		5	0	Tho. Suettenham		1	8	Will. Stocke		1	8
Nic. Grene		1	8	Rog. Welles		1	8	Johanna Goote		10	0
Ad. Suett		4	0	Joh. Jones		1	8	Johanna Vndurwod		3	0
Will. Frysbye		5	0	Will. Donnyngton		1	8	Tho. Reyu*er*[4]		5	0
Joh. Moore		1	8	Will. Belg*r*aue		3	4	Will. Corby		1	8
Will. Dawe		2	6	Joh. Launde		6	8	Wal. Asheby		3	4
Ric. Sharp		10	0	Gal. Willnale		1	8	Will. Broun		5	0
Ric. Boys		2	6	Tho. Spens*er*		1	8	Will. Donyngton		1	8
Will. Swan		6	8	Joh. Garton		3	4	Joh. Hardborugh		2	0
Rob. Thed		3	4	Nic. Palm*er*		3	0	Tho. Cardemaker		2	0
Will. Repynton		6	8	Johanna Hosier		2	0	Joh. Alen		3	4
Rad. Duffeld		3	4	Rad. Garton		13	4	Ric. Rasche		1	8
Will. Perte		1	8	Joh. Norm*a*nton		5	0	Ric. Ryvell		1	8
Ric. Gamill		2	0	Joh. Michell		10	0	Juliana Spycer		1	8
Will. Dey		1	8	Joh. Shotteswell		1	8	Tho. Bayly		1	8
Johanna Northwoode		6	8	Joh. Pyncherd		1	8	Dav. Wryght		1	8
Joh. Northwoode		10	0	Joh. Neuby		3	4	S*um*ma £11 19*s*. 0*d*.			
				Hugo Coruis*er*		1	8				

49 names. **Bayly-lane.**

	£	*s.*	*d.*		£	*s.*	*d.*		£	*s.*	*d.*
Joh. M*ar*ston		4	0	Joh. Vpton		1	8	Joh. Plumer		4	0
Sim. Vpton		1	8	Ric. Dyvett		4	0	Joh. Spenc*er*		5	0
Joh. Harborgh		3	0	Joh. Skill		1	8	Rad. Coton*er*		1	8
Joh. Sircocke		4	0	Joh. Malory		1	8	Joh. Wall		3	4
Joh. Whitley		3	0	Hen. Bate		3	4	Tho. Peut*er*ere		4	0
Hen. Watford		3	0	Joh. Crosbye		1	8	Joh. Bechamp		2	0
Rob. Herdwyk		3	0	Joh. Benett		5	0	Will. Broke		5	0
Joh. Bordall		3	4	Joh. Sperpoynt		1	8	Joh. Ronton		6	8

[1] leaf 53. [2] *Sic.* Read Gale. [3] *Sic.* Read Glenne. [4] ? Reyner.

Bayly-lane.

	£	*s.*	*d.*
Joh. Hull		4	0
Joh. Suetton		1	8
Joh. Mulner		1	8
Joh. Joyner		1	8
Joh. Wiche		1	8
Joh. Power		1	8
Ric Deister		1	8
Joh. Chamb*ur*		1	8
Joh. Frankelen		5	0
Will. Yate		4	0
Tho. Loke		2	0
Joh. Burbage		1	8
Joh. Gryme		3	4
Joh. Bayly		1	8
Rob. Gloucest*ur*		1	8
Joh. Oderyche		1	8
Will. Clerke		3	4
Pat. Kay		4	0
[1]Tho. Thorp		3	4
Joh. Crosse		4	0
Hen. Birde		4	0
Nic. Russell		2	6
Joh. Gilberd		2	0
Ric. Braytofte		5	0
Tho. Wirley		5	0

Summa £7 7*s.* 0*d.*

35 names.

Brode-yate.

	£	*s.*	*d.*
Rob. Melton		1	8
Joh. Locoke		1	8
Rog. Cooke		3	0
Joh. Capp*er*, cuteler		1	8
Will. Daubney		1	8
Will. M*ar*shall		1	8
Will. Spenc*er*		1	8
Will. Flekney		3	0
Joh. Barnard		2	0
Joh. Yong		1	8
Hen. Sircock		10	0
Wal. Paslowe		1	8
Ric. Busshebury		10	0
Joh. Pers, hosier		1	8
Ric. Freman, walker,		6	8
Tho. Sorche, cooke		1	8
Ric. Morell		1	8
Will. Prentes		3	4
Joh. George		1	8
Joh. Archer		1	8
Joh. Cardemak*er*		1	8
Egid. Allesley		6	8
Will. Shether		1	8
Joh. Darby		3	0
Tho. Bedford		1	8
Joh. Baker		1	8
Joh. Fisher		1	8
Rob. Praty		2	0
Ric. Couper		2	0
Tho Lyons		1	8
Joh. Colyns		1	8
Joh. Chaturton		1	8
Will. Drap*er*		1	8
Tho. Drap*er*		6	8
Rog. Walles		2	0

Summa £4 18*s.* 0*d.*

36 names.

Smytheford[-strett].

	£	*s.*	*d.*
Joh. Maynard		3	0
Dav. Burton		3	0
Ric. Hikelyng		3	0
Tho. Hosyer		3	0
Tho. Whitside		3	4
Joh. Yate		2	0
Will. Peut*er*ere		5	0
Joh. Tate, merc*er*		3	0
Tho. Carbonell		2	0
Joh. Bristow	1	6	8
Joh. Lynne		3	4
Joh. Bere		2	0
Tho. Broun		3	4
Magote Chaloner		1	8
Rog. Osteler		3	0
Joh. Blakeman		5	0
Joh. Oneley		10	0
Tho. Joy		1	8
Ric. Osburn		3	4
Joh. Kyngston		3	4
Joh. Owtrede		2	0
Joh. Egynton		5	0
Ad. Diere		4	0
Wall. Norfolke		3	4
Will. Happefford		3	4
Tho. Baxter		1	8
Will. Bredon		1	8
Joh. Braunston, jun.		2	0
Joh. Braunston, sen.		13	4
Will. Sloley[2]		3	4
Ric. Wymondeswold		3	4
Will. Jones, weu*er*		3	0
Joh. Bowyer		1	8
Tho. Ive		6	8
Joh. Forest, taylour		1	8
Joh. Russhoton, hosier		3	4

Summa £8 8*s.* 0*d.*[3]

78 names.

Spon-strett.

	£	*s.*	*d.*
Joh. Mersche		3	4
Joh. Hastlyffe		4	6
Joh. Watford		2	0
Joh. Essex		8	0
Tho. Pratt		1	8
Ric. Shurstooke		3	0
Joh. Sircet*ur*		2	0
Ric. Waren		1	8
Joh. Gurdelford		1	0
Will. Pratte		6	8
Joh. Bett		1	0
Joh. Menley		6	8
Nic. Barro		1	0
Joh. Lott		4	0
Joh. Warde		5	0
Joh. Stanley		1	6
Joh. Brere		2	0
Joh. Broun, drap*er*		6	8
Joh. Brett		3	0
Joh. Sewen		3	4
Joh. Honyb*ur*ne		3	0

[1] leaf 53, back. [2] In Warwickshire, near Arley.

[3] Really £7 10*s.* 0*d.* Here, as in many other places, it is impossible to reconcile the total with the various items.

Spon-strett.

	£	s.	d.
Hugo Rogeley		5	0
Egid. Corbrond		5	0
Tho. Tokebye		5	0
Rad. Ookes		1	4
Joh. Robardes		5	0
Rog. Maltby		1	4
Joh. Moole, coruyser		6	0
Will. Kerver		11	6
Joh. Deister		11	6
Will. Broun, wever		2	4
Joh. Chestur		3	6
Emma Marnam		4	0
Reginald Whitacre		1	4
Joh. Eire, weuer		2	8
Sim. Busteler		2	0
Ric. Welford		6	0
Joh. Wellyngton		5	0
Joh. Burbage		2	0
Hen. Holt		6	0
Hen. Mason		2	4
Will. Stockton		1	8
Joh. Harries		4	0
[1]Joh. Hoges		1	8
Tho. Divett		1	4
Tho. Lenton		2	0
Joh. Baxster		1	8
Will. Wellys		3	4
Joh. Perett		1	4
Joh. Thornton		1	0
Rog. Balle		3	4
Wal. Bulker		2	4
Hugo Steyne		3	4
Ric. Baxster		1	4
Margeria Ridale		2	0
Rob. Myles		1	0
Tho. Smythe		1	0
Tho. Straunge		1	0
Joh. Plasterer		5	0
Joh. Clyston		3	0
Mat. Withe		6	8
Ric. Capper		3	4
Rob. Grynder		1	0
Joh. Passynger		2	0
Joh. George		1	0
Laur. Deister		1	0
Rob. Baxster		3	4
Joh. Balle		2	4
Nic. Hull		1	0
Hugo Barbour		2	0
Vxor Tho. Goldsmythe		1	8
Tho. Samson		1	4
Will. Hardwike		1	8
Joh. Waren		1	6
Ric. Walford		4	0
Joh. Westley		1	0
Isabell Walker		1	0
Rob. Boteler		1	0

Summa £11 19*s*. 0*d*.

94 names.

Crose-chepyng.

	£	s.	d.
Rob. Flecher		2	6
Hen. Taunerer		1	8
Joh. Warde		2	6
Joh. Multon		2	0
Tho. Tate cum socio suo		1	8
Rob. Mylburne		3	4
Rob. Grubber		5	0
Joh. Huntley		3	4
Ric. Pulter		1	8
Joh. Fraiter		1	8
Ric. Botoner		6	8
Joh. Doughty		5	0
Hen. Banbury		2	6
Joh. Hewer		2	0
Joh. Nele		4	0
Margaret Breux		6	8
Gal. Draper		1	8
Ric. Harbourgh		2	6
Ric. Lane		2	0
Will. Radclyffe		5	0
Will. Hend		2	0
Rad. Chaundler		5	0
Joh. Parker		2	6
Joh. Frythe		3	4
Joh. Bryhtmer		3	3
Nic. Smythe		3	4
Will. Adderton		1	8
Joh. Appulby		3	4
Rob. Slye		1	8
Rog. Mulner		1	8
Ric. Joy		16	8
Hen. Adderton		1	8
Joh. Holland		1	8
Will. Humburston		1	0
Will. Marten		4	0
Joh. Gobett		1	8
Ric. Penson		2	6
Tho. Norwiche		2	6
Will. Bromwiche		I	4
Joh. Eborall		2	0
Joh. Nele, coruyser		1	0
Ric. Bryd		1	0
Johanna Gascoyne		5	0
Joh. Yong		1	0
Rob. Stookton		1	8
Tho. Chakeman		1	0
Joh. Bryde		4	0
Ric. Peyntour		2	6
Tho. Goldsmyth		2	0
Joh. Huett, mason		2	6
Moric. Bocher		4	6
Tho. Bassyngburne		3	4
Will. Potager		4	0
Ric. Brystocke		1	8
Tho. White		2	6
Rad. Bocher		2	6
Hen. Randull		5	0
Ric. Wooner		3	0
Gal. Woolpayner		1	8
Elyzabeth Lirpole		2	0
Joh. Newport		2	0
Joh. Hall		4	6
Tho. Lylynton		4	6
Will. Deyster		3	4
Joh. Northampton		2	0
Rob. Burman		4	0
ffratres Joh. White		1	8
Ric. Imayne		1	0
Hen. Cooke		2	6
Joh. Boise		3	4
Sim. Payne		1	8
Will. Bedon		1	8
Mat. Alerton		1	8
Isabella Huyton		16	8
Tho. Rastell		3	4
Tho. Swayn		2	6
Joh. Style, deister		5	0
Will. Pere, deister		3	4
Hen. Euerdon		1	8
Will. Meke		1	8
Will. Newporte		3	0
Will. Stoneley[2]		2	6
Will. Huett		4	0
Tho. Waren		2	6
Joh. Colyn, barbour		2	0
Will. Dilcocke		16	8
Will. Barbour		1	0
Will. Benett		3	4
Will. Darsett		5	0
Will. Hull, dubber[3]		2	0
Joh. Weston		1	8
Will. Dey		5	0
Will. Byneley		2	6
Joh. Bandy, barbour		4	0

Summa £15 4*s*. 6*d*.

[1] leaf 54. [2] leaf 54, back. [3] dubber = one who furbishes up old clothes.

71 names.

Byshop-strette.

	£	s.	d.
Rob. Gom*er*y		2	0
Ric, Biston		1	8
Rob. Bandy		1	8
Joh. Grene		3	4
Tho. Carde		2	0
Will. Withiforde		3	4
Joh. Coston		1	8
Joh. Kebull		3	4
Nic. Wiredrawer		1	8
Will. Thornton[1]		5	0
Tho. Sulby		1	8
Joh. Gold		3	4
It*em* *pro* Garett		1	8
Joh. Welford		6	8
Will. Warr[ewyk]		1	8
Sim. Pynne		1	8
Joh. Walg*r*aue		3	4
Gervasius Coole		1	8
Ric. M*ar*she		1	8
Joh. Lysturley		5	0
Hen Knott		3	4
Will. Staunton		3	8
Ric. Southam	1	8	4
Will. Listurley		2	0
Joh. Grynder		3	4

	£	s.	d.
Joh. Folvyle		2	0
Joh. Raignold		1	8
Will. Kemp		3	4
Joh. Barbour		1	8
Moric. Steynour		1	8
Joh. Atwoode		1	8
Hen. Walker		3	4
Joh. Stafford, myluer		3	4
Rog. Tailour		3	4
Edm. Drou*er*		5	0
Tho. Broun		1	8
Tho. Wodcok		1	8
Tho. Cleybroke		1	8
Hugo Cartwryght		1	8
Will. Savage		1	8
Will. Horsley		1	8
Will. Wilkyns		6	8
Will. Aubem		1	8
Hen. Hethe		3	4
Will. Dyvett		2	0
Joh. Augur		3	4
Joh. Lychfeld		10	0
Will. Alys		1	8
Wal. Tryg		3	4

	£	s.	d.
Ric. Thomason		1	8
Tho. Carter		3	4
Rob. Weston		3	4
Will. Coup*er*		2	0
Sim. Moore		2	0
Rog. Lessyngham		3	4
Will. Feld		1	8
Tho. Walg*r*aue		2	0
Will. Wymondeswold		6	8
Ric. Chetestur		3	4
Will. Crudworth		13	4
Joh. Boteler		1	8
Ric. Philleps		3	4
Joh. Gilberd		5	0
Will. Allesley		1	8
Ric. Speyc*er*		1	8
Will. Neuton		3	4
Hugo Shaw		3	4
Will. Cutt		1	8
Will. Bate		1	8
Ric. Clerke		1	8
Will. Humburston		1	0

Summa £11 17*s.* 4*d.*

S*um*ma tot*alis* Cv li. the w*i*ch C li. is paid as hit apperith the ij[cond] leff folowyng, and v li. is paid, that is to witt, iij li. to Laur. Cooke for his beryng the C li. to London, and xl s. to the collect*our*s of the shire in money and in Costes. Of the w*i*ch costes the messyngere þ*at* brought a com*m*ission to þe maio*ur* for to ret*ain* C li. of the collectors had vj s. viij d. £105. L. Cook has £3 0*s*. 0*d*. Collectors £2 0*s*. 0*d*.

[2] And aftur þ*at* the sayd o*ur* souer*aign* lorde in the said moneth of Ap*r*ill w*ith* oth*ur* lord*es* spirituall and temp*or*all, þ*at* is to say, the wurthy Cardynall, then bischop of Wynchest*ur*,[3] the bischop of Bathe,[4] the bischop of Ely,[5] and the bischop of Rouchest*ur*,[6] lord*es* spirituall; The duke of Yorke, the duke of Northfolke,[7] the Erle of War[ewyke], the Erle of Stafford,[8] the Erle of Huntyngdon,[9] the Erle of Arundell, the Erle of Oxenford,[10] the

April 23. The king with the lords spiritual and temporal, bishops,

dukes and earls,

[1] Possibly the painter of the stained-glass window at S. Mary's hall, and great window at York.
[2] leaf 55. [3] Cardinal Beaufort. [4] John Stafford.
[5] Phillip Morgan. [6] John Langdon. [7] John Mowbray.
[8] Humphrey Stafford, created Duke of Buckingham, 1444.
[9] John Holland. [10] John de Vere.

barons and bachelors, took water at Dover, and came to Rouen.

Erle of Devonschire,[1] the Erle of Vrmonde,[2] *with* other reu*er*ent barons and bachelers, the Sum*m*e of the retynew is. . . . .[3] And they toke þe wat*ur* at Douer, and Ryveden thorugh Godd*es* g*r*ace at Calys, and so comen to the Cite of Roan by the lond of Pykardy.

[4]EASTER LEET.

"Couentre." April 22.

¶ [V. f. p. held before Tho. Paynell, m., Joh. Prentes, Ric. Boton*er*, b., on Saturday in Easter week 8 Hen. VI.]

Jury.

Joh. Bristowe, Will. Dilcok, Laur. Coke, Hen. Peyto, Tho. Wyldegryse, Joh. Brafto*ft*, (*sic*) Ric. Joy, Joh. Leder, Joh. Parker, drap*er*, Joh. Bowyere, Joh. Michell, Joh. Braunston, Joh. Clerke, Joh. Everdon, Rob. Melburn, Will. Kerver, Joh. Deister, Will. ffrysby, Ric. Dene, Joh. Onley, Joh. Whalley, Joh. Doughty, Will. Swanne, Joh. Launde.

The ditch.

It*em*, they orden that ȝeu*er*ymen fey the towne dyke there as they haue ffyld hyt, or eny ffylth caste into hit, be-twene this and myssomer, yeu*er*-y-man [or 100 s. to the town-wall, to be raised by the chamberlains].

The gaoler and the prisoners' beds.

It*em*, they orden that John Stoke take but a peny ffor his owne bede, there as ij men lyne there-in or iij, and that he take no money ffor no bedde there as it is ȝeue on almes so to ley almes in,[5] and that ȝeu*er*-y-man that is prisener brynge in his bedde at his lyste, and take it a-wey when he woll, vp-on the peyn of fforfet off his office.

The town-clerk's chamber.

It*em*, they orden that the Toowncle*r*ke shall paye ffor the Chamb*ur* that he occupiethe yerly vj s. viij d. to the Trinite yeld.

The river.

[The mayor to search the river as is ordered in other leets; penalties contained ("contened") in previous orders.]

"Millers" must grind a strike for 1*d*.

Every miller taking toll

They orden that eu*er*y-man pay ffor a stryke of whette or Rye gryndyng j d., and ȝeue ony mylner take ony corne or tolle ffor eny gryndyng, that ȝeue hit be preued, that he make a-mendes and restitucion to the parti; and allso that they shuld paye at ȝeu*er*y defaute to the meir xx d., and

[1] Tho. Courtenay. [2] Jas. Butler. [3] Blank in MS.
[4] leaf 59. Scribe C. A difficult scribe.
[5] ? to keep the bed only for those too poor to pay.

to the bayles other xx d., wethe-oute grace. And that they be swore ȝeuery ȝere twye to be trewe; and whoso woll not be reweled be this ordynance that he pay as he was wonte to do off old tyme, and the mulners to be atte the large as a-ȝenes him, and not boundon to the peyne as hit ys boue seyde as a-ȝenns hem that woll not be rewled be the ordinaunce.

to pay 1s. 8d. both to the mayor and to the bailiffs; and other customers, who will not obey this rule, to pay as they were wont, and the millers to be free from penalty.

THE WIREDRAWERS AND THE CANOPY.

[1] Hit is to to haue in mynde, þat hit is ordenyd that the Crafte of the wiredrawers shall kepe the Canape ou*er* the hiȝe aut*ur* in saynt Mich*el* in Couen*tre*, as hit appearith by indent*ur* made, the w*i*ch tenou*r* folowithe in thies Wordes:—

Sept. 1, 1430.

This indent*ur* witnessithe that the furst day of September the yer of the raign of kyng Henr*e* the sixte aft*ur* the conquest the IXth, John Sheldon, Tho. Eldbek, Hen. Coton & Rob. Burges, wardeins of the wiredrawers of the Cite of Couen*tre*, w*ith* Joh. Stafford, Joh. Rocheford, Joh. Blakman, Joh. Benett, Will. Deist*er*, Will. Claybroke, Nich. Jones, Joh. Straunge & Tho. Stafford w*ith* oþ*er* whurthy men of the same Crafte in the name of all the p*er*sones of the Crafte, hauyng hur deuoc*i*on to allmyghty God & to the blessid Sac*ra*ment, the w*i*ch is all C*ri*sten mennys beleve, consideryng a devout thyng callyd the new Canape ou*er* the awt*ur* in the churche of saynt Michaels of the said Cite in the w*i*ch the blessid Sac*ra*ment is wurthely at this tyme kepte, the w*i*ch kepyng must haue cost & rep*ar*ac*i*on, cam before Tho. Paynell, then maiou*r* of the said Cite, Laur. Cooke, Tho. Wildgryse, Joh. Braitofto, Gyles Allesley, Joh. Bristowe, Will. Legburne, Chaplen, Ric. Sharp, Joh. Clerk, Joh. Eu*er*don, Joh. Prentes, Will. Swan, Joh. Franklen, Joh. Whalley, Ric. Godesley & oþ*er* moo in saynt Mary halle, p*ra*yng & desiryng of deuoc*i*on þat thei haue to þe said sac*ra*ment, & wurship to þe said Cite, to haue the kepyng and the gou*er*nance of the forsaid Canape & all thyng*es* longyng þ*er*to. The w*i*ch the said maiou*r* & oþ*er* wurthy men þ*er* beyng

"The companie of wiredrawers,"

out of devotion to the blessed Sacrament,

come before the mayor and others,

and request to be allowed to keep in repair the canopy over the high altar in S. Michael's;

[1] leaf 56, back. Scribe A.

which request is granted; and the matter entered in the Mayor's Register.

with hym consideryng hur desire & hooly deuocion grauntyth them hur peticion, thankyng hem of hur desire and good will. And at request of the wardens & oþer men of the said Crafte this indentur is registred in a boke callyd the meyres Regestur in saynt Mary hall beforesaid for perpetual remembraunce þerof to be had in tyme comyng. And this said indentur abydithe in Tho. Peynell bag in saynt Mary hall.

"Couentre." Oct. 4.

[1][V. f. p. held on Wednesday after Michaelmas 9 Hen. VI], Joh. Brystowe, Will. Dilcok, Joh. Leder, Hen. Peyto, Joh. Braytoft, Ric. Joy, Egid. Allesley, Ric. Sharp, Rad. Garton, Joh. Parker, draper, Joh. Bower, Rob. Melburn, Joh. Michell, Will. Byfeld, Will. Crudworth, Joh. Clerk, Joh. Euerdon, Joh. Breton, Joh. Deyster, Will. Swanne, Hen. Syrcok, Joh. Onley, Joh. Launde, Joh. Stille.

Bailiffs.

[Joh. Ronton, Ric. Busshebury.]

Orders of leet.

[Constables, who shall be chosen by the mayor and bailiffs, shall be of the more honest & discreet sort, according to the discretion and advice of the mayor & bailiffs for the time being.]

[The mayor to summon a hall of Forty-eight persons to inquire into the sheriff's interruption of the city's liberties, and how the cost of prosecuting the sheriff is to be borne, with all haste.]

Item, ordinarunt quod maior faciat vnam aulam de xlviij personis ad videndum pro interripcione (*sic*) libertatum ville de Couentre per vicecomitem facta & interipta (*sic*), & quomodo Costagium inde erit portatum ad prosequendum versus vicecomitem predictum Cum omni festinacione. Also atte the same tyme that they orden be the meirs avise ffor the balans and whutes (*sic*) after the fforme of the Statuta (*sic*).

[Balance and weights.]

A FIFTEENTH.

Michaelmas 1430.

[2][Collectors of the second fifteenth, conceded in Michaelmas term, 9 Hen. VI.

Gosford Street. Will. Bagett, Hen. Weston, Bened. Marchall, Joh. Stafford, Joh. Baker, deister. £5 16s. 0d.

[1] leaf 59, back. Scribe C. [2] leaf 57. Scribe A.

Jorden Well. Joh. Cressy, Joh. ffreman, Joh. Lee, Rob. Defford. £5 0s. 0d.

Muchpark Street. Will. Birde, Tho. Warmynton, Will. Charlton, Joh. Le, smythe. £5 0s. 0d.

Bailly Lane. Joh. Harbourgh, Joh. M*ar*ston, Joh. Spenc*er*, Tho. Peut*er*er. £3 10s. 0d.

Earl Street. Ad. Swett, Tho. Ryver, Will. Belg*r*aue, Nic. Palmer. £5 13s. 8d.

Broadgate. Tho. Drap*er*, Rog. Walles, Rog. Cook*es*, Rob. Praty. £2 6s. 8d.

Smithford Street. Joh. Tate, Joh. Blakman, Ad. Dier, Tho. Broun, weu*er*. £4 0s. 0d.

Spon Street. Ric. Wallford, Joh. Moole, Mat. White, Joh. Sisset*ur*, Wal. Prate. £5 13s. 8d.

Cross Cheaping. Will. Darsett, Joh. Hall, Ric. Chapman, Will. Bromwiche. £7 5s. 0d.

Bishop Street. Will. Wymondeswolde, Joh. Grynder, Hen. Knott, Ric. ffillypes. £5 13s. 0d. Sum of the second fifteenth. £50 0s. 0d.[1]]

And aftur þ*at* the said Tho. Paynell, meir, be comyssion to hym direct for to receive C li. of the collectours of the shyre of the second xv^{te} to make payment of the C li. þ*at* was lant to o*ur* [2]soue*re*n lord the xv^{ten} day of M*ar*che the viijth yer of the kyng þ*at* nowe is, as hit appearith the v leffe p*re*cedent,[3] the said maiour by vertu of the said com*m*ission the said C li. receyvyd, þ*at* is to say, l li. of the Collectours of the Shire, and l li. of the Collectours of th*is* Cite, and mad repayment to hem that lant the said C li. And the copy of the said comyssion abydithe in the maio*ur*s bag, Thom*as* Paynell; and the same com*m*yssion abidith in the said bag allso.

The mayor receives £100 from the collectors of the fifteenth; and with it repays the king's loan.

WEIGHTS AND MEASURES.

Hit is to haue in mynd, for-also-moche as hit is ordenyd þ*at* ther shuld be but one Weyght & one mesure thorout this Realme, the said maio*ur* sent to London for to haue the weightes acordyng to the weightes of thexechecour and thens brought xiiij li., vij li., ij li., j li.,

"Mayor to have oversight of sealing weights."

[1] Really £49 18*s.* 0*d.* [2] leaf 57, back. [3] *v.* p. 129.

in brass. And aftur that the said meire lett make an hall, the x day of December last past, to haue knowlege who shuld haue the said weightes in his kepyng, the ouersight of the weyng, and the sealyng of weightes þat ben to seale. And by the whurthy men, whos namys folowen, was ordenyd þat the maiour shuld comen with the Recorder Donyngton & othur lernyd men, and as thei set rule so to be holden in tyme comyng; wherupon the said maiour, the Recorder Donyngton, & othur lered men commenyd to-gethur of this mattur, and sett rule þat the said meire shuld haue the kepyng, ouersight of the weyng, and the sealyng of weightes þat byn for to seale.

Dec. 10.

A hall of worthy men decide the matter.

The worthy men; 54 names.

Laur. Cooke, Tho. Wildgrise, Hen. Peitoo, Joh. Leeder, Joh. Braitofte, Will. Byfeld, Joh. Prentes, Joh. Euerdon, Ric. Dene, Joh. Michell, Tho. Suettenham, Joh. Walley, Will. Swan, Hen. Sircoke, Will. Birde, Tho. Reyuer,[1] Joh. Clerke, Ric. Sharp, Joh. Warrant, Will. Frissby, Rad. Garton, Will. Belgraue, Joh. Ronton, Ric. Braytoft, Ric. Busshebury, Egid. Allesley, Joh. Bristow,[2] Joh. Egeston, Joh. Beachamp, Joh. Tate, Will. Crosse, Joh. Bowyer, Joh. Oneley, Joh. Braunston, Joh. Blakeman, Will. Keruer, Tho. Wirley, Joh. Deister, Mat. White, Rob. Melburne, [3]Ric. Bootoner, Joh. Wylowby, Joh. Doughty, Joh. Style, deister, Will. Dilcoke, Ric. Joy, Rob. Southam, Joh. Walgraue, Will. Wymynswold, Joh. Lysturley, Joh. Stafford, Joh. Lee, hosier, Joh. Catur, Tho. Elderkeke,[4] jun.

ACCOUNTS AND TOWN BUSINESS.

[Warden's accounts for 1428.

[5]Memorandum quod Will. Frisbye et Joh. Doughty, Custodes camere (etc.) computauerunt coram Thoma Paynell, maiore, de tempore Johannis Bristowe, et Onerantur cum iiii^{xx} x li. ix d. ob.

[Charge £90 0*s.* 9½*d.*

[Allowances for expenses

Vnde petunt allocari pro certis

1 ? Reyner. 2 "weuer" deleted follows. 3 leaf 58. 4 ? Elderbeke. 5 leaf 55, back.

and remissions £91 18*s.* 6*d.*

And thus they are in advance £1 13*s.* 8½*d.* But of this £91 18*s.* 6*d.*

there is owing 18*s.* 0*d.*

£8 5*s.* 0*d.*

1*s.* 6*d.*

£7 0*s.* 0*d.*

Total £16 4*s.* 6*d.*

Which (sum of) £15 18*s.* 6*d.* cannot be levied for divers causes. Therefore it is respited until next account. Paper in mayor's bag.

[Accounts for 1429.

[Charged with the foot of last account £15 18*s.* 6*d.*, and with £67 6*s.* 2*d.* Total £83 4*s.* 8*d.*

[Allowances £63 8*s.* 1*d.*

[Balance £18 16*s.* 8*d.*

[Owe £16 4*s.* 6*d.* by reason of its being respited as appears above.

[Chamberlains' accounts 1430.

[Charge £86 9*s.* 3*d.*; ex-

expens*is*, vacac*ionibus* & p*er*don*is* iiij^{xx} xi li. xviij s. vj d.

Et sic p*re*sunt xxxiij s. viij d. ob. Sed me*morandum* q*uo*d de p*re*dic*tis* iiij^{xx} xi li. xviij s. vj d.

Will. Darset d*ebet* xviij s.

Will. Kersley d*ebet* viij li. v s.

Joh. Pisfort d*ebet* xviij d.

Johanna Goote d*ebet* vij li.

S*um*ma xvi li. iiij s. vj d.

Q*uam* (*sic*) quidem (?) xv li. xviij s. vj d. no*n* possu*nt* adhuc leuari p*ro* diu*er*sis caus*is*. Ideo pon*itu*r in respect*u* vsq*ue* ad p*roximum* compo*tum*. & papir*us* istius Compot*i* remane*t* in baga Tho. Paynell, maior*is*.

Compot*us* Will. Frisby & Ric. Dene, custod*um* camer*e* (etc.), de temp*ore* Laur. Coóke maior*is*. Et oner*antur* de pede compot*i* xv li. xviij s. vj d. & oner*antur* cu*m* lxvij li. vj s. ij d. S*um*ma on*eracion*is iiii^{xx} iij li. iiij s. viij d. Vnde petu*nt* allocari p*ro* diu*er*sis expens*is*, vacac*ionibus* & p*er*don*is* lxiij li. viij s. j d. & sic reman*ent* in arreragi*is* xviij li. xvj s. viij d.[1]

D*ebent* xvj li. iiij s. vj d. de p*re*dict*is* xviij li. xvi s. vij d. [que] ponit*ur* in respec*tu* usq*ue* p*roximum* compot*um*, p*ro*ut p*atet* sup*r*a in compot*o* Will*el*mi Frysby & Joh*annis* Doughty. & papir*us* istius compot*i* reman*et* in baga Thome Paynell, maior*is*.

[2][Will. Swane and Hen. Sircoke are charged with £86. 9s. 3d. They ask allowance for divers expenses,

[1] £19 16*s.* 7*d.* [2] leaf 56.

penses £90 5*s.* 4½*d.*; deficit £3 16*s.* 1½*d.*

[In this mayor's and these chamberlains' time 14½ perches of the stone wall of the city near to the friars Carmelite, and the half of a round tower were built for £77 13*s.* 4*d.*

[The prior's written receipt for £10 paid by T. Paynell, due at the Michaelmas term in the 9th year of the king, remains in the mayor's bag.]

payments, vacancies and remissions £90. 5s. 4½d. And thus they are in advance £3. 16s. 1½d. as appears by the chamberlains' record in the mayor's bag. Total £3. 16s. 1½d.][1]

Mem. q*uod* temp*or*e Tho. Paynell, maior*is* (etc.). Will. Swanne & Hen. Sircoke, cam*er*arior*um*, xiiij perche & di*midium* muri lapide*i* Ciuitat*is* p*re*d*i*ct*e* iux*t*a *f*ra*t*res Carmelitar*um* & dimidietat*as* vni*us* turre (*sic*) rotunde ib*idem* composit*e* & construct*e* fueru*nt* p*ro* lxxvij li. xiij s. iiij d.

Mem. q*uod* acquietanc*ia* p*r*ior*is* et convent*us* Coventr*ie* de x li.[2] solut*is* p*er* manus Tho. Paynell maior*is* etc. p*ro* t*er*mino S. Mich*ae*lis anno nono *Regis* nunc, reman*et* in baga eiusdem Tho. Paynell.

THE WHITE FRIARS AND THE WALL.

"Carmelite friers liberty to make a banke against the town wall."

[3]Mem. þ*at* accord toke betwene Tho. Paynell, meir, and bailyffes and chamb*ur*leins & Com*in*ialtye of the Cite of Couentre on þ*at* one pa*r*tie, and the p*r*iour and Covent of the ffrere Carmelit*es*[4] of Couen*tre* on þ*at* oþ*er* side: That the said prio*ur* & Couent shull make w*ith*in ther Garden aft*ur*[5] the town wall a bank of Erthe Joynyng to the said wall on ther own Costes, in Lenght fro the four-square toure there vnto þe Rounde Toure, a-foore Laur. Cook*es* mylne on the Corner, & in height vnto the tabull[6] of the said wall Except ij fette, and rep*ar*acion þ*er*off shall make, as hit appearith in endenturs þ*er*off made more playnely. The w*i*ch endenturs abydon in Tho. Paynels Bag, w*ith* a obligac*i*on in the w*i*ch the said priq*ur* & couent arn boundon in x li. to kep the said Couena*u*ntes.

[1] There was a complaint of the difficulty of bearing the heavy burdens for murage about this time. In 1427 the mayor and community had licence to amortize lands and rents to the yearly value of £40 for the support of the town. Corp. MSS. B. 45. [2] The annual ferm, *v. supra,* p. 2.
[3] leaf 58. [4] *v.* Dugd. 122–3. [5] after = along. [6] A string-course.

WILL. DILCOCK, MAYOR, 1431.

[1] [Election of officers.] Jan. 25.

Electors. Laur. Cook, Hen. Peyto, Tho. Wildegryse, Ric. Joy, Egid. Allesley, Joh. Euerdon, Joh. Ronton, Ric. Bussheburу, Rad. Garton, Joh. Parker, Ric. Sharp, Joh. Bowyer, Ric. Botoner, Joh. Prentes, Will. Keruer, Will. Wymondeswold, Joh. Onley, Joh. Stille, Tho. Crosse, Will. ffrysby, Joh. Egeston, Joh. Doughty, Will. Crosse, Mat. White.

Officers. [m. Will. Dilcok; cor. Joh. Whalley; ch. Rob. Southam, Joh. Burton; W. Joh. Warrant, Rich. Dene; mace, Will. Oxton.]

EASTER LEET. "Couentre."

Apr. 7. Jury. [2][V. f. p. held before Will. Dilcok, m., Joh. Rontton, Ric. Bussheburу, b., on Saturday in Easter week 9 Hen. VI.]

Joh. Bristowe, Laur. Cook, Joh. Leder, Hen. Peyto, Tho. Wildgrese, Joh. Brayftot, Tho. Paynell, Ric. Joy, Joh. Euerdon, Ric. Sharp, Joh. Michell, Rad. Garton, Joh. Bowyer, Will. Byfold, Will. Crudworth, Joh. Clerk, Joh. Prentes, Ric. Botoner, Joh. Braunston, Will. Swanne, Joh. Onley, Joh. Dilcok, Joh. Doughty, Rob. Southam.

Orders of leet. Essoins permitted. The (*sic*) ordeyne that eueryman that will Cast asson[3] lawfully that he haue hit.

Allso the orden that the meire haue the ouer-sight off ffrayes & debates ffor ther (*sic*) ees off the Comen[4] pepul. And ther be no Constabull made but he be off good name & god ffame, be ouer-Syght of the meir. Also that no seriant somen no mo to wake but xvj persons anyght; & that the money that they take ffor to hire men withe, that thei hire men truly & duly & take no brybe, a-pon the peyn off vj s. viij d. at euery defaut to be rered to the town wall. Constables; sergeant to summon 16 men only to "watch" every night; and to take no bribes.

PRESENT TO THE DUKE OF GLOUCESTER.

May 20, 1431. [5]Hit is to haue in mynd that at the feste of Whitsontyd the yere of Kyng Herri the vj the ix, be avyse &

[1] leaf 60. [2] Scribe C.
[3] Bona fide reason for absence from a court of law.
[4] Written above the line. [5] leaf 60, back. Scribe of B type.

40 marks, a cup, 4 pipes of wine, 20 pikes, 12 breams, total £50.

ordenaunce of thes wurthimen foloweng, ther was gevon to the Duke of Gloucestre & to the Duchas[1] xl marc' & a Cuppe of siluer & ou*er*gilt, iiij pype wyn, xx pykes, xij bremes; the su*m*ma of all l li.

The worthy men; sixty-three.

Will. Dilcok, meire, Joh. Bristowe, Laur. Cooke, Joh. Leder, Hen. Peyto, Tho. Wildegrise, Joh. Braytoft, Ric. Joy, Egid. Allesley, Tho. Paynell, Joh. Euerdon, Joh. Ronton, Ric. Busshebury, Will. Byfeld, Will. Crudworth, Joh. Michell, Rob. Melburn, Joh. Braunston, Joh. Bowyer, Joh. Clerke, Joh. Prentes, Ric. Boton*er*, Ric. Sharp, Rob. Southam, Joh. Burton, Joh. Onley, Will. Kerver, Joh. Lychefeld, Joh. Deyster, Will. Wymondeswold, Mat. White, Joh. Stille, Joh. Sircoke, Joh. Tate, Tho. Wirley, Will. Derset, Will. ffrisby, Will. Swan, Joh. Warant, Ric. Dene, Joh. Lusterley, Joh. Dilcok, Joh. Egeston, Joh. Blakeman, Joh. Stafford, Rog. Cookes, Joh. Garton, Joh. Stretton, Bened. Marchall, Joh. Sheldon, Joh. Merston, Rob. Praty, Will. Marchall, Joh. Lee, hosier, Joh. Normanton, Joh. Brabson, Tho. Kemp, Will. Cortenale, Joh. Whalley, Joh. Lyme, Joh. Evesham, Joh. Revell, Joh. Shadde.

MICHAELMAS LEET.

"Couentre." Oct. 4, 1431.

[2]¶ [V. f. p. held on Thursday after Michaelmas 10 Hen. VI.[3]]

Jury of 26.

Laur. Cooke, Joh. Leeder, Tho. Wildgrise, Joh. Braytofte, Ric. Joy, Tho. Paynell, Joh. Eu*er*don, Joh. Mychell, Will. Crudworth, Ric. Sharp, Joh. Bowyer, Joh. Brampton, Joh. P*ar*ker, Joh. Prentes, Joh. Clerke, Ric. Boton*er*, Will. Byfeld, Joh. Deist*er*, wolma*n*, Joh. Dilcok, Will. Frissby, Joh. Oneley, Will. Wymondeswold, Rob. Southam, Joh. Burton, Joh. Warrant, Joh. Style.

Bailiffs.

[Joh. Lichefeld, Will. Keru*er*.]

Orders of leet.

Thei orden þat the maio*ur* be prevy to thelecc*io*n of offic*ers*; and þat ther be noo mysgou*er*nyd man offic*er*[4];

[1] The duchess was the duke's second wife, Eleanor Cobham, afterwards indited for witchcraft. This was the year of the Lollard rising under Jack Sharp, vigorously suppressed by Gloucester. Arrests were made at Coventry. Ramsey, I. 437.

[2] Scribe A., leaf 61, back.

[3] The words "*per sacramentum*" (by oath) follow.

[4] Cf. pp. 132, 137.

and þ*at* the bailiffes yeve þ*er* office*rs* ther fees as thei wer wont to doo; and þ*at* noo office*r* do noo se*r*uyce for nowght but for his wag*es*, as thei did of olde. Bailiffs' officers.

Thei orden þ*at* thei com as ofte tymes as þei woll in the weke, and þ*at* þei sell nott brede to noo huckster, vpon payn of forfeture [of] the same brede; and the said huksters lese[1] at eue*r*y tyme of defaute xij d. to the vse of the meir*e*. And þ*at* the baxste*rs* of the said Cite do sell bred in the same place and the same tyme, as well as thei off the contrei doo. "Bakers."

THE FIFTEENTH.

[2]Hit is to haue in mynd that thies p*er*sones foloweng wern the Collectours of xv^{te} peny in the tyme of Will. Dilcok beyng maio*ur*.

[3][*Gosford Street.* Joh. Baker, deiste*r*, Joh. Smyth, writillmaker,[4] Tho. Mason, Coruise*r*, Ric. Somur, weue*r*.

Much Park Street. Will. Cleybroke, Nic. Gryve, Will. ffythRobert, Rob. Hendman.

Earl Street. Joh. Wylouȝby, Ad. Suotto, Ric. Boys, Tho. Suettenham.

Smithford Street. Joh. Maynard, Joh. Lynne, Ric. Osburne, Tho. Carboncll.

Crosscheaping. Will. Radclyffe, Joh. Bryghtmer, Joh. Hall, Joh. Hewett.

Jorden Well. Joh. Shade, Tho. Ilagė, me*r*cer, Will. Deiste*r*, cardmake*r*, Tho. Elderbek.

Bayly Lane. Rob. Hardwyke, Ric. Dyvett, Joh. Atwall, Joh. Bechamp.

Broadgate. Joh. Cappe*r*, Joh. George, Will. Marchall, Rob. Saxton.

[5]*Bishop Street.* Joh. Kebull, Tho. Walg*r*aue, Hen. Knott, Joh. Boteler.]

WILL BYFELD, MAYOR, 1432.

[6][Election of new officers.] Jan. 25.

Laur. Cooke, Joh. Leder, Joh. Braitofte, Tho. Wildgrise, Ric. Joy, Joh. Brystowe, Tho. Paynell, Joh. Eue*r*don, Electors.

[1] lose, *N. E. D.* s. v. leese. [2] leaf 61.
[3] For sums collected from each ward *v.* p. 133. [4] *v.* Gloss.
[5] Curious omission of Spon Street. [6] leaf 62.

Joh. Lychefeld, Will. Keru*er*, Ric. Sharp, Joh. Bowyer, Will. Crudworth, Joh. Clarke, Joh. Braunston, Joh. Prentes, Ric. Boton*er*, Joh. Ronton, Joh. Oneley, Joh. Dilcocke, Will. Swane, Tho. Crosse, Will. Frissby, Joh. Doughty.

Officers. [m. Will. Byfeld; cor. Joh. Walley; ch. Joh. Willowbye, Will. Darsett; w. Tho. Wirley, Joh. Lee, hosier; mace, Will. Oxton.

J. Ps. The mayor, recorder, Laur. Cooke, Will. Dilcok, Tho. Wildgrise, Joh. Leder.

Key-keepers. The same without the recorder.]

EASTER LEET.

June 26 or 29. [1][V. f. p. held in the time of Will. Byfeld, m., Joh. Lychefeld, Will. Keru*er*, b., on Thursday SS. Peter and Paul 10 Hen. VI.]

Jury. Laur. Cooke, Will. Dilcoke, Joh. Leeder, Hen. Peytoo, Tho. Wildgrise, Joh. Braytofte, Ric. Joy, Tho. Paynell, Joh. Eu*er*don, Joh. Brampston, Joh. Mychell, Joh. Clarke, Joh. Prentes, Ric. Boton*er*, Ric. Bushebury, Will. Frysby, Will. Swan, Joh. Stylle, Hen. Sircoke, Joh. Warrant, Ric. Dene, Joh. Oneley, Joh. Dilcoke, Joh. Doughty.

Orders of leet. Town-ditch: those who have fouled it must cleanse it. They orden that the maio*ur* goo and ou*er*see the town dyke þ*at* hit be clansyd, and þ*at* the p*er*sons þ*at* haue caste muke or othur fylthe *with*in the dyke be chansyd (*sic*)[2] at þ*er* cost þ*at* haue fuld hit or cast any thyng[3] þ*er*in, Eu*er*y-man vpon the payn of xl s. betwen this and mydsom*er* to be rered to the town wall, and þ*at* þ*er* be noo more cast þ*er* from this tyme forthe, on the same payn to be reryd to the same vse.

"Murage." [Every man to be assessed ("extendid") according to his lands and movables for murage between now and Michaelmas.]

Bridges at Earl's Mill floodgates. They orden þ*at* John Rocheford & John Lee, hosier, to make the byrg*es* at the Erle myle flodyat*es* sufficyent for hors and man to passe and com ou*er* þ*at* wey *with*in vj dayes, [or a fine of 40 s. from each to the town wall.]

[1] leaf 63. June 29 occurred on a Sunday this year.
[2] ? charged. [3] Repeated in MS.

WEIGHTS AND MEASURES.

The morn aftur the fest of the Natiuite of our Lady the xth yere of kyng Henry the vj[te], thes wurthy men folowyng wern aduised þ*at* all the strykes wi*th*in the Cite of Couentr*e* shuld be serchid and made of one mesure & lyke, and none moore then othur, and that thei shuld be mesured aft*ur* a halffe st*r*ike, w*i*ch is made wi*th* a strype of Iron ourtheward.

Sept. 9, 1432.

Strikes to be made after one pattern, which has a strip of iron overthwart.

Joh. Weston, Recorder, Laur. Cooke, Hen. Peitoo, Tho. Wildegrise, Ric. Joy, Joh. Braytofte, Joh. Lychefeld, Will. Donyngton, Joh. Breton.

The Council.

And aft*ur* that, Will*iam* Byfeld, maio*ur*, lett do com afore hym all the strykes of this Cite, and made them of one mesur*e* aft*ur* the forme abouesaid.

MICHAELMAS LEET.

[1][V. f. p. held on Thursday after Michaelmas, 2 Hen. VI.] Will. Dilcok, Hen. Peitoo, Tho. Wildegrise, Joh. Braitofte, Ric. Joy, Joh. Euer*d*on, Joh. Clerke, Joh. Braunston, Joh. Prentes, Ric. Botone*r*, Joh. Ronton, Ric. Bushebury, Rob. Southam, Joh. Willoughby, Will. Derset, Will. Frysby, Ric. Dene, Hen. Sircoke, Joh. Deiste*r*, Joh. Eiston, Joh. Doughty, Joh. Oneley, Mat. White, Joh. Bowyer.

Oct. 2. Jury.

[Will. Swan, Joh. Warrant.]

Bailiffs.

Orders of leet.

[No bailiff to let to farm issues or fines to the sergeants-at-mace or any other, but to have and hold them as of old, under pain of £20 to the town wall.

& ord*inarunt* q*uo*d nulli ball*iv*i de cet*er*o debent conced*er*e nec dimittere exit*us* nec am*er*ciament*a* clauig*er*ib*us* nec alicui al*io* ad firma*m*, *sed* h*ab*eant & tenea*n*t ut ab antiq*uo* tenueru*n*t, s*ub* pen*a* xx li*brarum* ad vsum muri ciuit*atis* p*er* maior*em* leuand*arum*.

[The receiver of the Trinity guild payments not to be empanelled[2] so long as he holds the office.

Item, ord*inarunt* q*uo*d ipse qui est recept*or* den*ariorum* Gilde S. Trinitat*is* amodo non enpanellat*ur* (*sic*), qua*m*diu d*ictum* offi*cium* occupat.

[1] leaf 64, back.

[2] ? On the Leet Jury.

Sergeants to enter their own actions. Jailor to sell no ale in the prison.

Thei orden that the sergeant*es* somo*n* ther*e* playnth them-selff, and non o*þer* Clerk, and *þat* the Gayler sell no ale w*it*h*in* the gayle, but *þat* hit be (?) fett in the town be mesur*e* ensealyd, [or 20s. to the town wall.]

A FIFTEENTH.

Martinmas. Nov. 11, 1432.

[1]Thes byn the Collectours of the fourth p*ar*te of the xv^{ten}, wh*ic*h was paid at Martelmass the xj year of kyng Henre the vj^{te}.

Collectors.

Gosford. Joh. Baker, deist*er*, Joh. Smyth, wirtil-mak*er*,[2] Tho. Mason, Coruis*er*, Joh. Stretton. [£1 9s. 0d.]

Much-park. Will. Cleybroke, Nic. Gryve, Will. fiȝt-Rob*er*t, Rob. Hendman. [£1 5s. 0d.]

Erle. Ad. Swett, Ric. Boys, Tho. Swettenham, Tho. Reyu*er*. [£1 8s. 5d.]

Smyth[*ford.*] Joh. Maynard, Joh. Lynne, Ric. Osburne, Tho. Carbonell. [£1 0s. 0d.]

Crasch[*epyng.*] Will. Rad-Clyffe, Joh. Bryghtmer, Joh. Hall, Joh. Huett. [£1 16s. 3d.]

Jurden. Joh. Schade, Tho. Illage, m*er*c*er*, Will. Deist*er*, cardm*ak*e*r*, Tho. Elderbek. [£1 5s. 6d.]

Bayll[*y.*] Rob. Herdwyk, Ric. Dyvett, Joh. Bechamp, Ric. Parbroun. [17s. 6d.]

Brodeyate. Joh. Capp*er*, Joh. George, Will. M*ar*chall, Rog. Walles. [11s. 8d.]

Spon. Joh. Mershe, Joh. Essex, Joh. Sircetur, Joh. Mole. [£1 8s. 5d.]

Byschop. Joh. Kebull, Tho. Walgraue, Hen. Knott, Joh. Boteler. [£1 8s. 3d.]

THE WALL.

Joh. Clarke allows the town wall to be built on his land;

[3]Hit is to haue in mynd *þat* Joh. Clarke of Couentr*e*, m*er*chant, g*r*auntyd by his fre will *þat* the town wall shuld be made apon his lond lyeng in lenght a this halue the toure *þat* is mache-collyd[4] at the Bischop-yate, w*it*h

[1] leaf 63, back. [2] *v.* Gloss. Also rit, ritler, *E. D. D.*
[3] leaf 62, back. [4] machicolated.

fre entre & issue to the same aftur the forme as hit is now be-gon to be made. And this graunt was made in the presence of Will. Byfeld, maiour, & oþer persons folowyng:— Laur. Coke, Joh. Leeder, Joh. Braytofte, Tho. Wildgrise, Ric. Joy, Tho. Paynell, Joh. Lychefeld, Will. Keruer, Ric. Sharp, Joh. Bowyer, Joh. Braunston, Joh. Prentes, Ric. Botoner, Joh. Oneley, Joh. Dilcok, Will. Swan, Tho. Crosse, Will. Frisbye, Joh. Doughty, Will. Dilcoke, Hen. Peitou, Egid. Allesley, Tho. Wirley, Joh. Le, Joh. Whalley, Ric. Dene, Joh. Warrant, Joh. Wylouȝby, Joh. Mychell, Ric. Bushebury.

30 persons witness his grant.

And aftur the said graunt the said John Clerke, oþerways aduised, said þat þe seid town wall shuld nott goo that way. Wheruppon the said William Byfeld, meir, lett make an hall and callyd afore hym thes persons folowyng and the said Joh. Clerke. The which, all the mattur seyn, seld, & vndurstondon, ordenyd and grauntyd þat the said wall shuld goo and be made as hit was furst grauntyd.

But afterwards J. Clarke changes his mind;

nevertheless "a hall" of 73 townspeople insist on taking him at his first word.

Laur. Cooke, Bened. Marchall, Tho. Wildgrise, Joh. Whalley, Joh. Prentes, Joh. Dilcok, Joh. Bryan, Joh. Ashewell, Will. Deister, cardmaker, Will. Herdbourgh, Joh. Herdbourgh, Will. Byrd, Hen. Peitoo, Joh. Braytofte, Joh. Clerke, Tho. Yorke, Ric. Dene, Will. Charlton, Joh. Garton, Ric. Sharp, Joh. Willouȝby, Ad. Suett, Will. Swan, Walt. Asheby, Tho. Reyuer, Joh. Vndurwoode, Will. Frisby, Joh. Euerdon, Ed. Brogreue, Joh. Ronton, Hen. Byrde, Joh. Sircoke, Joh. Spenser, Joh. Bochamp, Tho. Wirley, Ric. Braytoft, Joh. Gryme, Joh. Franklen, Rog. Cookes, Ric. Bushebury, Tho. Ruyton, Rob. Pratty, Joh. Tate, Joh. Oneley, Joh. Blakemon, Joh. Braunston, Joh. Lynne, Tho. Paynell, Will. Keruer, Mat. White, Ric. Botoner, Rob. Melburn, Joh. Doughty, Ric. Joy, Joh. Hall, Will. Darsett, Joh. Kebull, Will. Peer, Hen. Rondall, Joh. Stoke, Rob. Southam, Joh. Walgraue, Will. Wymondeswold, Joh. Grynder, Joh. Stafford, mylner, Ric. Fillips, Joh. Augur, Will. Rad-Clyffe, Joh. Maynard, Tho. Swayne, Ad. Dyer, Tho. Broun, weuer, Joh. Freman, chaundeler.

Seventy-three names.

RIC. SHARP, MAYOR 1433.

Jan. 25. [1][Election of officers.]

24 Electors. Ric. Joy, Will. Dilcok, Laur. Cooke, Tho. Wildegrise, Joh. Braitoft, Joh. Bristowe, Joh. Michell, Joh. Clerke, Joh. Braunston, Joh. Prentes, Ric. Boton*er*, Will. Keruer, Ric. Bushebury, Rob. Southam, Tho. Crosse, Will. Frysby, Joh. Egeston, Joh. Deist*er*, Joh. Doughty, Joh. Oneley, Joh. Blakeman, Joh. Tate, Tho. Ruyton.

Officers. [m. Ric. Sharp; cor. Joh. Whalley; ch. Will. Brid, Rad. Chaundeler; w. Tho. Wirley, Joh. Lee; mace, Will. Oxton.

J. Ps. Ric. Sharp, m., Joh. Weston, rec., Laur. Coke, Joh. Leder, Tho. Wyldgrise, Hen. Peitoo.

Key-keepers. The same; except the recorder.]

WILL. CROSS' CHARTER.

Jan. 13, 1434.

[Let all present and to come know that we W. Crosse, ferryman, W. Legburne and J. Holbargh, chaplains, have delivered, enfeffed and by this present quadripartite charter confirmed to J. Garton, mercer, the heirs of his body lawfully begotten, a tenement with shops and all its appurtenances in the Bayly-lane,	[2]Sciant p*re*sent*es* et futuri, q*uo*d nos Will*elmus* Crosse de Couen*tre*, passeng*er*, Will. Legburne et Joh. Holbargh, capell*ani*, t*ra*didim*us*, feoffauim*us* et hac p*re*sent*i* cart*a* n*os*tra quaterp*ar*tita confirmauim*us* Joh*ann*i Garton, m*er*cer, de Couentr*e* & h*er*edib*us* de corp*or*e suo l*egi*time p*r*oc*re*at*is*, vnu*m* ten*ementum* cu*m* Shop*is* & om*n*ib*us* suis p*er*tinen*ciis* in Couen*tre* in le Balylane, quod Joh*annes* Mok*es* quond*am* tenuit; &
which J. Mokes formerly held, situated between the prior's tenement on one side, and that formerly held by D. Corby on the other side in breadth,	situat*ur* int*er* ten*ementum* p*r*ior*is* et convent*us* de Couen*tre* ex p*ar*te vna, et ten*ementum* q*uo*d Dauid Corby quond*am* tenuit ex p*ar*te alt*er*a, in latitudine,
and stretches itself in length from the said street to the prior's land called the Earl's orchard.	& extendit se in longitudine a p*re*dict*a* venella usq*ue* ad t*er*r*am* p*re*dict*orum* p*r*ior*is* et conuent*us* vocat*am* le Erles-orchard.
[We deliver also, and have confirmed to the said J. Garton	Tradim*us* (*sic*) etia*m* et confirmauim*us* p*re*fat*o* Joh*anni* Garton et h*er*edib*us* de (etc.)

[1] leaf 64, back. [2] leaf 66.

and his heirs 15 selions and a headland lying together beyond the New Gate at the end of Much Park, between the Trinity guild land formerly H. de le Mure's on each side in breadth, and in length according to the bounds there made.

[To have and to hold the said tenement (etc.)

to the said J. Garton and his heirs of the chief lords of the fees by the service thence due and by right accustomed for ever. And if it chance that the said J. Garton die without legitimate heir, which God forbid, then we will, and by these presents do grant that the said tenement (etc.) shall remain in its entirety to R. Praty, mercer, for the whole life of the same Robert, to be held of the chief lords of those fees for services due.

[And after the decease of the said Robert we grant that the said tenement, shop, land (etc.),

shall remain to R. Lyllyng, weaver, and his heirs;

and if R. Lyllyng die

without heirs then we grant that these

quindecim seliones[1] & vnam forearam terre simul iacentes ultra Novamportam Couentrie ad finem Parcimaioris, inter terram gilde S. Trinitatis quondam Henrici de le Mure ex vtraque parte in latitudine, & in longitudine secundum metas & diuisas ibidem factas. Habendum et tenendum predictum tenementum cum Shopa & omnibus pertinenciis suis, ac predictas quindecim seliones et forarea terre cum pertinenciis, prefato Johanni Garton & heredibus de (etc.) de capitalibus dominis feodorum illorum per seruicia inde debita & de iure consueta imperpetuum. & si contingat predictum Johannem Garton sine herede de (etc.) obire—quod absit :—Extunc volumus & concedimus per presentes quod predictum tenementum cum Shopa & omnibus pertinenciis suis, ac predicte quindecim seliones et forarea terre cum pertinenciis, integre remaneant Roberto Praty, mercer, de Couentria ad totam vitam ipsius Roberti, tenendum De capitalibus dominis feodorum illorum per seruicia inde debita et de iure consueta. & extunc post decessum predicti Roberti volumus et concedimus per presentes quod predictum tenementum cum Shopis (etc.) integre remaneant Ricardo Lyllyng, weuer, de Couentria et heredibus de (etc.) tenendum de capitalibus dominis (etc.). & si contingat predictum Ricardum Lyllyng sine herede de (etc.) obire, Extunc volumus & concedimus per presentes quod predictum tenementum

[1] v. Gloss

shall remain to J. Wyldgrise and others, and their heirs and assigns for ever. So that they by the advice of the mayor, within half a year after this remainder shall fall to them, shall sell the lands and tenement in the best way possible, and the money for the same lands and tenements received by the advice and assent of the mayor they shall distribute in works of piety for the soul of R. Garton, and for the souls for whom he was bound to pray. In testimony of which thing we have alternately affixed our seals. These being witnesses (etc.).

[Coventry Jan. 10, 1434.

[One part of this charter remains in a chest, called the wardens' counter, among the muniments, left there by the mayor, R. Sharp.

cum Shopis et omn*ibus* pertin*enciis* suis ac (etc.) integ*re* remaneant Joh*anni* Wildgrise, Will. Braytofte, Tho.[1] Bristowe, Hen. Sharp, Joh. Hampton, Joh. Bowyer, Joh. Eue*r*don, jun., Vmfrido· Swane, Joh. Burbage, jun., Joh. Praty, Joh. Broun, Tho. Kyrke & Will. Charlton, eor*um* he*re*dibus & assign*atis* imp*er*p*etuu*m. Ita q*uo*d ip*s*i, eor*um* he*r*edes uel assignati, terr*as* & tene*mentum* p*r*edict*a*, p*er* avisament*um* & assens*um* maior*is* Couen*trie* qui tu*nc* fue*r*it, infra dimidiu*m* annu*m* post remanere p*r*edict*um* eis evenire contig*er*it, vendant meliore modo q*uo* pot*er*int; & denar*ii* p*ro* eisdem t*er*r*is* & tene*mento* recept*i*, p*er* auisamentu*m* et assens*um* eiusdem maior*is*, distribuant in op*er*ibus pietat*is* p*ro* an*im*a Rad*ulfi* Garton, & p*ro* an*im*ab*us* p*ro* quib*us* iidem (*sic*) Rad*ulf*us te*n*ebat*ur* exorare. In Cuius Rei testi*monium* hiis Cart*is* quadripa*r*tit*is* sigilla n*ost*ra alt*er*natim apposuim*us*. Hiis testib*us* Ric*ardo* Sharp, m*er*catore, tu*nc* maiore (etc.) Rob. Southam et Will. Donyngton tu*nc* ball*iuis* (etc.) Tho. Wildegrise, Joh. Braytofte, Joh. Clarke, Ric. Dene & mult*is* aliis. Dat*um* apu*d* Couentr*iam* deci*mo* die me*nsis* Janu*arii* a. r. r. H*enrici* vj^ti post conq*ues*t*u*m duodecimo.

& vna pa*r*s istius cart*e* reman*et* in quad*am* Cista, vocat*a* le wardens Countre,[2] int*er* muniment*a* ciu*itatis* Couen*trie*, ib*id*em demissa p*er* manus Ric*ard*i Sharp tu*nc* maior*is*, etc.

[1] ? Will. [2] *N.E.D.* A table or desk for counting money; a bureau.

ACCOUNTS.

[Wardens' accounts for 1430.

[1]Compotus Joh. Warrant & Ric. Dene, Custodum camere ciuitatis Couentrie tempore Tho. Paynell maioris.

[Charge for which they must account £83 4*s.* 8*d.*

In primis onerantur cum iiij^{xx} iij li. iiij s. viij d.

[They ask allowance for expenses, remissions, vacancies and payments, and also for £14 8*s.* 5*d.* of a certain sum of £15 18*s.* 6*d.*, and £63 11*s.* 11*d.*

Vnde petunt allocari pro diuersis expensis, vacacionibus, perdonis & solucionibus, et etiam de xiiij li. viij s. v d. de quadam Summa xv li. xviij s. vj d. de pede compoti Will. Frysby & Ric. Dene,[2] lxiij li. xj s. xj d. & sic remanent in areragiis v li. iiij s. iiij d.

[Arrears (or balance of charge over expenses) £5 4*s.* 4*d.*

[Accounts for 1431.

Compotus predictorum Johannis & Ricardi Custodum camere (etc.) a tempore Will. Dilcoke maioris (etc.).

[Charge £67 6*s.* 2*d.*

In primis onerantur cum lxvij. vj s. ij d.

[Allowance £59 2*s.* 0*d.*

Vnde petunt allocari pro diuersis expensis, perdonis et solucionibus lix. ij s.

[Arrears £8 4*s.* 2*d.*

& sic remanent in arreragiis viij li. iiij s. ij d.

[For the two years total £13 8*s.* 6*d.*

& sic predicti custodes remanent in arreragiis pro illis duobus annis xiij li. viij s. vj d.

[Further allowances, 4 marks (£2 13*s.* 4*d.*).

Vnde petunt allocari de iiij marcis solutis Joh. Michell.

[For L. Cook £1 8*s.* 0*d.*

Item, pro Laur. Cooke xxviij s. qui remanent in manus (*sic*) eiusdem Laurencii.

[17*s.* 2*d.* remitted; and they ought to bring in balance in money by tale £8 10*s.* 0*d.*

Item, perdonantur de xvij s. ij d. Ad inducendum in pecuniis numeratis maiori viij li. x s. Excepto quod ipsi debent inducere xij s. vel vnum distres pro Will. Darsett.

[Except that 12*s.* on a distress from W. Darsett should be brought in.

[1] leaf 65. [2] p. 135.

[They have clear £7 18*s*. 0*d*. and the 12*s*. or distress;

& remanent de claro in pecuniis vij li. xviij s, et xij s. uel distres de Will. Darsett.

which £7 18*s*. 0*d*. they pay to their successors.[1]

Qui (*sic*) quidem vij li. xviij s. iidem Joh. Warrant & Ric. Dene soluerunt Thome Wirley & Johanni Lee custodibus camere.

[Accounts for 1432.

Compotus Tho. Wirley et Joh. Lee, custodum camere (etc.) tempore Will. Byfeld, maioris.

[Charge £65 18*s*. 6*d*., and with the foot of W. Frisby and R. Dene's account, for £7 0*s*. 0*d*. and 18*s*. from others. And with the foot of J. Warrant and R. Dene's account £7 18*s*. 0*d*., and for W. Dorset 12*s*.

In primis onerantur cum lxv li. xviij s. vj d. Item, onerantur cum pede compoti Will. Frisby et Ric. Dene,[2] videlicet cum vij li. pro Joh. Burton, xviij s. pro Will. Darsett, [3]pro Ric. Pisford. Item, onerantur cum pede compoti Joh. Warrant et Ric. Dene[4] cum vij li. xviij s. Item, pro Will. Dorset xij s.

[Total £82 7*s*. 0*d*.

Summa totalis oneracionis iiij^{xx} ij li. vij s.[5]

[Allowances, as appear in a book in the mayor's bag,

Vnde petunt allocari pro diuersis expensis ut patet in quodam libro existente in baga Ric. Sharp tunc maioris de lxiij li. xix s. ij d. ob.

£63 19*s*. 2½*d*., for vacancies £8 9*s*. 8*d*., for a priest 2*s*., for J. Fynche, 6*s*. 8*d*.

Item pro vacacionibus viij li. ix s. viij d. Item pro sacerdote ij s. Item pro Joh. Fynche vj s. viij d.

[Total £72 17*s*. 6½*d*.

Summa allocacionis lxxij li. xvij s. vj d. ob.

[Balance £9 9*s*. 6½*d*.

& sic remanent in areragiis ix li. ix s. vj ob.[6]

[Further allowances for certain debts owed by Laur. Cooke, J. Burton and W. Darsett,

[7]& vlterius iidem Tho. Wirley & Joh. Lee onerantur cum certis debitis que debentur per Laur. Cooke[8] & Joh. Burton & Will. Dorsett, que

[1] Their successors are liable for it, v. *infra*.
[2] v. p. 135. [3] Something omitted. [4] v. *supra*.
[5] Really £82 6*s*. 6*d*. [6] Really 5½. [7] leaf 65, back.
[8] Curious that a J. P. and member of the elective jury should be in debt.

£7 0*s*. 0*d*. £1 8*s*. 0*d*. £1 8*s*. 0*d*. 18*s*. 0*d*. 12*s*. 0*d*. 6*s*. 0*d*. £11 12*s*. 0*d*.	no*n* possu*n*t ad huc leuare; vi*delicet* pe*r* Joh. Burton vij li., pe*r* Laur. Cooke, de temp*ore* Ric. Dene xxviij s., et temp*ore* predict*orum* Tho. Wirley & Joh. Lee xxviij s., & pe*r* Will. Darsett temp*ore* Will. Frisby pe*r* tres annos xviij s., temp*ore* Joh. Warrant et Ric. Dene pe*r* ij^{os} annos xij s., temp*ore* predict*orum* Joh. Lee & Tho. Wirley vj s. vi*delicet* p*ro* vno anno. Summa xj li. xij s.
[Accounts for 1433.	Compot*us* Tho. Wirley & Joh. Lee, custod*um* cam*ere* (etc.) temp*ore* Ric. Sharpe, tunc maior*is*.
[Charge £74 18*s*. 10½*d*.	Qui on*e*rant*ur* cum iii^{xx} xiiij li. xviij s. x d ob.
[Allowance for divers expenses, vacancies, and other discharges, as appears in a paper in J. Mychell's bag, £73 11*s*. 10½*d*.	Vnde iide*m* custode*s* petu*n*t allocar*i* p*ro* diue*r*sis expens*is*, vacac*ionibus* & al*iis* desone*racionibus*, ut p*atet* in baga Joh. Mychell, maior*is*, in quod*am* papir*o* ib*idem* de lxxiij li. xj s. x d. ob.
balance £1 7*s*. 0*d*.	& sic remane*nt* in arrerag*iis* xxvij s.
[Further charge for certain debts owed by L. Coke, J. Burton and W. Dorsett viz. £11 12*s*. 0*d*. as appears above, and again with £1 8*s*. 0*d*. owed by L. Coke for 3 tenements in Gosford Street, and with 6*s*. by W. Dorsett for rent of a tenement formerly E. Lychfeld's. [Arrears £14 13*s*. 0*d*.	& ult*e*rius iidem custode*s* oner-ant*ur* cum ce*rtis* debit*is* que debent*ur* pe*r* Laur. Coke, Joh. Burton et Will. Dorsett, vi*delicet* cum xj li. xij s. ut p*atet* sup*r*a in compot*o* p*redictorum* custod*um* in p*r*imo a*nno*. & simili*ter* one*r*ant*ur* cum xxviij s. p*ro* Laur. Coke qui debent*ur* p*ro* iij^{bus} ten*ementis* in Gosford-strett de a*nno* vlti*mo* p*r*edict*orum* custod*um* et cum vj s. p*ro* Will. Dorsett de eodem a*nno* de Reddit*u* exeunt*e* de q*u*odam ten*emento* ejusdem Will*el*mi nupe*r* Edwardi Lychefeld. & sic reman*ent* in arerag*iis* xiiij li. xiij s.

JOHN MYCHELL, MAYOR, 1434.

Jan. 25. [1][Election of officers.]

24 electors. Egid. Allesley, Will. Dilcok, Laur. Cooke, Hen. Peitoo, Tho. Wildgrise, Joh. Braytofte, Ric. Joy, Joh. Rounton, Joh. Braunston, Joh. Clerke, Joh. Prentes, Ric. Bushebury, Will. Kerver, Joh. Lichefeld, Will. Swane, Joh. Warrant, Joh. Style, Joh. Doughty, Joh. Deist*er*, Will. Friseby, Joh. Egeston, Ric. Dene, Joh. Dilcoke, Joh. Oneley.

Officers. [m. Joh. Mychell; cor. Joh. Whalley; ch. Ad. Swett, Joh. Essex; w. Joh. List*ur*ley, Ric. Braytofte; mace, Will. Oxton.

J. Ps. Joh. Mychell, Will. Donyngton, rec., Egid. Allesley, Laur. Cooke, Tho. Wildegrise, Joh. Braytofte.

Key-keepers. Joh. Michell, m., Gil. Allesley, Laur. Cooke, Joh. Leeder, Hen. Peitoo, Tho. Wildegryse.]

WEIGHTS AND MEASURES.

Representatives from every ward take counsel about the "measures."

[2]Gosford[-strete.]

Laur. Cooke, Tho. Wildgrise, Joh. Stafford, Bened. Marschall, Joh. Stretton.

Jurden-well.

Joh. Prentes, Joh. Whalley, Joh. Rocheford, Joh. Lee, hosier, Joh. Dilcok, Joh. Bryan.

Much-p*ar*ke[-strete.]

Joh. Leeder, Joh. Braytofte, Hen. Peitoo, Joh. Clerke, Ric. Dene, Will. Charlton.

Erle-strett.

Ric. Sharp, Joh. Euerdon, Ric. Boton*er*, Joh. Warrant, Will. Swane, Ad. Swett, Will. Frysby.

Bayly-lane.

Joh. Rounton, Tho. Wirley, Joh. S*ir*coke, Joh. Spenc*er*, Joh Franklen.

[1] leaf 66, back. [2] leaf 67.

Brod-yate.

Egid. Allesley, Ric. Bushebury, Hen. S*ir*coke, Tho. Ruyton, Rog. Cookes.

Smyth[ford-strete.]

Joh. Bristowe, Joh. Braunston, Joh. Oneley, Joh. Blakmon, Joh. Egeston, Joh. Tate.

Spon[-strete.]

Will. Keru*er*, Mat. White, Joh. Essex, Joh. Grynder, Joh. Deister.

Crosch[epyng.]

Will. Dilcoke, Ric. Joy, Joh. Doughty, Joh. Style, Will. Dorsett.

Bischop[-strete.]

Rob. Southam, Joh. Lychefeld, Will. Wymondeswold, Joh. Listurley, Joh. Boteler.

The w*i*ch of eue*r*y ward, as hit is aboue-said, in saynt Mary hall called to-githur, apoynted that all the strik*es* of this Cite shuld be accordant to the standard made and delyue*r*ed vnto this Cite in the tyme of John sumtyme kyng of Inglond,[1] the w*hi*ch standard is halffe a st*r*ike wit*h* a barr of Iron ou*er*twart beyng in the maio*ur*is almory in the geyl-hall off Couentre.[2] **"Measures."** **A standard strike of brass in the mayor's aumbry at the gaol-hall.**

[3] Allso they orden that the maio*ur* now beyng do orden a strike of laten in allsoo goodly[4] as he may. Wherupon Joh. Mychell, maio*ur*, lett orden a st*r*ike of brass accordaunt to the standard of London sealyd and m*ar*kyd wit*h* a crown, and a Galon of brass accordant vnto the same, the w*i*ch abydithe in the kepyng of the meraltie. **Another strike, also a gallon of standard size;**

And allso þ*er* is ordeyned a st*r*ike of tree accordaunt vnto the Standard of theschekur. **a wooden strike.**

THE DUKE AND DUCHESS OF BEDFORD.

[5] Egid. Allesley, Will. Dilcok, Laur. Cooke, Joh. Leder, Hen. Peyto, Tho. Wildegrise, Ric. Joy, Joh. Braytoft, **Council of 62**

[1] In Magna Charta. v. *Statutes of the Realm*, I. 117.
[2] "Vte foliu*m*" is written below; the reverse of this page is almost blank.
[3] leaf 67, back.
[4] word omitted.
[5] leaf 68. Scribe of B. type.

Joh. Bristowe, Ric. Sharp, Will. Donyngton, Joh. Ronton, Rob. Southam, Joh. Braunston, Rob. Melburn, Joh. Clerke, Joh. Euerdon, Ric. Boton*er*, Joh. Prentes, Will. Kerver, Joh. Lychefeld, Ric. Busshebury, Will. Swanne, Joh. Warant, Joh. Willoghby, Joh. Willowby,[1] Ad. Suette, Joh. Esex, Joh. Lusterley, Ric. Braytoft, Joh. Whalley, Joh. Doughty, Will. ffrysby, Ric. Dene, Will. Darsett, Joh. Lee, Tho. Wirley, Hen. Sircok, Joh. Burton, Rad. Chaundeler, Joh. Stille, Joh. Deyster, Will. Bridd, Joh. Walgraue, Joh. Blakemon, Mat. Whit, Joh. Grynder, Joh. Asshewell, Joh. Stafford, Joh. Shadde, Joh. ffrankelen, Rog. Wilnale, Joh. Goolde, Will. Broun, Tho. Draper, Rog. Cockes, Joh. Boteler, Rob. Grubber, Nic. Gore, Joh. Bryan, Joh. Spenser, Joh. Walle.

ordain that "a present" be given to the Duchess of Bedford, and "to the Duke of Bedford," and sent to Fullbrook.

The whiche above writon han ordeyned that my lady, the duches of Bedford,[2] shuld haue l marke, & a Cowpe of siluer & ou*er*gilt, p*r*ic*e* v mark.

24 pike value £2 10*s*. 0*d*. 12 bream £1 16*s*. 0*d*. 12 tenches 16*s*. 0*d*. a tun of wine £7 6*s*. 8*d*. carriage 6*s*. 8*d*. total £12 15*s*. 4*d*.

Also they ordeyned that as-well the p*re*sent that was sent to my lord, the Duke of Bedford, vnto ffullbroke, that is to sey, xxiiij pykes,[3] p*r*ic*e* ls.[3], xij bremes [3]p*r*ic*e* xxxvj s.[3], xij tenches, [3]p*r*ic*e* xvj s.[3], & a Tune of rede wyn, vij li. vj s. viij d.[3], p*r*ice of all with the Cariage, vj s. viij d.[3], xij li. xv s. iiij d. As the seid l mark & the Cowpe of v marke shulde be leuyed be the wardes.

Other expenses £1 9*s*. 6*d*. Total (with 55 marks) £55 18*s*. 2*d*.

Also in dyuers costages made be iij tyme Rydyng to Fulbroke by dyuers officers & also be all the wurthy men of this Cite. S*um*ma xxix s. vj d. S*um*ma totalis lv li. xviij s. ij d.[4]

The duke to have 50 marks, 2 pipes of wine worth 22 . . .

[5]Mem. quod isti subsequent*es* ordinauerunt q*uo*d d*omi*n*us* Dux Bedford*ie* h*ab*eret l marcas, ij pipes vini p*r*ecii xxij . . . . . (desunt.)

See on the other side of the leaf.

Vacat quia alibi, ex alt*er*a p*ar*te folii.[6]

[The following gave to the duke of Bedford.

[7]Mem. q*uo*d isti subsequent*es* dederunt duci Bedford*ie* temp*or*e Joh. Michell maior*is* (etc.) Will. Donyngton & Rob. Southam balli*vo*r*um* (etc.)

[1] ? a repetition. [2] The duke's second wife, Jacquette of Luxembourg.
[3] Written above the line.
[4] ? £50 18*s*. 2*d*. But some items may have been omitted.
[5] leaf 68, back. [6] In margin. [7] leaf 69.

51 names.

Gos[ford Street.]

	£	s.	d.
Laur. Cooke		10	0
Tho. Wildegrise		10	0
Wal. Bonde		1	0
Joh. Boteler		1	0
Will. Capper		1	0
Joh. Baker		2	10
Joh. Watford		2	0
Ric. Skotte		2	10
Joh. Langton		1	6
Tho. Horsley		1	0
Tho. Cockes		1	0
Rob. Shukborgh		4	0
Will. Cockes		1	0
Joh. Brabson[1]		3	0
Tho. Stone		2	6
Joh. Stafford		3	4
Ric. Molle		1	6
Hugo Spencer		1	0
Joh. Sheldon		2	4
Will. Dawe		3	4
Will. Gilberd		3	4
Joh. Sheldon, jun.		2	0
Joh. Derby		1	6
Joh. Castell, wright		1	6
Tho. Smyth		1	6
Joh. Maydford		1	6
Hen. Skille		2	0
Joh. Holyes		3	4
Chris. Wright		1	0
Tho. Bowyer		1	0
Tho. Baker, draper		1	6
Joh. Asshewell		3	4
Joh. Breux			6
Hen. Coton		1	8[2]
Bened. Marchall		3	0
Alicia Breton		4	0[3]
Hen. Lambard			6
Joh. Stretton		3	0
Tho. Mason		2	6
And. Evesham		2	0
Ric. Somer		2	6
Joh. Manton		1	0
Tho. Reve		1	0
Ric. Cockes		1	6
Christiana Golofre		2	6
Joh. Eston		1	6
Will. Saunders		2	6
Ed. Deister		1	0
Sim. Baker		2	6
Joh. Evesham		2	6
Tho. Weue [? Weuer]		1	0[4]

S*umma* total*is* v li. xvj s. & inde no*n* recep*ti* xvj d.[5]

60 names.

Jurdenwell.

	£	s.	d.
Joh. ffreman, chaundler		2	2
Rob. Defford		1	4
Ric. Sherman		1	4
Tho. Elderbek		2	4
Joh. Porter			10
Joh. Brewer		1	8
Joh. Dilcok		3	8
Joh. Bryan		3	8
Joh. Cater		3	8
Joh. Whalley		3	8
Ric. Barbour		1	0
[6]Hugo Couper		1	4
Joh. Hawkyns		1	8
Tho. Barnwell			10
Joh. Rocheford		2	10
Rob. Shawe			8
Joh. Lee		3	8
Margerie Godfrey			10
Will. Cressy		1	0
Will. Shirley		2	6
Joh. Wade			8
Joh. Perkyns		1	4
Joh. ffynche		1	0
Joh. Egull		1	4
Tho. Thomas			10
Math. Tyler			8
Joh. Bette		2	0
Joh. ffolshull			10
Joh. Stoneley			10
Will. Castelton		1	8
Ric. Adam		1	1
Will. Oxton			10
Joh. Stanfeld			10
Will. Bulkley			8
Tho. Welles		2	0
Joh. Gamull		1	4
Joh. Hall		1	0
Joh. Pake			10
Hen. Cooke			10
Joh. Bradley		1	0
Tho. Dykens		2	2
Joh. Abram		2	10
Rob. Clerk		2	0
Tho. Maydford		2	10
Tho. Thruston[7]		2	2
Wal. Tyrell			10
Joh. Creke		1	0
Joh. Symond		2	4
Joh. ffremon			8
Will. Gale			10
Tho. Illage		2	6
Joh. Multon		1	0
Joh. Sutton		2	4
Rob. Grene			6
Joh. Shad		3	0
Ric. Recheford		2	6
Joh. Cressy		2	0
Ric. Clerk		1	8
Ric. Cotoner			8
Joh. Prentes		5	0

S*umma* v li. ij s. et vnde no*n* recep*ti* xxij d.[8]

[1] "bson" deleted, and "bon" substituted in another hand or ink; read Brabon.

[2] "inde re*cepti* xvj d." follows, added later.

[3] "inde re*cepti* ij s." added.

[4] "nich*il* inde re*ceptum*" added.

[5] Total £5 16*s.* 0*d.* of which 1*s.* 4*d.* has not been received.

[6] leaf 69, back.

[7] Thrustanus Walker, p. 87.

[8] Total £5 2*s.* 0*d.* of which 1*s.* 10*d.* has not been received. v li. xxj d. has been scribbled in the margin.

46 names.

Muchpark strete.

Name	£	*s.*	*d.*
Rob. Skille, sporiour			8
Will. Beverley		1	4
Will. Brid		2	6
Ric. Dene		3	4
Will. Grene		2	6
Will. Betley		3	4
Joh. Clerk		6	0
Tho. Wylot			6
Hen. Peyto		10	0
Rob. Mason, coruyer		2	0
Tho. Walsale, weuer		1	0
Joh. Leder		10	0
Johanna Byfeld		4	0
Tho. Waren		1	0
Joh. Ray		1	0
Tho. Norwyche			6
Hen. Hobbes		2	6
Alicia Attewall		1	0
Ric. Bromley, smyth		1	2
Joh. Lee, smyth		1	4
Ric. Jones, smyth			10
Joh. Derby, coruyser		2	0
Tho. Warmynton		2	6
Ric. Staffordshire		1	4
Will. Charlton		1	4
Tho. Peyntour		2	0
Joh. Gale		1	4
Will. Deys*ter*		2	0
Will. Cleybroke		2	0
Joh. Honey, mylner			8
Nic. Gryve		2	0
Will. Glasier		1	4
Joh. Witham, carter		1	0
Joh. Garton		2	6
[1]Joh. Braytoft } Will. Braytoft }		10	0
Will. Cortenale		1	0
Tho. Tyler			10
Tho. Tate		1	0
Rob. Hendeman			8
Ric. Knyghtley		1	0
Joh. Gosnore		2	6
Hen. Carter		1	4
Will. Southam		2	6
Ric. Tyler, mason			8
Tho. Abell			6

S*um*ma v li. et inde no*n* recep*ti* x d.[2]

55 names.

Erlstrete.

Name	£	*s.*	*d.*
Rob. Barbour		1	0
Joh. ffranklen		1	0
Margareta Horborgh		1	0
Joh. Lyones		1	0
Nic. Russell		1	8
Joh. Willowby		3	4
Tho. Morsby		1	0
Joh. Warant		5	0
Ad. Suette		1	8
Will. Broun		3	4
Wal. Assheby		1	8
Will. ffrysby		2	6
Joh. Motte		1	8
Tho. Reyuer[3]		1	8
Joh. Hawkyns		1	0
Ric. Sharp		6	8
Ric. Braytoft		3	4
Joh. Vnderwode		1	8
Will. Swanne		5	0
Tho. Swanne		1	8
Joh. Perpoynt		1	0
Rob. Thede		1	8
Will. Donyngton, hosier		1	8
Joh. Bryan		1	8
Will. Ednam		1	8
Joh. George		1	0
Will. Perte		1	0
Galf. Cunwey		1	8
Tho. Bayly		1	0
Joh. Radley		1	0
Agn. Crudworth		1	8
Johanna Brabson		1	0
Joh. Waterfall		1	0
Will. Dey		1	0
Tho. Glenne		2	0
Joh. Kyrkeby		1	0
Joh*anna* Northewod		3	4
Joh. Michell		6	8
Rob. Praty		1	8
Tho. Kyrke		1	8
Rob. Barnesley		1	0
Nic. Palmer		1	8
Joh*anna* Hosier		1	0
Tho. Crosse		3	4
Edm. Brogreve		1	8
Ric. Boys		1	8
Joh. Chacombe		1	0
Will. Tolas		1	0
Joh. Euerdon		5	0
Joh. Burton		5	0
Tho. Swettenham		1	8
Ric. Boton*er*		5	0
Will. Belg*r*ave		1	0
Will. Donyngton, Recordator		5	0
Ric. Revell		1	0

[5]S*um*ma v li. xiij s. iiij d. et inde no*n* rec*epti* ij s.

27 names.

Brodeyate.

Name	£	*s.*	*d.*
Alicia Illage		1	4
Locok, taylour			6
Joh. Blackamour		1	0
Will. Spenser		1	0
Tho. Spenser		1	0
[6]Will. fflekney		1	8
Joh. Bernard		1	4
Tho. Barbour			6
Tho. Ruyton, drap*er*		2	6
Joh. Yate		1	4
Hen. Sircok		5	4
Rog. Cockes		3	0
Wal. Paslowe			6
Ric. Busshebury			8
Will. Drap*er*			6
Wal. Chaterton			6
Nic. Gore		3	0
Ric. Cowper		1	0
Egid. Allesley		6	8
Will. Abram, shether		1	0
Joh. Cappe, coteler		1	6
Joh. Malory		1	0
Katherina ffremon		1	0
Joh. Huntley		1	0
Ric. Morell		1	0
Will. Dawbeney		1	0
Hugo Manton		1	0

[7]S*um*ma xlvj s. viij d.

[1] leaf 70. [2] £5 0*s.* 0*d.* of which 10*d.* has not been received.
[3] (?) Reyner; v. 13 Ryver. [4] *Sic.* (?) Colas; v. 79.
[5] £5 13*s.* 4*d.* Not received 2*s.* [6] leaf 70, back. [7] £2 6*s.* 8*d.*

41 names.

Smyth[ford strete.]

	£	s.	d.		£	s	d.		£	s.	d.
Joh. Maynard		2	0	Rog. Okburn		1	4	Wal. Northefolke		2	0
Will. Happeford		1	0	Will. Ive, smyth		1	0	Nic. Sadeler		1	0
Tho. Wodard		1	8	Joh. Hampton		1	0	Joh. Braunston		5	0
Tho. Whitside		1	8	Joh. Blackmon		3	4	Ric. Peche, Skynner			8
Will. Ruyde		1	0	Joh. Onley		3	4	Joh. Wilde		1	0
Joh. Tate		1	4	Tho. Joy		1	0	Will. Jones		2	0
Tho. Peuterer		3	0	Ric. Osbarne		3	4	Margeria Bowyer		2	0
Joh. Bristowe		10	0	Will. Melodyne		1	4	Marg*eria* Ive		3	4
Joh. Lynne		3	4	Joh. Kyngeston		2	0	Joh. Nele		1	0
Joh. fforest		1	0	Joh. Owterede		1	0	Rog. fflecher		1	0
Ric. Wymondes-wold		1	0	Ric. fflynte, osteler		2	0	Ranulph Plumer			8
Tho. Broun		3	4	Joh. Egynton		3	4	Rog. Profet, glou*er*			8
Reg. Bowyer		1	0	Joh. London		1	0	[2]*Summa* iiij li. & inde non *recepti* xij d.			
Joh. Gey [? Dey]		1	4	Tho. Leche		1	0				
				Joh. Wyponbury[1]		1	0				

85 names.

Croschepyng.

	£	s.	d.		£	s.	d.		£	s.	d.
Rob. fflecher		1	0	Joh. Barbour		1	0	Tho. Lyllynton		1	0
Dauid Hardwaremon			6	Joh. Sutton		1	0	Joh. Huet		1	0
Rob. Melburn		8	4	Ric. Drowht			10	Joh. Weston			8
Rob. Grubber		3	0	Nic. Grene		1	0	Ric. Peyntour		1	0
Will. Prentes		1	0	Tho. Bredon		1	8	Will. Deyster		1	8
Joh. Walle		2	0	Joh. Bandy		2	0	Joh. Halle		2	0
Joh. Doughty		3	4	Ric. Penson		1	8	Joh. Northemon		2	0
Joh. Gye		1	0	Tho. Norwyche		1	6	Ric. Wcuer		1	4
[3]Joh. Nele		2	0	Joh. Whight		1	0	Rob. Bron		1	8
Margareta Breux		2	0	Will. Hosier		1	0	Joh. Northampton		1	8
Hen. Peyntour		1	0	Will. Bromwyche		1	4	Hen. Rondull		2	0
Will. Hende			10	Tho. Bassingburn		2	0	Joh. Bette		1	4
Swanlond		1	0	Joh. Boteler		3	4	Ric. Bedon			8
Joh. Milner		1	0	Joh. Eborall		1	0	Rob. Mors		2	0
Ric. Lane		1	0	Joh. Iveley		1	0	Will. Huyton		6	8
Ric. Hardeborgh		1	0	Joh. Colyns		1	8	Ric. Spicer		1	0
Will. Radclyf		1	8	Tho. Aleyn			10	Tho. Swayne		1	4
Rad. Chaundler		3	4	Joh. Yong		1	0	Joh. Stille		4	0
Will. Bredon		1	0	Will. Mason		1	0	Rob. Seriaunt		1	0
Joh. ffrithe		1	0	Tho. Goldsmyth		1	0	Ric. Cade		1	0
Nic. Smyth		1	4	Will. Hulle		1	0	Joh. Warde		1	4
Joh. Appelby		2	0	Will. Darset		4	0	Will. Heyes		1	0
Will. Aderton			6	Will. Benet		1	4	Will. Meke			10
Nic. Wirdrawer		1	0	Will. Dilcok		6	8	Will. Huet		2	0
Joh. Suker		1	0	Joh. Barbour		1	0	Will. Stoneley		1	0
Ric. Joy		10	0	Will. Dey		2	6	Joh. Gelot		1	0
Thom. Holybrig		1	0	Rad. Hulle		2	0	*Summa* vij li. v s. et inde non *recepti* xiiij d.[4]			
Hen. Aderton		1	0	Joh. Imayne			10				
Joh. Barbour		1	0	Tho. White		2	0				
				Galf. Wolpyn*er*		1	2				

[1] Wappenbury, Warw. [2] £4 0*s.* 0*d.*; 12*d.* not received. [3] leaf 71.
[4] £7 5*s.* 0*d.* and 1s. 2*d.* not received.

49 names.

Baili lane.

	£	s.	d.
Joh. Merston, gurdeler		1	8
Joh. Harborgh		1	0
Joh. Byram		2	0
Joh. Whitley		1	8
Hen. Watford		1	0
Will. Warde		1	0
Joh. Sircok		2	0
Ric. Deister		1	0
Ric. Dyvet		1	8
Joh. Skille		1	4
Joh. Alen		1	8
Joh. Patenmaker		1	0
Tho. Jakemon, coruyser		1	0
Joh. Makesey		2	0
Tho. Wirley		2	0
Joh. Plymmer		2	0

	£	s.	d.
Joh. Spenser		2	0
Ric. Perbroun		1	4
Joh. Milet		1	0
Tho. Brid		1	4
Joh. Bechamp		1	4
Will. Booke		1	8
Ric. Julians		1	0
Joh. Ronton		5	0
Joh. Holt		2	0
Joh. Whiche		1	0
Joh. Yate		1	4
Hen. Walton			8
Ric. Hampton		1	0
Joh. ffrankelen		2	6
Joh. Power		1	0
Rob. Herdewyk		1	4
Tho. Loke		1	0
Joh. Burbage		1	0

	£	s.	d.
Joh. Gryme		2	0
Tho. Wadard, hosier		1	0
Joh. Bayly		1	0
Rob. Glouseter		1	4
Joh.[1]		1	4
Will. Clerk		1	8
Rob. Styff		1	4
Joh. Crosse		1	8
Hen. Brid		1	4
Sim. Harfrey		1	0
Joh. Bordale		2	0
Joh. Gilberd		1	4
Joh. Cardmaker			8
Will. Oteley			8
Joh. Lowthe			8

[2]*Summa* iij li. x d. et inde *non recepti* viij d.

61 names.

Sponstrete.

	£	s.	d.
Will. Awberey		1	0
Tho. Hastlyf		1	0
Joh. Grynder		3	4
Tho. Rastell		4	0
Joh. Essex		3	4
Alicia Paynell		3	4
Joh. Mersche		1	4
Ric. Shustoke		1	8
Joh. Sircetur		1	0
Joh. Waren		1	0
Will. Peer		3	0
Gerv. Cole		2	0
Joh. Menley		3	4
Will. Welles		2	0
Rog. Wilnale		2	0
Will. Pratte		2	0
Joh. Lote		1	8
Joh. Broun		2	0
Joh. Sewen		1	8
Joh. Honeyburn		2	0
Egid. Corbrond		3	0
Tho. Tokeby		2	0

	£	s.	d.
Joh. Molle		2	0
Will. Kerver		5	0
Joh. Deyster		4	0
Joh. Chester		2	0
Joh. Saunder		1	0
Sim. Busteler		1	4
[3]Joh. Eyre		1	0
Hen. Holt		1	8
Ric. Welford		3	0
Joh. Harres		1	8
Joh. Adley		2	0
Will. Stone		1	8
Nic. Smyth		1	0
Tho. Brid		1	0
Rog. Ball		2	0
Wal. Bulker		1	0
Will. Spenser		1	0
Hugo Steyne		2	0
Ric. Baxster		1	0
Tho. Smyth		1	0
Joh. Plasterer		2	0
Rob. Boteler		1	0

	£	s.	d.
Mat. White		3	4
Sim. Mores		2	0
Rob. Capper		2	0
Joh. Westley		1	0
Rog. Wales		2	0
Rob. Baxster		2	0
Joh. Balle		1	8
Rad. Okes		1	0
Hugo Barbour		1	4
Joh. Barkeby, baxster		1	4
Will. Hardewyk		1	8
[4]Lote, weu*er*			8
[4]Burbage		1	0
[4]Lenton			6
Reg. Whittawer			8
[4]Brasier			8
[4]Gurdelsford			6

[5]*Summa* v li. xiij s. iiij d. et inde *non recepti* xvj d.

EASTER LEET.

"Couentre." Apr. 7.

[6]¶ [V. f. p. held before Joh. Michell, m., Rob Southam, Will. Donyngton, b., on Wednesday after the Close of Easter, 12 Hen. VI.]

[1] Blank. [2] £3 0*s*. 10d.; of which 8*d*. not received.
[3] leaf 72. [4] Blank.
[5] £5 13*s*. 4*d*.; of which 1*s*. 4*d*. not received. Bishop Street omitted.
[6] leaf 72, back. Scribe B.

Jury.

Egid. Allesley, Laur. Cooke, Joh. Leder, Tho. Wilgrise, Ric. Joy, Joh. Bristowe, Ric. Sharpe, Joh. Ronton, Joh. Braunston, Joh. Euerdon, Joh. Clerk, Joh. Prentes, Ric. Botone*r*, Ric. Bussheburý, Will. Kerver, Will. Swan, Joh. Essex, Ad. Swette, Will. ffrisby, Ric. Dene, Joh. Doughty, Joh. Whalley, Ric. Braytoft, Joh. Onley.

Orders of leet. Joh. Onley and the conduit in Smithford Street.

They ordeyn that Joh. Onley haue þe co*men* seall þ*at* þe stondard of þe cundyte in þe Smythford-strete afore his yate shall not be doon awaye.

A road to be made.

Also they ordeyn þ*at* Isabell Huyton & Will. Huyton make þe weye that stretcheth fro Cheylesmor*e* Grene vnto Som*er*lesowe betwixt þis & Michelmasse next comyng, vppon the peyn of Cs. to the vse of þe Chambr*e*.

Taverners.

Also they ordeyn that þe Meir execute the orden*au*nce made for Tave*r*ners that sell wyne ayenst þe olde orden*au*nce [20s. to be raised at every trespass.]

"Recorder elected."

Also they ordeyn that Will. Donyngton be Recordo*ur* of þe Citie of Couent*r*e, als long as he is of goode beryng.

Hill Street bridge.

[The bridge in Hill Street to be made, half at the chamberlains' cost, and half at the cost of those having tenements in Hill Street.]

Palmers' Lane bridge.

Also that þe brige in the Palmer lane be made be þe wardeyns, & help of þe ward*is* þ*er*to adioynyng.

The mayor to send for the most sufficient persons for the council of Forty-eight. Disobedience to orders of the Forty-eight punished by a 6*s*. 8*d*. fine.

[1] Also they ordeyn þ*at* when þe mair hath nede to send for xlviij p*er*sones, that he send for þe most sufficient p*er*sones that shal-be at whome, & yf he come not when he is send for to lese xij d. at euery defalt, but yf he haue a resonable cause; & yf eny p*er*sone disobeye þe orden*au*nce made be þe xlviij, he so disobeyng to lose vj s. viij d. at eue*r*y tyme to þe vse of þe Chambr*e*.[1]

"Conduits."

And as touchyng the Cundyte they ordeyn that who-so make eny suspirall fro this tyme forward shall pay xl s. at eue*r*y trespasse to be rered to þe vse of þe Chambr*e*.

No grant under common seal to have suspiral.

Also they ordeyn þ*at* the Standard at Bablake be doon awaye, and þ*at* fro thys tyme forward ther be no graunte made vnder the co*mien* seall to no man to haue eny suspirall, etc.

1—1 Repeated almost verbatim, f. 90, p. 34. There the fine (6*s*. 8*d*.) is to go to the chamberlains.

See elsewhere for the Michaelmas leet. Require alte*rum* vis*um* tent*um* ad festu*m* S. Mich*ae*lis p*roximo* anno temp*or*e Joh. Eue*r*don, folio xviij° p*roximo* sequent*e*.[1]

[2] COLLECTION OF A FIFTEENTH.

Mar. 28, 1434. Thes ben the Collectours of the iiij parte of a xv peny graunted be a parlyment made in the Terme of Mich[aelmas] the yere of kyng Henry the vj the xij, to be payd at iiij tymes, the first at the fest of Ester the seid xij yere.

Gosford[-strete.]

Sim. Deyster, Ric. Somer, Joh. Stretton, Hen. Coton. £1 9s. 0d.

Jurd[*en*-well.]

Joh. ffreman, Tho. Dikons, Tho. Thurston, Tho. Elderbek. £1 5s. 6d.

Much[-park-strete.]

Rob. Mason, Tho. Tyler, Edm. Shermon, Rob. Hendmon. £1 5s. 0d.

Erll[-strete.]

Joh. Motte, Will. Donyngton, hosier, Edm. Brogreve, Nich. Palmer. £1 8s. 5d.

Baill[y-lane.]

Rob. Herdewyke, Joh. Gilberd, Tho. Jakemon, Joh. Harborgh. 17s. 6d.

Brod[-yate.]

Joh. Yate, Will. Dawberey, Hugo Manton, Ric. Morell. 11s. 8d.

Smyth[-ford-strete.]

Joh. Tate, Joh. Wilde, Ric. Wymondeswold, Joh. Hosier. £1 0s. 0d.

Spon[-trete.]

Joh. Hasclyff, Will. Welles, Tho. Rastell, Ric. Shirstoke. £1 8s. 5d.

[1] Joh. Euerdon's Michaelmas leet is included in this year, leaf 82, back. Joh. Michell's Michaelmas leet is found in part duplicated on leaf 64 (Byfeld's year), and on leaf 90 (Euerdon's year). v. *infra*. [2] leaf 68, back.

Crosch[eaping.]

Will. Deister, Will. Bromwiche, Tho. Swayne, Joh. ffrith, smyth. £1 16s. 4d.

Bissh[op-strete.]

Will. Kempe, Joh. Augur, Will. Humberston, Ric. ffillippes. £1 8s. 4d.

THE KING'S VISIT AND PRESENT.

[June 12, 1434.

[The following granted that the men of Coventry shall ride to meet the king, in green robes and red caps; and that the king should have £100 in ready money in a certain silver and gilt cup, for which the money should be levied by the wards; and that 48 of the council of the city should be called to S. Mary's Hall to confirm this ordinance.]

[1]Memorandum quod isti subsequentes concesserunt in aula B. Marie die Sabbati proximo post festum S. Barnabe apostoli [12 Henry VI], tempore Joh. Michell maioris, quod homines de Couentre equitabunt obuiando Regi cum viridibus Togis & Rubiis capiciis. Et dominus noster Rex predictus haberet C li. in pecuniis numeratis in quodam Cipho argenti & deaurato; & quod predicta summa & Ciphus essent leuata per wardas. Etiam ordinarunt quod xlviij discreti homines Ciuitatis predicte de consilio Ciuitatis predicte essent conuocati in aula predicta ad affirmandum ordinacionem predictam si voluerint.

Laur. Cooke, Egid. Allesley, Hen. Peyto, Tho. Wildegrise, Joh. Braytoft, Joh. Bristowe, Ric. Joy, Ric. Sharp, Joh. Ronton, Rob. Southam, Joh. Clerk, Joh. Euerdon, Rob. Melburn, Ric. Bussheburу, Ric. Botoner, Will. Kerver, Joh. Lychefeld, Joh. Waraunt. Will. Swanne, Joh. Braunston. 20 names.

[The following with the above-named discreet and reverend men have confirmed these ordinances, and ordained that they be observed. Note

Isti subsequentes cum prenominatis discretis & Reuerendis viris affirmauerunt et ordinaciones predictes obseruandas ordinauerunt. Et etiam Notandum est quod Ciphus predictus

[1] leaf 73.

that the cup cost 10 marks 2*s*. (£6 15*s*. 4*d*.), or 29 oz. at 4*s*. 8*d*. per oz. with the fashioning and gilding of the foot 6*s*. 8*d*. Total £7 2*s*. 0*d*.

constab*at* x marc*is* ijs.; videl*icet* xxix vnc*ie* qual*ibet* vnc*ia* iiijs. viij d.; cum fassione & p*ro* deauraci*on*e pedis eiusdem Ciphi vj s. viij d. S*um*ma x mar*ce* viij s. viij d.

Hen. Sircok, Joh. Yate, Baxster, Joh. Blakemon, Joh. Onley, Tho. Broun, Joh. Grynder, Joh. Menley, Joh. Doughty, Rad. Chaundeler, Ric. Penson, Will. Dorsette, Rob. Grubber, Joh. Goolde, Will. Wymondeswold, Joh. Rebull, Joh. Asshewell, Joh. Stafford, Tho. Elderbek, Joh. Recheford, Will. Bird, Joh. Garton, Tho. Warmynton, Will. ffrysby, Nic. Palmer, Joh. Spenser, Joh. Bechamp, Joh. Clerke, Ric. Botone*r*, Rog. Wilnale, Will. Bromwiche. 30 names.

[The following gave £107 2*s*. 0*d*. in money by tale according to the ordinance on the other part of the leaf.

[1] Isti subsequentes dederunt d*omi*no Regi C li. x marc*as* viij s. viij d. in pecuniis nume*r*atis sec*und*um ordinacionem ex alte*r*a pa*r*te folii ordinat*am*.

126 names.

Gosford-strete.

	£	s.	d.
Joh. Holy		3	8
Joh. Maltman, wirdrawer			4
Joh. Godyng, bocher			8
Hen. Weston		1	0
Hen. Skille		3	4
Joh. Mayford, weu*er*		4	0
Tho. Smyth, writelmaker		2	0
Wal. Purs		1	0
Joh. Castel, wright		3	0
Ric. Anabull, mason		1	0
Joh. Derby, wright		2	6
Joh. Sheldon, jun.		3	4
Joh. Tyrsethion		1	8
Joh. Gilberd, me*r*cer		4	6
Will. Dawe, Taylour		4	0
Joh. Sheldon, sen.		3	4
Hugo Spenser, Taylour		1	8
Ric. Molle, weu*er*		2	6

	£	s.	d.
Joh. Stafford, wirdrawer		4	0
Will. Rothwell, weu*er*		3	0
Tho. Weuer		3	4
Wil. Perte, wirdrawer			8
Joh. Preston, Taylour		1	3
Joh. Brabon, weu*er*		4	0
Will. Cokes, weu*er*		1	8
Laur. Cooke		10	6
Tho. Stretton		4	0
Rob. Burges, wirdrawer		1	3
Tho. Sporiour, wirdrawer			8
Joh. Wright		1	8
Tho. Cooke, baxster			4
Will. Corbet, weu*er*			4
Joh. Treves, weu*er*		1	3
Tho. Cockes, weu*er*		1	8
Tho. Horsley, weu*er*		1	0
Joh. Lenton, walker		2	6

	£	s.	d.
Joh. Knyȝt, wirdrawer		1	8
Joh. Clerke, laborer		1	0
Will. Sturdy		1	0
Tho. Chapman		1	0
Will. Saunders, deister		3	4
Will. Harres, deyster		1	8
Rog. Boteler		1	6
Sim. Deyster		3	8
Will. Lokier		1	3
Joh. ffyleng		1	0
Tho. Nedeler		1	0
Sim. Baxster			10
Tho. Hasting			11
Joh. Euesham		4	0
Will. Abram		1	7
Joh. Watres			8
Tho. Coke			8
Joh. Sawyer		1	0
Hayward			8
Joh. Rondull			8
Joh*anna* Nores			4
Joh. Rage		1	3

[1] leaf 73, back.

Gosford-strete.

Name	£	s.	d.
Hen. Stone			6
Wal. Bonde		2	6
Hen. Warmynton, wright		1	3
Will. Magson, carter		1	2
David Wright			6
Joh. Boteler		1	8
Rob. Wattes			8
Joh. ffrenshe			4
Will. Newnam		1	3
Joh. Clement			4
Will. Capper		1	3
Joh. Baker		3	8
Joh. Watford		2	6
Hugo Welford			3
Nich. Stoke			4
Will. Smyth, writel-maker,		1	0
Ric. Skotte		4	2
[1]Tho. Ston			4
Will. Caladon			4
Will. Miles			4
Will. Whiter			4
Tho. Button			4
Tho. Barbour			6
Ric. Mason			4
Tho. Mores		1	0
Gal. Molle			3
Tho. Barker, weu*er*			6
Joh. Spake, wir-drawer			6
Christopher Wright		1	8
Joh. ffennes, wir-drawer			6
Ric. Willy, card-maker			6
Tho. Bateman		1	0
Joh. Stere			4
Tho. Bowyer		2	2
Tho. Baxst*er*, drap*er*		2	6
Joh. Asshewell, m*er*c*er*		6	0
Joh.[2]		1	0
Joh. Plymmer		1	6
Ric. Colet		1	8
Tho. Bunsale,[3] tiler		1	0
Hen. Coton		2	6
Will. Bomye			4
Bened. Marshall		3	8
Alicia Breton		4	0
Joh. Baxster, hosier			8
Tho. Wene, weu*er*		1	8
Rog. Lambard		1	0
Tho. Wildegryse		10	6
Joh. Stretton, Taylo*ur*		3	8
Tho. Mason, coruyser		3	8
And. Evesham		1	8
Joh. Poche		1	6
Ric. Somer, weu*er*		3	8
Joh. Manton		2	8
Tho. Reve		1	8
Tho. Milwarde			8
Rad. ffolshull			8
Will. Andseld		1	8
Joh. Walker, deyster			4
Ric. Welles		1	1
Ric. Cockes, weu*er*		2	0
Joh. Sande		1	3
Tho. Hayle, walker		1	0
Hen. Tredsyn[4]		1	3
Christiana Golofur		3	8
Joh. Eston, deist*er*		3	0
Joh. Hethul		1	0
Eus. Golofer, deister		1	8

Summa £11 12*s.* 0*d.*[5]

129 names.

Jurden-well.

Name	£	s.	d.
Joh. ffreman, chaundeler		4	0
Joh. Pynder			8
Rob. Defford		2	0
Rad. Baron			4
Ric. Shermon		2	0
Tho. Elderbek		4	0
Joh. Porter		1	0
Ric. Taylour			8
Joh. Brewer		3	0
Joh. Dilcok		5	4
Tho. Wodcok			6
Joh. Prentes		6	8
Will. Gayton			4
Joh. Brian		5	4
Will. Marshall			4
Will.[2]			8
Joh. Cater		5	4
Hugo Neuton			4
Joh. Whalley		5	4
Joh. Taylour			6
Ric. Barbour		1	0
Hugo Couper		2	0
Joh. Hawkyns		2	4
Tho. Dernwell		1	0
Joh. Neve			8
Joh. Recheford		5	0
[6]Rob. Shawe		1	0
Joh. Lee		5	4
Margeria Godefrey		1	4
Will. Byg			6
Rog. Cressy		1	0
Will. Shurley		4	0
Tho. Smyth			8
Joh. Perkins		2	0
Joh. Wade		1	4
Joh. ffynche		2	0
Hen. Wen*e* [?Weu*er*]			4
Joh. Lokier			6
Joh. Deist*er*, pynn*er*			6
Will. Hurley			4
Will.[2] , Mason			6
Joh. Harres			8
Nic. Hinch			8
Joh. Toft, jun.			8
Will. Bradmere		1	0
Will. Milner			4
Joh. Milner			4
Ric. Willy, myln*er*			8
Mat. Tyler		1	0
Joh. Hosier			4
Rad. Giterner			4
Joh. Marchall			4
Rad. Clement			4
Joh. Egle		1	4
Tho. Thomas			8
Rob. Arglas			8
Joh. Tedyngworth			8
Will. Bette			8
Tho. Gilberd			4
Joh. ffolkeshull		1	4
Hen. Robyns		2	0

[1] leaf 74. [2] Blank. [3] Bonsall, co. Derby (Mr. Stevenson).
[4] ?Tredfyn. [5] £12 8*s.* 3*d.* erased. £11 8*s.* 10*d.* in margin.
[6] leaf 74, back.

Jurden-well.

	£	s.	d.
Joh. Stonley		1	0
Gil. Dubber			4
Joh. Egleston			4
Joh. Broun			4
Joh. Nicoll			4
Joh. Euesham			6
Ric. Clement			4
Tho. Merston			4
Rad. Plymer			8
[1] Castelton		3	0
Ric. Adam		2	0
Joh. Ekilsale			4
Will. Oxston			8
Will. Malyn			4
Joh. Stanffeld			8
Tho. Kirtley			8
Joh. Chapman			4
Rob. Coucher			4
Joh. Halle		1	8
Joh. Peuterer			4
Will. Patenmaker			4
Tho. Wynchestre			4
Will. Bulkeley			8
Tho. Bery			4

	£	s.	d.
Tho. Welles		3	4
Joh. Gamyll		1	8
Agnes Seuster			4
Pet. Tailour			4
Joh. Heywode			6
Greg. Hill			4
Joh. Heywode, coriour			8
Elys Tailour			4
Joh. Pake			6
Hen. Cooke			8
Joh. Bradley			8
Tho. Dykons		4	0
Joh. Abram		5	0
Tho. Horne			4
Joh. Dryffeld			6
Rob. Hosier			6
Rob. Clerk		2	8
Rog. Kyngeley			4
Isab. Hayle			4
Will. Bolton			8
Tho. Maydeford		4	0
Tho. Thruston		4	0
[1] [2]Wotton, weu*er*		1	0

	£	s.	d.
Rob. Archer			8
Joh. Belmon			4
Walt. Tyrell			8
Ric. Mildenale			6
Joh. Creeke[3]		1	0
Joh. Symond		4	0
Joh. ffreman		1	4
Dauid Baxster			6
Rob. Grene		1	8
Joh. Elderbek			8
Will. Gale		1	4
Tho. Illage		4	0
Joh. Multon		1	4
Joh. Sutton		3	4
Joh. Shadde		5	0
Ric. Recheford		2	8
Will. fflouter			4
Agn. Pynn*er*			4
Joh. Cressy		4	0
Ric. Clerk		1	8
Ric. Cotoner			8

Su*m*ma £10 4*s.* 0*d.*

93 names.

Much-park-strete.

	£	s.	d.
Rob. Eme, card-maker			8
Tho. Sherman			8
Will. Grove, card-maker			8
Rob. Skille, sporiour		1	4
Will. Beverley, smyth		2	0
Will. Brid		4	0
Edm. Sherman		1	4
Joh. Steyner			8
Ric. Dene		5	4
Joh. fford			8
Will. Grene		4	0
Will. Betley		4	0
Joh. Clerke		10	0
Tho. Willot			8
Hen. Peyto		13	4
Rob. Mason		3	4
Will. Jones			8
Tho. Walsale		2	0
Joh. Leder		13	4
Joh*anna* Byfeld		8	0
Tho. Waren		3	4
Joh. Brayn, smith			8
Joh. Yong, baker			8

	£	s.	d
Joh. Ray		2	0
Tho. Norewyche			8
Hen. Hobbes		4	8
Joh. Atwall		2	0
Margareta Walkelen			8
Joh. Lee, smyth		4	0
Ric. Bromley		2	0
Ric. Burfrey		1	4
Joh. Derby		3	4
Joh. Coruyser			8
Tho. Warmynton		4	0
Ric. Staffordshire		2	0
Wal. Neuton			8
Joh. Cockes, weu*er*			8
Joh. Braylesford			8
Hen. Benet			8
Joh. Yate			4
Hen. Balle		1	0
Tho. Kyldraught			8
Nic. Overton			8
Tho. Peynter		4	0
Will. Charlton		4	0
Joh. Cale[4]		2	0
Will. Deyster		4	0
Will. Cleybroke		3	4
Joh. Tirvile			8
Joh. Steyno*ur*			8

	£	s.	d.
Eleanora le Virgyn			8
[5]Tho. Burwey			8
Tho. Harres			8
Joh. Burnam			8
Joh. Hony, myln*er*		1	4
Alex. Myln*er*			8
Tho. More, mylner			8
Joh. ffilippes, quariour		1	4
Will. Peverell			8
Tho. Abell			8
Joh. Dyvet, carter		1	4
Ric. Tyler, mason		1	4
[1]Ston, werkman			8
Nic. More			8
Tho. Pawnton			8
Tho. Tough			8
Joh. Dilcok			8
Joh. Shergrynder		2	0
Nic. Gryve, Tiler		3	4
Will. ffermon			8
Will. Glasier		2	0
Kat*er*ina Asshow			8
[1]Onley, wir-drawer			8
Joh. Witham		2	0
Joh. Garton		4	0

[1] Blank. [2] leaf 75. [3] *Sic.* p. 125 Croke.
[4] *Sic.* ? Gale. [5] leaf 75, back.

Much-park-strete.

	£	s.	d.
Symond Mason			8
Joh. Braytoft		13	4
Tho. Tyler		2	0
Will. Osbern			4
Will. Molle			8
Tho. Tate		2	0
Rob. Hendeman		1	4
Ric. Knyghtley		2	0
Joh. Gosnore		4	0
Hen. Bug		2	0
Will. Southam		4	0
Rog. Shipston		1	4
Tho. Harper			4
Ric. Haddon			8
Ric. Coriour			4
Margareta Harries			8
Joh. Benet			8
Patr. Glasier			8
S*um*ma £10 0*s*. 0*d*.			

124 names.

Erll-strete.

	£	s.	d.
Rob. Barbour		1	8
Joh. ffrankelen		2	0
Matill Harborgh		4	0
Joh*anna* Skotte			8
Will. ffloure			8
Joh. Lyones		1	4
Nich. Russell		2	0
Joh. Caunter		1	4
Joh. Willowby		3	4
Tho. Morsby		1	4
Ric. Byfeld		1	4
Joh. Warant			[1]
Joh. Bere		1	0
Ad. Swete			[1]
Will. Broun			[1]
Walt. Assheby		2	8
Will. ffrisby			[1]
Joh. Motte		2	0
Joh. Hawkyns		1	4
Ric. Sharp			[1]
Joh. Bentley			8
Ric. Braytoft			[1]
Will. Cotoner		1	4
Tho. Reyuer		2	8
Tho. Owdeby		1	4
Joh. Colyns			8
Joh. Vnderwode		2	8
Tho. Swanne		2	8
Will. Swanne			[1]
Rob. Thede		2	8
Joh. Brian		2	8
Will. Donyngton		2	8
Joh. Perpoynt		2	8
[2]Jac. Glouer			6
Ric. Cologne			8
Joh. Goorge		2	0
Ric. Knyttesford		1	4
Agn. Crudworth		3	4
Tho. Bayly		1	4
Rad. Starky			8
Joh. Tempull			8
Joh. Radley		1	4
Will. Ednam		2	0
Will. Barbour			8
Will. Perte[3]		2	0
Galf. Drap*er*		3	0
Joh. Clerk		1	4
Joh*anna* Brabson		2	8
Tho. Shermon		1	0
Joh. Shoteswell		1	4
Will. Madam			4
Ric. Butterley			8
Will*elmus* s*er*uiens Joh*annis* Brabson			8
Will. Brewer			6
Will. Dey		1	4
Joh. Ryconjay			6
Will. Cowcher		1	4
Joh. Colman			6
Tho. Sturdy		1	4
Will. Broke			8
Joh. Ryvell			6
Joh. Waterfall		1	4
Agn. Couper			8
Tho. Glenne		3	0
Hen. Clerk		1	4
Joh. Hawton			8
Joh. Kyrkeby		1	4
Joh. Bedemaker, pynn*er*			8
Hen. Dalby		1	4
Alex. Barker			8
The Tail*our* that wedded the leches wyf			8
[1]			8
Nich. Broun			8
Joh*anna* Northewode		8	0
Joh. Michell		8	0
Rob. Praty		2	0
Rob. ffysher			[1]
Joh. Stanbury			8
Ric. Nasshe		1	0
Tho. Shawe		1	0
Agn. Nores			[1]
[1]			8
Tho. Kirke		2	8
Hen. Louth, Taylour			8
Rob. Barnesley		1	4
Joh*anna* Hosier		1	4
Nich. Palmer		2	8
Will. Crosse			8
Nich. Esterton			6
Tho. Crosse			[1]
Edm. Brogreve		3	0
Ric. Boys		3	0
Joh. Chacombe		2	0
Joh. Carles			6
Will. Daget		1	0
Will. Tolas [? Colas]		1	4
Joh. Euerdon		6	8
Joh. Burton		6	8
Will. Harold			8
Joh. Drayton			[1]
Tho. Swettenham		2	8
Alicia Annesley			2
Ric. Boton*er*		6	8
Will. Belgraue			8
David Wright		1	0
Will. Donyngton, Recorder		6	8
Ric. Revell		2	0
Will. Huyron			8
Ric. Welles, mason		2	0
Elys Skinner			8
Tho. Mason		1	0
[1] weu*er*			8
Joh. Bradley			8
Rob. Wildegryse		1	0
Joh. Gynne		3	5
Hen. Castron			8
Joh. Croncsford			8
Joh. Jones			8
Tho. Rede, skynn*er*			8
[4]Ric.[1]			4
,[1] Coruyser			8
Joh. Bullesdon, wright			8
Joh. Russheton			4
Tho. Ridware, skynner			8
S*um*ma £11 7*s*. 4*d*.			

[1] Blank in MS. [2] leaf 76. [3] ? Perce. [4] leaf 76, back.

105 names.

Brodeyate.

	£	s.	d.
Rob. Lemynton, Tailour			6
Alicia Illage		1	0
Joh. Mel[ton]			8
Joh. Locok			[1]
Joh. Blakamour		1	4
Will. Spenser		1	4
Will. ffekeney		2	0
Joh. Bernard		2	0
Tho. Barbour		1	0
Tho. Ruyton		3	0
Rog. Miln*er*, Tayl*our*			8
Joh. Hencote, Tail*our*			8
Joh. Yate			[1]
Joh. Yong			[1]
Hen. Sircok		6	0
Rog. Cockes		3	0
Rog. Coke			8
Joh. Marton			8
Walt. Paslowe		1	4
Ric. Busshebury		6	8
Joh. Cappe, coteler		2	0
Will. Cockes			8
Joh. Malory		1	4
vx*or* Ric. ffreman		1	8
Joh. Huntley		1	4
Rob. Persale			8
Ric. Morell		1	4
Ric. Bromley, goldsmyth		1	0
Ric. Essex			8
Joh. Nele, Taylour			8
Will. Dawbeny		1	8
Joh. Archer		1	0
Will. Marshall			8
Vx*or* Rob. Sporio*ur*			8
Ric. Twyg			8

	£	s.	d.
Hugo Manton		1	4
Rad. Duffield		1	4
Will. Draper			8
Will. Chaterton			3
Joh. Kele			4
Will. Barley			4
Will. Lyth[2]			4
Tho. Catter			4
Joh. Yerwell, coteler			4
Galf. Coteler			8
Will. Abram, shether		1	0
Will. Shether		1	0
Ric. Barwell		1	0
Nic. Pikstaff			8
Joh. White			8
Joh. Solihull, wright			8
Joh. Harres			8
Ed. Corio*ur*		1	4
Ric. Styward			8
Tho. Lokyngton			8
Bened. Stokton			4
Ric. ffletcher			3
Joh. Barbour			4
Wal. Kyppyng			4
Tho. Wastell			4
Nic. Gore		2	8
Sibell Janyns		1	0
Joh. Nicoll, Coriour			8
Alicia ffox			8
Moric*ius* Morewyk			4
Will. Walton, Cobeler			8
Egid. Allesley		6	8
Will. ffoster			4
Will. Grene, skole-maist*er*			4

	£	s.	d.
Will. Canley			4
Will. Coteler			4
Will. Westbury			4
[3]Joh. Pigou			4
Tho. Ruydyng			4
Tho. Parker			4
Marg*er*ia ffisher			2
Joh. Chapman			2
Ric. Bystowe			4
Clem. Wirdrawer			4
Marg*er*ia Onley		1	0
Joh. Basset			4
Rob. Peuterer			4
Ric. Couper		1	4
Joh. Heges			4
Will. Willcotys		1	0
Joh. Purs			4
Joh. Repyn[4]			4
Rob. Ingrewf			4
Hen. Westley			4
Joh. Bullesdon			4
Will. Wyresdale			4
Tho. Lyones		1	4
Joh. Yong			4
Dav. Welsheman			4
Joh. Melton			4
Ric. Garton			8
Tho. Warde			4
Will. Tyler, wright			4
Ric. Walsale			4
Joh. Hare, mason			4
Nic. Jones			4
Joh. Robyns			4
Ric. Waterfall			4
Rob. Illyot			4
Tho. Godfrey			4

S*um*ma £4 13*s*. 4*d*.

91 names.

Smythford-strete.

	£	s.	d.
Joh. Maynard		3	4
Rog. Profet		1	8
Alex. Bower			8
Will. Happeford		2	0
Tho. Wodard		3	4
Tho. Whitside		3	0
Will. Rede		2	0
Rob. Sherman		1	0
Joh*anna* Peuterer		1	4
Tho. Tate		2	0
Tho. Peuterer		3	4
Joh. Bristowe		13	4
Joh. Lynne		4	0

	£	s.	d.
Joh. fforest		2	0
Ric. Holt			6
Ric. Wymondeswold		2	0
Tho. Broun		4	0
Will. Ive, smyth		1	8
Joh. Kirkebank			8
Joh. Bowterode			4
Joh. Abowte			8
Hen. Balle			4
Reg. Bowyer		2	0
Joh. Dey		2	0
Rob. Barley			4

	£	s.	d.
Rob. Haliday			8
Simond Awdeley			4
Joh. Jabet		1	8
Ranulphus Plymner		1	0
Joh*anna* Holt			6
Rog. Rouke		2	0
Joh. Blakemon, jun.			8
Joh. Hony		1	0
Joh. Hampton		1	4
Tho. Plymer			8
Joh. Blakeman, sen.		5	0
Elena Rede			4
Joh. Onley		5	0

[1] Blank in MS. [2] ? Heth, *v.* p. 177. [3] leaf 77. [4] p. 177, Rypon.

Smythford-stretę.

	£	s.	d.
Tho. Joy		1	8
Ric. Osbern		4	0
[1] Will. Melodyne		2	0
Joh. Brewer			8
Joh. Hygreve		1	0
Joh. Kyngeston		3	4
Joh. Malory		1	8
Elys Taylour			10
Will. Gobeler			8
Joh. Outered		2	6
Rad. Bredon		1	4
Ric. Adlyngton			6
Tho. Whetecroft		1	0
Ric. fflynt		3	4
Agnes Colam			4
Margareta Abell		1	0
Will. Bolton, Coteler		1	4
Joh. Egeston		5	0
Joh*anna* Dier		2	0

	£	s.	d.
Tho. Leche		1	4
Joh. London		1	0
Joh. Wypenbury		1	8
Marg*eri*a Prescote		1	0
Joh. Glastenbury			8
Walt. Northfolk		3	4
Johanna Weram			6
Rob. Sturdy, Coteler			9
Joh. Peer			6
Joh. Adderbury			6
Tho. Hopkyns			8
Ric. Baxster			8
Ad. Deyster			4
Will. Heywode			8
Ric. Couper			8
Will. Bredon		1	0
Will. Mariot			8
Nich. Sadeler		1	4
Joh. Braunston, jun.		1	0

	£	s.	d.
Joh. Braunston, sen.		6	8
Elis Barbour			4
Joh. Metburn		1	0
Joh. ffrankelen, jun.			6
Ric. Peche, skynn*er*		1	4
Joh. Wilde		1	8
Will. Jones		3	0
Joh. Gode		1	0
Isabella Tyburton			6
Margeria Bowyer		4	0
Mar*geri*a Ive & Will. fil*ius* eius		6	0
Joh. Nele, su*m*nour		1	8
Joh. Swanlond		1	0
Joh. Nele, coruys*er*		2	0
Rog. ffletcher		1	4

S*um*ma £8 0*s.* 0*d.*

132 names.

Spon-strete.

	£	s.	d.
Will. Awbrey		1	0
Joh. Botte		1	0
Joh. Hasolyf[2]		1	8
Joh. Grynder		4	0
Joh. Stoneley		1	0
Tho. Rastell		4	0
Joh. Esex		5	0
Alic*ia* Paynell		6	8
Joh. Mersche		2	8
Ric. Shistoke		2	0
Tho. Pratte		1	4
Joh. Sissetur		1	8
Joh. Waren, coruyser		1	8
Joh. Gurdelesford		1	0
Will. Allesley		1	0
Will. Pere		3	4
Gervasius Cole		3	0
Will. Pars			6
Joh. Bette			8
Edw. Laborer			8
Joh. Menley		4	0
Will. Welles		2	8
[3] Rog. Iremonger		4	0
Will. Pratte		3	0
Joh. Derby, deist*er*			6
Joh. Lote		4	0
Tho. Irysshe		1	0
Joh. Broun		4	0
Joh. Brette		1	0
Joh. Sewen		3	0

	£	s.	d.
Ric. Pulter			6
Egid. Corbrond		3	4
Hugo Rogeley		1	0
Tho. Tokeby		3	8
Joh. Honyburn		3	4
Joh. Naylston			4
Joh. Molle		2	8
Will. Kerver		10	0
Joh. Deyster		6	0
Joh. Chester		3	0
vx*or* Will. Broun			6
Joh. Blakenale			6
Emma Marnam } Joh. Saunders }		2	0
Reg. Whittawer		1	0
Rob. Milner		1	0
Joh. Bullok			8
Hen. Taylour			9
Ric. Corby			6
Joh. Eyre		2	0
Rob. Hache			8
Simon Busteler		2	0
Ric. Rows			6
Joh. Brere		1	0
ffelicia Astley			8
Tho. Tewe			10
Joh*anna* Brysaldon			4
Joh. Lote		2	0
Joh. Knyghtley		1	4
Joh. Burbage		3	0
Hen. Holt		3	0

	£	s.	d.
Joh. Broun		1	0
Ric. Welford		4	0
Will. Stokton			6
Joh. Acaws			6

vide pl*ura* no*min*a de ista warda, qui (*sic*) solue-ru*n*t do*min*o Regi, ut sup*ra*, folio tercio sub-sequent*e* post ward*am* de Bayly-lane.[4]

[5] Pars warde Spon-strete.

	£	s.	d.
Joh. Harres		2	8
Joh. Hegges			8
Joh. Howdon[6]		1	0
Tho. Harper			6
Will. Roper			4
Joh. Cowper			6
Joh. Vpton		1	0
Joh. Pen		1	0
Tho. Lenton			8
Tho. Archer		1	0
Joh. Baxster			8
Joh. Wynfeldon			8
Tho. Morton			6
Joh. Stoke			6
Galf. Tygen		1	0
Dav. Yong			8

[1] leaf 77, back. [2] or Hastlyf. [3] leaf 78.
[4] I have transposed these names from leaf 81. [5] leaf 81. [6] Howden, co. York

Spon-strete.

	£	s.	d.
Joh. Benet, Typper			4
Joh. Wylnale			6
Joh. Thornton		2	0
Joh. Stone			6
Rog. Balle		3	0
Walt. Bulker		2	8
Ric. Rede		2	0
Hugo Steyne		4	0
Ric. Baxster		1	11
Joh. Gamull			6
Joh. Hamond			6
Will. Spenser		2	2
Joh. Cockes, walker			10
Tho. Caldwell		1	0
Will. Myles		1	6
Tho. Smyth		2	0
Will. Slede			4
Tho. Straunge		1	7
[1]Paunton			8
Galf. Capper			8
Joh. Plasterer		3	0

	£	s.	d.
[2]Joh. Levyng			4
Rob. Boteler		2	0
Laur. Huyson			8
Ric. Taylour			3
Moric. White		3	0
Mat. White		6	0
Ric. Kersyman			4
Ric. Capper		3	0
Joh. Bulkeley			6
Joh. Melton, sadeler			8
Joh. Chiry			6
Hen. Brown			6
Rog. Barton			6
Ric. Huyton			6
Joh. Smyth			6
Rob. Grynder		1	0
Hugo Milner		3	6
Joh. West			5
Will. Bate		1	4
Joh. Westley		1	0
Joh. Couper		1	0

	£	s.	d.
Rog. Wales		2	8
Joh. Wamburn			8
Rob. Bulkley		3	4
Joh. Balle		2	0
Tho. Bayly			6
Joh. Tykell			6
Rad. Okes		1	6
Hugo Barbour		1	8
Agn. Goldsmyth			6
Joh. Baxst*er*		2	0
Tho. Saumson			8
Will. Hardewyk		2	0
Ric. Walford			8
Joh. Hadley		3	9
Will. Stone		2	0
Nic. Smyth		1	0
Tho. Brid		1	4
Hen. Prynse			6
Nic.[1]			3

Summa £11 7*s.* 4*d.*

197 names.

[3]Bysshop-strete.

	£	s.	d.
Ric. Cardyff			8
Will. Yong			8
Joh. Auger		2	0
Joh. Lychefeld		8	0
Joh. Welles			4
Hugo Cartwright		1	0
Ric. Tomson		1	4
Rob. Crudworth, mynstrel			4
Walt. Trig		2	8
Tho. Carter		2	0
Joh. Wright			6
Rob. Weston		2	8
Joh. Shilton, Tailour			8
Rob. Barbour			8
Joh. Couper		1	4
Wil. Couper		2	0
Sim. More		1	0
Tho. Lesyngham			4
Rog. Lesyngham		2	0
Joh. Wodecote			1
Joh. Span, coruys*er*			6
Will. ffelde		1	4
Joh. ffreman		1	0
Tho. Walgraue		2	4
Tho. Smyth		1	0
[4]Joh. Plomer			4
Will. Trewman		1	0
Will. Richardson		2	0
Tho. Broun		1	0

	£	s.	d.
Ric. Tedde		1	0
Will. Wymonds-wold		6	0
Tho. Broun, weu*er*		1	8
Alicia Widowe			4
Tho. Cleybroke		2	0
Joh. Sandon			8
Tho. Hawkeslow		2	0
Tho. Smyth			8
Joh. Savaye			8
Ric. Pyne			6
Simond Wright		1	4
Rad. Smyth			4
Joh. Mathewe			4
Joh. Cleybroke			8
Edw. Pyne			4
Hen. Smyth			4
Paulus Weu*er*			4
Tho. Clerke, laborer			4
Will. Horsley		2	0
Will. Russheton			8
Persyvale Werkman[5]			4
Breymerus Mason[5]			8
Hugo Shaw, jun.			8
Nic. Harold, Bitter[6]			4
Will. Iressheman			4
Rog. Gose		1	0
Seruiens Tho. Staf-ford			4

	£	s.	d.
Tho. Stafford		2	0
Will. Aubenie			8
Will. Wylkyns		5	0
Joh. White		1	0
Tho. Sponer			8
Tho. Shawe			4
Sampson Wever[5]			4
Ric. Waren		1	0
Ric. Cockes, Coto-n*er*			4
Will. Daventry, glasier			4
Tho. Cockes, ffyssher		1	4
Joh. Walker			8
Will. Wythiford		4	0
Joh. Broun			4
Joh. ffethy			8
Joh. Bryn			4
Joh. Bylston			8
Galf. Taylour			4
Joh. Grene		3	4
Joh. Golde		5	0
Joh. Welford		3	4
Will. Chapman			4
Joh. Edward			8
Dav. Mores			4
Tho. Sulby		1	4
Agn. Maltman			4
Hen. Wright			4

[1] Blank in MS. [2] leaf 81, back. [3] leaf 78. [4] leaf 78, back.
[5] Not clear whether occupation or surname. [6] *v.* Gloss.

Bysshop-strete.

	£	s.	d.
Joh. Kebull		3	4
Joh. Waldyf		1	0
Rob. Baxster			4
Ric. Cockes, baxster			8
Will. Smyth, weuer			4
Ric. Chichester		2	6
Joh. Stokton			4
Joh. Hampton		4	0
Pet. Milner		1	0
Joh. Sompton		1	0
Ric. ffillipes		3	4
[1] Bardford			4
Will. Rolf			4
Tho. Weuer			8
Will. Humburston		2	0
Joh. of the Hoode			4
Tho. Barbour, weuer		1	0
[2] Ric. Harberd			8
Will. Neuton		2	6
Joh. Chacombe, coruyser			8
Tho. Sadeler			8
[1] Wright			4
Hugo Shawe		5	0
Will. Bate		1	0
Joh. Powes, wright			8
Matill. Profetto & *filius* eius		2	0
Tho. Eton			4
Ric. Clerk		1	4
Ric. Spicer		2	4
Tho. Waren, wright		1	4
Eliott Coruyser[3]			4
Joh. Seele			4
Johanna Palmer			6
Will. Warrewyk		2	0
Johanna Walgraue		4	4
Joh. Tebbe		1	0
Joh. Lyncoln		1	4
Will. Lichefeld		1	0

	£	s.	d.
Rob. Cooke			4
Rob. Southam		10	0
Will. Garet			8
Will. Lusterley		1	8
Tho. Wodcok		2	0
Will. Bette			8
Joh. Barres			4
Tho. Chester, glouer			4
Joh. Couper		1	8
Nic. Hulle		1	0
Hen. Hulle		1	0
Ric. Pisford			8
Joh. ffolvile		2	0
Joh. ffyndon			8
Joh. Reynold			8
Will. Kemp		3	4
Tho. *seruiens* Will. Kemp			4
Tho. Wardyghter			4
Hugo Ryse			4
Ric. Lorde			4
Seruiens Joh. Lusterley			8
Rog. Holbeche		1	0
[1] Mores, Bocher		3	4
Ed. Bitter			4
Rob. Wright			4
[1] ffyndon, jun.			4
Thom. Sponer			4
Nic. Laborer[3]			4
Will. Sowle			4
Will. Smyth, laborer			4
Ed. Drouer		5	0
Moric. Sawyer			4
Rog. Taylour		3	4
Tho. Smyth			8
Joh. Stafford		2	6
Joh. Bitter			4
Alex. Barker		1	4
Joh. Dormesa			4

	£	s.	d.
Ric. Wyche[4]			4
Will. Smyth, wright			8
Nic. Cook			4
Hen. Baxster			4
Ric. Alrestre			4
Will. Bydell			4
Rob. Owtrede			4
Joh. Alys			4
Nic. Taylour			3
[1] fforest, wright			4
Will. Brynton			4
Will. Tuttebury			3
[1] Morley, walker			4
Margareta Stanffeld			4
Hen. Deyster			4
Will. Wyngode			8
Ric. Glouer		1	0
Laur. Bette			8
Will. Sawyer			6
[5] Joh. Tewe			4
Joh. Pynne			4
Hen. Walker		1	8
Joh. Attewode		1	4
[1] Walsale, weuer			8
Moric. Steynour			8
Ric. Bylston			4
Joh. Stokes, Tailour			8
Tho. Sewker			4
Rob. Denyver			4
Will. Raby			4
[1] Halywode			4
Will. Tryske[6]			4
Tho. Tebbe			4
Ric. Tomkyns			4
Joh. Delamare			4
Tho. Wakefeld			4
Galf. Polle			4
Joh. Parker			8

Summa £11 6*s.* 0*d.*

149 names.

Cros-chepyng.

	£	s.	d.
Rob. ffletcher		1	8
Dav. Bulwyk			8
Will. Tauerner			8
Joh. Multon, spicer			8
Rob. Melburn		6	8
Rob. Grubber		6	0
Will. Prentes		2	0
Joh. Otewalle		4	0
Tho. Garton		1	0

	£	s.	d.
Joh. Doughty		6	0
Guydo Draper[3]		2	0
Joh. Henware			6
Joh. Nele		4	0
Margareta Breux		5	0
Hen. Banbury		1	4
Will. Hende		1	4
Tho. Swanlond		1	4
Joh. Milner		2	0

	£	s.	d.
Ric. Lane		1	8
Ric. Harborgh		1	8
Will. Radclyf		3	0
Rad. Chaundeler		5	0
Will. Bedon		2	0
Joh. ffrithe		1	8
Nic. Smyth		3	0
Joh. Marchall			6
Will. Aderton		1	4

[1] Blank. [2] leaf 79. [3] Not clear whether occupation or surname.
[4] A certain Ric. Wiche was burnt as a Lollard in London in 1439.
[5] leaf 79, back. [6] Probably Thirsk, co. York.

Cros-chepyng.

	£	s.	d.
Joh. Apelby		3	4
Tho. Kerdyf		1	0
Nic. Taylour, wirdr*awer*		1	4
Will. Syvetare		1	4
Joh. Wright		1	4
Joh. Purdon			8
Margareta Jatkyns			8
Nic. Burbury		1	0
Joh. Manton			4
Ric. Joy		10	0
Pet. Shefeld			6
Joh. Bylston			8
Tho. Holybryg		1	0
Hen. Aderton		2	0
Will. Dyvet		1	8
Alicia Parker			10
Joh. Lokier			8
Laur. Sutton		1	4
Joh. Bylston, barbour		1	4
Ric. Illage			6
Joh. Sutton		1	8
Tho. Goloffre			8
[1] Ric. Drought		1	4
Nic. Grene		2	0
Tho. Bredon		3	0
Joh. Bandy		3	0
Joh. ffysher			8
Ric. Penson		3	0
Tho. Norwyche		3	0
Joh. Wetoft		3	0
Will. Hosier		1	8
Tho. Bayly			8
Tho. Bassingburn		4	0
Joh. Boteler		4	0
Joh. Eborall		1	8
Joh. Iveley		1	4
Joh. Brasse			8
Joh. Colyns		3	4
Joh. Yong		1	8
Joh. Shenston			8
Tho. Alen		2	0

	£	s.	d.
Will. Mason		2	0
Tho. Goldsmyth		1	8
Joh. Botte [? Bette]		3	0
Ric. Bedon		1	4
Joh*anna* Cooke		1	0
Simon Payne		1	8
Tho. Doff			6
Joh. Marchall			6
Tho. Clerk, coriour			6
Mat. Allerton, wayte		2	0
Joh. Coucher			4
Joh. Maysbroke			4
Rob. Mors		3	4
Joh. fflaxhale			6
Will. Huyton		6	8
Ric. Spicer		2	0
Hugo Cariour			6
Tho. Swayne		3	4
Joh. Stille		6	0
Rob. Seriaunt		1	8
Joh. Cade			8
Joh. Coriour			6
Joh. Warde		3	0
Will. Heyes		2	0
Hen. Euerdon			8
Will. Meke		2	0
Will. Nuport			6
Will. Huet		4	0
Will. Stoneley		1	0
Joh. Shepey, Coriour			4
Joh. Prentes			4
Will. Gylyon		1	0
Juliana Dyssher			8
Joh. Colyns, barbour		2	8
Joh. Launder			8
Tho. Cobeler			6
David de le Priory			4
Joh. Blokley			8
Edw. Dilcok		10	0
Will. Barbour			8

	£	s.	d.
Joh. Baker de Priory			4
Will. Boteler			6
Joh. Hayly		1	0
Joh. Barbour		1	4
Will. Garen			4
Will. Dey		5	0
Will. Bynley		1	4
Agn. Westbury			8
Ric. Peyntour		2	0
Joh. Weston, su*mn*our		1	8
Joh. Huet, mason		2	8
Joh. Wright, bocher		1	4
Tho. Dokon			4
Will. Lyllynton		1	4
Tho. Lyllynton		2	0
Golf. Wulpyn*er*		2	0
Joh. Vynsent			8
Will. Norton		1	4
[2] Tho. Whyght		2	8
Joh. Imayne		2	0
Ric. Imayne			4
Rob. Hare		2	0
Nich. Boch*er*			8
Hen. Wydwell		1	4
Rad. Hull		3	0
Joh. Wynwyke			8
Hen. Taverner			8
Hen. Rondull		4	0
Joh. Marchall			8
Will. Manton			4
Joh. Northampton		4	0
Ric. Lyrpull		1	11
Rob. Burn		4	0
Joh. Bynley			8
Ric. Wouer [? Weuer]		3	4
Elisabeth Lyrpull		1	0
Joh. Nuport		2	0
Joh. Halle		4	11
Joh. Lyllynton		1	4
Will. Deyster		3	4
Tho. Leyghton		1	0

S*um*ma £14 10*s.* 0*d.*

82 names.

Bayly-lane.

	£	s.	d.
Joh. Merston		3	0
Joh. Thorp			4
Will. Langcastell			4
Joh. Harborgh		2	0
Joh. Bryan		3	0
Joh. Hornby			8
Joh. Whitley		2	8
Rob. Spenser			8

	£	s.	d.
Tho. Dyvet		1	0
Hen. Watford		2	0
Will. Wylde			4
Will. Warde		1	4
Joh*anna* Bryd			4
Joh. Sircok		4	0
Will. Harborgh		1	0
Ric. Deyster		1	8

	£	s.	d.
Ric. Godefrey			6
Ric. Dyvet		3	0
Hen. Wright			4
Will. Oteley		1	4
Nic. Edwarde			8
Joh. Alen		2	8
Joh. Bradley			8
Joh. Cardmaker		1	0

[1] leaf 80. [2] leaf 80, back.

Bayly-lane.

	£	*s.*	*d.*		£	*s.*	*d.*		£	*s.*	*d.*
Joh. Boteler		1	8	Joh. Bechamp		2	6	Rob. Herdwyke		2	6
Joh. Straunge			4	Joh. Wyche, peut-				Tho. Loke		2	0
Will. Wright		1	0	erer			8	Joh. Burbage		1	8
Tho. Jakemon		1	8	[1]Will. Broke		4	0	Joh. Gryme		3	4
Will. Westley			8	Joh. Louthe		1	0	Rog. Wodard		1	4
Ric. Goddesley			8	Joh. Langestell			6	Tho. Gryme		1	0
Katerina Crossely			4	Ric. Julyans		1	4	Joh. Bayle		1	4
Will. Grauncester			8	Joh. Ronton		10	0	Rob. Gloucester		2	0
Joh. Maxsey		4	0	Joh. Hulle		3	4	Will. Clerke		3	0
Wal. Clerke			6	Joh. Yate		2	0	Joh. Oderyche		2	0
Ric. ffurnes			8	Joh. Joyner		1	0	Rob. Styff		2	0
Tho. Wyrley		4	6	Joh. Wyche		2	0	Joh. Crosse		3	0
Joh. Plymer		3	0	Tho. Coriour			4	Joh. Haddon		1	0
Joh. Spenser		4	0	Hen. Walton			8	Hen. Brid		1	8
Ric. Tokeby		1	0	Ric. Clerke		1	4	Simon Harfrey		1	0
Rad. Cotoner		1	0	Ric. Plymer		2	0	Joh. Bordale		3	0
Ric. Perbrown		2	0	Joh. Skille		2	0	Joh. Gylberd		2	8
Joh. Mylet		1	0	Joh. Chambur			6	Hen. Typper			4
Tho. Peuterer		2	8	Joh. ffrankelen		4	0	Alicia ffloytour			4
Ric. Smale			8	Joh. Power		1	4	*Summa*	£7	0*s.*	0*d.*

MICHAELMAS LEET.

[2][3][V. f. p. held on Monday after Michaelmas, 13 Hen. IV.]

Oct. 4.

Jury of 23.

Egid. Allesley, Laur. Coke, Joh. Leder, Hen. Peyto, Tho. Wildegrysse, Joh. Braytoft,[4] Ric. Joy, Joh. Bristowe, Joh. Ronton, Joh. Brampston, Joh. Clerk, Joh. Euerdon, Joh. Prentes, Ric. Botone*r*, Will. Kerver, Joh. Licheffeld, Ric. Busshebury, Will. Swanne, Joh. Waraunt, Joh. Esex, Ad. Swette, Joh. Stelle, Dyst*er*, Ric. Braytoft.

[Will. ffrysby, Joh. Doughty.]

Bailiffs.

They orden that breusters selle a galon of good ale whill hit is newe ffor ob. q^a^., and when h*i*t ys stale ffor j d., eue*r*y man & eue*r*y woman, a-pon the peyne off vj s. viij d. at eue*r*y defaute to þe vse of þe Cite; allso þ*at* they Galon, pottell and quart be made acordant to the stondart.

Orders of leet. A gallon of new ale for ¾*d.* and stale for 1*d.*

Also the orden that the seriauntes off the stresse Rolle warn eue*r*y man, [5]be hym self or his neyghbour,[5] that is in the Roule defendant eue*r*y fourtenyght ones or elles eue*r*y iij wekes atte lest, eue*r*y se*r*iaunt opon þe peyne of xl d. at eue*r*y trespas, to be leuyed to þe vse off

The sergeants to warn those who have been distrained upon, or 3*s.* 4*d.* fine.

[1] leaf 81. [2] leaf 90, duplicated leaf 64. [3] Scribe C.
[4] MS. Brayftot. [5—5] Interlined and not on f. 64.

After the third holding of the court the defaulter is to be arrested.

þe Towne. And þ*at* no man ffro þ*is* tyme ren no lenger in þe stresse Role issues ne indymentes[1] (*sic*) but iij Courte dayes, & then to be returned to a Capias, and so attached to Com to onsuere.

The attendance of the Forty-eight.

Also the ordeyne that they meire tak xlviij off þe most worthiest men that arn at home p*re*sent, eue*r*y man that Comyth not [see for penalties p. 157].[2]

The river.

The ordeyne tha[t] the Reuer be elarged be oue*r*seiȝt off þe meire, and þ*at* eue*r*y man voide hit ffor his parte[3] off hys ten*ement*, vpon þe peyne off xx s.

The ordeyne þ*at* the Comen se*r*geant Clense and haue away all þe filth at þe Costes off the towne wit*h*-Inne þis moneth, vnd*ur* þe peyne off di*midie* ma*rce* to be paied by they Chamburlens.

A swain for the swine.

[4] They orden that they haue a swon as þey were wont to haue, and þ*at* they þ*at* [5]that haue their swyn before hym paye hym,[5] or elles the Comyn sergeuant distreyne hym ffor þe payment by sufficiant distresse.

"No orders off Crafts to be good except Alowed by þe mayor & his bretheren." Millers.

["Caves" and ordinances made by the crafts are all void; none to be made without the assent of the mayor and council, on pain of a £20 fine to the town wall.]

The orden þ*at* melners Grynde ffrohensfurth for vjd. a quarte*r*, and so afte*r* that rate without Toll [6]takyng, vppon the peyn of di*m*. marc*e* at eue*r*y de*faut*.[6]

A FIFTEENTH.

Nov. 11, 1434.

[7][The following collected the fourth part of a fifteenth "de *festo* S. Martini Ep*iscop*i," 13 Hen. VI.]

Gosford[*-street.*] Joh. Sheldon, Joh. Brabon, Tho. Stoone, Hen. Coton. £1 9s. 0d.

Jurdenwell. Tho. Eldurbek, Joh. Sutton, Cardmake*r*, Will. Gale, Joh. Rocheford. £1 5s. 6d.

Much[*park-street.*] Rob. Mason, Tho. Tiler, Ed. Sharman, Tho. Tate. £1 5s. 0d.

[1] "ne in indytement*es*," f. 64. Insignificant variations between the two versions are not noted.

[2] Here the duplication ends.

[3] & or "a" in MS. The writing is slovenly and almost illegible with frequent deletions. [4] leaf 90, back.

[5—5] In the hand of scribe B, who fills up the gap left by scribe C. Probably the former supervised the latter's writing.

[6–6] In Scribe B.'s hand. [7] leaf 82. Scribe A.

Erle[*-street.*] Joh. Moote, Will. Donyngton, Joh. Clerke, tailo*u*r, Ed. Brogreve, Rob. Thede. £1 8s. 5d.

Baill[*y-lane.*] Rob. Herdwike, Joh. Gylberd, Tho. Jakemon, Joh. Harbourgh. 17s. 8d.

Brodeyate. Joh. Yate, Joh. Locok, Joh. Yong, sporiour, Ric. Morrell. 11s. 8d.

Smyth[*ford-street.*] Joh. Maynard, Tho. Carbonell, Joh. Wylde, Will. Melodyne. £1 0s. 0d.

Spoon-[*street.*] Ric. Austen, Capper, Ric. Shustoke, Will. Wellys, Joh. Sewyn. £1 8s. 5d.

Crosch[*epyng.*] Will. Deist*e*r, boch*e*r, Will. Bromwiche, Sim. Payn, Joh. ffryth, smyth. £1 16s. 4d.

[1]*Welstrett.* Will. Kemp, Joh. Awger, Will. Humburston, Ric. fylipes. £1 8s. 3d.

JOHN EVERDON, MAYOR, 1435.

[2][Election of new officers.] Jan. 25.

Electors. Ric. Sharp, Laur. Cooke, Tho. Wildegryse, Joh. Braytoft, Ric. Joy, Egid. Allesley, Joh. Bristowe, Joh. Braunston, Joh. Clerke, Ric. Boton*e*r, Joh. Warant, Rob. Southam, Ric. Bussheb*u*ry, Will. Swanne, Joh. Egeston, Joh. Deyster, wollemon, Tho. Wyrley, Joh. Lee, Tho. Crosse, Joh. Onley, Will. Wymondeswold, Joh. Dilcok, Will. Brid, Joh. Boteler.

Officers. [m. Joh. Euerdon; cor. Joh. Whalley; ch. Will. Brown, drap*e*r, Joh. Brian; w. Joh. Lusterley, Ric. Braytoft; mace Will. Oxton.]

[They ordain that an assize of novel disseisin shall be purchased against W. Dorsett, dyer, concerning an annual rent of 6*s*. coming from a tenement of which the mayor and community are seised.]

Eciam ordinat*um* est ad hunc diem q*uo*d assisa noue diss*eisin*e erit p*er*quisit*a*[3] (*sic*) p*er* maiore*m* & Co*m*-*mun*itatem (etc.) v*er*sus Will. Dorsette de Couentre, deist*er*,[4] de quodam annuo Reddit*u* sex solid*orum* exeu*n*te de quodam ten*emento* in Couentre nup*er* Edwardi Lichefeld, vnde maior & Co*mmun*itas p*re*dict*i* fueru*n*t seisi*a*ti, etc.

[1] Usually Bishop Street. [2] leaf 83, Scribe of B. type.
[3] *i. e.* prosecuted. *v.* Gloss [4] *v.* p. 135. Dorset was to be evicted.

J. Ps. [Joh. Euerdon, m., Will. Donyngton, rec., Ric. Sharp M. G. S. T., Laur. Cooke, Tho. Wyldegryse, Joh. Braytoft.

Key-keepers. The same except the recorder and Joh. Braytoft.]

EASTER LEET.

"Couentre." April 23. Jury of 25.

[1][V. f. p. held before Joh. Everdon, m.,[2] on Saturday in Easter week, 13 Hen. VI.] Laur. Cooke, Ric. Sharp, Joh. Bray[to]ft, Ric. Joy, Joh. Bristowe, Egid. Allesley, Joh. Michell, Joh. Rontton, Joh. Braunston, Joh. Clerke. Joh. Prentes, Ric. Botone*r*, Ric. Busshebury, Will. Kerver, Joh. Warant, Will. Swanne, Rob. Southam, Hen. Sircok Will. Bird, Joh. Brian, Tho. Wyrley, Joh. Lee, hosier, Ric. Dene, Joh. Onley, Joh. Whalley.

Orders of leet. No fuller to stretch cloth on the tenter that is sold for wet cloth.

They orden that no walker off the Cite of Couentre ne non oder man Shall Rakke no Clothe on the Tey[n]tur that schall be solde ffor wette-clothe, [or 6s. 8d. to the town wall.]

Cloth to be stretched to the utmost.

And yffe ony man that woll haue hys Clothe Rakked, that þe walkers abovesayde and all other Rakk hit to the vtmast as they han don affore this tyme, but they shull make non hengers[3] off Clothe so Rakked, apon the peyne to lose at eue*r*i defaute vj s. viij d. to the vse of the Towne walle to be rered.

The saddlers and painters to be contributory to the card-makers' pageant.

The orden that the Sadelers and the peyntours off The Cite of Couentre be fro this tyme fforward Contrebetory vnto þe paiont off the Cardemakers, and tha[t] þey paye as the Cardemakers don yerly, vppon the peyne off C s. to be payd to þe vse off þe Chamburlens.

LOAN TO THE KING.

May 26, 1435. King's letter

[4]Memorand*um* that ther was a letter send be our soue*r*en lorde the kyng to the meire and bayllyves and oder notabull pe*r*sons, and to the good comi*n*alte of the Cite of Couentre, for to Cheues[5] of V[c] marc', of the whiche l*ett*re the Tenour folowth in thes wordes :—

Be the kyng.

Trusty and wel-beloued, for alsomyche as we now late

[1] Scribe C., leaf 88, back. [2] Bailiffs omitted. [3] *v.* p. 188.
[4] leaf 83, back. Scribe of B. type. [5] = to raise (money).

instantly required, as well be solempne ambassates as be *lettres* of our holy fadur, the pope, the generall conceile, our broder the emperour, Vncle of Burgoyne, and many oder, to entende vnto the menes of pees to be tretede bitwix vs & our aduersarie in our Reaume of ffraunce, be condessended to send our solempne ambassiate of the lordes of our blode and oder in grete noumbre to mete with thambassiatours of our seid aduersarie at Arras[1] the furst dey of Jule next comeng; for whiche cause of necessite we must sende also atte same tyme in-to our seid Reame of ffraunce a great armee to holde the felde, the whiche thyng, as ye in your discression can well consider, may in no wyse be don namely so soone withe-outten grete eid of cheuesance of our trewe ffrendes and subgittis, to the whiche aid attis tyme we han founde our leal vncle, the Cardenall,[2] and the remenaunt of our counsell and oder about our person, as well spirituele as temporell, as well willed as our hert can desire; notwithestondyng that many of hem at our prayer shall goo vnto the seid conuencion in ther persons. We desire & preye you that consideryng the grete goode whiche we trist to our Lorde shall ensue of pees[3] thynges before rehersed, ye confourmyng you vnto oder of your astate, like as ye han do right kyndely at all tymes, ye wold attis tyme lene vnto vs the summe of V^c marc, for the whiche our Tresorer of Englonde shall make vnto you be autorite of parlyment such surtees for your repayment as he makithe vnto our seid leall vncle, the Cardenall, and the remenant of our counsell, and oder that lene semblable summes and gretter vnto vs in this necessete. The whiche summe we prey you to be delyuered vnto our seid Tresorer at London atte oeptaues[4] of the Trynite next comeng atte ferrest, as ye desire the wurship and wele of vs, and the conseruacion of bothe our Reames. Yeuen vnder our priue seale at Westm[ynstre], the xxviij day of May.

concerning the council of Arras,

asking for a loan

of 500 marks,

upon the same security as Cardinal Beaufort and others,

to be delivered on the octave of Trinity Sunday.

[1] Congress of Arras was opened Aug. 4, 1435. It was an unsuccessful attempt at mediation between the French and English.

[2] Cardinal Beaufort.

[3] ? Something omitted.

[4] "oeptaves" occurs in 1389 in *Proc. and Ord. Privy Counc.*, I. p. 12*a*. (Mr. Stevenson).

Wheruppon the meire & the baillies & odur wurthy & discrete men of this Cite lat make an halle of all the substance of this Citie, among whom this letter Rad and vnderstonden, [it] was Grauntede that our seid soue*r*en
£100 granted, lorde shulde haue C li. be wey of lone, and that shuld be gedered be the wardes of this Cite in the forme as herafter folouthe.

91 names.

Spon-strete.

	£	s.	d.
+Will. Tailour		1	4
+Ric. Shermen		1	0
+Joh. Bette		1	0
+Ric. Capmaker		5	0
+Joh. Gryndar		5	6
+Joh. Stonley		1	0
+Tho. Rastell		6	8
+Joh. Esex		6	0
+Alicia Paynell		6	8
+Joh. Marche		1	4
+Ric. Shustoke		3	4
+Joh. Sirseter		2	0
+Joh. Gurdelsford		1	0
+Will. Allesley			8
+Agn. Goldsmyth			8
+Will. Peere		6	0
+Gervas. Cole		4	0
+Joh. Menley		6	0
+Will. Welles		3	4
+Rog. Wilnale		4	0[1]
+Will. Pratte		3	4
+vx*or* Joh. Lote, wright		2	0[2]
+Tho. Irisshe			8[3]
+Joh. Broun		5	0[4]
+Joh. Brette		1	0
+Joh. Sewyn		1	2
+Egid. Colbrond		5	0
+Joh. Molle		3	4
+Tho. Tokeby		2	0
+Joh. Honyburn		3	4
+Will. Keru*er*		10	0
+Joh. Deister		6	8

	£	s.	d.
+Joh. Chester		3	4[5]
+[6]Joh. Blakeney		1	0
+Reg. Whittawer		1	0
+Rob. Milner		1	4
+Ric. Bulloke		1	4
+Hen. ffisher, Tailo*ur*			8
+Joh. Eyre		3	4
+Sim. Busteler		3	4
+Rob. Bulkeley			8
+Tho. Tewe			6
+Joh. Lote		3	0
+Joh. Burbage		2	0
+Hen. Holt		3	4
+Ric. Burbage		1	4
+Tho. Broun		1	8
+Ric. Welford		6	8
+Joh. Harres		4	0
+Nic. P*er*ines, Barker			8
+Rob. Smyth			8
Coruyser			8
+Gal. Tygull		1	0
+ Chaundeler			8
+Joh. Brasier		1	0
+Rog. Balle		3	4
+Wal. Bulker		3	4
+Hugo Steyne		4	0[7]
+Will. Baker		1	0
+Will. Spenser		2	0
+Tho. Cauldenall			8
+Rob. Miles		1	0
+Tho. Walker		2	0

	£	s.	d.
+Tho. Straunge		1	8
+Gal. Capper		1	0
+Joh. Plasterer		5	0
+Rob. Boteler		2	0
+Hugo Wright			8[8]
+Laur. Yrn			8
+Will. Deist*er*, weu*er*			8
+vxor Math. White		5	0
+Sim. Mores		4	0
+Hugo Muln*er*		1	0
+Joh. Peuterer			8
+Elias Drap*er*		1	0[9]
+Joh. Westley, weu*er*		1	0
+Tho. Pratte		1	4
+Rog. Wales		1	2
+Joh. Whamburn		1	0
+Rob. Baxster		4	0[10]
+Joh. Balle		1	8
+Wal. Northefolk		4	0
+Rad. Okes		1	8
+Hugo Barbour		3	0
+Agn. Smyth			8
+Joh. Inglond, baker		2	0[11]
+Tho. Saunsom		1	8
+Ric. Walford		1	8[11]
+Joh. Hadley		3	4
+Will. Stone		3	4
+Nic. Smyth		1	8

S*um*ma £11 6*s*. 8*d*.

[1] "*þer* ffynch" added in different ink. The crosses which precede the names have also been added later, probably when the payments were made.
[2] re*cepti per* Joh. Lote, weu*er*.
[3] xij d. vij c? added. [4] *per* fil*ium*. [5] re*cepti per* Starky.
[6] leaf 84. [7] *per* Suettenham & Goolde.
[8] re*cepti per* Marsche, taylo*ur*. [9] *per* fil*ium*. [10] *per* Starky.
[11] *per* maiore*m*.

Smythford-strete.

59 names.

Name	£	s.	d.
+Joh. Maynard		5	0
+Rog. Profette, glou*er*		3	0
+Alex. Bowyer		1	0
+Will. Happeford		3	0
+Tho. Wodward		5	0
+Joh. ffynch		3	4
+Will. Reede		3	0
+Rob. Coton*er*		1	0
+Joh*anna* Peuterer		3	0
+Tho. Peuterer		5	0
+Joh. Bristowe		10	0
+Joh. Lynne		6	0
+Joh. fforest		3	0
+Ric. Wymondeswold		2	0
+Tho. Broun		5	0
+Will. Ive		1	2[1]
+Reg. Bowyer		4	0
+Joh. Dey		3	0
+Ranulph Plumer		1	8
+Alanus Tayler		1	0
+[2]Rog. Osborn		3	0
+Joh. Hampton		1	0
+Tho. Plomm*er*		1	0
+Joh. Blakemon		6	0
+Joh. Onley		6	8
+Tho. Joye		2	0[2]
+[3]Rog. Osborn		6	0
+Will. Melodyne		3	0
+Ric. Co[u]pper		1	0
+Joh. Hygreve		1	0
+Joh. Kyngston		4	0
+Joh. Malory		1	6[4]
+Rad. Bredon		2	0
+Ric. fflynt		4	0
+Tho. Whetecroft		1	0[5]
+Joh*anna* Dyer		2	0[6]
+Joh. London		1	4
+Marg. Prescote		2	0
+Joh*anna* Sherman		1	0[7]
+Ric. Baxster		1	6
+Will. Bylton		1	6
+Will. Bredon, skynn*er*		2	0
+Tho. Leche		3	0
+Will. Mariot		1	0
+Nic. Sadeler		2	0
+Joh. Braunston		6	8[8]
+Joh. Medburn		1	0
+Ric. Peche		1	4
+Joh. Wylde		2	6
+Will. Peerte		1	0[9]
+Joh. Good		1	8
+Marg*er*ia Bowyer		3	0[10]
+Will. Donyngton, hosier		4	0
+Marg*er*ia Ive		5	0
+Joh. Nele		3	0
+Joh. Barbour		3	0
+Tho. Whitside		5	0
+Rog. ffletcher		2	0
+Rog. Costantyne		1	0[8]

S*umm*a £7 10*s*. 6*d*.

Croschepyng.

129 names.

Name	£	s.	d.
+Rob. ffletcher		1	8
+Agn. Bulwyk		1	0
+Agn. Molton		1	8
+Rob. Melburn		10	0[11]
+Rob. Grubber		6	0[8]
+Joh. Walle		4	0[8]
+Tho. Weuer		1	8
+Joh. Doughty		6	8
+Guido Weston		2	0
+Joh. Huewer			8
+Joh. Nele		4	0
+Will. Hende		1	4
+Tho. Swonlond		1	8[12]
+Ric. Carde		1	0
+Ric. Lane		1	10
+Ric. Harborgh		2	0
+Will. Prentes		2	0
+Rad. Chaundeler		6	0
+Will. Bedon		2	0[13]
+Joh. ffrithe		1	0
+Joh. Sheldon		2	0
+Will. Aderton		1	8
+Ric. Pult*er*, deist*er*		1	8
+Tho. Carde		1	4
+Nic. Wirdrawer		1	4
+Nic. Bunbury[14]		1	0
+Will. Syvekar		1	0
+Joh. *seruiens* Joh. Walle		1	0
+Joh. Yong, coruys*er*		2	0
+Tho. Alen		1	8
+Will. Mason		3	0
+Tho. Goldsmyth		2	0
+Ric. Joy		16	0
+Pet. Shefeld		1	0
+Joh.[15] Bilston		1	0[16]
+Tho. Holybryg		1	4[17]
+Rob. Purdon		1	0
+Hen. Adderton		2	0
+Will. Dyvette		2	0
+Will. Radclyff		1	8
+Joh. Sutton		2	0
+Will. Stretford		1	0
+Joh. Barbour		1	8
+Ric. Hillage		1	0
+Tho. Glouer		1	0
+Ric. Drought		1	8
+Nic. Grene		1	3
+Tho. Bredon		3	4
+Joh. Bandy, barb*our*		4	0
+Joh. Savage, ffissher		1	4
+Ric. Penson		1	3
+Tho. Norwyche		4	0
+[18]Joh. Wyttoft		3	4
+Will. Hosier		2	0
+Will. Bromwyche		2	0
+Tho. Bayly		1	0
+Joh. Eborall		2	0
+Tho. Paynton		1	0[19]
+Joh. Nele, coruyser		3	0
+Joh. Brasse		1	0
+Joh. Colyns		3	0
+Agn. Westbury		1	0
+Joh. Boteler		5	0
+Ric. Peuterer		2	0
+Reg. Goldsmyth		1	0[20]
+Ric. Smale		1	0

[1] *per* J. Wylde. [2–2] Added in different ink and hand.
[3] Interlined "Ric." leaf 84, back. [4] *recepti per* R. Hedon.
[5] per (?) Joh. filium & executores. [6] *per* Shustoke. [7] *per* Kyngeston.
[8] *per* ffynch. [9] *per* Bartram. [10] *per* W. Donyngton [illeg.].
[11] *per* W. Beuyngton. [12] per H. Banberry. [13] *recepti per* Ric. Bedon
[14] Substituted for Bowyer. [15] Interlined Will. [16] *per* W. [illeg.].
[17] *per* vxorem. [18] leaf 85. [19] *per* J. ffynch. [20] *per* Nic. Welles.

Croschepyng.

Name	£	s.	d.
+Joh. Huet		2	4
+Will. White		1	8
+Joh. Vynsent		1	0
+Gal. Wolpyn*er*		2	0
+Will. Norton		1	8
+Tho. White[1]		3	0
+Joh. Sadeler			6
+Rob. Harry		2	0
+Rad. Hulle		3	4
+Joh. Wynwyk		1	0[2]
+Hen. Tavern*er*		1	0
+Hen. Rondull		3	4
+Joh. Marshall		1	0
+Joh. Northampton		5	0
+Ric. Lirpull		1	0
+Rob. Broun		3	4
+Ric. Weu*er*		3	4
+Joh. Ymayne		2	0
+Joh. Neuport		2	0
+Joh. Halle		4	11
+Joh. Lyllynton		1	0
+Tho. Deist*er*, boch*er*		1	0
+Will. Deist*er*		3	0
+Tho. Leyghton		1	0[3]
+Joh. Botte		1	8[4]
+Ric. Bedon		1	8
+Joh*an*na Cooke		I	0
+Sim. Payne		1	8
+Tho. Dovy		1	0
+Ric. Loder		1	0
+Mat. Elerton		1	8
+Rob. Mors		3	4
+Joh. Stille		5	0
+Jac. Seriaunt		2	0
+Rob. Seriaunt		1	8
+Will. Huyton		10	0[5]
+Ric. Spicer		2	0
+Hugo Cariour		1	0
+Tho. Swayne		4	0
+Ric. Cadde		1	0
+Will. Hayes		2	0
+Hen. Euerdon			6[6]
+Will. Meeke		1	8
+Will. Huet		3	4
+Will. Stonley		1	0
+Tho. Sulby		1	8
+Joh. Bynley		1	0[7]
+Joh. Colyns, barbour		2	8
+Joh. Tailour		1	0[8]
+Tho. Gest		1	0
+Joh. Blokley		1	0[9]
+Edw. Dilcok		10	0[10]
+Will. Barbour		1	0
+Joh. Baker		1	0[11]
+Will. Boteler		1	0[11]
+Joh. Hayle		1	0
+Will. Benet		4	0
+Will. Darset		6	0
+Will. Hulle		1	8
+Joh. Barbour		1	8
+Joh. Weston		1	8
+Will. Dey		5	0
+Will. Bynley		1	8

*Su*mma £14 18*s*. 11*d*.

67 names.

Bysschopstrete.

Name	£	s.	d.
+Joh. Kebull		5	0
+Will. Walker		3	4
+Joh. Goold		6	8
+Joh. Grene		3	4
+Will. Wythiford		5	0[12]
+Joh. Lyncoln		1	8
+Joh. Lusterley		8	0
+[13]Will. Warrewik		3	4
+Hen. Rastell		1	8
+Hen. Knotte		2	4
+Rob. Southam		15	0
+Will. Garet		1	8
+Tho. Wodcok		3	4[14]
+Joh. Coper, baker		1	8
+Joh. ffolvyle		2	0
+Joh. Reynoldes		1	8
+Will. Kempe		6	8
+Joh. Mores		3	4
+Alicia Nores		1	8
+Ed. Drouer		10	0
+Rog. Taylour		5	0
+Joh. Stafford, myln*er*		3	4
+Ric. Glover		1	0
+Joh. Attewode		1	8
+Moric. Steyn*our*		1	6
+Will. Coper		3	4
+Rog. Lesyngham		2	0
+Joh. Appelby		3	4
+Joh. Wodecote		1	8
+Will. ffelde		1	8
+Joh. Trewman		1	8
+Will. Richardson		1	8
+Tho. Broun		3	4
+Ric. Tedde		1	8
+Will. Wymondeswold		7	2
+Joh. Walde*g*raue		6	8
+Tho. Waldegraue		1	8
+Joh. Broun		1	8[15]
+Tho. Cleybroke		1	8
+Joh. Hawkeslowe		1	8
+Sim. Wright		1	0
+Will. Horsley		2	0
+Ric. Mason de Dogl[ane]		1	8
+Hen. Hethe		1	8
+Tho. Stafford		1	8[15]
+Will. Wilkyns		3	4[16]
+Will. White de Dog-l[ane]		3	4
+Joh. Lichefeld		15	0
+Ric. Tomson		1	8
+Wal. Trig		3	4
+Hen. Weston		3	4
+Joh. Couper		1	8
+Tho. Waren		1	8
+Ric. Clerke		1	8
+Pet. Miln*er*		1	8
+Hugo Shawe		5	0
+Will. Neuton		3	4[17]
+Joh. Brasier de Angleslane		1	8
+Will. Humberston		1	8
+Joh. Warde, deist*er*		1	8
+Ric. ffelippes		3	4
+Ric. Spicer		3	4
+Joh. Hampton		6	8
+Ric. Chichester		3	4
+Ric. Baxter		1	8
+Joh. Welford		6	8
+Alex. Barker		1	8
+Joh. Tebbe			10

*Su*mma £11 6*s*. 0*d*.

[1] Substituted for Wright. [2] *per* ffynch. [3] *per* maiore*m*.
[4] *scilicet* Bette *pro* Botte. [5] *recepti per* Southam. [6] W. Welles, weuer.
[7] *per* vx*orem*. [8] *recepti* viij d. [9] *per* Lirpull. [10] *per* H. Locok.
[11] *per* W. Barbour. [12] *per* Starky. [13] leaf 85, back.
[14] *per* Ric. Welford. [15] per maiore*m*. [16] execut*ores*. [17] *recepti* xx d.

Brod-yate.

82 names.

Name	£	s.	d.
+ Alicia Illage		2	0
+ Joh. Melton			8
+ Hen. Louthe[1]			4
+ Joh. Blakamour		1	4
+ Will. Spenser		1	4
+ Tho. Spenser		1	4
+ Will. ffekeney		2	0
+ Joh. Bernard		2	0
+ Will. Stafford et soci*us* suus		1	0
+ Tho. Ruyton		3	4[2]
+ Rog. Miln*er*, tailour			8
+ Joh. Hencote			8
+ Hen. Sircok		6	0[3]
+ Rog. Cockes		3	0
+ Rog. Cooke			8
+ Wal. Paslowe		1	4[4]
+ Ric. Busshebury		6	8[5]
+ Joh. Cappe, coleter		2	0
+ Joh. Locok		1	4
+ Joh. Malory		1	4
+ Joh. Bradley			8
+ Kat*er*ina Bradley		2	0[6]
+ Joh. Huntley			8
+ Rob. Persale			8
+ Joh. Dalton			8
+ Will. Holt		1	4
+ Ric. Esex		1	4
+ [7]Joh. Nele, Taylour			8
+ Joh. Archer		1	0

Name	£	s.	d.
+ Will. Archer[8]		1	0
+ vxor Rob. Sporio*ur*			8[9]
+ Ric. Twyg			8[3]
+ Hugh. Manton		1	4
+ Rad. Duffeld		1	4
+ Will. Drap*er*		1	0
+ Will. Chaterton			8
+ Tho. Wytham			4
+ Will. Hethe			4
+ Will. Barley			4
+ Gal. Rose, coteler			8[10]
+ Will. Abram, shether		1	4
+ Will. Ryder, shether		1	0
+ Ric. Barwell		1	4
+ Nic. Pykstaff			4
+ Tho. Lokyngton			8
+ Benedict Stokton			8
+ Edw. Coriour		1	4[11]
+ Joh. Barbour			8
+ Wal. Kyppyng			8
+ Joh. ffawkes			4
+ Tho. Wastell			4
+ Nic. Gore		3	4
+ Cecilia Janyns		1	4
+ vx*or* Joh. Vnderwode		1	0
+ Alicia ffaux			8
+ Will. Walton, Cobeler			4

Name	£	s.	d.
+ Egid. Allesley		6	8
+ Will. Grene, skolemaist*er*			8
+ Joh. Coly			4
+ Ric. B[r]ystowe			4
+ Clemens Wirdrawer			4
+ Joh. White, grynder			4
+ Marg*er*ia Onley		1	0[12]
+ Marg*er*ia Lylyngton			8[13]
+ Joh. Basset			4
+ Ric. Coup*er*		2	0
+ Ric. Machon		1	0
+ Will. Wylcote		1	4
+ Joh. Purs			6
+ Joh. Rypon			4
+ Hen. Westley			4
+ Joh. Persyvale			4
+ Tho. Lyones		1	4
+ Joh. Otley			4
+ Joh. Melton			4[14]
+ Will. Tyler, wright			4
+ Ric. Garton		1	0
+ Joh. Bere			4
+ Tho. Mason			8
+ Joh. Hare, mason			2
+ Tho. Warde			4
+ Tho. Godfrey			4

S*um*ma £4 13*s*. 0*d*.

Bayli-lane.

62 names.

Name	£	s.	d.
+ Joh. Merston		3	4
+ Joh. Thorp			6[12]
+ Joh. Langcastell			6[12]
+ Joh. Wylkyns		2	0
+ Joh. Bryan		3	4
+ Joh. Whitley		3	4
+ Hen. Watford		2	4
+ Will. Warde		1	8
+ Joh. Sircok		4	0
+ Ric. Deist*er*		2	0
+ Ric. Dyvette		4	0
+ Will. Oteley		1	4
+ Tho. Dey		1	0[15]

Name	£	s.	d.
+ Joh. Alen		3	0[16]
+ Joh. Cardmaker		1	4
+ Joh. Boteler		2	0
+ Joh. Straunge			6
+ Joh. Worstedman		1	0[3]
+ Will. Wright		1	8
+ Tho. Jakeman		2	0
+ Ric. Goddesley			8
+ (?) Will. Grauncestre			8
+ Tho. Wirley		6	0
+ Joh. Plymmer		2	8
+ Joh. Spenser		4	0
+ Ric. Tokeby		1	0

Name	£	s.	d.
+ [17]Hugo Shyryf		1	0
+ Ric. Perbroun		3	0
+ Joh. Millet		1	0
+ Tho. Peut*er*er		3	0
+ Joh. Beauchamp		2	6
+ Joh. Whiche, pe[u]terer		1	0
+ Will. Broke		4	0[4]
+ Joh. Louthe		1	0
+ Ric. Julyans		1	8
+ Joh. Ronton		10	0
+ Joh. Hulle		3	4
+ Joh. Baron		1	0[18]

[1] ? Lonche. [2] *per* Brogreve. [3] per maiore*m*. [4] *per* Starky.
[5] *per* Bartram. [6] *per* fili*um* recepti. [7] leaf 86.
[8] Deleted. Marshall added in different ink. [9] *per* Barley fili*um*.
[10] per Rog. Cooke. [11] *per* Joh. Wyche, cl*ericum*.
[12] *per* W. Allesley. [13] *per* ffili*um* [14] (?) *pro* Melton.
[15] *per* Beauchu*mp*. [16] *per* R. Starky.
[17] leaf 86, back. [18] *per* Southam.

Bayli-lane.

Name	£	s.	d.
+Editha Mowton		1	0[1]
+Joh. Hony		1	0[2]
+Joh. Bradley			8
+Hen. Walton			8
+Joh. Colyns			8[3]
+Ric. Plymmer		2	8
+Joh. Skille		3	0
+Millesant Frankelen		2	0[4]
+Joh. Power		1	4
+Rob. Herdewyk		2	0
+Tho. Loke		2	0
+Joh. Burbage		1	0
+Joh. Gryme		4	0
+Tho. Gryme		1	0
+Joh. Bayly		3	0
+Rob. Gloucestre		2	0
+Will. Clerke		3	8
+Joh. Oderiche		2	4
+Rob. Styff		2	0
+Joh. Crosse		3	4
+Hen. Brid		2	0
+Simon Harfrey		1	0
+Joh. Bordall		3	4
+Joh. Gilbard		2	8

Summa £6 18*s*. 0*d*.

62 names.

Erl-strete.

Name	£	s.	d.
+Rob. Barbour		1	8
+Joh. ffreman		3	4
+Matill. Harborgh		4	0
+Joh. Watford		1	8
+Joh. Lyones		1	0[5]
+Nic. Ruffeld		3	0
+Joh. Chaunter		1	0
+Ric. Clerke		2	0
+Ric. Byfeld		1	8
+Joh. Warant		10	0
+Will. Gilbard		3	4
+Joh. White		3	4[6]
+Will. Broun		6	8
+Wal. Assheby		4	0
+Will. ffrisby		6	8
+Joh. Motte		2	8
+Joh. Hawkyns		1	8
+Ric. Sharp		13	4
+Ric. Braytoft		6	8[7]
+Tho. Owdeby		1	0
+Tho. Swan		1	8[7]
+Will. Swanne		8	0
+Rob. Thede		3	0
+Joh. Bryan		2	0
+Joh. Perpoynt		1	8
+Will. Ednam		3	4[8]
+Joh. George, fflecher		3	4
+Ric. Knyttesford		2	0
+Agn. Crudworth		3	4[9]
+Tho. Bayle		3	0
+Joh. Radley		2	0
+Ric. Alen		6	8
+Joh. Clerke		2	0
+Johanna Brabson		3	0
+Will. Dey		1	8[8]
+Will. Coucher		1	8[10]
+Tho. Glenne		3	4[11]
+Hen. Dalby		2	0
+Johanna Northwode		13	4
+Joh. Michell		13	4
+Rob. Praty		1	8[12]
+Rob. ffissher		1	0
+Ric. Nasshe		1	0
+Tho. Shawe		1	0
+Agn. Nores		1	0[7]
+Tho. Kirke		3	4
+Nic. Palmer		1	8
+Tho. Crosse		10	0
+Rob. Barnesley		1	8
+Ed. Brogreve		5	0
+Ric. Boys		5	0
+Joh. Chacombe		2	0
+Joh. Euerdon		10	0[13]
+Johanna Burton		5	0
+Joh. Eyres[14]		1	0
+[15]Tho. Suettenham		3	4
+Joh. Kirkeby		1	8
+Ric. Cotoner		10	0
+Will. Donyngton		6	8
+Tho. Welles		3	4[16]
+Joh. Gynne		2	0
+Tho. Wapunbury		1	0

Summa £11 17*s*. 4*d*.

87 names.

Much-park-strete.

Name	£	s.	d.
+Rob. Eme, cardmaker		1	0
+Tho. Sherman			10
+Will. Grove, cardmaker			8[17]
+Rob. Skille, sporiour		2	0
+Will. Bayle, mercer		2	0[18]
+Will. Brid, gurdeler		6	8
+Ed. Sherman		1	4
+Ric. Dene, mercer		6	8
+Joh. fforde, Sharman		1	4
+Will. Betteley		6	8
+Joh. Clerke		13	4
+Tho. Willot, tailour			8
+Rob. Mason, coruyser		2	4
+Will. Jones, coruyser		1	0
+Tho. Walsale		2	0
+Johanna Byfeld		10	0
+Joh. Brayne, smyth		1	4
+Joh. Yong, baker		1	4
+Joh. Ray		2	0
+Tho. Norwiche, coruyser		1	4
+Hen. Hobbes, smythe		5	0
+Alicia Attewalle		2	0
+Joh. Lee, smythe		2	8

[1] *per* Lyrpull. [2] *per* Starky. [3] *per* meyorem. [4] *per* J. Gryme.
[5] *per* Solond. [6] *per* Johanna Swett. [7] *per* maiorem.
[8] *per* Will. Swan. [9] *recepti per* W. Allesley.
[10] *scilicet* Joh. Coucher. [11] *per* Southam. [12] *per* Gayton.
[13] *pro* Kirke. [14] Eyles substituted. [15] leaf 87. [16] *per* Joh. Palmer.
[17] *per* W. Cleybrooke. [18] *recepti per* Warant.

Much-park-strete.

	£	s.	d.
+Ric. Bromley, smythe		2	4
+Ric. Burfrey, smythe		1	8
+Joh. Derby, coruyser		2	4
+ Tho. Warmynton, hosier		6	8
+Ric. Staffordshire		3	0
+Joh. Brayleford, wev*er*			8
+Margaret Harres			8[1]
+Joh. Smythe			8[2]
+Joh. Yate, cardmaker			8
+Hen. Balle, coruyser			8
+Tho. Kildraught, pavier		1	0[3]
+Will. Solant, hosier		1	0
+Joh. Bry[s]towe, wever		1	0
+Rob. Pavier			8[3]
+Nic. Ouerton			8
+Tho. Yorke, peyntour		5	0
+Will. Charlton		4	0
+Ed. Goldsmythe			4
+Joh. Cale [Gale]		3	0
+Will. Cleybroke		2	4

	£	s.	d.
+Joh. Steynour			8
+Nic. More			4
+Joh. Elmes, mason			8
+Joh. Tyrvill, wev*er*			8
+Joh. Bayly, pinn*er*			8[4]
+Tho. Burwey, wright		1	4
+Gobett ?, Bruer			8
+Tho. Harres		1	4
+Joh. Burnham			8
+Joh. Lebbes			4[5]
+Tho. Harper			4
+Joh. ffolshull, wirdr*awer*			8
+Joh. Hony, mylner		1	4
+Alex. Milner		1	4
+Joh. ffillippes, quari*our*		1	4
+Will. Peverell			8
+Joh. Dyvette, cart*er*		1	4
+Tho. Abell			8[6]
+Will. Stone, werkman			8
+Alicia Stafford			8[7]
+Tho. Pawnton			8
+Tho. Tough			8[8]

	£	s.	d.
+Tho. Tate, m*er*cer		1	4
+Nic. Gryve, tyler		4	0
+Joh. Sheregrynder		2	6
+Will. Cortonhale		1	8
+Katerina Assho			8
+ leche			8[4]
+Will. Glasier		2	0
+Will. ffermon, tailour			8
+Joh. Witham		2	8
+[9]Pat. Glasier		1	4
+Joh. Garton, m*er*c*er*		5	0
+Sim. Mason			8
+Joh. Braytoft, m*er*cer		20	0
+Tho. Tyler, skynn*er*		1	4
+Ric. Baker		2	0
+Joh. Makesey		6	8
+Rob. Hendemon		1	4
+Ric. Knyghtley		2	0
+Katerina Gosnore		1	0[10]
+Hen. Boohghe, sharman		2	6
+Will. Southam		5	4
+Tho. More, myln*er*			8

S*um*ma £10 0*s*. 6*d*.

91 names.

Jurd[an-well.]

	£	s.	d.
+Ric. Clerke		3	4
+Tho. Elderbek		5	4
+Joh. Porter		1	0
+Ric. Yate			8
+Ric. Tayler			8
+Joh. Brewer		3	4
+Joh. Dilcok		6	8[11]
+Tho. Wodecok			8
+Joh. Prentys		1	0
+Joh. Bryan		0	0
+Will. Smythe		4	0
+Will. Thomas			8
+Will. Marchall		1	0
+Joh. Cater		8	4
+Ric. Barbour		1	4
+Joh. Whalley		10	0

Mil-lone.

	£	s.	d.
+Hugo Cowper		2	0
+Joh. Hawkyns		3	0
+Tho. Barnewell			8
+Joh. Rochcford		8	0
+Rob. Shawe		1	0
+Joh. Lee		10	0
+Wal. Tyrell		1	4
+Margaret Godefroy		1	4[12]
+Tho. Baxster		1	0
+Rog. Cressy		1	0
+Tho. Smyth			6
+Will. Shurley		5	0
+Joh. Perkyns		2	0[13]
+Joh. Wade			10

	£	s.	d.
+Joh. Horneby		2	0
+Tho. Bette		1	0
+Will. Bradmere			10
+Joh. Eglee		2	4
+Tho. Thomas		2	0[14]
+Will. Bette		4	0
+Joh. Folshull		1	0
+Joh. Stoneley		1	0[15]
+Joh. Skynn*er*			6

Neu-strete.

	£	s.	d.
+Tho. Merston			4
+Will. Castelton		3	4
+Ric. Adam		2	6
+Will. Oxton		1	0[3]
+Tho. Kirteley			8

[1] *per* Solond. [2] *per* Benet Marchall. [3] *per* maiore*m*.
[4] *per* W. Allesley. [5] *per* Alvea*m* (? Aliciam) matre*m* sua*m*.
[6] *per* Bartram. [7] *per* Ric. Tyler. [8] *per* Cale. [9] leaf 87, back.
[10] *per* Bordale. [11] *per* Prentes. [12] *per* Lee. [13] *per* filiu*m* suu*m*.
[14] *per* vxore*m*. [15] *per* Wade.

	£	s.	d.
+Joh. Stanffeld			10
+Joh. Camelle		2	0
+Joh. Pake		1	0
+Tho. Dykonnes		5	0
+Rob. Clerke		4	0
+Will. Bolton			8
+Rad. Plymmer		1	0
+Tho. Maydeford		5	3
+Tho. Threston		5	3
+Joh*anna* Abram		2	0
+ Wotton, weu*er*			8
+Rob. Archer			8
+Joh. Creeke		1	0[1]
+Joh. Smythe			4
+Joh. ffreman		1	4
+David Baxst*er*			8
+Rob. Grene		1	0
+Joh. Elderbek			10
+Will. Gale		1	8

	£	s.	d.
+Tho. Illage		6	8
+[2]Joh. Multon		1	4
+Joh. Sutton		5	3
+Joh. Savage			8
+Joh. ffrankelen		5	0
+Joh. Shadde		6	8
+Ric. Recheford		4	0
+Ric. Weley			4[3]
+Will. ffouter			4
+Joh. Cresse, m*er*cer		4	0
+Ric. Coton*er*		1	0
+Joh. Barre, deyster			4
+Joh. Lokier de Mil-lone			4
+ Peynt*our* of the New-strete			3
+Joh. Barres, card-maker			4

	£	s.	d.
+Agnes Sewster			2
+Tho. Bere			4
+Gregorius Hulle			4
+Will. Byg			4
+Tho. Thymeler			4
+vx*or* Joh. Bradley			4
+Elias Tailour			4
+Joh. Egleston			4
+Tho. Recheford			4
+Ric. Clement			3
+Pet. Tailour			4
+Ric. Willy, myln*er*			4
+Joh. Clyfford, myln*er*			4
+ Lokier de New-strete			4

S*um*ma £10 4*s*. 1*d*.

Gosford.

(cætera desunt.)

[£11 12*s*. 0*d*. delivered to the Gosford Street collectors, because they had not enrolled the names of the ward; of which £11 12*s*. 0*d*. Will. Swan, mayor (1438) received 12*d*. for R. Burges, and 8*d*. for Rob. Wattes, because S. Baker says he paid.

[Total £100 7*s*. 4*d*.]

& vnde xj li. xij s. delib*er*an*ur* collectorib*us* ib*id*em, videl*ic*et Joh. Stafford, Hen. Skille, Joh. Asshewell, Joh. Stretton, Will. Dawe & Simon Baker, p*ro* eo q*uo*d no*n* h*ab*ueru*n*t nomi*n*a dicte warde de Gosford irrotulat*a* vt p*ate*t; de quib*us* xj li. xij s. Will. Swan, maior, recep*it*[4] xij d. [pro] Rob*er*to Burges & viij d. p*ro* Rob*er*to Wattes, eo q*uo*d Sim. Baker dic*it* q*uo*d ips*e* soluit.

S*um*ma to*tal*is C. li. vij s. iiij d.

THE WORKERS IN IRON.

Sept. 14, 1435. A bill delivered to the mayor,

[5]Hit is to haue in mynde that in the fest of the Exaltacc*io*n of the Holy Crosse a bille foloweng was delyu*er*ed to John Euerdon, meire of the Cite of Couentre, in thes wordes:

To the Reu*er*ent Meire of the Cite of Couentre & to halle the wurthy men of the same; for-alsomyche as hit

[1] p*er* vx*orem*. [2] leaf 88. [3] p*er* Elderbek sen.

[4] Some words looking like "xx s. xij d. p*ro* Will. Sturdy, iam mortuo" are crossed out. "&" is also inserted. [5] leaf 89.

is necessarie & nedefull to euery gouernour of Cite & of Town to se suche rule & gouernaunse may be hadde be the whiche the kynges peapull may be truly rulede & demened: Be hit known to you that but yif certen ordenaunses of Craftes withe-in this Cite, & in speciall the Craft of wirdrawerz, be takon good hede to, hit is like myche of the kynges pepull, & in speciall poor chapmen & Clothemakers, in tyme comeng shullon be gretely hyndered; and as hit may be supposed the principall cause is like to be amonges hem that han all the Craft in her own hondes, That is to sey, smythiers, brakemen, gurdelmen & Cardwirdrawers; for he that hathe all thes Craftes may, offendyng his consience, do myche harme. First in The smethyng, yif he be necligent & mysrule his Iron, that he wirkithe, be onkynd hetes or elles in oder maner, the whiche, when hit is so spilt, is not to make no maner chapmannes ware of, Neuerthelater for his own eese he will com to his Brakemon & sey to hym;—"Here is a ston of rough-iron, the whiche must be tendurly cherysshet." & then the Brakemon most nedes do his maisters comaundement, and dothe all that is in hym; & then when the Brakemon hathe don his ocupacion, That that the mayster supposithe wil-not in no wyse be holpen atte gurdell, Then hit shall be solde for hoke wire. And when hit is made in hokes and shulde serue the ffissher to take fisshe, when hit comythe to distresse, Then for febulness hit all-to brekithe, and thus is the ffissher foule disseyued to hym[1] grete harme. And then that wire that the mayster supposithe wille be cherisshed atte gurdell, he shall com to his girdulmon and sey to hym as he seid to the brakemon:—"Lo, here is a stryng or ij, that hathe ben mysgouerned atte herthe; my brakemon hathe don his deuer, I prey the do now thyne." & so he dothe as his maister biddethe hyme. And then he gothe to his cardwirdrawer, & seithe the same to hym, and he dothe as his maister bidDithe hym. And then when the Cardmaker hathe bought this wire thus dissayvabely wrought, he may not know hit tille hit com to the Crokyng,[2] & Then hit crachithe and farithe foule; so

concerning the "wire-drawers,

cardmakers, smiths," and the deceits that spring from the union of the workers in iron, who are able to pass on badly tempered iron

to brakemen

and to be sold for fish-hooks,

and to girdle-makers,

and to card-makers,

[1] ?his. [2] "Crooking," bending, curving.

the Cardmaker is right heuy ther-of, but neu*er*-the-later he sethe be-cause hit is Cutte, he must nedes helpe hymself in eschueng his losse, he makithe cardes ther-of as well as he may. And when the Cardes ben solde to the clothemaker & shuldon be ocupied, anon the tethe brekon & fallon out, so the clothemaker is foule disseyued. Wherfore, sirs, atte reue*re*ns of God in fortheryng of the kynges true lege peapull & in eschueng of all disseytes, Weithe this mater wysely, & ther as ye see disseyte is like to be, therto settithe remedy be your wyse discressions. For ye may right welle know be experience that & the smythier & the brakemen[1] wern to-gider & no mo, and the cardwirdrawers & the Middlemen[2] to-gider and no mo, Then hit were to suppose that ther shuld not so myche disseyuabull wire be wrought & sold as ther is; ffor & the Craft were severed in the man*er* as hit [is] seide aboue, Then the Cardwirdrawers and the myddelmen most nedes bye the wire[3] that they shull wirche of the smythiers, and yif the cardwiredrawer were ones or thies disseyued withe ontrewe wire he wolde be warre, and then wold he sey vnto the smythier that he bought that wire of:—"Sir, I hadde of you late badde wire. Sir, amend your honde, or, in feithe, I wille no more bye of you." And then the smythier, lest he lost his Custemers, wolde make true goode; and then, withe the grase of Godd, The Craft shuld amend, and the kynges peapull [be] not disseyued withe ontrewe goode.

to the great harm of the king's liege people. It is proposed that the crafts should be separated.

Oct. 8. 1435. The mayor sends to the worthymen of the Leet for advice.

¶ The whiche bille the seid meyre atte lete holdon the Monday next after the fest of seynt Mich[ael] thennes next sueng at Couentre send to all the wurthymen of the seyd lete to take her avyse theropon, and ther the seyd bille afore hem was radde, herde and vnderstonden; And for-alsomyche as the mater of this bille is grevous & Nuyefull[4] to the co*m*en pepull, and for oder greuaunse vnto the seid wurthymen attis seid lete shewed, They willeng goode ordenaunses and goue*r*nanses in this seyd

[1] Not in *N.E.D.* in this sense. *v.* Gloss. Mr. Stevenson points out to me that a brakeman was evidently the artificer who converted iron into wire, coarse at first, then drawn finer by the cardwiredrawers. The "brake" was his tool or implement.

[2] middle = the waist. [3] "of" deleted. [4] *i.e.* hurtful.

Cite to be hadde [1]In distruccion of all mysrules & mysgouernaunses the seyd wurthymen in the seyde lete han ordened that fro this tyme fortheward that the Jurneymen of Cardwiredrawers & gurdelmen with-In the seyd Cite wurche in ther own howses, and they haue eese ther-to, and not in ther mayster howses; and that ther werke be truly wrought withe-outen Gyle or disseyte, or ony colour of disseyte; and that they vse no craft but that alon, apon the peyne of xx li. at euery defaut to be rered to the vse of the Town walle withe-outon ony grase; and that ther maysters constreyne hem non oderwes to doo, apon the same peyne. And also that Smythiers and Brakemen wirche to-gider in ther mayster howses, or elles ther may [be] best serued to her eese; and that they wirche ther wyre of trew metell & Truly do therto her labour with-outon any disseyte or Colour of disseyte, so that hit be trewe Chapmannes ware; and that they ocupie neder Cardwiredraweng ne gurdeldraweng, but only smethyng and brakyng, apon the peyn to lose xx li. at euer[y] defaut to be rered to the vse of the Town Walle [2]at euery defaut[2] witheouten ony grase. Also that no smythier ne Brakemon fro this tyme in tyme to come bye ne selle be colour ne sotell Imagynacion ne Cardwyre ne mystermannes wyre, [3]the whiche may be hynderyng or grevyng to the kynges lege pepull oder-weys then is ordend afore, apon the peyne to lose at euery defaut xx li. to be payde as hit is aboue-seyd withe-outen ony grase.

The Leet orders that cardwire drawers and girdlemen are to be united, the journeymen working in their own houses,

or £20 fine,

and smiths and brakemen to be united,

but not to engross any further trade, under the same fine.

All metal sold to be good.

The whiche ordenaunse be John Euerdon then meyre seyn & vnderstonden, lete come afore hym & his Counsell Certen persons of the seid Craft of wirdrawers, whose names fowlon (*sic*) her-after, that is to sey :—

The craft of wiredrawers summoned before the mayor and council.

Joh. Brian, Tho. Elderbek, Joh. Blakeman, sen., Joh. Sheldon, sen., Will. Deister, Ric. ffillipes, Wal. Bonde, Hen. Hethe, Pet. Milner, Ric. Recheford, Will. Horsley, Clemens Kirton, Joh. Elderbek, Joh. Oone, Will. Stoneley, Will. Doubrigge, Tho. ffalkes, Joh. ffeldyng, Rob. Grene, Nic. Ouerton, Will. Chetell, Wal. Neuton, Will. Cleybroke, Tho. Hastyng, Rob. Burges, Joh. Knyght, Will. Bayly, Joh. Spake, Hen. Tredsyn, Will.

Their names.

[1] leaf 89, back. [2—2] A repetition. [3] "of" deleted.

Onfeld, Will. Abram, Joh. Mathewe, Tho. Symthe, Joh. Straunge, Joh. Stafford, Joh. Harries, Ric. Thom*as*, Rad. ffolkeshull, Tho. Reve, Joh. Manton, Hen. Coton*er*, Joh. Peche, Joh. Breux, Tho. Dernwell, Will. Shurley, Tho. Bateman, Joh. Stonley, Tho. Thomas, Tho. Stafford, Joh. Rocheford, Will. Shurley, Joh. ffolkeshull, Joh. Sheldon, Joh. Smythe.

The division of occupations.

The whiche p*er*sons aboue-writon, the ordenaunses aboue-writon to hem redde, the seyde ordenaunses so to kepe agredon, And for-alsomyche as Joh. Stafford, Joh. Blakemon, sen., Tho. Elderbek, Joh. Sheldon the yonger, & Tho. Stafford & Ric. ffillippes & Wal. Bonde heldon for the most p*ar*t as well smethyng, brakyng, Middelyng[1] and cardwiredraweng, They afore the Meire agredon & graunted to ocupye her craft as her-after folouth:—That is to sey, John Stafford [2]graunted to ocupie the craft of smethyng & brakyng, John Sheldon the yongur the same, John Blakemon the same, John Sheldon the elder, Ric. ffillipes, Wal. Bonde, Hen. Hethe, Pet. Milner, Tho. Smyth, Tho. Stafford, the same; & to leve and not to ocupie neder cardewirdraweng, ne girdull; & Tho. Elderbek & all thes oder g*r*aunted to ocupie Cardwirdraweng & gurdull, & neder Smethyng ne brakyng.

MICHAELMAS LEET.

Oct. 3. Jury.

[3][V. f. p. held on Monday after Michaelmas, 14 Hen. VI.] Ric. Sharp, Laur. Cooke, Joh. Braitofte, Ric. Joy, Joh. Brystowe, Joh. Mychell, Joh. Clerke, Joh. Rounton, Joh. Braunston, Ric. Bushebury, Joh. Prentes, Ric. Boton*er*, Joh. Lichfeld, Will. Kerver, Joh. Warant, Will. Swane, Rob. Southam, Will. Broun, drap*er*, Joh. Bryan, Will. Byrde, Joh. Lee, Ric. Braytoft, Joh. Whalley, Joh. Oneley.

Bailiffs.

[Hen. S*ir*coke, Joh. Deist*er*.]

Orders of leet. The "jayler fees."

Allso they orden þ*at* the gailward of the geill of Couen*tre* fro this tyme forward take of no man þ*at* is p*r*isoner for his bed but for a Wek iijd., and for one nyght ob.; and if he haue a bed of his own þ*at* he pay a penny a Weke for his chamb*ur*.

[1] *i. e.* girdle-making. [2] leaf 90. [3] leaf 82, back. Scribe A.

Allso thai orden that the Jorneymen of wirdrawers and of all oþer Craftes within this cite except hakmen[1] and smythers wurche in hur own houses and nott in hur masters housz; And that þer masturs constrayne them no othur wyse to doo, a-pon peyn of xx li. at euery defaute. Wiredrawers work in their own houses.

Allso the smythes of this Cite shall fro thys tyme forwarde show straungers horsies as-well on Sondais as on othur weke-days, euery man a-pon the payn of xld.; and euery barbour þat he shaue any straunger on Sonday as-well as oþer dais, apon the peyn aforsaid.[2] Shoeing and shaving on Sunday.

Allso thei orden þat the lane þat is adioynyng vnto the Wemen-feld, þe which John Plumer holdith, be no more stoppid ne dychid, but þat ther be a yate and a style þer, so þat the way of old tyme may be had and not stoppid, vpon the peyn of vjs. viijd. Right of way.

Thei will þat the carpynters be associate vnto þe Tileres & pynners to maynten hur pagent and hur lyuerey þat now is; & that the maiour call the substance of the Crafte of Carpynters and sett hem to-geþer as one felawshipe.

JOHN RONTON, MAYOR, 1436.

[Easter and Michaelmas Leets.]

[[3]V. f. p. before Joh. Rontton, mayor, Hen. Sircok and Joh. Deyster, bailiffs, on Saturday in Easter week, 14 H. VI.] Ric. Sharp, Laur. Cooke, Tho. Wildegryse, Joh. Braytoft, Egid. Allesley, Joh. Bristowe, Joh. Michell, Joh. Everdon, Joh. Lichefeld, Joh. Prentes, Joh. Clerke, Will. Kerver, Ric. Busshebury, Will. Swanne, Will. ffrisby, Joh. Doughty, Joh. Whalley, Joh. Lee, hosyer, Joh. Spenser, Rob. Grubber, Joh. Lusterley, Joh. Onley, Joh. Walgrave. Couentre. Apr. 14, 1436. Jury of 23.

The[4] orden þat þey prior be not suffered to make no more off þe Stan wall vndur þey[4] priory in Seynt Mich[aels] Churcheyerd vnto the tyme tha[t][4] hyt may be proued be þey priours euydence that he hath Ryght therto. Orders of leet. "Wall on south side St. Michaells Church."

Also they orden tha[t] ffro thys tyme fforward the pre- Four persons assess fines.

[1] I do not know the significance of this word; but it is evidently the same artificer as the brakeman. [2] *v.* Introd.

[3] Scribe C, leaf 92, back. [4] Characteristic of this Scribe.

sentementes off þe letes, when þey schuld be afered,[1] tha[t] þey schuld be a-ferred be iiij wurthy persons, be þey meire ffor þey tyme being to be Choson.

The wall. Item, the orden that the Chaumburlens off the Cite off Couentre now beeng[2] do make off The Towne wall thys yere alsomyche as the stent off þe Towne . . .[3] ?

[The ordinance made at the last leet to be kept under the penalties there specified.]

The last leet. The Conferme þe ordenaunce made in þe last lete, & þat they peyne off þe seid lete be sewed aȝeynes hem that Breketh the seid ordinaunce.[4]

The Red-ditch. They ordeyne þat the meire take with hym the worchipfulmen off þe lete, and make siȝt off they Red-Diche with-in shorte tyme, that þe defautes theroff may be amended as nede axeth.

Expenses to be shared by chamberlains and property owners. The wille the Chaumburlens shulde make and paye ffor that oon halfe, and they that han the Rent in the Hul-stret shuld pay the oder halff, as hit hath ben ordeyned afore.

Oct. 4, 1436. [[5] V. f. p. held on Thursday after Michaelmas, 15

Jury. Hen. VI.] Ric. Sharp, Laur. Cooke, Tho. Wildegrysse, Joh. Braytoft, Joh. Bristowe, Joh. Michell, Joh. Euerdon, Joh. Licheffeld, Joh. Braunston, Joh. Clerke, Ric. Busshebury, Joh. Prentes, Ric. Botoner, Will. Kerver, Joh. Warrant, Will. Swanne, Rob. Southam, Will. ffrisby, Joh. Doughty, Will. Brid, Joh. Lusterley, Ric. Braytoft, Joh. Bryan, Joh. Whalley.

Bailiffs. [Tho. Wirley, draper, Joh. Esex.]

[The bailiffs to repair the cuckstool at their expense.

Ordinatum est quod Ballivi (etc.) repareant (*sic*) & emendent le Cokestole de eorum expencis, (*sic*) etc.

[Present and future bailiffs to pay the recorder, as others have done in time past, and he is to have his livery without impediment.]

Item, ordinatum est quod Ballivi que iam sunt, et eciam qui fuerint, soluant Recordatori, qui nunc est, sicut alii Balliui soluerunt tempore prefato,[6] & quod ipse habeat suum lyuerey sine aliquo impedimento.

[1] *v.* Gloss. [2] Characteristic of this scribe.
[3] Illegible words follow.
[4] *v.* p. 185. Probably the ordinance concerning the workers in iron is here intended. The repetition is curious.
[5] leaf 93, repeated leaf 95. [6] ? preterito.

They orden that what man or woman that letteth the Be[s]tt*es* to haue ther ffre passage þ*at* they lesse[1] at eu*er*y deffaute xl d. 3*s*. 4*d*. fine from any one stopping the passage of the beasts.

JOHN LEEDER, MAYOR, 1437.

Easter and Michaelmas Leets.

[[2] V. f. p. held before Joh. Leder, m., Tho. Wirley, Joh. Esex, b., on Saturday in Easter week, 15 Hen. VI.] Joh. Michell, Laur. Coke, Tho. Wildgrysse, Joh. Braytoft, Egid. Allesley, Joh. Bristowe, Ric. Sharp, Joh. Everdon, Joh. Ronton, Rob. Southam, Joh. Braunston, Joh. Clerk, Joh. Prentes, Ric. Botone*r*, Ric. Bussheb*u*ry, Will. Kerver, Joh. Warrant, Will. Swanne, Will. ffrisby. Joh. Doughty, Joh. Deister, Joh. Whalley, Tho. Suettenham, Will. Bridde. Apr. 6. Jury.

[Orders of leet.

[Present and future mayors shall have from the bailiffs 13*s*. [4*d*.] every sessions of the peace, for a breakfast for the bailiffs and clerks.

Ordinauerunt q*uo*d Maior qui est, & qui p*ro* temp*or*e erit, h*ab*ebunt de Ball*iu*is ville de Couentre, tam qui nu*n*c sunt, seu qui p*ro* temp*or*e eru*n*t, xiij s.[3] ad q*uam*l*ib*et cessionem pac*is* etc., ad faciend*um* qual*ib*et die Cessionis pac*is* Ball*iu*is ac cle*r*ic*is* vnu*m* Jantaculu*m* etc.

[The mayors to have all forfeitures accruing from the breaking and bringing to nought of orders of leet; as well those now forfeited, as those in the future to be forfeited.]

Item, ordinauerunt quod Maior, qui est & p*ro* temp*or*e erit, h*ab*ebit omnes fforisfact*ur*as de ordinac*ion*ib*us* pe*r* let*as* fract*is* & pe*r*dit*is* tam qui (*sic*) nu*n*c sunt forisfacte, q*ua*m qui temp*or*e futuro eru*n*t fforisfacte.

Also the orden that eu*er*y walker withe-in this Cite ffro this tyme fforwarde walke no Cloth & wete hym, but yeff the seyde Cloth bere the lengeth off xxiiij yerdes atte leste, and eu*er*y dosse*n* xij yerd*es* atte lest, and yeff so be that hit wol-not bere the seyde lengeth than that the walker Teynter hym out to the lengethe off xv yerdes, so that a chapman may knowe the Clothe that he b[y]eithe wheder hit be wette; so that eu*er*y walker to Fullers; pieces of cloth to be 24 yards long, and every dozen 12 yards long; the fuller to stretch it out on the tenter to 15 yards.

[1] v. *N. E. D.* leese = lose. [2] leaf 93, back.
[3] 4*d*. omitted, *v*. p. 190.

half a mark fine; and 13*s.* 4*d.* kepe this rule and ordinanse, apon the peyne to lose at eue*r*y dose*n* di*midiam* marc*am*, and at eue*r*y hole Cloythe xiij s. iiij d. And that eue*r*y Cloth or dose*n* that ys sold ffor wet-cloth, tha[t] he bere the brede as he shewthe, apon the same peyne, and þ*at* ther be non hangres[1] vpon the Cloth.

Cuckstool. [The bailiffs to make the "Cokstoll aȝens the feste of Whisontyde" or pay 40s. to the mayor.]

The mayor to assess the tenements for murage. Also they ordeyne that the Meire do to extent the tene*mentz* off the thown off new after Chartre off the kyng[2] wole be-twix thys and Michelmas.

"Search of Tile-makers." Also tha[t] the meire *with* hys Councell haue the oue*r*-sight off Tyle-makyng, that hyt be as hyt was off olde tyme.

Rents. Also the orden that the wardens off the Town geder vp all the smale rent*es* th*a*[t] the Chaumberlens haue geddryd affore tyme.

"Conentre." Oct. 5, 1437. [[3]V. f. p. held on Saturday after Michaelmas, 16 Hen. VI.] Joh. Michell, Laur. Coke, Tho. Wildegrise, Joh. Braytoft,[4] Egid. Allesley, Joh. Bristowe, Rob. Southam, Joh. Brampton, Joh. Clerke, Joh. Prentes, Ric. Botone*r*, Ric. Busshebury, Joh. Licheffeld, Will. Kerver, Joh. Warant, Will. Swane, Will. ffrisby, Joh. Doughty, Hen. Sircok, Joh. Deyste*r*, Ric. Braytoft, Joh. Lusterley, Joh. Spenser, Joh. Whalley.

Bailiffs. [Will. Brown, draper, Will. Darsett, dyer.]

[The Trinity guild to have the Bablake-gate of the mayor and chamberlains for a term of 99 years, for the yearly rent of a red rose at the feast of S. John Baptist.]

Ordinant eciam q*uo*d Magiste*r* Gilde S. Trinitat*is*[5] Couentre, fratres et sorores eiusdem Ciuitat*is* & Successores sui h*ab*eant et teneant portam vocat*am* le Bablake-yate de Maiore etc. & Came*r*ariis etc. usq*ue* ad fine*m* te*r*mi*ni* quaterviginti nouemdecim annor*um*. Reddendo inde annuati*m* eisdem Maiore (*sic*) etc. & succes*sor*i*bus* suis vnam Rosam rubiam ad festu*m* Natiuitat*is* S. Joh*ann*is Bap*tis*tem (*sic*), si petat*ur*.

[1] ? A torn piece depending from the rest.
[2] For murage patents *v.* Dugd. 98, and Corp. MSS. B. 42, 45.
[3] leaf 96. [4] MS. Brayftot.
[5] MS. inserts "fratres" here.

WILL. SWAN, MAYOR, 1438.

[1] Tempore Will. Swanne.

(*No entries.*)

WILL. KERVER, MAYOR, 1439.

[2] [Election of officers.] Jan. 25.

Electors. Joh. Braytoft, Laur. Cooke, Joh. Leder, Joh. Bristowe, Ric. Sharp, Joh. Ronton, Joh. Warant, Will. Broun, Joh. Braunston, Rob. Southam, Joh. Doughty, Hen. Sircok, Tho. Wirley, Joh. Clerke, Ric. Botoner, Will. Warset [Darset], Will. Broun, Will. ffrisby, Joh Prentes, Joh. Deyster, Joh. Lee, Joh. Lusterley, Will. Brid, Ed. Brogreue.

[m. Will. Kerver; cor. Joh. Whalley; ch. Tho. Bassyngburn, Ric. Osborn; w. Tho. Suettenham, Joh. Goolde; mace, Will. Westeley.]

The waits. Hyt is ordeyned that they Trumpet schall haue the rule off the whaytes,[3] and off hem be Cheffe.

EASTER AND MICHAELMAS LEETS.

Apr. 11. 1439. [4][V. f. p. held before Will. Kerver, m., Joh. Spenser, Joh. Bryan, b., on Saturday in Easter week, 17 Hen. VI.]

By oath of the electors. Per sacr*amentum*, Joh. Braytoft, Joh. Leder, Tho. Wildegrise, Joh. Bristowe, Joh. Michell, Joh. Ronton, Will. Swanne, Joh. Warant, Joh. Bramston, Joh. Clerke, Joh. Prentes, Ric. Bottoner, Joh. Licheffeld, Ric. Busshebury, Will. ffrysby, Joh. Doughty, Hen. Sircoke, Joh. Deister, Joh. Esex, Tho. Wirley, Joh. Broun, Joh. Whalley, Ric. Braytoft, Joh. Beauchamp.

Orders of leet. Presentment. E. Lichfield has granted leaden pipes to convey water from the conduit over the Sherbourne, Qui present*ant* & dic*unt* that where-as Edward Licheffeld off Couentre graunted vnto the meire and the Com*in*alte off the Cite off Couentre and to ther successouros for*euer*more[5] that they schall have certen pipes of lede lyeng within the[6] tenement of the seyde Edward, be the which water[7] ffro the Condite Thorogh hys seide tenem*ent* vnto the[8] ou*er* Shurburn atte ende of the seyde tenem*ent* being, may be brought; off the whiche pipe[9] of

[1] leaf 97. [2] leaf 99. [3] "wayt*es*" deleted.
[4] leaf 100. [5] "forthermore" crossed out.
[6] "y" crossed out. [7] "waytours" crossed out.
[8] "seid" deleted; ? omission, or "ov*er*" redundant.
[9] "thei" follows.

which pipes W. Darsett

lede[1] the seide meire and Com*in*altc haue ben seased.[1] And nowe long tyme sithem (*sic*) Will. Darsate,[2] notwithestondyng the seid g*r*aunte, off hys Euell wille the tyme of the seyde g*r*aunt notheng haveng ne clayneng[3] in the seide teneme*nt*, pipes off lede to the valu off[4]

has broken and taken awny.

in the seid teneme*nt* beeng, and ther layde after the graunt aboue-seyde, hath broken, takon awey and the watur stopped, to grett nosaunse off the Com*in*alte off the seid Cite.

The justices' feed.

The worshipull men off thys lete wollen [that the bailiffs pay 13*s.* 4*d.* towards the expenses of the mayor and justices at every session].[5] Allso they wolle that the se*r*iaunte*s* off this Cite se*r*ue all warrantes off the Courte

Sergeants to serve warrants without fee.

w*ith*in they sum off xl d. w*ith*-out takyng of money, like as hyt was ordeyned by a lette made in the tyme off John Michell last past etc.[6]

The river again!

They wolle that they Meire and the Bailles make syght oue*r* the ryuer, and they defautes That they ffynde that they warne the tenantes duellyng ther to amende they defautes by a ce*r*ten day, vpon a peyne, and yeffe the

Fine 6*s.* 8*d.* to be shared between the mayor and bailiffs.

amende not her defaute*s* that vche trespaso*u*r pay to they meire and Baill*ies* di*midiam*[7] marc*am* to be depa*r*ted be-twen he*m*.

The master of S. John's Hospital to have the pasture below Swanswell Pool in severalty, with a foot-way.

Volunt quod mag*ister* S. Joh*ann*is Bapt*iste*,[8] ffratres & sorores infra no*min*ati h*ab*eant & teneant Campu*m* & pastura*m* Swanneswelpole infra [nominata] in sep*ar*ati, Cu*m* via pedestre & nulla alia via, p*r*out h*ab*uer*unt* a temp*or*e antiquo, etc.

"Scoole."

[9]They orden that they Meire with vj off hys Councell go vnto the prior and Co*m*ien[10] the matier, Wyllyng hym

The education difficulty.

to occupye a skole of Gramer, yffe he like to teche hys Brederon and Childerun off the aumbry, and that he wol-not gruche ne meve the contrari, but tha[t] eue*r*y mon

The prior not to feel aggrieved.

off this Cite be at hys ffre chosse to sette hys chylde to skole to what techer off Gramer that he likyth, as reson askyth, etc.

1 Words deleted. 2 One of the 24; bailiff 1437; *v.* p. 171.
3 claymeng. 4 Blank in MS. 5 *v.* p. 187.
6 *v.* p. 169–70, but not given.
7 "C" deleted. 8 Sharp, *Antiq.* pp. 155–60.
9 leaf 100, back. 10 commune = talk over.

They ordeyne that the[1] Close the pa*r*cels that ben sowen, and that they lett they remenand be opon to lett Comyn bestes off they town haue her Comyn; and Fremans-quarell to be Comyn, as hyt hath ben off olde tyme; and an a-nother ffeld that John Northampton holdyth to be Comyn, eue*r*y man vpon the peyne of xx s. at eue*r*y deffaute. "Comons" to be open.

They ordeyne that ffrom thys tyme fforward that any muk or ffilth be Cast ther by eny pe*r*son, but ȝif the Comyn seriant do execucion he schall lese his office; also John Braunston hath g*r*aunted an house to on that will kepe they seide town yende, and Ric. Busshebury hath g*r*aunted xx s. for to fey hyt. The cleansing of the town-end.

They ordeyne that they meyre and the mastur off the Tr*ini*te Gilde comyne with Will. Pere, deyster, ffor he graunted xx s. ffor they Byrge (*sic*), and that hyt be made be the oue*r*siȝt of they seyd meyre and w*ith* other off hys peyrs in schort tyme. W. Pere and the bridge.

They ordeyne that they meyre and they Bayles shall chesse[2] in eue*r*y warde ij aletasters, the wich schall taste boythe bred and ale, so tha[t] they be able pe*r*sones and discrete, and that the se off the ale that hyt be solde after the meyors Cryo,[3] and that pe*r*sone defauton they seyd ale-tasters schall eue*r*ychone of hem haue at eue*r*y defaute a Gallon off the best ale, and the remenaunde to be sold by they meyr eue*r*y gallon ffor a ob.[4] "Ale-tasters."

They ordeyne that frome thys tyme fforward suche mane*r* vpholders[5] w*ith*in Comprehened be pursewed as they were pe*r*sones sole, and onswere ffor ther owne dedez, and all other in lyke Case. Upholders.

They ordeyne that Michell Pa*r*ker come not nor sell not with-in the (?) Cont*re* off Couentre, vppon they [peyne] off inp*r*isonment. M. Parker expelled from the (?) country of Coventry.

[6]¶ [V. f. p. on Saturday after Michaelmas, 18 Hen. VI.] Joh. Braytoft, Laur. Cooke, Joh. Leder, Tho. Wildegrise, Joh. Bristowe, Egid. Allesley, Ric. Sharp, Joh. Michell, Couentre. Oct. 3. Jury.

1 *i.e.* they. 2 chose. M.E. chese, O.E. cēosan (Mr. Stevenson).
3 v. *supra*, pp. 23 *sqq.*
4 Some omission. Informers are to have the ale. *v.* p. 25.
5 Either persons of some body corporate, or maintainers of suits.
6 leaf 99, back.

Joh. Ronton, Will. Swan, Joh. Warrant, Joh. Braunston, Joh. Prentes, Ric. Boton*er*, Joh. Clerke, Ric. Busshebury, Joh. Doughty, Joh. Deister, Will. Broun, Joh. Essex, Tho. Wirley, Will. ffrysby, Joh. Walley, Will. Perre.

Bailiffs. [Ric. Braytoft, Joh. Lusterley.]

Constables to be chosen by the mayor and 5 [of his] peers.

Ordinaverunt q*uo*d deinceps om*n*es Constabul*ar*ii sunt el*ecti* p*er* maiorem & quinq*ue* soc*ios* etc.

J. Burton's house.

[The mayor, by the recorder's advice, to enter into the house in Earl Street, once Joh. Burton's.]

"Woll to be sold in the hall."

They ordeyn that all men that bye any wolle in the Cite off Couentre that hyt be brouth to the hall and ther to be weyed, payng therffore acordyng to the statut,[1] and that the Swerdberer and they meyr se*r*iant haue the oue*r*syt off the weyng, & that they seyd wolle be clene & able wi*th*-ouȝt ffileth or muk as the statut wyll.[1]

Brewers and regraters. "Against setting up corn before it be brought to the market, forfeit 40*s*."

They ordeyn that they Breusters off thys Cite of Co[uentre that] Brue ther ale to sale tha[t] þe brue after they p*ro*clamacyon and ordynance off lete, eue*r*y bruster vppon the peyne of xx s., and eue*r*y typuler vppon they peyne off di*m*. mark, ffor that schall be rered by the Meir and Bailles; also what mane*r* bruester, or ells,[2] that regraton ony mane*r* Corn with-in they Cite or withowt in they hynderyng off þe market, he schall lose xl s. atte eue*r*y defaute.

"The office of Town-Clerkshipp."

Alsoy (*sic*) they ordeyne that Symkyn Birches enjoy and haue off the office off Toun-cle*r*kship terme off hys lyffe, takyng therffore Salaries and fees due and Custum*m*ed.

"Carted ? ffornihtenonor."[3]

Alsoy they ordeyn that Will. Powet, Capper, and his p*ar*omou*r* be Caried and lad thorowe þe town in a Carre in exaumpull off punnyshment off syne, and that alle other that be p*ro*ved in they same syne, ffrom thys tyme fforward shall haue the same peyne.

Vegetable refuse to be removed.

They ordeyne that eue*r*y man or woman that sett ouȝt ony bladys[4] in they seyde lane, but yffe they leffe[5] hyt, they schall paye atte eue*r*y deffaute xj d. (*sic*).

[1] *v.* p. 193. [2] ells = other. [3] fornicator.

[4] This is the only instance of the use of this word in South Britain known to Dr. H. Bradley, who kindly tells me that blades = vegetable refuse, *i. e.* cabbage-leaves, etc., is common in Scotland.

[5] "lift," remove.

JOH. ESSEX, MAYOR, 1440.

Easter and Michaelmas Leets.

Couentre. Easter leet. Apr. 2, 1440. Jury of 24.

[1] [V. p. f. before Joh. Essex, m., Ric. Braytoft and Joh. Lusterley, b., on Saturday after Easter, 18 Hen. VI.] Joh. Braytoft,[2] Laur. Cooke, Tho. Wildegrys, Joh. Michell, Joh. Bristowe, Will. Swanne, Will. Kerver, Joh. Warrant, Joh. Braunston, Joh. Clerke, Joh. Prentes, Ric. Botoner, Ric. Busshebury, Joh. Doughty, Will. ffrysby, Rob. Southam, Hen. Sircoke, Will. Broune, Joh. Spenser, Joh. Bryan, Tho. Wirley, Joh. Whalley, Ric. Dene, Joh. Lynne.

[Orders of leet. The mayor and council ordered to undertake the assize of water; every miller to pay 6*s.* 8*d.*; half to the wall, and half to his craft, at every trespass.

Volunt quod assis*a* aque fiat p*er* Maiorem & Consili*um* suum, p*ro*ut ex antiquo cons[uetum est], et quod quil*ibe*t molend*inarius* soluat p*ro* quodl*ibe*t (*sic*) t*r*ans*gressione* vj s. viij d. v*iz*. di*m*. muro etc., aliud di*m*. arti molend*inariorum*, p*ro*ut bill*a* exigit etc.

[Whoever buys salt fish according to the custom of the town is to distribute it among his neighbours at the same rate at which they were first bought, or pay a fine of 40*d.* to the wall, and 40*d.* to the fishmonger's craft.]

[3] Volunt q*uod* quicu*n*qu*e* emant pises (*sic*) sals*os*, sec*und*um officiu*m* hui*us* ville distribuat (*sic*) int*er* conuisine*s* (*sic*) suos ad vend*endum* secu*ndum* id q*uod* prius Empt*i* sint[4] etc. Et qui in cont*r*ariu*m* fac*iat* soluet vj s. viij d. p*ro* qual*ibe*t trans*gressione*, etc. v*idelicet* xl d. muro ville etc. & xl d. arti eiusd*em* piscen*arii*.

The wool to be weighed at the wool-hall.

Thei wyll that the wolles be weyed at the hall and that the wardens see hyt and take ffor her labur a-Cordyng to the Statute to the p*r*ofyt off the Towne.[5]

Accounts.

[Kerver,[6] the wardens and chamberlains whose accounts

[1] leaf 101, back. [2] MS. Baytoft.

[3] See Bateson, *Leicester*, I. 78, and *Law of Breteuil* (Eng. Hist. Rev. Jan. 1900). The custom allowing bystanders in the trade to go shares in a bargain was prevalent. It kept down prices, and helped to discourage regratery.

[4] I am not at all sure of this reading. It looks like "empt' suis" in MS.

[5] Statutes of the Realm, I. 390, II. 64, 292.

[6] The late mayor.

are due to be ready with them on Thursday "com seven-yght."]

Couentre. Oct. 1, 1440. Jury.

[1] [V. f. p. held on Saturday after Michaelmas, 19 Hen. VI.] Joh. Braytoft, Laur. Cooke, Joh. Leder, Egid. Allesley, Will. Swan, Will. Kerver, Joh. Ronton, Joh. Michell, Joh. Warrant, Joh. Prentes, Joh. Doughty, Ric. Busshebury, Ric. Botoner, Tho. Wyrley, Hen. Sircoke, Joh. Braunston, Rob. Southam, Joh. Spenser, Will. ffrysheby (*sic*), Joh. Clerke, Joh. Bryan, Will. Pir, Piere (*sic*), Ric. Osburne, Ric. Dene.[2]

"One fyned ffor sueing out of this Court," *i. e.* in the Hundred court; offender to pay 100*s*.

[3] Mem. that on Ric. Molle, weue*r*, because he sued on Will. Harries, deiste*r*, in þe hundreth contrarie to the ordenau*n*ce of diue*rs* lete*s* made in tyme past that no man shuld enplede other but in þe kynge*s* Courte in Couentre, but yf hit were be writte of thyng doon within þe seid Cite, vppon peyn of C s., be auctorite of þis seid lete, was demed to pay C s., be þe Maire & wardeyns to be rered.

Latrines leased to W. Pere for 99 years, as appears by his bill filed at the leet.

It*em*, at þis same lete at þe speciall petic*i*on of on Will. Pere the sege houses[4] in þe West-orcherd were graunte to hym for te*r*me of $\overset{xx}{\text{iiij}}$ ȝer & xix, to paie to þe towne xij d., and he to newe bylde theym, & the brige there, & so to kepe & repair theym sufficiently duryng þe seyd te*r*me, vt pe*r* billa*m* dicti Will. Pere in d*i*c*t*a leta filat*am* [? plenius apparet.]

"Wel-stret." "A way from Well Street to Hill Street gate" stopped.

It*em*, it was ordeyned at þe same lete þ*at* ij co*m*en lanes in þe Well-strete, whech then wer stopped, shuld be opened ayen & so kept be þe maire & Bayleffs within a weke þen next suyng, vppon [the peyn of] vj s. viij d.; þe on lane lay there vnto a well betwixt þe housez of Lusterley & Hen. Knotte*s*, and þe other ley into þe Hill-strete be the towne-dych.

"Couentre." Jan. 25.

JOHN WARRANT, MAYOR, 1441.

[5] [¶ Election of officers.]

Electors.

Will. Swan, Joh. Leder, Tho. Wyldegrys, Joh. Braytoft, Joh. Mychell, Joh. Ronten, Will. Kerver, Joh.

[1] leaf 101. [2] No record of bailiffs' election.
[3] Scribe B. [4] *v.* Gloss.
[5] leaf 102. In marg. "vacat his q*uia* ex alt*er*a pa*r*te." Warrant's leet is leaf 102, back.

Lusterley, Rob. Southam, Will. ffrysby, Joh. Spenser, Joh. Bryan, Hen. Sircok, Joh. Clerke, Joh. Doughty, Ric. Botoner, Tho. Wyrley, Ric. Braytoft,[1] Joh. Prentes, Will. Birde, Ric. Osberne, Joh. Lee, Will. Pere, Joh. Lynne.

[m. Joh. Warant; cor. Sim. Birches; ch. Ric. Boyes, Ric. Scot; w. Ed. Brogreve, Joh. Walgraue; mace, Will. Oxton.] Officers.

EASTER AND MICHAELMAS LEETS.

[2][V. f. p. held before Joh. Warrant, m., Joh. Whalley, Ed. Drouer, b., on Saturday after Easter, 19 Hen. VI.] "Couentre." Apr. 22.

Will. Swanne, Tho. Wyldegrice, Joh. Braytoft, Joh. Leder, Joh. Bristowe, Joh. Michell, Will. Kerver, Joh. Essex, Hen. Syrcok, Rob. Southam, Joh. Prentes, Joh. Doughty, Will. ffryseby, Joh. Brampston, Joh. Clerk, Ric. Braytoft, Joh. Bryan, Will. Brome [Broune], Joh. Golde, Joh. Walgraue, Ed. Brogreve, Ric. Boyes, Joh. Lee. Jury.

[R. Eme and all others, who play in the Corpus Christi pageant, shall play well and sufficiently, so that no impediment may arise in any play, on pain of 20*s*. to the town-wall.

Ordinatu*m* est q*uod* Rob. Eme et om*n*es alii qui ludunt in festo Corporis *Christi* bene & suficiente*r* (*sic*) ludant; Ita q*uo*d nulla impedic*io* fiat in aliquo ioco, sub pe*n*a xx s. cuiusl*ibe*t deficient*is* ad vsus muri levando*rum* pe*r* maiorem & Came*rarios* etc.

[The mayor, bailiffs and other honest men shall ride to see to the bounds before Michaelmas.

Item, ordinant q*uo*d Maior & Balliui pe*r* se ipsos & alios p*ro*b*os* ho*min*es ville de Couentre semel cit*ra* fes*tu*m S. Mich*ael*is arch*angel*i p*roxi*m*o* futur*um* equitent ad vidend*um* metas & bundas franch*isarum* de Couent*ria* etc.

[The mayor to put into execution all the articles of his proclamation under the penalties contained therein.]

[The mayor and his peers to look to the defaults mentioned below, and all other defaults to be revealed.

Volunt q*uo*d Maior et Compares sui videant def*ec*tus inf*ra*-specificat*os* & om*n*es alios def*ec*tus tocius reveli (*sic*)[3] etc.

[1] MS. Brayftot. [2] leaf 102, back. [3] (?) ville.

[T. Shopes of the Priory, miller, shall be at mercy 6*s.* 8*d.* for stopping up the flood-gates. 20*s.* fine for any further offence to be levied by the chamberlains.

It*em*, Thom*as* Shopes, miluer, de Prioratu, sit in m*isericord*ia, v*idelicet*, vj s. viij d. p*ro* obstupac*io*ne de lez flodeȝatez in the Priory. Et quod deinceps bene se geret, sub pe*na* xx s. p*ro* quol*ibe*t def*ec*tu pe*r* came*r*arios levand*orum*.

[The wardens to take into their hands certain tenements in Much Park Street, which A. Swete held, on condition that they see to the gutters, and repair other defaults therein, according to the petition of Joan, Ad. Swete's wife.

Volunt quod Ga[r]duani recipia*n*t tene*menta* infra-specificat*a*, [1]v*ideli*-*cet*, tene*men*ta in le Mu[c]hep*ar*k-strete q*ue* Ad. Swete nuper tenu[i]t,[1] in manis (*sic*) suas, sub Condic*io*ne q*uo*d vidia*n*t (*sic*) gutteras, & alios def*ec*tus ib*ide*m emende*n*t, p*ro*[ut] pet*itu*r etc. [1]p*er* Joha*n*nam, vx*or*em p*re*dicti Adam Swete.[1]

[W. Oxton to remove the under-mentioned butts, situated at the muck-hill in Little Park Street, without challenge of any one, by the mayor's command, and those now being made to be made in another place, provided that no one shoot in the cock-fighting place.

Volunt q*uo*d Will. Oxton amm[o]-veat lez butes infra specificat*os*, [1]situat*os* apud le Mukhill in þe Litilp*ar*k-strete,[1] sine cont*r*adict*io*ne alic*u*i*us* per prece*ptum* Maioris, & modo facientes faciant in alio loco; & p*ro*uiso q*uo*d nullus deinceps sagittet in le Cokfytyng place, etc.

[Will. Oxton, sergeant-at-mace, to have the power of arresting and presenting; so that he does not suffer any warrants to be taken, and to have the gate at the Bishop Gate, so that he repair it well and sufficiently.

Volunt q*uod* [1]Will. Oxton, co*m*ien se*r*iant,[1] h*ab*eat potestatem attach*i*-*andi* & p*re*sentandi [ali] q*uem*,[2] Ita p*ro*uiso quod non (?) sinat aliqua pre-ce*pta* *s*umend*a*; & quod habeat portam [1]apud le Bishopȝate[1] etc., Ita quod bene & sufficiente*r* rep*ar*et illam.

[They wish that if any persons indicted be arrested when the bailiffs of the town have first taken the mainprise, the bailiffs ought to aid the

Volunt quod si huius*modi* ind[i]c-[t]ati[2] decete*r*o arestati existe*r*int (*sic*) Ita q*uod* ball*ivi* ville de Couentre prius ceper*int* (?) m*anucapcionem*, ipsi bal-l*ivi* debent adiuuare g*r*avatem[3] (*sic*)

1—1 Interlined in another ink. 2 doubtful. 3 gravatum.

aggrieved party to prosecute or otherwise release the mainprise.]

ad *prosequendum* vel (?) al*iter*[1] resoluant m*anucapcionem* etc.

[2][V. f. p. held on Thursday after Michaelmas, 20 Hen. VI.] Will. Swanne, Tho. Wyldegryce, Laur. Coke, Joh. Braytoft, Joh. Bristowe, Joh. Michell, Will. Kerver, Hen. Sircok, Ric. Boton*er*, Joh. Clerke, Joh. Lychefeld, Joh. Doughty, Joh. Prentes, Rob. Southam, Ric. Braytoft, Will. ffryseby, Ric. Bussebury, Tho. Wyrley, Joh. Spenser, Joh. Bryan, Joh. Walg*r*aue, Tho. Swettenham, Ric. Boyes, Joh. Golde. Oct. 5. Jury.

[Joh. Lee, Joh. Lyme.] Bailiffs.

[They ordain that the mayor and recorder choose 12 worthy persons, their neighbours, and by their discretion it may be provided if the outer liberty be ridden, and let it be done as [of old time it was accustomed.]

It*em*, ordinant q*uo*d Maior & Recordat*or* elegant (*sic*) xij dignas p*er*sonas, convicinos suos, sibi, & p*er* discrec*iones* ipsor*um* p*r*ouideat*ur* si lib*er*tas exte*r*ior equitet*ur* vel (?) legit*ime*, & sic fiat p*r*out etc.

[No one dwelling in Coventry to be collector of the Fifteenth in the county without the liberties or 100*s*. fine.

It*em*, ordinant q*uo*d deinceps nullus qui Conmorat*ur* (*sic*) infra villam de Couentre sit Collector xv[me] in Com*itatu* Warre*wicie* ext*r*a lib*er*tatem ville p*re*d*icte* cont*r*a tenorem Carte[3] eiusdem ville [or 100*s*. fine to the town use.]

[Neither W. Aubrey nor any one else to receive into his hostelry coal, barley, or other grain, by way of regratery, whereby the market is damaged, or 40*s*. fine.

It*em*, ordinant quod nec Will. Aubrey nec aliquis alius inf*r*a villam de Couentre capiat nec recipiat inf*r*a hospiciu*m* suu*m* carbones, ordium (*sic*), nec aliquod aliud granu*m* via reg*r*atre, Ita quod foru*m* ib*ide*m in aliquo deteriorete*ur* [or 40*s*. to the mayor.]

[The persons under-specified[4] are to be governed according to the mayor, recorder and their craft, like the rest of their craft, or pay 20*s*. to the town wall.][5] Rebellious crafts-people to be ruled by the mayor, etc.

[1] alt*er*. [2] leaf 103. [3] Pat. 11 R. II. p. 2 m. 29 (Dugd. 98).

[4] infra cont*ente*.

[5] Probably this was a new attempt to strike or make a journeymen's guild. In January 1441 the corporation obtained a confirmation of previous grants, forbidding the formation of new guilds. Corp. MS. B. 47.

[The bailiffs are to be present with the mayor and J. Ps., and if the latter have attributed misdoing to any one, as this bill supposes, against the law, they (the former) are to make amends to the injured party. And no bailiff to arrest any one against the good custom of the city.]

Volunt q*uo*d Ball*iv*i sint p*r*esentes Coram maiore, Justic*iariis* pacis infra Ciuitatem Couentr*ie*, & si p*r*edicti fecissent[1] offenc*io*nem alicui, p*r*out suppo*n*it*ur* pe*r* bill*am*, cont*r*a legem, emendent p*ar*ti lese. Et quod null*us* Ball*ivus* decet*er*o attach*iet* aliquem cont*r*a bonu*m* vsu*m* Ciuitat*is* p*r*e-dicte, [or 100*s*. to the town's use.]

JOHN BRAYTOFT, MAYOR, 1442.

"Couentr*e*." Jan. 25.

[2][Election of officers.]

Electors. Tho. Wylgrys, Laur. Cooke, Joh. Leder, Ric. Sharp, Joh. Michell, Will. Swanne, Will. Kerver, Joh. Essex, Joh. Whalley, Joh. Lusterley, Rob. Southam, Will. ffrisby, Joh. Prentys, Joh. Clerk, Tho. Wyrley, Joh. Bryan, Joh. Spenser, Joh. Doughty, Ric. Boton*er*, Will. Birde, Joh. Golde, Will. Pere, Ric. Deane, Ric. Austen.

Officers. [m. Joh. Braytoft; cor. Joh. Whalley, ch. Gerv. Cole, Joh. Rechford; w. Ed. Brogreve, Joh. Walgraue; mace, Will. Oxton.]

EASTER AND MICHAELMAS LEETS.

"Couentre." Apr. 7.

[3]¶ [V. f. p. held before Joh. Braytoft, m., Joh. Lee, Joh. Lynne, b., on Saturday after Easter, 20 Hen. VI.]

Jury. Tho. Wi[l]degrys, Joh. Leder, Joh. Bristowe, Ric. Sharp, Joh. Michell, Will. Swanne, Will. Kerver, Joh. Essex, Joh. Warant, Ric. Braytoft, Joh. Clerk, Will. ffrysby, Joh. Doughty, Tho. Wirley, Joh. Spenser, Joh. Lusterley, Joh. Whalley, Ric. Boton*er*, Joh. Prentes, Rob. Southam, Hen. Sircok, Tho. Swettenham, Joh. Walg*r*aue, Ric. Dene.

[Orders of leet.

[The wardens to pay 13*s*. 4*d*. every Christmas to the Corpus Christi guild master until £9 10*s*. 0*d*. is paid,

Item, ordinant q*uo*d Gardinani (*sic*) soluant annuatim M*agist*ro Gilde Corp*or*is *Christi* xiij s. iiij d. quousq*ue* ix li. & x s. plenar*ie* persolut*i* fue*r*int p*r*efat*is* Mag*ist*ro & Successorib*us*

[1] It looks like "feoffent." [2] leaf 103. Scribe B.
[3] leaf 103, back. Scribe of C type but more legible.

suis annuatim ad f*estu*m Nat*ivitatis* D*omi*ni, quos (*sic*) quidem ix li. & x s. eid*em* Mag*istr*o plene persolut*os* (?)[1] Thome Stratton p*ro* negociis que ad opus ville de Couentr*ia* p*ro*fecit[1] (*sic*) etc.

and the master is to give the money to T. Stratton for the business which he undertook for the town's profit.

Volunt q*uo*d Maior p*ro*videat pauiatores ad pauiand*as* stratas p*ro*ut infra desideratu*r*, & p*ro* stipend*io* inde soluend*o* leuant*ur* (*sic*) p*er* districc*ion*em ; si aliquis h*ab*eat aliquod lib*eru*m tenementu*m* infra villam de Couentre etc.

[The mayor to provide paviors to pave the streets, and the wages shall be raised by distraint; if any one have a free tenement within the town [he shall pay, etc.].

Et quoad porcos tam inf*r*a villam q*ua*m ext*r*a, co*mmun*is Sub-b*allivus* h*ab*eat illos ad Co*mmun*es (*sic*) parcu*m*, et levat p*ro* quol*ibe*t pede ob., & ipsemet h*ab*eat pecuniam sic leuat*am* etc.

[The common sub-bailiff shall have the pigs, within as well as without the town at the pound, and take ½*d.* for each foot, and have the money himself.

Et quoad domos infra specificatas[2] ordinant & p*ro*uident quod nullus deinceps euellant (*sic*) domos aliquas infra vill*am* nisi reedificat illud (*sic*), sub pe*n*a soluend*i* p*ro* tene*mento* vaca*nte* x s. x li. & sic secu*n*d*u*m ratam, & quod Maior & Ball*iv*i h*ab*eant vna*m* di*midiam*, & Came*r*arii h*ab*eant aliam di*midiam* etc. ad exe*r*cend*a* etc.[3]

[No one henceforward to pull down a house without rebuilding it, under pain of paying £10 [for one of] 10*s.* [rent] and so according to that proportion, the mayor and bailiffs to have one half and the chamberlains the other for the exercise [of their office].

Et q*uo*d co*mmun*is Sub-b*alliuus* mu*n*dat Co*mmunem* parcu*m* infra quindenam p*r*oxi*mo* seq*uentem*, sub pe*n*a xl d.

[The common bailiff to cleanse the pound within 15 days or 3*s.* 4*d.* fine.

Volunt q*uo*d co*mmun*is Subball*iuus* p*re*muniat vbi necesse est, p*ro*ut infra fit menc*io*, *et* tunc q*uo*d om*n*es defe*c*tus emendant*ur* cit*r*a f*estu*m

[The sub-bailiff to give warning where need is, and all defaults to be emended before

[1] Probably some word omitted. We should expect "qui quidem . . . persolvantur" (Mr. Stevenson).

[2] MS. specificat*ur*.

[3] *v.* p. 223.

Nativity of S. John Baptist.

Nativitatis S. Joh*anni*s Bap*tis*te p*roximo* futur*um*, [or 6*s.* 8*d.* fine at every default, half to the mayor and half to the chamberlains.]

[They [the waits] are to have their livery on condition that they have a trumpet, and the escutcheons (badges) on security being found; that is to say, they shall have a dozen of cloth worth 20*s.* due to them for their livery from the wardens, against Corpus Christi.

Volunt quod h*ab*eant vesturas suas p*r*out billa ista exigit etc. sub Condic*ione* quod h*ab*eant vnu*m* Trumpet, p*r*out infra fit menc*io* etc. & les skecons[1] sub securitate invent*a* h*ab*ebunt etc., v*idelicet* h*ab*ebunt vnam xij panni (*sic*) p*ro* vestura etc. sibi debit*a* pe*r* Gardianos p*r*ecii xx s. etc. erga f*es*t*u*m Corpo*r*is *Christi* etc.

[All leet ordinances from aforetime to be observed under the penalties contained therein to be levied to the town's use.]

"Couentre." Oct. 6. [2]¶ [V. f. p. held on Saturday in the octave of Michaelmas, 21 Hen. VI.]

Jury. Tho. Wyldegrys, Joh. Leder, Joh. Bristowe, Joh. Michell, Will. Swanne, Will. Kerver, Joh. Esex, Ric. Braytoft, Joh. Clerk, Will. ffrysby, Rob. Southam, Joh. Doughty, Joh. Prentes, Hen. Sircok, Ric. Botone*r*, Tho. Wyrley, Joh. Lusterley, Joh. Brampton. Ed. Drouer, Joh. Deister, Joh. Whalley, Joh. Bryan, Tho. Swettenham, Joh. Gold.

Bailiffs. [Ric. Dene, Joh. Grynder.]

[Orders of leet.

[The wardens to have the rents of the town by the watering-place for the next year, and not the chamberlains; and for every pig doing damage there, they shall take 4*d.* upon delivery, and also they shall collect in the town for their expenses.]

Volunt q*uo*d h*ab*eant reddit*um* Gardinor*um* ville ib*id*em iuxta le Wateryng-plase pe*r* vnu*m* annu*m* p*roximo* futur*um*, et q*uo*d Came*r*arii p*ro* p*roximo* anno non pe*r*cipiant reddit*u*m ib*ide*m etc. & insupe*r* quod Capiant pro quodl*ibe*t (*sic*) porco i*bid*em dampnu*m* facient*e* iiij d. p*ro* deliberac*ione* h*ab*end*a* etc., ac eciam coliant[3] (*sic*) in villa p*ro* costag*iis* suis fact*is* etc.

[1] Sharp, *Cov. Mysteries*, 208. [2] leaf 104. [3] ? colligant.

THO. WYLDGRISE, MAYOR, 1443.

[1][Election of officers.] Jan. 25.

Joh. Warant, Joh. Leder, Joh. Bristowe, Joh. Michel, Will. Swan, Will. Kerver, Joh. Essex, Joh. Lusterley, Will. ffrisby, Joh. Doughty, Joh. Prentys, Ric. Botoner, Joh. Brian,[2] Tho. Wirley, Joh. Clerk, Joh. Spenser, Ed. Drover, Joh. Lee, Will. Pere, Joh. Golde, Ric. Boyes, Ric. Scotte, Joh. Boteler, Joh. Biram. Electors.

[m. Tho. Wilgris; cor. Joh. ffynch; ch. Ric. Alen, Will. Kemp; w. Tho. Warmyngton, Tho. Rastell; mace, Will. Oxton.] Officers.

EASTER AND MICHAELMAS LEETS.

[3][V. f. p. held before Tho. Wylgris, m., Ric. Deane and Joh. Grynder, b., on Saturday in Easter week, 21 Hen. VI.] Apr. 27, 1443.

Joh. Warant, Joh. Leder, Will. Swan, Will. Kerver, Joh. Essex, Joh. Listerley, Ric. Braytoft, Rob. Southam, Hon. Sircok, Joh. Clerk, Will. Broun, Joh. Whalley, Ed. Drover, Will. ffrisby, Joh. Doughty, Joh. Briane, Joh. Lee, Joh. Lynne, Joh. Spenser, Ric. Botoner, Joh. Prentys, Tho. Wirly, Edm. Brogreve, Joh. Walgraue.

[The bitters to repair the Broad-well, so that no water flows into the place where the horses stand, before the feast of the Ascension, or every one having a horse standing there to pay 6*s.* 8*d.*; and no horse is to come there, under the same penalty.

Qui volunt & ordinant q*uo*d lez Bitters[4] emendant le Brodewell q*uo*d aqua non emanet in locu*m* vbi equi stant ibi cit*r*a festu*m* Ascen*sionis* Do*mi*ni p*r*ox*imo* futur*um*, s*u*b pena cuiu*slibe*t qui h*abe*t equu*m* illuc venient*em* vj s. viij d., & int*er*im null*us* equus ibi pe*r*mitt*er*e (*sic*) evenire (*sic*), s*u*b eade*m* pe*n*a.

[A good iron grating to be made in Little Park Street at the cost of the wardens on their land, and whoever has lands or tenements adjoining the Redditch [shall contribute

Item, volunt & ordinant q*uo*d fiat vnu*m* bonu*m* gredeyron ferri in le Litel-pa*r*k-strete ad cust*agia* Gardianor*um*, [5]& vlt*er*ius q*uo*d quil*ibe*t qui h*abe*t te*r*ras vel ten*ementa* adiac*entes* ad le Reddych sup*er* solu*m* suu*m*[5]

[1] leaf 105. Scribe B. [2] Repeated and deleted. [3] leaf 105, back.
[4] Repairers, 'beaters,' from bete = O.E. bētan, to mend, etc. (Mr. Stevenson).
[5—5] This seems an interpolated and incomplete sentence.

thereunto] for the cleaning of the same ditch; it is to be of reasonable length and breadth, namely, 4 inches only between each bar stretching in depth (?).[1]

. . . . . p*ro* mu*n*dac*io*n*e* eiusd*em* fossat*i*, *raci*onabil*is* latitud*in*is & altitud*in*is, v*idelicet* iiij police*s* int*er* quaml*ibet* barra*m* solu*mmodo* extend*entes* in altu*m* etc.

[Latrines to be taken away from the Red-ditch before Whitsuntide or 6*s*. 8*d*. fine; so are others between Attelborough-place and Gowers-place and wherever else is necessary.]

Et q*uod* quil*ibet* qui h*a*b*et* latrina*m* sup*er* fossatu*m* p*red*ic*tu*m auferat ea*m* cit*r*a fest*um* Pente*c*os*tes* p*r*oxi*mum* etc. s*u*b pe*na* vj s. viij d. & si*mi*lit*er* om*nes* al*ie* a Attilburgh-place vsq*ue* tene*me*n*tum* voc*atum* Gowers-place, & alib*i* vbi necesse e*s*t infra villa*m* etc.

"Couentre." Michaelmas leet. Oct. 5, 1443. 24 electors.

¶ [V. f. p. held on Saturday after Michaelmas, 22 H. VI.] Joh. Warant, Joh. Leder, Joh. Bristowe, Ric. Sharp, Will. Swanne, Will. Kerver, Joh. Essex, Joh. Lusterley, Ric. Braytoft, Rob. Southam, Joh. Clerk, Joh. Braunston, Will. ffrisby, Joh. Doughty, Joh. Whalley, Ric. Botone*r*, Tho. Wirley, Joh. Spenser, Ed. Drover, Joh. Lee, Joh. Lynne, Joh. Brian, Ric. Boyes, Tho. Swetnam.

Bailiffs. [Will. Pere, Joh. Walgrave.][2]

RIC. BRAYTOFT, MAYOR, 1444.

Jan. 25. [3][Election of officers "in aula S. M*ar*ie, loco ad hoc consueto."][4]

Electors. Will. Kerve*r*, Joh. Leeder, Joh. Bristowe, Ric. Sharp, Joh. Mychell, Will. Swan, Joh. Essex, Joh. Warrant, Joh. Listerley, Joh. Clerk, Joh. Prentes, Will. Frisby, Rob. Southam, Ric. Botone*r*, Joh. Whalley, Ric. Dene, Joh. Lee, Tho. Wyrley, Joh. Bryan, Joh. Spense*r*, Joh. Goolde, Ric. Boyse, Ric. Skott, Gerv. Cole.

Officers. [m. Ric. Braitofte; cor. Joh. Fynche; ch. Ric. Clerk, Will. Clerke; w. Tho. Warmynton, Tho. Rastell; mace, Will. Oxton.

J. Ps. Ric. Braitofte, m., Will. Donyngton, rec., Will. Keru*er*, M. G. S. T., Joh. Leeder, Tho. Wildgrise, Joh. Bristowe.

[1] The bars were to be perpendicular and not horizontal (Mr. Stevenson).

[2] A much corrected sheriffs' and bailiffs' oath follows, leaf 107, back; other versions transcribed, *v*. p. 224.

[3] leaf 108. Scribe A.

[4] First mention of S. Mary's Hall in this connection.

Ric. Braitoft, Ric. Sharp, Joh. Leder, Tho. Wildgrise, Joh. Bristow.]

Key-keepers.

QUARREL BETWEEN THE WEAVERS AND CORVESERS.

Feb. 26 or Sept. 24, 1444. "Varyans betwen þe weavers and Coruesers." The weavers and corvesers

[1]ffor-alsomoche as hit was notiffied & Relac*io*n made vnto þe meir*e*, that is to sey Ric. Braytoft, þ*at* c*er*ten debates & stryves wer had betwen the Crafte of Weu*ers* & the Crafte of Coruisors, The said maio*ur* in keping of the peace, and allso willyng good rule & rest to be had betwen the said Craftys, mad to com a-for hym bothe the said Craft*is* chargyng hem to kep the peace, and allso to bryng hym in Wrytyng the matt*ur* & greua*unce* þat was betwen them. And so the Thursday next aft*ur* the fest of saynct Math[ew][2] thapostle the said Craft*is* brought vnto the maio*ur* in wrytyng the cause of ther greuance. Submittyng themselffe w*ith* due submission to abyde the rule of the maio*ur* & his Counsell. Wherupon the maio*ur* & his councell, whos [names] heraftur folowen, the complaint*es* of bothe p*ar*ties herd & vndurstond, haue ordenyd & p*r*ouyded that the Crafte of coruysers shuld Restore and satisfie vnto John Wamb*ur*ne of Couentr*e*, weu*er*, xl d., þ*at* is to say the said xl d., the hoode & the pair*e* of Glouys þ*at* wer taken awey fro*m* John Feythyng, s*er*ua*un*t vnto the said John Wamburne, when the seid John Feithyng was betyn. And ou*er* þ*at* the seid Craft of Coruysers shull pay for the betyng & for anoþ*er* trespas that was doon in the house of John Symond*es*, Coruis*er*, in despyte of the weu*er*s vj s. viij d.

bring a written account of their mutual grievances, submitting to the arbitration of the mayor and council.

The corvesers are to restore 40*d.* a hood, gloves, and 6*s.* 8*d.*,

Allso the said maio*ur* & his counsell orden that þe Crafte of Coruise*rs* shall pay to Thom. Burdeux, weu*er*, C s.[3] in satisfacc*io*n of the t*r*espas doon to hym the tyme þ*at* he was beeton be c*er*ten p*er*sons of the said Crafte of coruisers, for the w*i*ch he was in dispair of his lyffe. Allso þ*at* the Crafte of weu*ers* for dyu*er*s offences made by the coruisers to dyuers men of the weu*ers* shall haue C s., the said C s. to be eton and dronken among the fellauship of both Craftys.

and 100*s.* in compensation; and another 100*s.* to be spent at a feast between the two crafts.

[1] leaf 108, back.
[2] Sept. 21. St. Matthias' is Feb. 24. It might be either saint.
[3] "The said C s. to be eton and dronken" obliterated.

And on no account shall new names for cloths be used.

Allso þei orden that noo man of the Crafte of Coruysers fro this tyme forward shall vse ne new namys as in Callyng blake of lyre[1] Queyr*es* anamelynges ne non oþ*er* suche namys of noo thyng þ*at* longyth to þe[2] Crafte.

J. Wamburn, weaver, to make satisfaction

Allso thei orden þ*at* John Wamburn, weue*r*, for hymselffe & Will*i*am Pars, weue*r*, for the offence þ*at* thei made to John Maynard shall pay to John Maynard & Wyll*i*am Ward, coruyse*r*, xl d. in satisfacc*i*on of thoffens & t*r*espas þ*at* wer made to John Maynard & Will*ia*m Ward.

to the corvesers;

and the craft of weavers

Allso þei orden th*a*t all the Crafte of weue*r*s shall pay and satisfie to þe Crafte of Coruyse*r*s xx s. for thoffens & t*r*espas don to Benet Stockton, coruise*r*, in dispite of the Crafte of coruise*r*s; and þ*at* xx s. to be disposid in mete & drynk a-mong the felauship of both Craftes.

to contribute 20*s*. to a drinking.

Names of mayor's council in this affair, 36 in all.

No*mi*na consilii maior*is* in hoc casu. Will. Donyngton, Recordator, Will. Kerv*er*, M. G. S. T., Joh. Leeder, Tho. Wildegryse, Joh. Bristow, Joh. Mychell, Will. Swane, Joh. Warrant, Joh. Listurley, Joh. Lichefeld, Joh. Clerke, Rob. South*a*m, Joh. Prentes, Ric. Botton*er*, Will. Frisbye, Joh. Doughty, Will. Broun, Tho. Wirley, Joh. Bryan, Joh. Spenc*er*, Joh. Whalley, Joh. Lynne, Joh. Grynder, Joh. Lee, Tho. Warmynton, Joh. Goolde, Ric. Boyse, Ed. Brogreve, Tho. Swettenham, Will. Clerke, Will. Pier, Joh. Walgraue, Ric. Dene, Ric. Alen, Tho. Rastell, Ric. Austen.

Those new-fangled names

[3]Allso hit is ordenyd by the maio*ur* and his forseid Councell þ*at* if any man of the Crafte of coruise*r*s vse to call, or in tyme comyng call, any new namys in ther crafte, as callyng blake of lyre Queyers a-namelyng*es*, or any other suche feynyd names, but onely suche namys as haue ben vsed afore tyme, that allso ofte as they do soo, or any of them doo soo, they shall forfett xx s. in money, x s. to the maio*ur* & x s. to the baylyff*es* for the tyme beyng at eue*r*y t*r*espas.

to be tabooed or 20*s*. fine.

[1] v. *N. E. D.* lyre. A kind of cloth from Lire in Brabant. "Queyres anamelynges" seems a fine-sounding nonsense word such as is found in drapers' catalogues now; perhaps from cuir = leather, and enamelling.

[2] "to the" repeated.

[3] leaf 109.

THE CARDMAKERS' PAGEANT.

The pageant of the card-makers, saddlers, painters and masons to be supported by the united fellowship.

ffor-alsomoche as the Crafte of Cardemakers, Sadelers, Masons, and peyntors of the Cite of Coventre be long tyme I-past haue byn as oone fellauship in beryng Costys, charg*es* and all oþ*er* dueties of old tyme to ther pagent & to the said felauship longyng. And now late, þ*at* is to say in the tyme of Ric. Braytoft, maio*ur* of the said cite, the said felauship for c*er*ten causes among hem movyd wer lyke to dep*ar*te and to breke þ*er* felauship. Wherfor c*er*ten p*er*sons of[1] the said Craftez, shewyng to the maio*ur* the causz of ther g*r*evance, besought hym in this matt*ur* to sett due Remedye. And so by goodly leysur the maio*ur*, callyng a-fore hym & his counsell all the said hoole fellauship, Rehersid vnto them the g*r*evouse complaynt*es* þ*at* wern made to hym by c*er*ten p*er*sons of the said felauship. The for-namyd felauship willyng to be Ruled compromytted hem to abyde the Rule and ordynau*n*ce of þe meire and his councell. And so by aduyse of the said meire and his councell, hit is ordenyd that the said iiij Craftes shal-be oone felauship beryng Costes, charg*es*, and all oþ*er* dueties to her pagent and to þ*er* felauship longyng. And þ*at* thei shall yerely chose new masturs a-pon saynt Thomas day in *Christ*inmas weke in the forme and mane*r* folowyng: That is to say, þ*er* shal-be of eue*r*y of the said Craftys iij men in a place consuette wit*h*in the said cite; and ther in the fest of saynt Thomas thai shall chose of eue*r*y of the said iiij Craftes oone Mast*ur* for the yer folowyng. And if so be þ*at* any of the said Craftes a monethe afore the said fest be reasonable cause vnfayned may excuse hyme that thei may not be at þe Elecc*i*on of the masturs at the said feeste, That then the Crafte or the Craftez þ*at* may nott be ther shall bryng in iij menys names of the Crafte þ*at* may not be þ*er* at þe elecc*i*on, and what-soeue*r* the iij p*er*sonnes wit*h* oþ*er* þ*at* shal-be a-pon the elecc*i*on doo, Thei þ*at* ben awey to agre þ*er*to; and also sone as the masturs be chosen that same day or thei dep*ar*te the new masturs so chosen shall take þ*er* consuett Othe. And allso eue*r*y p*er*son of the said Craftys

[1] MS. of of.

shall pay yerely to the masturs xij d. and all oþ*er* dueties, customes, and laufull charg*es* þ*at* long to þe pagent & to the said felauship; and all money þ*at* shal-be reryd [1]for makyng of new brethren or els in other wais to the Craft*es* renued, as hit is gadred hit shal-be put in a co*m*en box þ*er* to be kepte to the vse of the said felauship and to the wurship of this cite. Allso eue*r*y mastur of þe seid iiij Craftes shall haue due Correcc*io*n of his own Crafte of all the p*r*iue poynt*es* þ*at* long to his Crafte, w*ith*out medelyng or ent*ur*mettyng[2] of any oþ*er* Craftys. Allso þ*at* þ*er* shall no man of the said iiij Craftes play in no pagent on Corpus *Christi* day save onely in the pagent of his own Crafte, w*ith*out he have lycens of the maio*ur* þ*at* shal-be for the yer. Allso þ*at* eue*r*y man that hath any money of forfett*es* þ*at* have byn made, or els money for makyng of bredren afore this tyme in the said Craftes, that hit be brought in be-twen this & the fest of All Saynt*es* next comyng, and that to the maio*ur*. And also þ*at* all þe masturs of the said felauship þ*at* have not accomptid a-fore this tyme þ*at* thay mak þ*er* a-compte be-twene this and the fest of All Saynt*es* next comyng, and all the arereage, if any be, þ*at* hit be brought in the same day and delyue*r*yd unto the co*m*en box. And allso þ*at* all masturs þ*at* now byn, and all the masturs of the said felauship þ*at* shal-be heraft*ur*, yerle shall make þ*er* acompte, eue*r*y mastur for his tyme at the fest of Estur. P*r*ovyded allwey þ*at* the Crafte of masons, ne none of hem, shall not be chargid to com to noo buryeng, weddyng, ne offryng of the said Craft*es* on workedais. And who of the said felliship disobeith this ordyna*u*nce, or forefettyth in any of them, shall pay at eue*r*y forfett xli to þe maio*ur* of the Cite of Coue*n*tre that tyme beyng w*ith*outen any g*ra*ce.

No craftsman of the fellowship to play but in this pageant.

Nomina concilii maior*is* in hoc casu.

Names of the mayor's council. 58 councillors.

Will. Keru*er*, Tho. Wildgrise, Ric. Sharp, Will. Swan, Joh. Warant, Joh. Lysturley, Will. Peir, Rob. Southam, Joh. Clerk, Will. Frisby, Joh. Lychfeld, Will. Broun, Hen. S*ir*cok, Joh. Spens*er*, Joh. Prentes, Joh. Bryan,

[1] leaf 109, back. [2] Interfering.

Joh. Braunston, Joh. Grynder, Ed. Drou*er*, Ric. Boton*er*, Sim. Birches, Will. Braytofte, Ric. Osburne, Joh. Lynne, Joh. Lee, Ric. Clerke, Ric. Boise, Ric. Skott, Tho. Warmynton, Ed. Brogreue, Tho. Rastell, Gerv. Coole, Tho. Suettenham, Ric. Alen, Joh. Gryme, Ric. Wymondeswold, Will. Bird, Rob. Eme, Joh. Honyburne, Joh. Franklen, Ric. Clerke, Joh. Swan, Joh. Perpoynt, Tho. Elderbek, Joh. Sircok, Joh. George, Ric. Dyvett, Tho. Bristow, Joh. Stafford, Ric. Capper, Rob. Bradmedow, Rob. Barnsley, Tho. Bradmedow.

WARWICK'S LOAN.

[1]Memorand*um* that thies wurthy men, whose names heraft*ur* folow, haue lant vnto my lord of Warr[ewik] C marc' of st*er*lyng to be paid atte fest of saynt Martyne in Wynt*ur* next comyng, as hit appearith by a obligac*i*on in the w*i*ch obligac*i*on Tho. Port*er*, Squyer, and Hen. S*ir*cok, of Couentre ar bound vnto Ric. Braytoft, Meire, Tho. Wyldgrise and to Ric. Sharp; the w*i*ch obligac*i*on remaynyth in the hondes of Ric. Braytoft, meire.

Loan to my Lord of Warwick, 100 marks. £66 13*s*. 4*d*.

[Ric. Braytofte, £3. 13s. 4d.; Will. Keru*er*, Joh. Leeder, Joh. Mychell, Will. Pier, Joh. Listerley, Joh. Ronton,[2] £2. 0s. 0d. apiece; Joh. Bristowe, £1. 13. 4d.; Will. Swan, Joh. Essex, Joh. Warrant, Joh. Lychefeld, Ed. Drouer, Ric. Boton*er*, Tho. Wirley, Joh. Bryan, Hen. S*ir*coke, Will. Brown, drap*er*, Joh. Grynder, Joh. Lynne, Sim. Birches, Ric. Clerke, hosier, Joh. Spenc*er*,[3] Ric. Alen, Ric. Boise, Ric. Osbarn, Will. Braitofte, Ed. Brogreue, Ric. Capper, Joh. George £1. 0s. 0d. each; Ric. Dene, Joh. Lee, 13s. 4d. apiece; Tho. Wildgrise £5. 0s. 0d.; "Magist*er* gilde S. T*r*initat*is* p*ro* gilda etc." £20. 0s. 0d.[4]]

The master of the guild £20.

[1] leaf 110. [2] Sum either xls. or xxs. [3] "hosier" deleted.

[4] A deleted passage adds: & vlt*ra* hoc maior h*abe*t Cs. quos (*sic*) Cs. gilda s*an*cte T*r*init*atis* Couent*re* eru*n*t (*sic*) solut*i* p*er* Tho. Rastell & Joh. Warde, hosier, et ad q*uod* obligat*i* su*n*t in q*uod*a*m* Script*o* obligat*orio* reman*ent*e in manib*us* m*agist*ri, et eru*n*t solut*i* in *f*est*o* Pasche p*roximo* futur*o*, i. e. "that the mayor has 100 s. which the Trinity Guild will pay by (*per*) Tho. Rastell and Joh. Warde, hosier, and in which they are bound by a written bond in the master's hands, payable at the following Easter." There is also the explanation of the deletion :—"This is drawen & crossed bycause the Cs. is in the su*m*me of the Trinite gilde, for afore the Su*m*me was xv li."

EASTER LEET.

Apr. 20. [1] [V. f. p. held before Ric. Braytoft, m., Will. Pier, Joh. Walg*r*aue, b., on Monday after the close ("Clauis") of Easter.]

Jury. Will. Keru*er*, Tho. Wildegrise, Joh. Bristowe, Will. Swanne, Joh. Essex, Joh. Warrant, Joh. Leeder, Joh. Clerke, Rob. Southam, Hen. S*ir*coke, Joh. Prentes, Will. Broune, Tho. Wirley, Will. Frisby, Ed. Drou*er*, Joh. Bryan, Joh. Lee, Joh. Whalley, Ric. Dean, Joh. Grynder, Ric. Clerke, Joh. Lysturley, Tho. Warmyngton, Ed. Brogreue.

The Red-ditch. [Any one who has a tenement adjoining the Red-ditch to make clean against (erga) the tenement on both sides before the Nativity of S. John Baptist or 6*s.* 8*d.* fine, 1*s.* 8*d.* to the mayor and 5*s.* to the wardens.]

[The cunduits to be locked from 9 o'clock at night to 4 in the morning; and no brewer to take from them water for brewing, but only to prepare food, or 40*s.* [? 40*d.*] fine, 1*s.* to the mayor and 2*s.* 4*d.* to the wardens. Entrails not to be washed there under the same penalty for every time.

Volunt & ord*inant* q*uo*d le Conduyt*es* sint serat*i* a ix hora in nocte usq*ue* ad horam quart*am* in mane, & q*uo*d null*us* co*mmun*is pandoxator capiat ib*ide*m aq*u*am ad b*r*asiand*um*, *sed* solu*m*mod*o* ad parand*a* cibaria sua, s*u*b pe*n*a xl s.[2], vi*delicet* xij d. m*aiori* et ij s. iiij d. gardian*is* etc. & q*uo*d null*us* deinceps lavet lez poodyng*es* ad le condit*es* s*u*b cons*im*ili pe*n*a, & tociens q*u*otiens etc.

[Everybody shall clean the river Sherbourne against his holding, beginning at Crow mill, and thus as far as the Priory; and the Hill-mill brook the same, before Whitsuntide or 40*s.* [? 10*s.*] fine; 3*s.* 4*d.* to the mayor, and 6*s.* 8*d.* to the wardens. No manure to be swept into the gutter or 4*d.* fine. And no one put or throw

Item, volunt & ord*inant* q*uo*d quil*ibe*t mu*n*det rivilum de Shurburn erga tenur*am* sua*m* incipient (*sic*) ap*u*d le Crow myll, & sic usq*ue* ad Prioratu*m*. & le Hillmyl-broke simili*ter* cit*r*a fe*stu*m Penthecosthes (*sic*) p*r*oxi*mo* futur*um*, s*u*b pe*n*a xl s.[2] vi*delicet* m*aiori* xl d. & vj s. viij d. Gard*ianis* ad vsum ville. & q*uo*d null*us* de cet*er*o inf*r*a villam Scopat muke seu vilia in le chanell, sub pe*n*a iiij d. tociens q*u*otiens. & quod

[1] leaf 115, back. The king's regnal year is omitted. [2] An error here.

muck or ? posts in the river or the same penalty. The mayor is to appoint 2 or 4 men in each ward sworn to present defaults.]

nullus deinceps iactat nec ponat muk *vel* past in rivilum *sub* pe*na* iij s. iiij d., levand*orum* in forma p*redicta*. & q*uo*d maior ordinat in q*uolibe*t vico ij*os* uel quatuor ho*min*es ad p*re*sentandos defectus in p*re*missis ad hoc Jur*atos*.

LOAN TO THE KING.

[1][The following "worthi men" lent ("lant") £100 to the King, "the vj^{t} Henry."] 1444. £100 loan raised

64 names. according to wards.

[Gosford Street.

Collectors:—Joh. Barbour, Ric. Skott, Joh. Stafford, Joh. Baker, deist*er*. Total £11 12*s*. 0*d*.]

	£ s. d.			£ s. d.			£ s. d.	
Wal. Bond	1	0	Joh. Sheldon, jun.	5	0	Tho. Stone	5	0
Hen. Warmynton	2	0	Will. Dawe	6	0	Will. Gilberd	5	0
Rog. Wyly	3	0	[2]Barbur, gent.	4	0	Joh. Atturton	2	0
Baldwin Metley	2	0	Joh. Braban	6	8	Tho. Wildgryse	13	4
Joh. Kebull	1	0	Joh. Cok*es*	2	0	Tho. Mason	5	0
Tho. Hall	2	0	Ric. St*er*lyng	1	0	Ric. Som*er*	5	0
Joh. Baker, d[e]ist*er*	6	0	Ric. Anabuls	2	0	Joh. Manton	4	0
Will. Bocher	2	0	Tho. Smythe	1	0	Tho. Horsley	2	0
Ric. Skott	6	8	Joh. Stafford, sen.	6	0	Rob. Smyth	2	0
Will. Lambard	2	0	Joh. Straunge	4	0	Joh. Travas	2	0
Joh. Langton	5	0	Will. Smyth, wolman	5	0	*Christ*iana Golofre	5	0
Ad. Gawge	5	0	Will. Jones	4	0	Greg. Boteler	1	0
Will. Cook*es*	4	0	Joh. Hall, drap*er*	2	0	Joh. Eston	3	0
Wal. Tirrell	2	0	Ric. Bocher	3	0	Will. Harres	2	0
Mat. Curtes	2	0	Tho. Bowyer	4	0	Eust. Golofur	5	0
Ric. Cookes	5	0	Ric. Tiler	4	0	Ad. Ismay	3	0
Laur. Cooke	13	4	Ric. Collett	4	0	Sim. Baker	5	0
Ric. Toly	2	0	Tho. Kynnesbury	2	0	Johanna Eucsham	5	0
Ric. Foston	3	0	Joh. Stafford, jun.	2	0	Joh. Rage	3	0
Will. Rothewell	2	0	Rob. Nevell	5	0	Agn. Capper	2	0
Joh. Langcastell	1	0	Will. Haddon	3	0	Will. Knyght	2	0
Ric. Molle	3	0						

*Sum*ma £11 12*s*. 0*d*.

51 names.

[Jordan Well.

Collectors:—Joh. Franklen, Joh. Shade, Rob. Eme, Ric. Alwold. Total £10 4*s*. 1*d*.]

	£ s. d.			£ s. d.			£ s. d.	
Ric. Allwold	6	0	Tho. Eldurbek	3	4	Will. Broun	12	0
Rob. Newton	6	8	Joh. Hawkyns	1	8	Joh. Brian	12	0
Rob. Eme	6	0	Will. Crampe	5	0	Joh. Squyer	5	0

[1] leaf 110, back. [2] Blank.

	£	s.	d.		£	s.	d.		£	s.	d.
Joh. Cat*er*		6	8	Joh. Prentes		9	0	Will. Castelton		3	4
Ric. Barbour		1	0	Joh. Hawkyns,				Rad. Plumer		5	0
Joh. Whalley		12	0	wright		1	0	Joh. Chacombe		1	8
Ric. Rage		1	8	Joh. Recheford		8	0	Tho. Dikons		3	0
Ric. Cleibrooke		1	8	Joh. Lee		10	0	Will. Flecher		2	0
Ric. Tomson		1	0	Joh. Street		1	8	Will. Bowre		1	8
Joh. Elderbek		1	0	Joh. Pyncherd[1]		5	0	Joh. P*ar*kyn		1	8
Joh. Peche		6	0	Tho. Smyth		1	8	Joh. Oufeld		1	8
Joh. Franklen		6	0	Will. Dowbryge		1	8	Will. Bolton		3	4
Joh. Shadde		6	0	Joh. Maidford		4	0	Tho. Gybons		1	8
Ric. Recheford		5	0	Nic. Ourton		1	0	Tho. Bagett		6	0
Will. Flout*er*		1	0	[2]Joh. Barret, mylner		1	0	Tho. Tatte		1	8
Ric. Clerke		6	0	Joh. Egull		6	0	Will. Glouer		1	0
Tho. Hakett		1	8	Joh. Folkeshull		1	8	S*um*ma £10 4*s.* 1*d.*			
Joh. Heyne		1	8	Joh Stoneley		1	8				

60 names.

[Bayly Lane.

Collectors:—Joh. S*ir*coke, Joh. Oderiche, Tho. Jakeman, Ric. Tokeby. Total £6 18*s.* 0*d.*]

	£	s.	d.		£	s.	d.		£	s.	d.
Joh. M*ar*ston		1	0	Will. Jhonson		1	10	Rob. Skyll		2	6
Will. Crowe		1	0	Joh. Baker		1	2	Joh. Power		1	4
Joh. Barton		1	4	Tho. Joyn*er*		1	8	Joh. Whitley		3	4
Joh. Byram		4	0	Tho. Wirley		5	4	Will. Clerke		4	0
Nic. Knyght		1	4	Joh. Spens*er*		5	4	Joh. Gryme		4	0
Joh. Bordale		3	0	Hugo Shryve		2	0	Joh. Olyffe		2	0
Hen. Watford		2	6	Ric. Berbroun[3]		4	0	Rob. Gloucest*ur*			8
Will. Swyfte		1	4	Tho. Brydd		3	4	Tho. Hobbes		1	0
Will. Dubber		1	8	Rob. Peuterer		1	0	Joh. Bayly		3	4
Hen. Wright		1	2	Joh. Bechamp		4	0	Ric. Oderyche		2	0
Ric. Dyvett		4	0	Tho. Fawkys		1	4	Joh. Crose		2	8
Joh. Whitehede			8	Nic. Carre		1	8	Tho. Swettglade			8
Steph. Wilkyns		1	0	Will. Broke		3	4	Joh. Wilkyns		2	4
Joh. Buteler		1	8	Joh. Ronton		8	0	Rad. Merc*er*		1	8
Ric. Tau*er*ner		1	0	Joh. Hull, baker		4	0	Rob. Coryour		1	4
Bartillmew Broderer		1	0	Tho. Loot			8	Joh. Skyll			8
Will. Westley		1	0	Ric. Smale		1	8	Joh. Sircoke			8
Will. Bilston		1	0	Hugo Newton		1	3	Joh. Odryche		2	8
Will. Mason		2	0	Ric. Hampton		3	4	Tho. Jakeman		2	8
Hen. Barker		1	3	Ric. Deister		2	0	[4]Ric. Tokeby		2	0

54 names.

[5][Broadgate.

Collectors:—Tho. Spens*er*, Joh. Eborall, Ric. Essex, Joh. Malory. Total £4 13*s.* 0*d.*]

	£	s.	d.		£	s.	d.		£	s.	d.
Alicia Illage		3	0	Tho. Spenc*er*		2	0	Joh. Radley, tailour		2	0
Joh. Nele, tail*our*		1	4	Ric. Vlnere, m*er*c*er*		1	0	Tho. Bristow		3	4
Will. Bedford		1	4	Rad. Duffeld		1	0	Joh. Eborall		1	4
Joh. Blackamoore		2	0	Ed. Brogreve		5	0	Walt. Paslow		1	0
Will. Spenc*er*		2	0	Joh. Locok		1	4	Rog. Stanley		1	4

[1] The schoolmaster. [2] leaf 111. [3] Perbroun, p. 177.
[4] Total wanting. [5] leaf 111, back.

	£	s.	d.
Will. Dyngley		1	0
Rob. Wodward		3	0
Joh. Capp*er*		3	4
Joh. Crampe		1	4
Joh. Swettenham		1	4
Joh. Malory		1	8
Tho. Goldsmyth		1	8
Joh. Spens*er*, merc*er*		1	8
Joh. Dalton		2	0
Rob. Persale		1	0
Ric. Morell		1	8
Alic. Bristow & Katerina Brykhull		2	0
Will. Drought		1	4
Will. Dawbney		2	0
Rog. Myln*er*		1	0
Joh. Hopton		1	0
Hen. Hend, tail*ou*r		1	0
Hugo Manton		2	0
Joh. Mynfold		1	8
Ric. Clerke		1	8
Will. Draper		1	4
Will. Chaterton		1	4
Joh. Riconjay		1	0
Will. Abraham		2	0
Hen. Rog*er*s		1	0
Tho. Napton		1	0
Joh. Derby		2	0
Hen. Sircok		6	0
Joh. Hony		2	0
Egid. Allesley		3	0
Will. Canley		1	0
Joh. Crose, husbondman		2	0
Alic. Newbold		1	4
Will. Baryngton		1	4
Tho. Lyones, weu*er*		1	0
Joh. Purs		1	4
Will. Wirisdale		1	0
Joh. Hare, mason		1	0

Summa £4 13*s.* 0*d.*

56 names. [Smithford Street.

Collectors :—Ric. Wymondeswold, Joh. Maynard, Joh. Yale, Ric. Flynte. Total £7 10*s.* 6*d.*]

	£	s.	d.
Ric. Braitofte		8	0
Joh. Brystowe		8	0
Joh. Braunston		4	0
Joh. Lynne		6	8
Joh. Maynard		4	4
Joh. Fremon		5	0
Tho. Wodward		5	0
Joh. Fynche		3	0
Galf. Bowyer		3	4
Joh. Wirthynton		2	0
Tho. Carbonell		1	8
Tho. Grene		1	0
Ric. Wymenswold		2	6
Tho. Broun		3	0
[1] Will. Ive		2	6
Joh. Dey		1	8
Rad. Plumer		2	0
Tho. Cholley		1	0
Rog. Rouke		2	0
Joh. Barley		1	0
Joh. Brown		2	6
Joh. Hampton		2	6
Tho. Plymmer		1	4
Joh. Blakemon		6	0
Elias Barbour		1	0
Tho. Joy		2	0
Ric. Osbern		6	0
Will. Melody		2	6
Joh. Higreve		1	4
Joh. Wiponbury[2]		2	0
Tho. Shistocke[3]		1	0
Joh. ffiynte		2	0
Ric. fflynte		4	0
Tho. Rastell		6	0
Joh. Abell		2	8
Joh. London		1	4
Joh. Coucher		2	6
Tho. Capper		1	8
Will. Coup*er*		1	4
Kat*er*ina Sadeler		2	0
Will. Bredon		1	0
Tho. Leche		2	10
Will. Marriott		1	0
Nic. Kent		2	6
Joh. Metburn		1	0
Ric. White		2	0
Will. Pars		2	6
Joh. Yale		2	0
Joh. Wilde		2	6
Joh. Forest		2	6
Joh. Brewer*e*		3	4
Gal. Flecher		1	0
Averey Harley		1	0
Tho. Walker, skynn*er*		1	0
Tho. Whiteside		4	0
Joh. Flecher*e*		1	0

Summa £7 10*s.* 6*d.*

95 names. [Spon Street.

Collectors :—Joh. Mershe, Will. Saunders, Joh. Harries, Joh. Sewon. Total £11 6*s.* 8*d.*]

	£	s.	d.
Joh. Waredrop			8
Tho. Shermon		1	4
Will. Horram		2	0
Joh. Grynder		6	8
Will. Saunders		6	4
Will. Tuttbury		2	8
Joh. Essex		8	0
Tho. Kyrvale		2	8
Ric. Shustoke		3	0
Tho. Heyward			8
Rob. Whitacur[4]		3	4
Tho. Coucher		1	4
Tho. Garnett		3	4
Hen. Rastell			8
Joh. Whittawer		2	8

[1] leaf 112 [2] Wappenbury, Warwick. [3] Shustoke, Warwick. [4] Whitacre, Warwick.

	£	s.	d.
Leticia Menley		4	0
Laur. Huyron		2	8
Rog. Pepur		2	8
Will. Bayley		2	8
Ric. Walford		1	8
Joh. Kyngston		2	8
Joh. Honyburn		6	4
Will. Wellys		3	4
Egid. Corbrond		5	0
Tho. Tokeby		1	8
Will. Ednam		1	4
Joh. Lotte		4	0
Joh. Conwey		1	4
Joh. Blaknale		2	0
Joh. Moole		2	0
Rob. Cokk*es*		2	4
Will. Keru*er*		8	0
Joh. Deist*er*		6	8
Joh. Wynnesdon		2	8
Joh. Glou*er*		3	4
Ric. Duffeld			8
[1]Hen. Nele		1	4
Tho. Hynkley		2	0
Joh. Deister		2	0
Reignald Neuton		1	4
Ric. White		1	0
Joh. Shaw		2	0

	£	s.	d.
Hugo Laurence		1	4
Simon Busteler		2	0
Tho. Reffus			8
Hen. Fisher		1	4
Ric. Barnbroke			8
Will. Blaknale		1	4
Tho. Gilbard		4	0
Ric. Holte		2	0
Sim. Mores		1	8
Joh. Burbage		1	4
Rob. Rep*er*		2	0
Tho. Broun		2	8
Ric. Stone		3	0
Joh. Hadley		4	0
Rob. Roodes		1	4
Rob. Roop*er*			8
Will. Barnebrok		4	0
Joh. Wutton		1	0
Gal. Tigon		2	8
Rob. Fairfax		1	4
Joh. Thornton		2	0
Rob. Loote		2	0
Ric. Palmer		2	0
Wal. Bulker		2	8
Rad. Wryght		3	0
Ric. Rede		1	4
Wal. Wellys		1	0

	£	s.	d.
Will. Spenc*er*		3	4
Tho. Caldon		2	0
Rob. Smyth		2	0
Will. Hamond		1	0
Alanus Snape		2	0
Joh. Daw		1	0
Joh. Plasterer		2	0
Rob. Boteler		1	8
Joh. Aldreskole		1	0
Nic. Keriche		1	0
Will. Deister		1	0
Rob. Dubber			6
Will. Fisher			6
Joh. Coup*er*		2	0
Hen. Dalby		2	8
Rog. Wales		2	8
Joh. Wamburn		2	0
Rob. Baxster		3	4
Ric. Pope		1	0
Wal. Norfolke		3	4
Ric. Barbour		1	4
Hugo Barbo*ur*		4	0
Joh. Wirley		2	0
Joh. Chadley[2]		1	0
Rob. Sturdy			6
[3]Rog. Burnes		2	8

54 names. [Much Park Street.

Collectors :—Tho. Waren, Will. Abray, Joh. Garton, Ric. Staffordschir*e*. Total £9 18*s*. 6*d*. (*sic*)]

	£	s.	d.
Joh. Leeder		13	4
Joh. Clarke		10	0
Tho. Bate		6	8
Ric. Dene		6	8
Sim. Birches		10	0
Tho. Warmynton		6	8
Will. Braitofte		10	0
Will. Brydd		5	0
Joh. Clifford		2	6
Ed. Hensham		1	8
Hen. Bugg		2	0
Tho. Illage		3	4
Rob. Stook*es*		2	0
Tho. Wylott		2	0
Tho. Norwyche		3	4
Tho. Waren		4	8
Joh. Ingland		4	0
Hen. Hobbes		6	8
Ric. Bromley		5	0

	£	s.	d.
Joh. Derby		6	8
Ric. Staffordshir*e*		3	4
Will. Cleibroke		6	8
Will. Corbett		2	6
Joh. Forde		4	0
Ric. Burfrey		4	0
Ric. Knyghtley		3	0
Tho. Tyler		4	0
Joh. Garton		5	4
Will. Awbray		3	4
Joh. Ardern		3	4
Rob. Smith		3	4
Anna Grove		2	0
Will. Eton		2	0
Joh. Cale [? Gale]		2	6
Joh. Sowre, myln*er*		5	0
Tho. Tough		2	0
Joh. Shergryndar		2	0
Will. Weston		2	0

	£	s.	d.
Joh. Folkeshull		2	0
Joh. Ravon, pynn*er*		1	8
Joh. Crofte		2	0
[4]Castell, wryght		2	0
Joh. Haley		1	8
Joh. Makesey		1	8
Will. Solans[5]		1	8
Tho. Cooke, baker		2	0
Hen. Tailo*ur*		1	8
Agnes Onley		2	0
Will. Forbur		1	8
Joh. Mylner		1	8
[4]Tyrvyn, wev*er*		1	0
Will. Poverete			8
Will. Swyndryver		1	0
[4]Bateman		1	8

Summa £10 0*s*. 6*d*. (*sic*).

[1] leaf 112. [2] Hadley, p. 174. [3] Sum wanting.
[4] Blank. [5] Solant, p. 179.

64 names.

[[1] Bishop Street.

Collectors :—Will. Boteler, Will. Warwyke, Hugo Shawe. Total £11 6*s.* 0*d.*]

	£	s.	d.		£	s.	d.		£	s.	d.
Joh. Kebull		5	0	Rob. Weston		5	0	Joh. Warde,			
Ric. Bylston		1	8	Wal. Tryg		1	8	steynour		1	4
Will. Horsley		5	0	Joh. Bristow, weuer		1	0	Joh. Bruer		3	4
Will Herdwyke		1	8	Joh. Lichefeld		10	0	Hen. Benett		1	8
Joh. Goolde		6	8	Rog. Chapman		1	8	Gal. Strette		3	4
Rob. Reve		1	8	Ric. Tedd		1	8	Ric. Pisforde		1	8
Joh. Bylston		1	8	Joh. Atwode		5	0	Joh. Couper		3	4
Joh. Symondes		1	8	Will. Trewman		3	4	Joh. Folvill		1	8
Will. Withiford		5	0	Nic. Joones		1	8	Joh. Stafford		3	4
Tho. Spicer		1	8	Tho. Walgraue		1	8	Will. Byddell		1	8
Ric. Cokkes		5	0	Will. Felde		1	8	Will. Kemp		8	0
Ric. Chichesture		3	4	Joh. Wodcote		1	8	Rog. Tailour		5	0
Rob. Harberd		1	8	Joh. Appulby		5	0	Ed. Drouer		10	0
Ric. Spicer, grasier		5	0	Tho. Kekwike		1	8	Joh. Mores		5	0
Will. Ronkorne		1	8	Will. Couper		5	0	Tho. Brown		1	8
Ric. Fylippes		3	4	Will. Warwyk		5	0	Tho. Cleybroke		5	0
Will. Rolfe		1	8	Joh. Walgraue		10	0	Joh. White, bocher		3	0
Hugo Shaw		5	0	Ric. Glouer		1	8	Joh. Massey		1	8
Joh. Belper		1	8	Joh. Stanfeld		1	8	Joh. Cleibrok		1	8
Ric. Clerke		3	4	Joh. Lysturley		10	0	Joh. Raignold		1	8
Tho. Waren		1	8	Hen. Knott		1	8	Joh. Powle		1	8
Joh. Couper		5	0	Rob. Southam		6	8	Summa £11 6*s.* 0*d.*			

64 names.

[Earl Street.

Collectors :—Tho. Swettenham, Ric. Alyn, Ric. Austen, Rob. Bradmedow.][2]

	£	s.	d.		£	s.	d.		£	s.	d.
Joh. Warrant		10	0	Nic. Palmer		5	0	Joh. Bentley		1	0
Ric. Sharp		13	4	Tho. Dey		3	0	Tho. Hipstoones		2	0
Will. Swan		13	4	Rob. Barnsley		3	4	Joh. Asheburne		2	0
Joh. Mychell		13	4	Ric. Bartram		2	11	Baldw. Smythe		2	0
Will. Donyngton		10	0	Tho. Bradmedow		3	0	Joh. Symon		1	0
Joh. Northewode		10	0	Ric. Boyse		6	8	Will. Willaston		2	0
[3]Ric. Austen		1	8	Tho. Swettenham		4	0	Tho. Abell		2	0
Will. Frisby		5	0	Tho. Falkes		4	0	Will. Cotoner		1	8
Agn. Willouȝby		5	0	Joh. Harbourgh		3	0	Ric. Rashe		1	8
Rob. Bradmedow		1	4	Hen. Clerk		2	0	Tho. Parkyns		1	8
Wal. Asheby		6	8	Joh. Bradley		2	0	Ric. Chacombe		2	0
Will. Chawderell		2	0	Tho. Stafford		2	0	Rob. Heywode		2	0
Ric. Julyans		4	0	Will. Holme		2	0	Nic. Esterton		1	8
Ric. Alen		6	8	Hen. Shaw		2	0	Pet. Swett		2	0
Joh. Perpoynt		3	4	Joh. Pynchbek		2	0	Will. Nores		1	0
Joh. Douse		2	0	Joh. Alderews		2	0	Joh. Gilbard		1	8
Joh. George		10	0	Joh. Oldenhall		1	4	Will. Perkes		1	8
Agn. Crudworth		4	0	Bened. Corker		2	0	Steph. Pynner		2	0
Tho. Bayly		4	0	Joh. Clerk		2	0	Summa £11 17*s.* 4*d.*			
Ric. Clerk		6	8	Tho. Parker		3	0				
Joh. Goodwyn		6	8	Will. Dawe		2	0				

[1] leaf 113. [2] Sum wanting. [3] leaf 113, back.

98 names. [Cross Cheaping.

Collectors:—Joh. Northampton, Joh. Hall, Ric. Penson, Joh. Radcliff, Joh. Botte.][1]

	£	s.	d.
Tho. Goldsmyth		5	0
Ric. Drought		1	8
Rob. Mason		3	4
Joh. Dey		3	4
Ric. Wood & Rog. Constantyne		6	8
Joh. Golofre		1	8
Will. Byrynton		3	4
Joh. Walle		1	8
Joh. Doughty		10	0
Joh. Guye		3	4
Joh. Nele		3	4
Joh. Maidford		3	4
[2] Kardyffe, tyler		1	8
Ric. Lane		3	4
Ric. Goldsmythe		1	8
Will. Mason		1	8
Tho. Alen		3	4
Hen. Mason		3	4
Will. Rowlett		1	8
Joh. Colyns		5	0
[3] Joh. Nele		3	4
Joh. Corell		1	8
Tho. Paunton		3	4
Will. Donyngton		1	8
Will. Hosier		5	0
Joh. Whittofte		3	4
Joh. Savage		3	4
Will. Defford		1	8
Ric. Boto*ner*		10	0
Reg. Bere, goldsmyth		5	0
Rob. Mason		1	8
Joh. Huett		3	4

	£	s.	d.
Joh. Bett		1	8
Tho. Bredon		3	4
Ric. Charite		3	4
Nic. Grene		1	8
Tho. War*ner*		1	8
Ric. Drought		1	8
Joh. Barbur		3	4
Will. Warde		1	8
Will. Darsett		10	0
Will. Benett		5	0
Joh. Barbour		1	8
Will. Hewent (*sic*)		3	4
Will. Humburston		3	4
Editha Chaundeler		3	4
Tho. Wolffe		3	4
Will. Bedon		3	4
Rad. [2] *ser*iant		1	8
[2] Dalby		1	8
Will. Atterton		3	4
Tho. Swayne		3	4
Tho. Kerdiffe		1	8
Will. Suger		1	8
Joh. Manton		1	8
Agn. Joy		3	4
Hen. Aderton		3	4
Ric. Bealson		1	8
Will. Hull		3	4
[4] Hen. Randull		3	4
Agn. Bynley		1	8
Ed. Dilcoke		3	4
Joh. Colyns		3	4
Will. Whit		1	8
Tho. White		1	8
Tho. Okeham		1	8

	£	s.	d.
Tho. White		1	8
Joh. Exsale		1	8
Will. Norton		1	8
Gal. Wulpyn*er*		3	4
Joh. Imayne		1	8
Wal. Broun		1	8
Will. Peire		10	0
Gerv. Cole		6	8
Tho. Haddon		3	4
Will. Ryngley		1	8
Hen. Baker		1	8
Rob. Fawkes		1	8
Joh. Style		3	4
Will. Huett		3	4
Hen. Banbury		3	4
Ric. Leeder		1	8
Ric. Bedon		3	4
Tho. Skott		3	4
Will. Northampton		2	1
Nic. Randull		1	8
Will. Deyster		5	0
Joh. Deister		1	8
Tho. Kirvall		1	8
Joh. Bynley		3	4
Ric. Weu*er*		3	4
Rob. Burn		3	4
Joh. Northampton		2	1
Joh. Hall		2	1
Ric. Penson		2	1
Will. Radclyffe		2	1
Joh. Boote		2	1
Su*m*ma £14 17*s.* 1*d.*			

And for suertie of the said C li. & repayment to be had, the said maio*ur*, Ric. Braitofte, hath p*r*ouyded; and by his labour he hath gooten a patent of o*ur* soue*r*eign lord, þe kyng, and a Taile. Of the w*hi*ch payment the teno*ur* folow*i*th as hit appear*i*th hereaftur in the leffe folowyng. The w*hi*ch patent w*ith* the taile remanyth in the co*m*en Coofur in saynt Mary Hall etc. And aftur, that is to say, in Lenton then nextt folowyng, the said patent and Taile wer delyue*r*ed to Will*i*am Essex of the Exchekur to gett the next assigment that may be had. — Security — a patent and a Tally.

*Su*m*ma* to*t*al*is* C li. v s. ij d. — Sum total £100 5*s.* 2*d.*

[1] Sum wanting. [2] Blank. [3] leaf 114. [4] leaf 114, back.

[Money not taken.
Margery Peyntour 2*s.*; W. Shirley 1*s.* 8*d.*; Ric. Cardyffe 1*s.*

Vnde p*er*donat*ur* M*ar*gerie Peyntou*r*, ut p*atet* in Ward*a* de Much [park-strete] ijs. Ite*m*, Will. Shirley in Ward*a* de Jurd[en-well] xx d. It*em* Ric. Cardyffe xij d.

[Letters patent, security for the debt.

[Henry King of England etc. to all to whom these present letters shall come, greeting. Know ye that since the mayor and men of Coventry have lent us £100 in our urgent necessity, we wishing to dispose and ordain for the repayment of the said sum, by the advice and assent of our council, have granted for us and our heirs that the said mayor and men shall be repaid well and faithfully the said £100 from the Parva Custuma in the port of London by the collectors of the said custom at the term of payment of the same by virtue of a tally levied upon the said collectors therefor at the receipt of the Exchequer and delivered to the said mayor and men.

And in case the said mayor and men are unable to obtain payment of the said £100, then we will that whenever any subsidy, by whatever name it may be known, or sums of money

[1] Henricus (etc.) Sal*utem*. Sciat*is* q*uo*d cum maior et hom*ines* ville de Couentr*ia* Cent*um* libr*as* in vrgent*i* necessitate n*ost*ra nobis grat*is* mutuau*er*int, Nos, p*ro* resoluc*ione* su*m*me p*redicte* p*re*fat*is* maiori & ho*minibus* fidel*iter* facienda dispone*re* & ordinare volentes, de auisamento et assensu consilii n*ost*ri, concessim*us*, ordinauim*us* et assignauim*us* p*ro* nobis, h*e*redibus & successorib*us* n*ost*ris, q*uo*d p*re*dict*i* maior & ho*mines*, h*e*redes, executore*s* & assignati sui de p*re*dict*is* C li. de p*ar*ua custuma[2] in portu Londo*nie* p*er* manus Collect*orum* eiusdem Custume ad t*er*minu*m* soluc*ionis* eiusdem virtute talii (*sic*) sup*er* ipsos collect*ores* inde ad Recept*um* Scaccarii n*ost*ri leuate, & p*re*fat*is* maiori & ho*minibus* lib*er*ate, bene & fidel*iter* resoluent*ur*. & in casu q*u*o p*re*dict*i* maior et ho*mines* de dict*is* centu*m* libr*is* solui nequeant, extu*n*c volum*us* et concedim*us* p*er* p*re*s*e*ntes q*uod* q*uando*cu*n*q*ue* subsidiu*m* aliquod q*u*ocu*n*q*ue* no*mine* censeat*ur*, seu

[1] leaf 115.

[2] Parva Custuma, certain import duties paid on wool, wool-fells and leather by aliens, and on general merchandise, cloth, wax, tin and wine by aliens and natives.

shall be granted to us by the clergy or community of our kingdom the said mayor and men may have at their choice tallies and assignments for sums of money to be paid thence from other revenues and profits whatever belonging to us, arising from time to time, for all that which is lacking to them of the said sum of £100, lent to us, as aforesaid, by the said mayor and men, payment to be made by the hands of the collectors or the receivers of the same, until payment shall have been fully made of the said sum.

We will, moreover, and concede by these presents, that the treasurer of England for the time being shall have power and authority from time to time to change such assignments and tallies made in favour of the said mayor and men, but unpaid, and to alter them according to the will of the said mayor and men, and their heirs and assigns.

In testimony whereof we have caused these letters patent to be made.

Myself being witness at Westminster Aug. 24.]

pecuniar*um* su*m*me pe*r* cleru*m* seu co*mmun*itatem Regni n*ostr*i Anglie nobis concedi contig*er*it, p*r*edict*i* maior, ho*min*es, h*er*edes, executo*res*, & assign*ati* sui ad elecc*io*nem et ad libitu*m* sua h*ab*eant & p*er*cipiant tallias et assignac*io*nes de denario*rum* su*m*mjs inde ac aliis reuenc*ioni*b*us* et co*m*moditatib*us* nobis p*er*tinen*tibus* quobuscu*n*q*ue* (*sic*) de temp*or*e in temp*us* p*r*oue[nie]nt*ibus* de & p*ro* om*n*i eo q*uo*d sibi defu*er*it solut' (*sic*) de dict*a* su*m*ma Centu*m*librar*um* [que] pe*r* p*r*efatos maiorem et ho*min*es nob*is*, ut p*r*emittit*ur*, mutuat*ur*, pe*r* manus Collecto*rum* siue Recepto*rum* eoru*n*dem q*u*aliter*cu*n*q*ue assign*and*-*orum*, quousq*ue* eiisdem (*sic*) maiori & ho*min*ib*us*, h*er*edib*us*, Executori*bus* & assignat*is* suis de su*m*ma p*r*edict*a* plenar*ie* fu*er*it p*er*solut*um*. Volum*us* insup*er* & concedim*us* p*er* p*r*esentes q*uo*d Thes*aurarius* Anglie p*r*o temp*or*e ex*ist*ens h*ab*eat p*ot*es*t*atem & auctoritatem o*mn*es hui*us*mod*i* assignac*io*nes & tallias p*r*efat*is* maiori et ho*min*ib*us* sic f*a*ctas, et no*n* solut*as* de temp*or*e in tempus mutare, easq*ue* ad libitu*m* ipso*rum* maior*is* & ho*min*um, heredu*m*, executo*rum* & assign*atorum* suo*rum* reformare. In cui*us* Rei testi*moni*u*m* has l*it*era*s* n*ost*ras fieri fecim*us* patent*es*. T*es*te me ipso ap*u*d Westm[onasterium] xxiiij^{to} die Augusti a*nn*o R*egni* n*ostri* vicesimo secu*n*do.

Sturgeon.

MICHAELMAS LEET.

[1]¶ [V. f. p. held on Saturday after Michaelmas, 23 Hen. VI.] Couentre. Oct. 3.

Will. Keruer, Joh. Leeder, Tho. Wildgryse, Will. Swane, Joh. Essex, Joh. Warrant, Joh. Listurley, Rob. Southam, Hen. Sircoke, Joh. Clerk, Joh. Prentes, Tho. Wirley, Will. Frissby, Joh. Bryan, Ed. Drover, Joh. Lee, Joh. Lynne, Ric. Dean, Joh. Bristow, Will. Braitofte, Ric. Cleke, Tho. Warmyngton, Tho. Swettnam, Will. Clerke. Jury.

[Ed. Brogreue, Ric. Boyes.] Bailiffs.

[Orders of leet.

[The gratings from the Little-park-street to Jordan-well to be taken away, except that in the Little-park, under the pain contained in the last leet.

& ordinant quod omnes lez grates a le Lytull-parke-strett usque le Jurdenwell auferentur, (*sic*) illo in le Lytull-parke-strett excepto; sub pena in vltimo visu *ffranciplegii* posita, videlicet vj s. viij d.

[The chamberlains to cleanse as much as is occupied in the common market; and every one to cleanse about his tenement, as far as it stretches, and no one to cast dung to the injury of his neighbours, or 12*d.* fine.[2]

& volunt quod camerarii mundent in communi foro tantum quantum occupatur ad vsum ville. Et quod quilibet tenens mundat erga tenementum suum, ita late ut ipse pauement se extendit, & quod nullus iactet fimum ad nocumentum vicinorum suos (*sic*) sub pena xij d. tociens quotiens, per communem sub-ballivum leuandorum.

[No one to keep pigs in any place in the city to the injury of his neighbours, or 6 s. 8 d. fine.] "Swyne"

RIC. BRAYTOFT, MAYOR, 1445. Jan. 25,

[3][Election of officers.] Electors.

Ric. Sharp, Joh. Leder, Tho. Wildegryse, Joh. Michell, Will. Swanne, Will. Kerver, Joh. Esex, Joh. Warant, Joh. Lusterley, Joh. Lee, Will. Braytoft, Joh. Wildegryse, Tho. Wyrley, Joh. Bryan, Rob. Southam, Joh. Spenser, Joh. Walgraue, Ric. Dene, Ric. Skotte, Ric. Alen, Geruas. Cole, Will. Kemp, Will. Brid, Ric. Osberne.

[1] leaf 116. [2] "dirt [in the] streets" in margin.
[3] leaf 122. Another scribe.

Officers. [m. Ric. Braytoft; cor. Joh. ffynche; ch. Joh. Baker, deyster, Joh. George; w. Joh. Stafford, wirdrawer, Ric. Austen; mace, Will. Oxton.

J. Ps. Ric. Braytoft, m., Will. Donyngton, rec., Ric. Sharp, M. G. S. T., Joh. Leder, Tho. Wyldegryse, Joh. Brystowe.

Key-keepers of the common seal chest. The same, except the recorder.

Key-keepers of the chest where the common measure and other jewels are in S. Mary's Hall. Ric. Braytoft has two keys, Ric. Sharp, M. G. S. T., two, Joh. Leder one, Tho. Wildegryse one, Joh. Bristowe one.]

[1] THE MAYOR'S COUNCIL AND ARBITRATORS.

[Names of the Mayor's Council.]

19 councillors. Ric. Sharp, Joh. Leder, Tho. Wildegryse, Joh. Mychell, Will. Kerver, Joh. Esex, Joh. Lusterley, Ed. Brogreve, Ric. Boyse, Hen. Sircok, Joh. Walgraue, Rob. Southam, Joh. Bryan, Ric. Alen, Tho. Warmynton, Joh. Lee, Will. Braytoft, Joh. Wyldegryse, Joh. Grynder.

[These men elected by the mayor to see where there is debate among the people for fixing gutters, posts or the like within the liberty, and adjudicate therein, taking 6*d*. each for their labour from any one to whom the land is adjudged.]

Memorand*um* q*uo*d isti homi*n*es subscripti el*ect*i sunt p*er* Maiore*m*, videl*icet* p*er* Ric. Braytoft Maior*em*, etc. ad vidend*um* vbi aliquod debat*um* est & discordia int*er* aliquos ho*min*es Ciuitat*is* Couent*rie* p*ro* fixac*ione* gutturar*um*, postar*um* vel alior*um* consimiliu*m* infra lib*er*tate*m* Ciuitat*is* Couent*rie*, & eadem[2] tunc adiudicand*um*, capiend*o* p*ro* eor*um* labore quil*ibe*t vj d., videl*icet* de ipso cui te*r*ra adiudicat*a* [est].

Joh. Huet, mason, Ric. Tyler, Hen. Dalby, wright, Tho. Gylous, wright.

THE FIFTEENTH.

[[3]The wards that paid the half fifteenth conceded in Ric. Braytoft's time.[4]]

Spon-strete. Will. Saundres, Joh. Mershe, Joh. Harries, Joh. Sewen. [£2. 16s. 10d.]

[1] leaf 122, back. [2] Repeated and deleted. [3] leaf 125.
[4] Parliament conceded a half fifteenth March 1445. The heading is "tem-

Smyth[ford-street]. Joh. Yale, Gal. Bowyer, Joh. Wylde, Ric. fflynte. [£2. 0s. 0d.]

Croschepeng. Joh. Norhampton, Ric. Penson, Joh. Halle, Will. Radclyf. [£3. 12s. 6d.]

Bysshop-strete. Ric. Spycer, Tho. Parbroun, Will. Warrewyk, Will. Horsley. [£2. 16s. 6d.]

Brodeyate. Tho. Spenser, Joh. Eborall, Ric. Esex, Joh. Malory. [£1. 3s. 4d.]

Erl-strete. Rob. Bradmedow, Tho. Bayly, Tho. ffalkes, Rob. Barnesley, Joh. Alderwes. [£2. 16s. 10d.]

Jurden-well. Joh. Shadde, Rob. Eme, Ric. Alwolde, Joh. ffrankelen. [£2. 11s. 0d.]

Bayly-lone. Joh. Syrcok, Tho. Jakeman, Ric. Godedo riche, Joh. Ordericho. [£1. 15s. 0d.]

Much-park-strete. Will. Abrey, Ric. Staffordshire, Joh. Arderne, Tho. Waren. [£2. 10s. 0d.]

Gosford - strete. Will. Dawe, Tho. Stonew, Rob. Neuell, Joh. Manton. [£2. 18s. 0d.]

EASTER LEET.

[1][V. f. p. held before Ric. Braytoft, m. Ed. Brogreve, Ric. Boys, b. on Saturday after Easter, 23 Hen. VI.] Apr. 3, 1445.

Tho. Wilgris, Joh. Leder, Joh. Bristowe, Will. Swanne, Will. Kerver, Joh. Essex, Hen. Sircok, Rob. Southam, Joh. Clerk, Joh. Prentys, Tho. Wirley, Will. Frisby, Joh. Bryan, Ed. Broun, Joh. Lee, Joh. le Lynne, Ric. Bere, Joh. Grynder, Joh. Walgraue, Joh. Baker, Deist*er*, Joh. Stafford, Wiredrawer, Ric. Austen, Gerv. Cole, Will. Clerk, m*er*cer.

[Orders of leet.

[Any one having a dwelling who entertains bawds or keeps common women unless he turn

[2]Ord[inatum] e*st* q*uo*d quil*ib*et h*ab*ens tene*mentum* infra villa*m* de Couentr*ia* & suburbia eiusd*em* qui tenet v*e*l hospitat aliq*uas* bawedes, v*e*l susten*tat* v*e*l custod*it* co*m*en women, nisi eos (*sic*) amoueat & ext*ra* tene*mentum* suu*m* ponat t*a*les sup*er*

p*ore* Ric. Braytoft tunc maiore (etc.) anno xx sec*und*o"; the "xx" being interpolated as an afterthought. It was the second year of Ric. Braytoft's mayoralty; but the 23rd year of Henry VI.

[1] leaf 125, back. Scribe of C type. [2] Scribe B.

them out upon warning shall lose 20*s.* at every default; half to the church, and half to the bailiffs.

premunicionem ei inde factam per aliquod (*sic*) officiarium maioris & ballivorum, perdat ad quolibet (*sic*) defectum xx s., videlicet x s. ad opus ecclesie, & x s. ad opus ballivorum.

[Gardens beyond the walls are to be done away with before Whitsuntide or 6*s.* 8*d.* fine.]

Item, ord[inatum est] quod omnia gardina supra murum, & extra eiusdem Ciuitatis vbicunque sint, auferantur citra festum Pentecostes proximo, sub pena vj s. viij d. per Camerarios levandorum ad opus ville.

PROCESSIONS.

Processions on Corpus Christi and the watch at midsummer.

[1]Pur le Ridyng on Corpus *Christi* day and for Watche on Midsomer even.

The furst craft. ffyshers and Cokes. Baxsters and Milners. Bochers. Whittawers and Glouers. Pynners, Tylers and Wrightes. Skynners. Barkers. Coruisers. Smythes. Weuers. Wirdrawers. Cardmakers, Sadelers, Peyntours and Mason[s]. Gurdelers. Taylours, Walkers and Sherman. Deysters. Drapers. Mercers.

COST OF A CHARTER.

58 councillors meet to take counsel. Aug. 10, 1445.

[2]Memorandum that the Tewsday in the fest of saynt Laurance the yere of the reigne of Kyng Herry the syxst after the Conquest xxiij[ti], In the tyme of Richard Braytoft, Meire of the Cite of Couentre, after the goode Rule & custome of the seyde Cite of long tyme hadde & vsed for goode gouernaunce ther-of, at seynt Mary halle ther werne gedered lviij persons & moe of the most wurthiest that at that tyme wern at home whose names here folowon, The wheche per. . . . . .[3]

Ric. Braytoft, Will. Donyngton, · Tho. Wyldegryse 20s.[4], Joh. Leder, · Joh. Mychell 20s.[4], Joh. Bristowe, Will.

[1] leaf 122, back. Same scribe as leaf 43. See for the subject of these processions Sharp, *Coventry Mysteries*, 159–206.

[2] leaf 123. Scribe of B type.

[3] Break in MS.

[4] Sum in another hand. Roman numerals in MS. I have reproduced the dots by certain names.

Swanne, Will. Keruer, Joh. Esex, Joh. Norwode, ·Joh. Lusterley 13s. 4d.[1], ·Edm. Brogreve 13s. 4d.[1], ·Ric. Boyse 13s. 4 d.,[1] Joh. Deyster, Joh. Clerke, Joh. Walg*r*aue, ·Ed. Drover 13s. 4d.[1], ·Will. Kempe 6s. 8d.[1], Joh. Prentes, ·Ric. Boton*er* 13s. 4d.[1], ·Will. Browne 13s. 4d.[1], Joh. Doughty, ·Tho. Wyrley 13s. 4d.[1], ·Joh. Spenser 13s. 4d.[1], ·Joh. Lynne 13s. 4d.[1], Ric. Dene, ·Will. Piere 13s. 4d.[1], ·Joh. Grynder 13s. 4d.[1], ·Joh. George 6s. 8d.[1], ·Joh. Baker 6s. 8d.[1], ·Joh. Stafford, sen. 6s. 8d.[1], ·Ric. Awsten 6s. 8d.[1], ·Geruas. Cole 6s. 8d.[1], ·Ric. Alen 6s. 8d.[1], ·Will. Clerke 6s. 8d.[1], ·Tho. Warmynton 6s. 8d.[1], Will. Braytoft, ·Joh. Goolde 6s. 8d.[1], ·Joh. Blakeman, Nic. Palmer, ·Joh. Honeyburne, Joh. Freman, ·Reg. Bere 6s. 8d.[1], ·Ric. Attewode 6s. 8d.[1], Joh. Sircok, ·Ric. Dyvette 6s. 8d.[1], ·Joh. Gryme 6s. 8 d.[1], ·Joh. Shadde 6s. 8d.[1], ·Rob. Eme 6s. 8d.[1], Tho. Stone, weu*er*, Ric. Fyllypes wirdr[awer], Tho. Skotte, Joh. Mershe, ·Joh. Maynard 6s. 8d.[1], ·Tho. Rastell 6s. 8d.[1], ·Nic. Kente 6s. 8d.[1], ·Joh. Hadley 6s. 8d.[1], Joh. Beauchampe.

"The inhabitans paid þe charges of the Charter." £100 to be raised.

The whiche wurthymen abouen writon ordeyned that ther shuld be rerede C li., for to be payde in the forme that herafter suethe, for dyvers costes & expenses made in sueng for a Charter[2] of enlargeng the ffrawnches & lib*er*te of this Cite of Couentre, That is to sey eu*er*y man that hathe ben meyre shall pay xx s.; and every man that hathe ben Baylyff shall pay xiij s. iiij d.; and eu*er*y mane (*sic*) that hathe ben eder chamburlen or Wardeyne, or abell, or lyke to be, shall pay vj s. viij d. And all that remaynethe & may not be leviede be this mene to be leuyede of the Trinite yelde & Corpus *Christi* yelde, and of the Wardens of this Cite. And all the money that is thus gederde & payde to be payde ageyne to euerye p*er*son lyke as he hathe payde hit when the C li. that our souereyne lorde the kyng owethe vs is payde.

Every late mayor 20*s*. and bailiff 13*s*. 4*d*., chamberlain 6*s*. 8*d*., the rest from the guilds' and wardens' accounts.

Payment to be made by the following.

Memorand*um* that thes men writon on that oder parte of this lef han graunted to pay eu*er*y man after the ordenaunce aboue rehersede.

[1] See note 4, previous page.

[2] Corp. MSS. B. 48. Confirmation of ancient charters with grant of fair beginning on the Friday after Corpus Christi.

29 persons. [1] · Ric. Sharp 20s.[2], · Hen. Syrcok 13s. 4d.[2], · Ric. Clerke, hosier 6s. 8d.[2], · Joh. Byram 6s. 8d.[2], · Joh. Garton 6s. 8d.[2], · Rob. Bradmedowe 6s. 8d., · Ric. Clerke, cardmaker 6s. 8d.[2], · Will. Deyster, bocher 6s. 8d,[2] · Tho. Goldsmythe, m*er*cer 6s. 8d.[2], Joh. Brabon, Ric. Skotte, deyster, Joh. Recheford, Ric. Alwode, shermon, Derby, couryser, · Ric. Bromeley, smyth, 6s. 8d.[2], · Hugo Shade 6s. 8d.[2], Rob. Burne, bocher, · Tho. Whyte, bocher, 6s. 8d.[2], · Tho. Wodarde, hosyer 6s. 8d.[2], · Will. Warrewyke, deyster, 6s. 8d.[2], + Joh. Wytley, gurdeler, 3s. 4d. ex dono, + Joh. Bayly, gurdeler, 2s. 8d. ex dono, + Joh. Crosse, gurdeler, 3s. 4d. ex dono,[2] · Will. Dawe, taylour 6s. 8d.[2], + Rob. Nevell 3s. 4d. ex dono, + Ric. Cockes 3s. 4d. ex dono, · Ric. Whyte, baker, 6s. 8d. ex mutuo, · Hen. Stevenson 6s. 8d., · Ric. Osbern 6s. 8d.

MICHAELMAS LEET.

Michaelmas leet. Oct. 2, 1445. [3][V. f. p. on Saturday after Michaelmas, 24 H. VI.] Tho. Wilgris, Joh. Leder, Will. Swanne, Will. Kerver, Joh. Essex, Joh. Lusterley, Hen. Sircok, Joh. Clerk, Joh. Licheffeld, Will. Broun, Joh. Prentes, Joh. Bryan, Joh. Lee, Ric. Dene, Joh. Lynne, Joh. Grynder, Joh. Walg*r*aue, Will. Perc, Tho. Wirley, Joh. Baker, Joh. Stafford, Wiredrawer, Will. Kemp, Ric. Osburne, [4]Joh. Bristowe.

Bailiffs. [Will. Braytoft, Ric. Alen.]

[All craftsmen to be governed by masters and governors of their crafts, or 100*s*. fine. And if any one cannot agree with the masters of the craft for the fines and customs, then the mayor to have the management of the matter.]

Ord[inatum] e*st* q*uo*d o*mn*es ho*min*es, qui aliqua arte infra ista*m* Ciuitate*m* vtunt*ur*, sint gube*r*nati p*er* M*agist*ros & gube*r*natores eiusd*em* arti*s*, sub pena C s. tociens quocie*ns*. & si aliquis p*ro* finib*us* & cons*uetu-dinibus* eiusd*em* artis cu*m* prefat*is* m*agist*ris & gub*er*natorib*us* concordar*e* non pot*er*int, tu*nc* Maior p*ro* temp*or*e h*ab*eat gube*r*naci*on*em in mat*er*ia illa moderand*a*.[5]

[1] leaf 123.
[2] Sum in another hand. Those who gave the sum outright (ex dono) have a cross by their names; the one who loaned it (ex mutuo) and the others, who (probably) promised it, a dot.   [3] leaf 126. Scribe of C type.   [4] Scribe B.
[5] On the ceaseless struggle between the corporation and the crafts see Introduction.

Also hit is ordeyned þat þe Bakers of þis Citie shall haue license & liberte to bake & sell aboue the market vj d. in a quarter, be-cause they shall not come & bye corne in þe market at Couentre vppon the market day, nether ffriday nor Monday, nor haue no corne brought to their houses vppon þe said market dayes. And if eny of[1] theym do þe contrarie in eny of þe premissez they shall lose at euery defalt vj s. viij d. without favour in þat partie. The bakers not to buy corn in the market on market-days.

[None to wash entrails, vessels, nor singe hogs, nor do any other filthy operation there, or 12*d*. fine.

Item ord[inatum] est quod nullus lauat poodynges, lomes[2], nec synge hogges, nec aliquod aliud vile ibidem faciat, sub pena xij d. tociens quociens.

[Any mercer who comes to Coventry to sell mercery to stand in the Drapery to sell it as [the custom is], and not to walk about in the town, or 6*s*. 8*d*. fine.]

Item, ord[inatum] est quod quilibet mercerus vel Chapman qui de cetero veniet ad villam de Couentria [ad] vendenda mercimonia, quod stet in le Draperie [ad] ea vendenda prout etc. & quod non ambulet circumquaque in villa, sub pena vj s. viij d. tociens quociens.

Also hit is ordeyned that þe Mair & Baillyfs of þis Cite & their successours in all maner pleez to be pleded afore them to hem semyng feyned, fals, forreyn, or forged, be þe which þe kynges Court afore hem shuld be put oute of Jurisdiccion, to make suche examynacion of þe partie or þe attorne as they seme best for þe knolach of the trouth, and whom they fynde defectyfe in þe premissez to commyt them to prison & to make fyne after þat þe lawe woll etc. Mayor and Bailiffs to examine parties in suits that seem to them suspicious.

Also they ordeyn that no Coke of þis Cite frohensfurth sell no derrer a goode goose but for iiij d., a pyg for vij d., a quarter of a pyg for j d. ob., the hed j d. & no derrer, vppon þe peyn to lose at euery def[alt] iiij d. "Cookes"; a goose 4*d*., a pig 7*d*..

Also they ordeyn that euery man that taketh down eny tenement within þis Cite, and will not bild hit aȝeyn within a yere, yf þe tenement be worth x s. be yer to lese þerfor x li., & yf þe rent be xx s. then to lese xx li., & so forth aftur þe rate.[3] For rebuilding of houses.

[1] "of" repeated. [2] Vessels. [3] *v.* p. 199.

THE BAILIFFS' OATH.

Oath of the bailiffs.

[1]Sacra*mentu*m balli*uoru*m ville de Couentre.

Yee shall be gode and truwe to the kyng of Englond and his heires and to the ffraunches of Couentre, and hyt mayntene and sustenene; and all fermes and fees that the Baillyes of this cite haue vsed to pay in d[u]e dischargyng of this same franches trewly pay and doe, and trewe Jugges be in youre offices in all mat*er*s afore you moved, or duryng youre office to be moved, alsowell to the pore as to the[2] ryche wyth-out any fauo*u*r to be shewed in anywise; ne non extorc*i*on ne oppress*i*on doe to the pepull; and also[2] ret*u*rne all wryttes, warantes and preceptes, that be be you to [be] executed in discharge of all this Cite duryng this next yere comyng etc.[3] & also ye shall well & truly contynue in p*ro*pre p*er*sone eue*r*y courte day, ses-sions of the peace and plee riales to be holden with-in the Cite of Couentre, duryng the t*er*me of youre offes, and not dep*ar*te out of the said ffraunches at no tyme duryng youre seid offes with-oute licens of the meire beyng duryng youre seid offis, so help vs (*sic*) God and halidame.

THE BARBERS' RULES.

Ordinances of the barbers, and confirmation of the same.

[These ordinances in English were formerly ordained in the time of T. Skotte and W. Bate, masters of the barbers, on the feast of the Translation of S. Edward, Oct. 13.

1421.

And now on Oct. 16, 1445, the same are confirmed by R.

[4] Ordinac*io*nes artis Barbiton-sor*um*. Et confirmac*i*o ear*um*.

¶ Memorand*um* q*uo*d isti articuli & ordinac*io*nes in verb*is* anglicanis subsequent*ibus* dudum ordinat*i* fuer-unt in arte de Barbitansoribus[5] temp*or*e Tho. Skotte & Will. Bate, Magistrator*um* barbitonsor*um* Ciui-tatis Couentre, die Lune in festo T*r*ansl*ationis* S. Edwardi Reg*is* a. r. r. H. quinti post conq*uestu*m nono vt aparet etc. Et iam videl*ice*t xvj die Octobr*is* a. r. r. H. vj[ti] xxiiij

[1] leaf 124, back. A fresh scribe. [2] deletions.
[3] "so help you God and holy dame" deleted. The whole oath is copied on a spare piece of paper, and written closely as room failed.
[4] The same scribe as the writer of the bailiffs' oath. [5] *Sic.*

Braytoft, mayor and the council of the city.]

pre*dic*te ordinacio*n*es pe*r* Ric. Braytoft, maiore*m* Ciuitat*is* p*redic*te, & consiliu*m* eiusd*em* Ciuitat*is*, affirmantu*r* & allocantu*r*.[1]

ffirst, hit is ordeyned that what man of the same craft that is warned in resonabull tyme be the maysters of the seide Craft or be ony oder in her name to com to ony dyner, drynkyng, or ony oder mater that is to do within the seyde Craft, and he wil-not come at his our that he is p*re*fixed or lymeted, withe-outon he haue a resonable cause of excusacion, he shall pay to the Maisters of the seide craft that tyme beeng a lb. of wax at eu*er*y defawte. "Barbers; A company; their orders." 1st rule: Fine for non-attendance: a pound of wax.

Also hit is ordeyned & stabuld that what man of the same Craft is rebell ageyne the maysters or ageyne ony oder of the same Craft in the Mayster p*re*sence, and the Maister bid hym be in pece or hold hym stille & he wil-not, he shall paie at eu*er*y defawt j lb. of wax. 2nd rule: Fine for insubordination the same.

Also hit is ordeyned that what man of the same Craft that cometh vnto the seide Cite, & he be not prentes of the same craft with-in the seide Cite, and he sette vp a shoppe withe-in this Cite, he shall make fyne or pay to the Maysters of the seide craft xx s, or elles withe-in the summ*e* as the maysters & he may acorde; and yif they mow not acorde then to be demede & demened[2] be the meire that tyme beeng. 3rd rule: Barbers, not having been apprenticed in the city, on setting up shop, pay a fine of 20*s*. (or less) to the craft.

Also hit is ordeyned that what man of the seide Craft that is duelleng withe-in the seide Cite that settethe awerke ony man of the same Craft, but yif he haue ben prentes atte seide Craft, or elles that he can his Craft well & sufficiently, the whiche may be p*ro*ued be the maysters of the seide Craft, or be lefall & lawd[ab]ul pe*r*sones of the same craft, that he be abull to serve truly & duly the comen pepull that is with-in the seyde Cite, what man that wurchithe ony man of the seide craft in contrarie-wyse he shall forfet at eu*er*y defawt x s. to the Towne walle, & x s. to the comen boxe of the seyde Craft. 4th rule: Only late apprentices or competent workers to practise the craft or 20*s*. fine.

Also that no man shall take no prentes to the seide Craft no lesse yeres then vij yere, apon the same peyne. 5th rule: 7 years apprenticeship;

[1] "The" follows. [2] = governed.

no Sunday shaving; And that no man of the same Craft wurche ne shave apon the Sonday,[1] but yif he aske licence & leve of the Maisters of the saide Craft; and but yf he be a seke man or a weyfareng man that comethe to this Cite that hathe nede to-be shavon, apon the peyne whoso maybe foundon in suche defawte to pay x s. at euery defawte to the seide Maysters. or 10s. fine.

JOHN LUSTERLEY, MAYOR, 1446.

Jan. 25. [[2]Election of officers.]

Electors. Ric. Sharp, Joh. Leder, Tho. Wyldegryse, Joh. Mychell, Will. Swanne, Will. Kerver, Joh. Esex, Joh. Warant, Joh. Grynder, Joh. Walgraue, Ed. Brogreve, Joh. Wyldegryse, Joh. Clerk, Ric. Boyse, Joh. Lee, Ric. Dene, Will. ffrysby, Will. Piere, Geru. Cole, Will. Kempe, Ric. Clerke, Ric. Osberne, Tho. Warmynton, Joh. Spenser.

Officers. [m. Joh. Lusterley; cor. Joh. ffynche; ch. Reg. Bere, Joh. ffreman; w. Joh. Stafford, Joh. Catur; mace, Will. Oxton.]

[Ric. Braytoft (outgoing mayor) to be present during the next year in processions, and in worshipful conferences to go and be next to the mayor so as to aid and counsel him.]

Et Insup*er* ordinaverunt & p*r*oui-d*eru*nt q*uo*d Ric. Braytoft, qui iam exstat maior, p*er* totu*m* p*r*ox*imum* annu*m* sequ*entem* erit p*r*esens in p*ro*-cessionib*us* & dignis congregac*i*oni-b*us* [et] eat & sit p*r*ox*imus* maiori etc. ad essend*um* sibi in auxiliu*m* et consiliu*m* etc.

J. Ps. Joh. Lusterley, m., Will. Donyngton, rec., Ric. Sharp, M. G. S. T., Joh. Leder, Tho. Wildegryse, Joh. Bristowe.

Custodians of keys of the common chest. [The same except the recorder.

Custodians of the chest where standard measures and jewels[3] kept. [The same as the custodians of the keys.]

EASTER LEET.

Couentre. Apr. 20, 1446. ¶ [4][V. f. p. held before Joh. Lusterley m., Will. Braytoft and Ric. Alen b., on Wednesday after Easter, 24 H. VI.]

[1] Cal. Pat. R. 1391–96, p. 720.
[2] leaf 129. Scribe of type p. 102.
[3] "le strike & al*ia* Jocal*ia*."
[4] leaf 130, Scribe of C type.

Ric. Sharp, Joh. Leder, Tho. Wilgris. Joh. Warant, Will. Kerver, Joh. Grynder, Hen. Sircok, Joh. Clerk, Joh. Deist*er*, Ric. Boton*er*, Joh. Spenc*er*, Will. ffrysby, Joh. Doughty, Tho. Wirley, Joh. Lee, Joh. Lynne, Joh. Walg*r*aue, Ric. Dene, Will. Pere, Ed. Brogreve, Tho. Warmyngton, Joh. Stafford, weu*er*, Rag. Bere, Joh. ffreman. 24 Jurors.

[Orders of leet.

[Every one having lands or tenements lying by the river from Crow-mill to Gosford-gate, to cleanse it opposite his tenement before Whitsuntide, or 20*s.* fine levied by the mayor for this cleaning. And the mayor to see to it that where the river has been encroached on by any one, that it shall be put right.

[1] Ord[inatum] e*st* q*uo*d quil*ibe*t, qui h*abe*t te*r*ras vel tenem*en*ta adiac*entia* commu*n*i Riuilo in Co[uentria] a Crowemyll vsq*ue* Gosford-ȝate, mu*n*dat (*sic*) riuil*um* p*re*d*ict*u*m* erga tene*mentum* suu*m* cit*r*a festu*m* Pentecost*es*, s*u*b pena xx s. p*er* maiore*m* leuand*orum* ad mu*n*dac*io*nem Riuili p*re*d*icti* disponend*orum*. Et q*uo*d maior etc. p*ro*videat vbi rivilus p*re*d*ictus* p*er* aliqu*e*m art*a*t*us* sit, q*uo*d p*er* ips*u*m emendet*ur* cit*r*a d*ict*u*m* festu*m* etc.

[Whoever lives between the Bear and Smithford-brook to pay 4*d.* towards clearing the river or provide a labourer to do it before the festival.

& q*uo*d quil*ibe*t com*m*orans a signo voc*ato* le Bere vsq*ue* Smythford-broke soluat ad mu*n*dac*io*nem Riuili p*re*d*icti* iiij d. vel inveniat vnu*m* laborante*m* p*er* die*m* ad id faciend*um* cit*r*a d*ictum* fest*um*.

[Latrinæ on the Red-ditch to be removed before Whitsuntide or 20*s.* fine.] The Red-ditch.

At this [lete] the armytage at Gosford-grene was gra*u*nted vnto on John Thorpe of Couentre, Taylloʋ*r*, at his petic*io*n, vppon þ*at* condic*io*n þ*at* he shuld sufficiently kepe the rep*araci*o*n* þ*er*of. "Armitage at Gosford greene."

FRIAR JOHN BREDON'S SENTENCE.

[2] Hit is to haue in mynde that the last day of Aprill the yere of Kyng Herry the vj after the conquest xxiiij at Couentre in a place called seynt Marie halle apered xlviij p*er*sones of the moste wurthiest that tyme beeng Ap. 30, 1446.[3]

[1] Scribe B. [2] leaf 129, back. [3] (?) *v.* p. 228.

with-in this Cite be the comaundement of John Lusterley then meyre & his counsell after the good rule & custome withe-in the seyde Cite of long tyme vsed & had to comen & to trete for the p*r*ofet & wele of the seyde Cite. And in speciall for declaracion of a centens yevon for the priour & Couent of the Cathedrall churche of our Lady of Couentre ayeynest John Bredon,[1] ffrere mynor of Couentre, in the Court of my lordes of Caunturbury etc. The names of whiche xlviij here-after folowon. Joh. Lusterley, m., Will. Donyngton, rec., Ric. Sharp, Joh. Leder, Tho. Wyldegryse, Joh. Bristowe, Ric. Braytoft, Joh. Michell, Will. Keruer, Will. Swanne, Joh. Warant, Will. Braytoft, Ric. Alen, Will. ffrysby, Will. Broun, Tho. Wyrley, Hen. Sircok, Ric. Boton*er*, Joh. Doughty, Joh. Walg*r*aue, Joh. Lichefeld, Joh. Spenser, Tho. Swetenham, Will. Clerke, Joh. Byrame, Joh. Baker, deist*er*, Ric. Skotte, deist*er*, Joh. Brabon, Tho. Stone, weu*er*, Joh. Stafford, sen., Joh. Catur, Joh. Shadde, Joh. Lee, Ric. Dene, Tho. Warmyngton, Joh. Lynn*e*, Joh. Grynder, Joh. Deyster, Joh. ffremon, Reg. Bere, Will. Betley, Geru. Cole, Tho. Skot, Will. Warrewik, Joh. Goolde, Joh. Appulby, Will. Radclyff, Ric. Penson, Tho. Goldsmyth, Tho. White.

Mayor's 50 councillors.

"xxj persons to be the mayors Councell."

The provisions of 12 or more councillors to be ratified by the 48.

The whiche xlviij[2] p*er*sones a-fore-writon then & there ordeyned & p*r*ouyded for ease of hem, That the meyre shuld calle xij p*er*sones or moe after his discression for co*mmun*icacion & avyse to be had in any mater, & what the seyde xij p*er*sones ordeyned, the fornamed xlviij to conferme & alowe etc. Wherapon the Seturday the ij day of Aprill[3] a*nno* He*n*. vj^{ti} xxiiij then next sueng at seynt Mary halle abowe-seyde apered xxj p*er*sones warned after the Custome & ordenaunce aboue-seyde: Whereof the names her-aft*er* folown:

Apr. 2,

Ric. Sharp, Ric. Braytoft, Will. Donyngton, Joh. Leder, Tho. Wildegryse, Joh. Bristowe, Will. Swanne, Will. Keruer, Joh. Warant, Joh. Grynder, Will. Braytoft, Ric. Alen, Joh. Northewode, Will. Betley, Joh.

[1] *v. ante*, p. 97. Friar John complained that the funeral candles became the property of the prior and convent, instead of falling to those that ministered to their parishioners.

[2] Exclusive of the mayor and recorder. [3] ? date; *v.* p. 227.

Walgr*a*ue, Ed. Brogreve, Ric. Boyse, Sim. Birches, Hen. Sircok, Joh. Wildegryse, Will. Browne.

The whiche xxi p*er*sones & the meire aforseyde of oon assent & advise pr*o*uyded & ordeyned procutores for all the co*mmin*alte of the Cite of Couentre ayeynst the p*r*iour & Couent aforseyd, That is to sey Will. Betley, Will. Saundres, Joh. Walg*r*aue, Sim. Birches, Tho. Goldsmyth, Ric. Wode & Tho.[1]

21 councillors appoint procurators in the Bredon affair.

[2]And then on the Wednesday next foloweng in p*r*esence of thes p*er*sones, that the names sewn in writeng, a procresy for the meire & the co*mmin*alte aforseyde, in the mater aforenamed at seynt Mari-halle vnder the comen seale & the meires Seale was sealede etc.

And on Apr. 6 the following 22 in all act as "proxy" in the matter.

Joh. Lusterley, meire, Mayst*er* Tho. Chesterfeld,[3] Joh. Menley, vicar*ius*,[4] Ric. Sharp, Tho. Wildegryse, Joh. Leder, Joh. Bristowe, Ric. Braytoft, Will. Kerver, Will. Braytoft, Ric. Alen, Will. Betley, Hen. Sircok, Will. Broun, Joh. Lee, Joh. Walgr*a*ue, Ed. Brogreue, Ric. Boyse, Magist*er* Joh. Twys, official etc.[5], Joh. Stafford, sen., Sim. Burches, Joh. Crokez.

MICHAELMAS LEET.

¶ [6]V. f. p. held on Saturday after Michaelmas, 25 Hen. VI.]

Coventre. Oct. 1, 1446.

Joh. Warant, Tho. Wilgris, Ric. Braytoft, Joh. Essex, Will. Kerver, Joh. Leder, Joh. Bristowe, Joh. Grynder, Joh. Clerk, Tho. Wirley, Will. ffrysby, Joh. Spenser, Joh. Lee, Joh. Lyne, Joh. Walgr*a*ue, Ric. Boton*er*, Hen. Sircok, Ed. Brogreve, Ric. Boys, Tho. Swetenham, Ric. Clerk, hosier, Joh. Catur, Reg.[7] Bere.

Jurors.

[Gerv. Cole and Will. Kemp.]

Bailiffs.

[Order of leet.

[The Priory floodgates to be drawn up and opened when-

[8]Volunt & ordinant q*uo*d lez fflod-ȝat*es* in le Priory deinceps om*ni* temp*or*e necessario & oportuno s*i*nt

[1] Blank. [2] leaf 130. [3] Vicar of S. Michael's.

[4] Vicar of Trinity.

[5] One who exercises the jurisdiction of a bishop or archdeacon. The reason of the presence of so many ecclesiastics in the "proxy" is because the matter in dispute was an ecclesiastical one. After reading a recantation containing a fulsome apology to the prior and convent, Friar Bredon, sharing the fate of most reformers, was banished the city.

[6] leaf 130, back. Scribe of C type. [7] MS. Ragnaldus. [8] Scribe B.

ever necessary, lest any harm or evil happen to the inhabitants, as from this cause has happened many times before, or 100*s.* fine from whomsoever is in default.]

te*m*pestiue tract*e* & ap*er*te, ne in def*ect*u eiusd*em* eueniat aliquod dampnu*m* v*e*l malu*m* Ciuitatib*us* (*sic*) & inha*bi*tantib*us* isti*us* ville, sicut m*ul*tocie*ns* p*er*antea ea de causa eueniebat etc. s*u*b pena C s. leuand*orum* de ipso qui e*st* defect*iuus* inde etc.

THOMAS WIRLEY, MAYOR, 1447.

Jan. 25. [[1] Election of officers.]

24 electors. Joh. Esex, Ric. Braytoft, Joh. Leder, Tho. Wyldegryse, Joh. Bristowe, Joh. Michell, Will. Swanne, Will. Kerver, Joh. Waraunt, Ric. Boyse, Will. Braytoft, Joh. Wildegrise, Joh. Clerke, Will. ffrisby, Ric. Dene, Joh. Lee, Joh. Spenser, Ric. Alen, Ric. Clerke, Ric. Austen, Joh. Baker, Joh. Jeorge, Joh. Byram, Joh. Goolde.

Officers. [m. Tho. Wirley; cor. Joh. ffynche; ch. Rob. Bradmedowe and Will. Warrewyke; w. Joh. Stafford and Joh. Catur; mace, Will. Oxton.]

J. Ps. The mayor, recorder, Joh. Esex, M. G. S. T., Joh. Leder, Ric. Sharp, Joh. Bristowe.

Custodians of the common chest. Ric. Braytoft, Ric. Sharp, Joh. Leder, Tho. Wyldegryse, Joh. Bristowe.

Custodians of the common chest where the common measure[3] is. Ric. Braytoft.[2]

EASTER AND MICHAELMAS LEETS.

Couentre. Apr. 15, 1447. [[4] V. f. p. held before Tho. Wirley m., Gerv. Cole, Will. Kemp, b., on Saturday in Easter week, 25 Hen. VI.]

Jurors. Joh. Essex, Joh. Leder, Will. Swan, Joh. Warant, Will. Kerver, Joh. Lusterley, Joh. Grynder, Joh. Clerk, Hen. Sircok, Will. ffrisby, Joh. Lee, Joh. Lynne, Joh. Walgraue, Will. Pere, Ed. Brogreve, Ric. Boys, Ric. Deane, Will. Braytoft, Ric. Alen, Joh. Stafford, Joh. Catur, Joh. Baker, deist*er*, Rob. Bradmedawe, Tho. Swetnam.

[1] leaf 131. [2] Rest blank. [3] modiu*m* co*mmun*e.
[4] Scribe B. leaf 131, back.

[Orders of leet.

[Householders to cleanse the Red-ditch and the gutter running from the Peacock to the West Orchard opposite to their houses, twice a year.

Volunt & ordinant q*uo*d quil*ibet* qui h*ab*et te*rr*as seu tene*men*ta adiacent*es* fossat*is* in C*ouentre* voc*atis* le Reddych, & *simi*liter le Gutter, qui ven*it* de le Pecok vsq*ue* le Westorchard, mu*n*dant[1] (*sic*) ffossat*a* illa erga tene*mentum* suu*m* p*ro*priu*m* bis p*er* annu*m* & in anno [or 6*s*. 8*d*. fine, half to the mayor and half to the bailiffs.]

[The Priory floodgates to be emptied and an assize taken, and so of the other floodgates by the river; and all the embankment as far as the Sills be emptied as is just.

It*em*, volunt (etc.) q*uo*d le fflodeȝates in l*e* Priory sint vacuat*e* & assisat*e* & o*mn*es al*ie* fflodeyat*es* p*er* Riuil*um* infra lib*er*tate*m* etc. & totu*m* le Bullwark[2] vsq*ue* le Silles[3] sit vacuat*um*, p*ro*ut iust*um* es*t*, [or 100*s*. fine.]

[The Corpus Christi riding to be observed.]

Et q*uo*d le Ruydyng in festo Corp*or*is C*hrist*i fiat p*ro*ut ex antiquo te*m*p*or*e consueuit etc.

¶ [V. f. p. held on Saturday after Michaelmas, 26 Hen. VI.] Couentre. Sept. 30, 1447.

Joh. Leder, Ric. Braytoft, Ric. Sharp, Will. Kerver, Joh. Warant, Will. Swan, Joh. Lusterley, Joh. Bristowe, Joh. Grynder, Hen. Sircok, Will. ffrisby, Joh. Lee, Joh. Lynne, Ric. Boton*er*, Ric. Dene, Joh. Walgraue, Will. Pere, Ed. Brogreve, Ric. Boys, Will. Braytoft, Ric. Alen, Joh. Stafford, Joh. Catur, Ric. Austen. Jurors.

[Ric. Clerk, drap*er*, Ric. Scotte, deist*er*.] Bailiffs.

[Orders of leet.

[The ordinance concerning chandlers of Joh. Braytoft's time is confirmed and to be put into execution; i. e. no one is to sell 1 lb. of candles at any other price than 1*d*. a pound.]

Et ordinant ac confirmant ordin*a*c*io*nem te*m*p*or*e Joh*annis* Braytoft,[4] M*aioris*, nup*er* fact*am* de lez Chaundelers de vendic*io*ne candel*arum* etc. & om*n*ino ponat*ur* iam in execuc*io*nem, v*idelicet*, q*uo*d null*us* eoru*m* vendat vna*m* libra*m* Candel*arum* nisi t*an*tu*m* p*ro* j d. [or pay the fine previously ordained, 20*s*., *i. e.* 6*s*. 8*d*. to the mayor and 13*s*. 4*d*. to the bailiffs.[5]]

[1] A stroke of "m" missing. [2] An embankment.
[3] Sill, a beam or rafter; the bottom part of fixed bench, pen or other wooden erection (*E. E. D.*). [4] Mayor 1425, 1442. [5] *v*. p. 234.

Butchers. Item, it is ordeyned þ*at* no Bochou*r*, inhabitant within þis Cite, frohensffurth scalde no mane*r* of best*is* within þis Cite, but only in the scaldyng-house in þe Palmers-lane, þ*er*to ordeyned [or 6*s*. 8*d*. fine.]

Brewers. "No bruer nor maltster to fetch water at Conduits." And also þ*at* no bruer frohensfurth fet watir fro þe Cundite to brue or stepe with, vppon þe same peyn.

"Tilers-semy-tile." Also hit is ordeyned that no tyler frohensfurth ley no seny [? semy] tyle ne crased[1] tyle, nor that þe seid tylers set no man in warke onlesse he can his Craft, [or 6*s*. 8*d*. fine each time].

JOHN WALGRAVE, MAYOR, 1448.

Jan. 25. [[2]Election of officers.]

23 electors. [3]Ric. Braytoft, Joh. Leder, Joh. Bristowe, Will. Swanne, Will. Kerver, Joh. Esex, Joh. Lusterley, Ric. Boyse, Ric. Sharp, Joh. Leder, Will. ffrisby, Gerv. Cole, Ric. Dene, Will. Piere, Will. Kempe, Ric. Boton*er*, Will. Braytoft, Joh. Wyldegrise, Joh. Goolde, Reg. Bere, Will. Clerke, Ric. Austen, Joh. Boteler.

Officers. [m. Joh. Walg*r*aue; cor. Joh. ffynche; ch. Ric. Wode, Joh. Byram; w. Joh. Garton, Ric. Dyvet; mace, Will. Oxton.]

J. Ps. Joh. Walg*r*aue, m., Will. Donyngton, rec., Ric. Braytoft, M. G. S. T., Joh. Leder, Ric. Sharp, Joh. Bristowe.

Custodians of keys. [The same, except the recorder.

Custodians of keys of chest where the common measure is. [The mayor, Ric. Braytoft, M. G. S. T., Ric. Boyse, M. G. C. C., the chamberlains and the wardens.]

EASTER AND MICHAELMAS LEET.

Couentre. Mar. 30, 1448. [[4]V. f. p. held before Joh. Walgraue m., Ric. Clerk and Ric. Austen, b., on Saturday after Easter, 26 Hen. VI.]

Jurors. Ric. Braytoft, Ric. Sharp, Joh. Leder, Will. Kerver, Joh. Essex, Joh. Warant, Will. Swan, Tho. Wyrley, Ric. Boys, Joh. Grynder, Joh. Clerk, Ric. Boton*er*, Joh. Baker, Deist*er*, Ed. Brogreve, Will. Braytoft, Ric. Alen, Gerv. Cole, Will. Kemp, Joh. Garton, Joh. Stafford, Joh. Catur, Will. Warewyk, Ric. Divet, Will. Clerk.

[1] Crased = broken, cracked.
[2] leaf 133.
[3] Scribe of type p. 102.
[4] leaf 133, back.

[No one to do damage in pastures, closes, or other places in cutting branches, under the penalty of 12*s*. And that no one break the pavement to place branches on it on St. John's and St. Peter's eves, but every one to have coal and large fuel on the same penalty.

Volunt (etc.) q*uo*d nullus deinceps fac*iat* dampnu*m* in pastur*is*, claus*is*, seu aliis locis in scindendo ramos vel samples,[1] s*u*b pena cui*us*l*ibe*t delinquent*is* xij s. Et q*uo*d nullus decet*ero* frangat pauimentu*m* ad ponend*um* in eo ramos in vigil*iis* Natiuitat*is* S. Joh*ann*is Bap*tis*te & S. Petri ;[2] *sed* h*ab*eat quil*ibe*t carbones & grossu*m* ffocale s*u*b eade*m* pena.

[The poulterers to stand and sell victuals before the Priory door about the Bull Ring as far as the end of the Little Butchery.]

It*e*m volunt & ordinant q*uo*d lez pulters deinceps stent & vend*ant* victual*ia* sua ante portu*m* (*sic*) Priorat*us* circa le Bulryng vsq*ue* fine*m* de le Litel-bochery.

[3]¶ [V. f. p. held on Monday after Michaelmas, 27 H. VI.] Couentre. Michaelmas leet. Sept. 30, 1448.

Ric. Braytoft, Joh. Leder, Ric. Sharp, Will. Swan, Will. Kerver, Joh. Essex, Joh. Warant, Ric. Boys, Ric. Boton*er*, Joh. Grynder, Joh Lynne, Ric. Alen, Joh. Lee, Ed. Brogreve, Ric. Dene, Will. Pere, Will. Braytoft, Gerv. Cole, Will. Kemp, Hen. Sircok, Joh. Wildegrys, Joh. Cole, Ric. Wode, Joh. Garton. Jurors.

[Joh. Stafford, Joh. ffreman] Bailiffs.

[Orders of leet.

[Any one who withstands the mayor and bailiffs in the performance of anything appertaining to their office to have a week's imprisonment, and at the second offence a fortnight's.]

[4]Ord*inatum est* q*uo*d quil*ibe*t qui deinceps contradic*it* vel obstat Maiori & Ball*iv*is hui*us* Ciuitat*is* in execuc*ione* alic*uius* rei p*er*tinent*is* offic*iis* suis etc. h*ab*eat imp*r*isonament*um* vni*us* septi*m*ane absq*ue* aliqua p*er*donac*ione*, & ad *secun*d*um* def*ectum* h*ab*eat imp*ri*s*onamentum* xv^e [=quindene.]

[Much-park-street to be repaired (emendetur) before Christmas, or 100*s*. fine from every one failing, and the work to begin next Monday.] Much-park-street.

[1] Young trees left in woods for timber. *E. E. D.* s. v. samplars.
[2] On the bonfires on Midsummer night *v.* Sharp, *Coventry Mysteries*, 175–206.
[3] leaf 134. Scribe of C type.
[4] Scribe B. Probably new guilds were being formed in defiance of the corporation: *v.* Introduction.

[As soon as Will. Donnyngton withdraws from his occupation or dies, then immediately T. Litelton[1] shall have the office in the same manner and form as other recorders have had and enjoyed it, taking the accustomed fees, so that he remain within the city.]

Item, ord*inant* (etc.) q*uo*d q*ua*m cito Will. Donyngton, nu*n*c Recordator hui*us* Ciuitat*is*, de occupac*io*ne officii sui se dimiserit seu decess*er*it, q*uo*d tu*n*c imme*dia*te Tho. Litelton[1] h*ab*eat & gaudeat officiu*m* p*re*d*ictum* eisd*em* m*od*o & forma quib*us* cet*er*i Recordat*ores* ante hec temp*or*a h*ab*uerunt[2] & gauisi fueru*n*t, capiendo inde feoda consuet*a*. Ita q*uo*d maneat infra Ciuitate*m* etc.

The gutters. [The ordinance as ordained aforetime about sweeping the gutters ("lez Canell") in the streets to be put into execution; 12*d*. for every default.]

[The sergeant of the brewers-gild and the crier to wait upon the mayor on pain of losing their offices.]

Item, ord*inatum est* q*uo*d le s*er*iaunt de Breust*er*s ylde[3] & le Cryer sint intendentes sup*er* Maiore*m* s*u*b pena dimittend*i* offic*ia* sua.

Chaundlers. [The tallow-chandlers to sell candles at 1*d*. a pound or 6*s*. 8*d*. fine.[4]]

[All inn-keepers to have a lamp hanging before their doors until 9 o'clock at night, or 6*s*. 8*d*. fine.]

Ite*m*, om*n*es hostilar*ii* h*ab*eant lucerna*m* pendend*o* (*sic*) ad hostiu*m* suu*m*, vsq*ue* ix hora*m* in nocte, s*u*b pe*n*a vjs. viijd.

The fullers' and tailors' crafts separated. Ite*m*, at þis lete be auctorite of þe same þe walkers wer*e* seue*r*ed fro þe Crafte of Taillo*u*rs at þe desir of þe seid walkers, as appereth be their peticion filed in þe seid lete etc. & also be agreme*n*t of þe Taillo*u*rs as ther appereth etc.[5]

The bridge. Item, hit is ordenyed at þe same lete for they feying & clensyng of þe birge[6] in þe West-orchard that eue*r*y hall durr*e* shuld paye jd., and þ*er*uppon Will. Pier gra*u*nted to kepe þe Birge & þe rep*aracion* þ*er*of.

The gutter. [The gutter running from the Peacock to the West-orchard to be cleansed every quarter of a year or 40*d*. fine from every one failing.]

[1] *v*. p. 235.
[2] MS. hēuerūt.
[3] See below MS. leaf 304.
[4] Fine 6*s*. 8*d*. here, not 20*s*. *v*. p. 231.
[5] See Introduction.
[6] bridge.

EDMUND BROGREVE, MAYOR, 1449.

[Election of officers.] Jan. 25.

Electors. [1]Ric. Braytoft, Joh. Leder, Will. Keruer, Joh. Esex, Will. Swanne, Joh. Warant, Tho. Wyrley, Ric. Boyse, Will. Braytoft, Will. Piere, Ric. Boton*er*, Joh. Wylgryse, Joh. Lee, Ric. Dene, Gerv. Cole, Will. Kempe, Ric. Austen, Joh. Goolde, Joh. Baker, Tho. Warmynton, Joh. Cater, Rob. Bradmedowe, Will. Warrewik, Will. Clerke.

Officers. [m. Edm. Brogreue; cor. Joh. ffynche; ch. Ric. Charite, Tho. White; w. Joh. Garton, Ric. Dyvette; mace, Will. Oxton.

J. Ps. [Ed. Brogreue, m., Will. Donyngton, rec.,—and at the Easter view of frankpledge last past Tho. Litelton [2] was chosen recorder and a justice of the peace in the name (no*mine*) of the same Will. Donyngton—Ric. Braytoft, Joh. Leder, Will. Swan, and Joh. Walg*r*aue.

Custodians of the keys of the common seal chest: [The same except the recorder.

and of the standard measure[4] chest.[5] [The mayor, Ric. Braytoft, Ric. Boyse, the wardens and (probably) the chamberlains.[3]]

EASTER LEET.

Couentre. Apr. 19. [6][V. f. p. before Ed. Brogreve, m., Joh. Stafford and Joh. Freman, b., on Saturday after Easter, 27 Hen. VI.]

Ric. Braytoft, Joh. Leder, Joh. Brystowe, Will. Swan, Joh. Warant, Will. Kerver, Joh. Essex, Tho. Wirley, Joh. Walg*r*aue, Ric. Boys, Hen. Sircok, Ric. Dene, Joh. Grynder, Will. Braytoft, Ric. Alen, Gerv. Cole, Will. Kemp, Ric. Austen, Ric. Charite, Joh. Golde, Tho. Warmyngton, Joh. Bryan, Rob. Bredmedowe, Joh. Garton.

[Orders of leet.	Volunt et concedu*nt* p*er* auctori-
[The leet ordain that the	tate*m* huius visus q*uo*d Will. Donnyngton, Recordator hui*us* Ciuitat*is*,

[1] leaf 135. Scribe of type p. 102.
[2] Tho. Littleton (1402–81) of famous memory. Author of the legal work on "Tenures."
[3] The chamberlains not mentioned, but after a blank the words "ha*b*ent alium" occur, and after another blank the word "Camere."
[4] modum de standardo. [5] siste. [6] leaf 135, back.

recorder have yearly for term of his life £10 payable quarterly, viz. 10 marks (£6. 13*s*. 4*d*.) from the bailiffs, £1. 13*s*. 4*d*. from the Trinity gild, 16*s*. 8*d*. from the Corpus Christi gild and the wardens respectively, and that W. Donyngton shall henceforward be of counsel to the city as he was before ex-officio.]

ha*b*eat & p*er*cipiat annuati*m* ad t*er*mi*num* vite sue de eade*m* Ciuitate x li. leg*alis* monete ad iiij[or] anni te*rmin*os soluend*as*: vi*delicet* dece*m* marc*as* de Ball*iv*is (etc.), & xxxiij s. iiij d. de M*agis*tro G. S. T., xvj s. viij d. de M*agis*tro G. C. C. & xvj s. viij d. de Gardianis etc. Et q*uo*d pre-dict*us* Will. Donyngton deinceps sit de concilio eiusd*em* Ciuitat*is* sic*ut* ante hec temp*ora* fuit ex officio Recordat*oris*.

THE KING'S LOAN.

[[1]The underwritten lent the king £100 in Ed. Brogreve's time; the money paid by the wards.]

60 names.

[Smithford-street.[2]]

	£	s.	d.		£	s.	d.		£	s.	d.
De[3] Ric. Braytoft		10	0	Ric. Clerke		1	0	Ric. Coucher		2	6
De[3] Joh. Bristowe		8	0	Joh. Hampton		2	6	Joh. Marfood		1	0
Joh. Lynne		6	8	Tho. Plymmer		1	0	Katerina Sadler		2	0
Joh. ffremon		6	8	Margareta Blake-man		3	8	Tho. Strete		1	0
Joh. Maynard		5	0	Elias Barbur		1	0	Tho. Leche		2	6
Tho. Wodard		4	0	Tho. Joy, tailour		2	0	Will. Mariot		1	0
Joh. ffynche		2	6	Ric. Osbarne		6	0	Ric. White		2	0
Ric. Knede, baker		2	0	Will. Melodye		2	6	Nic. Kent		2	6
Gal. Bower		2	0	Joh. Hygreve, lokier		1	4	Joh. Halle		3	4
Joh. Malory		2	6	[3]Gal. Cappar		1	0	Joh. Wirthyngton		1	4
Joh. Crulle		3	4	[4]Joh. Gote		1	4	Joh. Braunston		1	0
Joh. Lorde		1	4	Rob. Balle		1	0	Joh. Yale		2	6
Will. Jones		1	0	Joh. fflynt		2	6	Joh. Wilde		2	6
Ric. Wymondeswold		1	6	Tho. Drake		1	4	Joh. Spenser		1	0
Tho. Broun		2	0	Ric. fflynt		5	0	Joh. Forest		2	6
Will. Ive, smyth		1	8	Tho. Rastell		6	0	Joh. Bruer		3	4
Joh. Dey		1	4	Joh. Abell		2	6	Tho. Colclow		1	6
Rob. Halyday.		1	0	Tho. Wyndull		1	0	Joh. fflecher		1	4
Rad. Plymmer		2	0	Joh. London		1	4	Will. Alyson		2	6
Tom. Cholley		1	0	Joh. Wyponbury		1	8	S*um*ma £7. 10*s*. 6*d*.			
Rog. Rouke, hosteler		2	0								

63 names.

[Broadgate.[5]]

	£	s.	d.		£	s.	d.		£	s.	d.
Joh. Illage		3	0	Thurstanus Lye		1	8	Will. Bedford		1	4
Ric. Prese		1	0	Joh. Houe		3	4	Tho. Spenser		1	4
Hen. Barker		1	8	Will. Spenser		2	0	Ed. Brogreue		6	8

[1] leaf 136.

[2] Collectors:—Tho. Broun, Gal. Bower, Joh. Wirthyngton, Will. Ive, Smyth. £7. 10*s*. 6*d*.

[3—3] "*De*" is repeated before all the names on this leaf.

[4] leaf 136, back.

[5] Collectors: Joh. Mirifeld, Hugo Manton, Rob. Wodeward, Joh. Oldenhale.

[Broadgate.]

Name	£	s.	d.
Joh. Radley		2	0
Tho. Bristowe		3	4
Joh. Eborall		2	0
Rog. Stanley		1	0
Will. Dyngley		1	0
Joh. Cappe, coteler		3	4
Joh. Thronton		1	8
Joh. Dagette			8
Avericius Bower		I	4
Tho. Goldsmyth		1	0
Will. Taylour, cooke		1	0
Rob. Perseele		1	0
Joh. Dalton		2	0
Joh. Sothurnewode			8
Alicia Brikstoke		2	0
Ric. Esex		2	0
Will. Bache, [? Bathe] tauern*er*		1	0
Joh. Nele, taylour		2	0
Joh. Opton, barbour		1	0
Hen. Hende		1	0
Tho. Squyer		2	0
Will. Draper		1	0
Will. Chaterton		1	0
Gal. Coteler		1	0
Hen. Roger, Glouer		1	0
Will. Bentley			8
Rog. Milnar, taylor			8
Joh. Locoke			8
Joh. Rewe		1	0
Joh. Ricongay		1	0
vx*or* Will. Abram		1	0
Tho. Napton		2	0
Ric. Dawbeney			8
Hen. Sircok		6	0
Tho. Lokynton			8
[1]Joh. Smyth, pyn*ner*		1	0
Will. Canley			8
Joh. Ruyton, drap*er*		2	0
Alic. Newbold		1	0
Joh. Hulle, s*er*iaunt		1	0
Joh. Clement			8
Joh. Symson		1	0
Joh. Lokkey		1	8
Joh. Sherde			8
Ric. Huyton			8
Will. Baryngton		1	0
Tho. Lyones			8
Joh. Crosse		1	8
Joh. Andrewe		2	0
Joh. Hare, mason			8
Tho. Warde			8
Nic. Glasier		1	0
Ric. Patrike, cori*our*		1	0
Tho. Byrton			8

S*um*ma £4. 13*s*. 0*d*.

61 names.

[Bayly-lane.[2]]

Name	£	s.	d.
Tho. Wirley		6	8
Tho. Joyner		1	0
Joh. Hampton, ply*m*mer		1	8
Joh*an*na Spenser, vidua		3	4
Ric. Lyng, pewterer		1	4
Will.[3] , glouer		2	8
Hugo Shireff		3	4
Ric. Parbroun		3	4
Will. Goldsmyth		1	0
Ric. Goldsmyth		1	4
Rob. Burnell, peut*er*er		3	4
Joh. Beauchamp		4	0
Tho. ffawcus		1	4
Joh. Alderwas		3	4
Joh. Bradley		1	0
Ric. Takeby		3	4
Ric. Halyday		1	4
Hugo Purser		1	0
Ric. Hampton		3	4
Joh. Hulle		1	0
Ric. Deyst*er*		1	0
Rob. Skille		3	4
Joh. Power		1	4
Joh. Straunge		3	4
Will. Clerke		4	0
Joh. Gryme		4	0
Joh. Clyff		1	0
Rob. Glouceter		4	0
Tho. Hobbes		3	4
Joh. Ordrige		3	4
Joh. Bayle		3	4
Joh. Crosse		3	0
Joh. Hogges		1	4
Tho. Sweteglade		1	8
Will. Dubbar, capper		1	0
Hen. Wright		1	8
Joh. Barton		2	0
Joh. Byrome		4	0
Rob. Lythe		1	4
Tho. Gryme		1	8
Hen. Watford		3	4
Will. Swift, pynn*er*		2	0
Rog. Costantync		3	4
Joh. Syrcok		2	8
Ric. Dyvet		4	0
Joh. Whitehede		1	4
Nic. Russell		1	0
Tho. Burley		3	4
Joh. Butler		1	0
Tho. Jakemon		4	0
[4]Will. Westley		1	8
Will. Mason		3	4
Rob. Coriour			8
Will. Cardyff		1	0
Will. Crowe		1	0
Joh. Bayly		1	0
[3] Burdews, purser		1	0
Joh. Castell		1	0
Ric. Taverner		1	0
Joh. Bolter		1	0
Joh. Smyth		1	0

S*um*ma £6. 18*s*. 0*d*.

[1] leaf 137.

[2] Collectors:—Joh. Byrame, Will. Clerk, Rob. Glouceter, Will. Mason, coruys*er*.

[3] Blank. [4] leaf 137, back.

69 names.

[Jorden-well.[1]]

	£	*s.*	*d.*
Ric. Alwolde		6	8
Will. ffouter		1	0
Rob. Eme		6	8
Tho. Elderbek		3	4
Joh. Haukyns		1	8
Will. Crompe		6	8
Tho. Towker		1	0
Will. Betley		10	0
Joh. Caţur		10	0
Ric. Barbur		2	0
Joh. Whalley		12	0
Ric. Rage		1	0
Ric. Couper		1	8
Eliz. Brian		2	0
Tho. Michell		2	0
Tho. Austen		2	0
Joh. Elderbek		1	0
Margare Androwe		1	0
Joh. Peche		6	8
Hen. Staffordshire		2	0
Joh. Swettenham		3	4
Joh. ffranklen		6	8
Joh. Shadde		6	0
Ric. Recheford		3	6
Joh. Smyth		3	4
Christiana Prentes		2	0
Joh. Recheford		8	0
Tho. Hoten		1	0
Joh. Lee		13	4
Joh. Pynchard		6	8
Joh. Strete		1	8
Will. Douebrigge		1	8
Joh. Oldbury		1	8
Will. Potter		4	0
Joh. Maydeford		4	0
Joh. Wake		1	0
Nic. Ourton		1	8
Tho. ffrogette		1	0
Joh. Egull		2	6
Joh. ffolkeshull		1	8
Ric. Wygons		1	0
Joh. Swyft		1	0
Joh. Boure		1	0
Will. Castelton		3	4
Rad. Capper		1	8
Rog. Boteler		1	8
Joh. Hosier		3	4
Rad. Plym*m*er		5	0
Will. Shurley		1	0
Joh. Jacome		1	0
Tho. Sweteng		1	0
Tho. Dykons		1	8
Will. Fletcher		3	0
Rob. Bocher		1	0
[2]Tho. Milner		2	0
Hen. Tredsyn[3]		1	0
Will. Bolton		1	8
Ric. ffrynes		2	0
Tho. Elcok		1	0
Tho. Smyth		1	0
Ric. Clerke		4	5
Rob. Stretton		2	0
Ric. Patage		1	0
Margareta Taţe		2	0
Joh. Hall		1	0
Hugo Pollard		1	8
Jacobus Barber			6
Hen. Dalton			8
Joh. Yonge			6

S*um*ma £10. 4*s*. 1*d*.

95 names.

[Much-park-street.[4]]

	£	*s.*	*d.*
Joh. Leder		6	8
Will. Braytoft		10	0
Tho. Warmynton		6	8
Sim. Burches		10	0
Ric. Dene		5	0
Ranulph. Barbur		1	0
Rob. Gidlowe		1	3
Rob. Wykesley		1	0
Ric. Gurdeler			6
Joh. Savage		1	0
Joh. Bruer, boch*er*		1	8
Will. Bridde		2	0
Joh. Clyfford		3	4
Hen. Bugge		1	8
Hen. Thysilton		1	0
Tho. Parker		3	4
Ad. Wale		1	0
Nic. Dilcok		1	8
Rob. Stokkes		1	4
Ric. Glouer, taylour			8
Joh. Cokke, sadeler		1	0
Joh. Hayly		1	8
Tho. Norwhiche		3	4
Ric. Knightley			6
Jacobus Horne		1	0
Tho. Waren		4	8
Tho. Willot			8
Joh. Inglond		5	0
Joh. Coucher		1	0
Joh. Barbur		1	0
Hen. Hobbes		6	8
Tho. Tyler		4	0
Ric. Bromley		5	0
Joh. Lokier		1	0
Joh. Weston			8
Joh. Derby		6	8
Ric. Staffordshire		3	4
Will. Madame			6
Joh. Onley		1	0
Will. Wright			8
Bernard. Clokmaker			8
Will. Corbette		2	6
Ric. Geene		3	4
Ric. Burfrey		1	8
Joh. Joynour		1	0
Joh. Garton		6	8
Tho. Ingre			6
Joh. Sharp			8
Will. Jowderell		2	0
Tho. Hagette			8
Dom*in*a,[5] barbur[6]		2	0
Joh. Ardurn		4	0
Tho. Westron		2	0
Will. Awbrey		5	0
[7]Joh. Skinner			8
Hen. Taylour		1	8
Rob. Garrette		3	4
Tho. Chapell		1	8
Tho. Paunton		2	8
Joh. Gale		2	0
Tho. Tough		2	0
Joh. Croft		3	4
Joh. Ravon		1	8
Tho. Garnet		1	0
[5]Tynker		1	0

[1] Collectors :—Joh. Cater, Ric. Clerke, cardmaker, Ric. Recheford, Joh. Egull.
[2] leaf 138. [3] or Tredfyn.
[4] Collectors : Ric. Bromley, Tho. Tyler, Joh. Ardurn, Will. Corbette.
[5] Blank. [6] A woman barber. [7] leaf 138, back.

[Much-park-street.]

Name	£	s.	d.
[1]Sampson		3	4
Will. Peverell		1	0
Joh. Brasier		1	0
Rog. Carter		1	0
Joh. ffolkeshull		1	0
Tho. Brayne		2	0
Joh. Carreke		2	0
Nic. Milner		1	0
Tho. Bateman		1	0
Hen. Wodeward			8
Will. Turvyle		1	8
Will. Claybroke		3	4
Joh. [2]Compton		1	0
[1]Tournour			8
Hen. Skylle			8
Joh. Shurley		2	0
Tho. Cooke		1	0
Will. Solond			8
Tho. Abram			8
Ric. Barker		1	0
Joh. Elmes		1	8
Tho. Jones			8
Joh. Emmottes		2	0
Joh. ffildeng			8
Will. Hynton			8
[2]Cooke de Charter-house			6
Tho. Mayke, smyth			6
Rob. Donam			8
Joh. Walker			8
Will. Stone, mason			8

Summa £10. 0*s*. 6*d*.

85 names.

[Spon-street.[3]]

Name	£	s.	d.
Joh. Wardroper, taylour		1	8
Tho. Doue, hosier		2	0
Will. Orme, deist*er*		3	4
Joh. Gryndar		6	8
Will. Saundres		6	0
Will. Tuttebury		4	0
Joh. Esex		8	0
Joh. Mershe		2	8
Joh. ffoster, coruys*er*			8
Ric. Barnebroke		1	4
Rob. Whitaker		2	8
Tho. Ryngley		5	0
Gerard. Crumpe, deist*er*		1	8
Joh. Wyllyams		3	4
Joh. Holme		1	0
Liticia Menley		6	8
Laur. Huyron		3	4
Rob. ffalke		3	4
Tho. Colmere		1	4
Will. Bayly		3	4
Joh. Garnet		1	4
Joh. Honyburn		3	6
Ric. Went		1	8
Egid. Corbronde		6	0
Tho. Tokeby		1	8
Will. Pynchebeke		5	0
[4]Will. White		5	0
Joh. Conwey		2	0
Joh. Clyfton		2	0
Tho. Grene		2	8
Will. Keruer		8	0
Joh. Deyster		6	8
Joh. Wynsden		4	0
Joh. Lote		4	0
Will. Walker		3	4
Joh. Broun, p*ar*doner		1	8
Hugh Larons		1	4
Joh. Shawe		1	8
Sim. Busteler		1	8
Tho. Skylton		2	0
Rob. Turnour, rop*er*[5]		1	0
Will. Blakenale		1	10
Tho. Gilbard			[1]
Ric. Holte		1	8
Rob. Bulkley		1	8
Will. Sponne, barker		1	8
Will. Bayly		5	0
Rob. Roper		1	4
Tho. Broun, weu*er*		2	4
Tho. Shustoke		1	4
Will. Stone, barker		1	8
Joh. Hadley		2	0
Nic. Bayly		1	8
Rob. Rodes		1	4
Will. Barnbroke		3	4
Will. ffraunses		1	0
[1]Jones, walker		1	4
Ric. Palmer		1	8
Joh. Godfrey		1	4
Tho. Barbur		2	0
Rob. fforte		1	8
Rad. Wright		4	0
Hugo Parre		2	0
Rob. Smyth, walker		2	0
Tho. Gybons, wright		1	8
Rob. Toppe		1	8
Joh. Davy		2	0
Hen. Dalby		3	4
Will. Deyster		1	0
[1]ffouler, grasier		3	4
Joh. Taylour		2	0
Joh. Couper		2	0
Rog. Wales		2	4
Joh. Wamburn		2	0
Nic. Lee, weuer		1	0
Wal. Norfolk		4	0
Ric. Barbur		2	0
Will. Shipston		2	0
Tho. Couche		2	8
Tho. Onyon		1	0
Hugo Forde, barbur		4	0
Joh. Wadley, clerk		2	0
Tho. Manston		1	8
Will. Capper		2	0
Rog. Burnes		4	0

Summa £11. 6*s*. 8*d*.

[1] Blank. [2] Interlined Will.
[3] Collectors: Joh. Honyburn, Will. Spenser, Wal. Norfolk, Tho. Gilbard.
[4] leaf 139. [5] or rep*er*. (?) deleted.

78 names.

[Gosford-street.[1]]

	£	s.	d.
Will. Clerk, taylour		1	0
Hen. Warmyngton		2	0
Joh. Wyldy		5	0
Baldw. Metley		3	0
Joh. Hasteng		2	0
Joh. Kebull		1	6
Deonysia Halle		1	6
Joh. Messyngham		1	0
Joh. Baker, deist*er*		8	0
Will. Bocher, deyst*er*		3	0
[2]Will. Harres		3	0
Joh*anna* Skotte		6	0
Greg. Butler		1	0
Will. Lambard		1	0
Joh. Rouke		1	0
Joh. Langton		3	0
Ad. Gawge		5	0
Tho. Cockes		5	0
Will. fflaxhale		2	0
Mat. Curtes		2	0
Ric. Cockes		5	0
Alic. Cooke, vidua		6	8
*Christ*iana Golofur		5	0
Ric. ffoston		2	0
Joh. Laurans, myln*er*		1	0
Joh. Grene, weu*er*		2	0
Will. Hadcokke		3	0
Ric. Molle, weu*er*		1	0
Joh. Lancaster		2	0
Rob. Blyburgh[3]		3	0
Joh. Sheldon, jun.		3	0
Will. Dawe, taylo*ur*		6	0
Agn. Onley		2	0
Joh. Elage		1	0
Alicia Brabon		3	0
Joh. Chambur		1	0
Will. Baxster		2	0
Tho. Stevons		1	0
Tho. Smythe		1	0
Tho. Barbur		1	0
Joh. Stafford sen.		10	0
Will. Broun, barbur		1	0
Will. Smythe, wolleman		4	0
Will. Jones, weu*er*		4	0
Ric. Bocher		4	0
Tho. Bower		5	0
Joh. Tyrsitheon		1	0
Ric. Polton, hosier		2	0
Tho. Colette		5	0
Joh. Bere, walker		1	0
Joh. Stafford, jun.		3	0
Rob. Newell		5	0
Tho. Mountford		1	0
Will. Haddon		3	0
Joh. Wildegrise		5	0
Will. Gylbard		5	0
Phelipp*us* Draper		3	0
Isabella Wildegrise		6	8
Will. Knyght, weu*er*		3	0
Tho. Stretton		2	0
Tho. Mason		5	0
Tho. Stone		5	0
Joh. Draughton		1	0
Rob. Wode		1	0
Rog. Taylour		1	0
Ric. Somer		5	0
Joh. Manton		5	0
Rad. ffolkeshull		1	0
Joh. Travas		1	8
Eustac. Golofur		5	0
Joh. Eston, deyst*er*		3	0
Will. Smyth, deist*er*		3	0
Joh. Sore		1	0
Ad. Ismay		1	0
[4]Horsley, glouer		1	0
Sim. Baker, deist*er*		5	0
Joh*anna* Evesham		4	0
Joh. Archer		1	0

S*um*ma £11. 12*s.* 0*d.*

119 names.

[Cross-cheaping.[5]]

	£	s.	d.
Hen. Adurton, m*er*cer		4	0
Rob. Mason		3	4
Ric. Drought		1	8
Joh. Dey, merc*er*		3	4
Ric. Wode		6	8
[6]Joh. Charite		1	8
Will. Byryngton		3	4
Joh. Walle		3	0
Joh. Boteler		3	4
Emma Doughty		5	0
Will. Marshall, coruys*er*		1	8
Joh. Hewer		1	0
Guido Wyston		4	0
Tho. Maydeford		3	4
Ric. Charite		5	0
Ric. Cardyf		1	8
Ric. Lane		2	0
Will. Radclyf		3	0
Tho. Wolff		3	4
Will. Bedon		3	4
Joh. Sponne		1	0
Nic. Taylour, wirdraw*er*		3	4
Will. Dyvette		3	4
Joh. Newman		1	0
Joh. fferby		1	0
[7]Dalby		4	0
Tho. Swayne		3	4
Tho. Cardyf		1	8
Will. Suker		1	8
Rich. fflecher		1	0
Joh. Manton		2	0
Ric. Bocher, wirdrawer		3	4
Hen. Addurton, hosier		3	4
Joh. Turner		1	0
Rob. Barbur		1	0
Auicia Humberston		2	0
Joh. ffareman		2	0
Joh. Bette		3	4
Will. Hende, coruyser		1	0
Nic. Rundull		3	0
Ric. Drought, sen., coruys*er*		3	4
Tho. Warner, coruyser		1	8
Hen. Meryngton, barbur		1	8
Reg. Bere		5	0

[1] Collectors: Joh. Wyldegryse, Eust. Golofur, Tho. Cockes, Joh. Stafford, jun.
[2] leaf 139, back. [3] Blythborough, Suffolk. [4] Blank.
[5] Collectors: Gui. Wyston, Will. Deist*er*, boch*er*, Will. Haddon, Tho. Bredon. [6] leaf 140.
[7] Christian name illeg. ?Edwardus.

[Cross-Cheaping.]

	£	s.	d.
Tho. Okeham		2	0
Ric. Boton*er*		6	8
Joh. Savage		3	4
Will. Sporiour		2	0
Joh. Whittofte		3	4
Joh. Batter		1	8
Will. Donynton, hosier		1	8
Tho. Paunton		3	4
Will. Rawlot		1	8
Joh. Nele, coruys*er*		3	0
Joh. Colyns		3	4
Joh. Golofur		1	8
Hen. Mason		2	0
Tho. Alene		3	4
Will. Mason, coruys*er*		1	8
Tho. Whitside		2	0
Joh. Botte, coruys*er*		2	0
Ric. Bedon		3	4
Will. Edwarde, weu*er*		1	8
Tho. Clerke, coriour		2	0
Hen. Banbury		3	4
Will. Wright		1	0
Tho. Skotte		3	4
Hen. Baxstor		1	8
Will. Swayne		1	8

	£	s.	d.
Will. Peer		6	8
Gerv. Cole		6	8
Tho. Ronton		2	0
Phelipp. Large		2	0
Joh. Smythe		2	0
Will. Horsley		3	0
Joh. Stille		3	4
Joh. Hoton		1	8
Will. Cobbes		3	4
Tho. Cawdrey		1	8
Tho. Irysshe, weu*er*		1	8
Tho. Hynkley, myln*er*		1	8
Joh. Couper		1	0
Will. Huet, coruyser		3	4
Joh. Nicols		1	4
Joh. Newman, boch*er*		2	0
Joh. Deyst*er*, boch*er*		3	4
Joh. Bynley, boch*er*		3	4
Tho. Whyte, boch*er*		5	0
[1] Will. Northampton		2	0
Joh. Halle		1	8
Ric. Weuer		1	8

	£	s.	d.
Rog. Lillynton		1	8
Rob. Burn		3	4
Joh. Northampton		3	4
Hen. Rondull		3	4
Will. Benet		3	4
Joh. Colyns		6	4
Agn. Westbury		1	0
Agn. Bynley		1	8
Tho. Nicols		1	0
Ric. Russheton			10
Dav. Mores, boch*er*		1	0
Wal. Bocher		2	0
Joh. Imayne		2	0
Galf. Wolpynn*er*		3	4
Will. Norton		1	8
Tho. Parker, boch*er*		3	4
Joh. Exsale		1	8
Nic. Swalynton		1	0
Tho. White		1	8
Will. White		1	8
Tho. Fawkes		3	0
Will. Boteler		1	0
Joh. Welbek		3	4
Will. Hulle, dubber		3	4
Ric. Penson			8
Will. Deyst*er*			9
Tho. Haddon			7
Tho. Bredon			7

Summa £14. 17*s*. 1*d*.

87 names.

[Bishop-street.[2]]

	£	s.	d.
Joh. Kebull		5	0
Ric. Bylston		1	0
Will. Horsley		2	0
[3] Will. Hardwike		1	8
Joh. Goolde		6	8
Rob. Reve		3	0
Joh. Bylston		1	8
Joh. Symondes		2	0
Alan. Snape		1	8
Joh. Bruer		5	0
Tho. Hulle, baker		1	0
Tho. Spyser			8
Joh. Brasier		1	0
Tho. Walker, coruys*er*		1	0
Joh. Trewman		1	8
Will. Warrewyk		6	8
Joh. Walgraue		10	0
Ric. Glouer, weu*er*		1	0

	£	s.	d.
Tho. Kelmestowe, deist*er*		1	0
Joh. Stansfeld		1	8
Will. Wright		1	0
Hen. Knotte		1	8
Rad. Bykenhull		1	4
Agn. Ly[n]colne		1	0
Joh. Reynold, weu*er*		2	0
Rob. Huet		1	0
Ph. Caytowayte		1	0
Joh. Arowe, weu*er*		1	8
Laur. Barton, ffisher		1	0
Tho. Parbron		1	5
Will. Thomas, weu*er*		1	8
Will. Baxst*er*, bocher		3	4

	£	s.	d.
Tho. Barbur		3	4
Ric. Cokkes		5	0
Elizabeth Chychestur		1	8
Rob. Harbard		2	0
Ric. Spyser		5	0
Joh*anna* ffyllippes		1	4
Nic. Jones		1	8
Ric. Couper, peynter		1	8
Joh. Thorp		5	0
Margareta Evesham		1	0
Joh. Powes		1	8
Matill*da* Profete		1	0
Will. Rolff		1	8
Ric. Clerke		1	5
Joh. Goodeknaue		5	0
Rob. Weston		5	0
Tho. Jabette		1	0

[1] leaf 140, back.
[2] Collectors: Joh. Appulby, Will. Horsley, Ric. Clerke, Tho. Parbron.
[3] leaf 141.

[Bishop-street.]

	£	s.	d.
Ric. Botell		3	4
Joh. Lychefeld		10	0
Joh. Rob*ertz*		3	4
Joh. Parkyns, weu*er*		1	4
Ric. Cawdrey, keru*er*		2	0
Will. Couper		5	0
Tho. Kekewyke		1	8
Joh. Apulby		2	0
Joh. Wodecote		1	8
Tho. Walg*r*aue		1	8
Joh. Smyth		1	8
Will. Bamb*our*		1	8
Joh. Attewode		5	0
Rog. Chapmon		2	0
Tho. Broun, g*r*asier		1	8
Joh. White		3	4
Will. Benefeld, fissh*er*		1	8
Will. Russheton		1	2
Joh. Cleybroke			8
Sim. Lawe			8
Tho. Cleybroke		5	0
Tho. Broun, weu*er*		2	0
Joh. Mores, g*r*asier		5	0
Ed. Drouer		10	0
Rog. Taylour		5	0
Will. Kempe		8	8
Rob. Crofton		1	8
Joh. Stafford, myln*er*		2	0
Joh. Reynold, barker		3	4
Joh. ffolvile		1	8
Joh. Couper		3	4
Ric. Pysforde		1	8
Ad. Hulle		1	0
Joh. Pysford		3	4
Will. Bydell		1	0
[1]Ric. Myles		1	0
Rob. Betriche		1	0
Will. Bowman			8

S*um*ma £11. 6*s*. 0*d*.

80 names.

[Earl-street.[2]]

	£	s.	d.
Tho. Clerke		1	0
Joh. Heyne		2	0
Ric. Osteriche		3	0
Ric. Awsten		6	8
Rob. Bradmedowe		6	0
Ric. Clerke, poticary		2	0
Wal. Assheby		3	0
Joh. Gawge		3	0
Tho. Dey		3	0
Tho. Bayly		3	0
Wal. Ludlowe		1	0
Will. Glover		1	0
Will. Vale		6	8
Joh. Davy, ffysher		4	0
Joh. a Lee, card-maker		1	0
Tho. Ipstones		2	0
Will. Dawe, passong*er*		3	0
Will. Coton, card-maker		2	0
Rad. Calbek		2	0
Joh. Assheburn		3	0
Joh. Gylbard		1	8
Joh. Chaunter		2	0
Ric. Spake		3	0
Joh. Warant		10	0
Joh. Michell		13	4
Will. Corby		1	0
Joh. Davy		2	0
vx*or* nup*er* Will. ffrisby		3	0
Joh. Smythe		2	0
Ric. Sharp		13	4
Agnes Crudworthe		3	0
Joh. Parkyns, shermon		1	0
Joh. Bentley		3	0
Will. Swane		13	4
Joh. Shemyng		2	0
Ric. Alen		6	8
Tho. Tate		1	0
Joh. Perpoynt		3	0
Ric. Peche, skynn*er*		2	0
Joh. Anedam, shermon		1	0
Jac. Grene			7
Will. fforde		1	0
[3]Legburn, taylour		1	0
Tho. Ethorp[4]		1	0
Will. Chaundeler		1	0
Joh. Baker, Tayl*our*		1	0
Hen. Shawe		1	0
Rob. Adurton		3	4
Joh. Wyrley		1	0
Ric. Pratte		1	0
Joh. Pynchebek		3	0
Will. Arnold		1	0
Ric. Clerk, draper		6	8
Joh. Bradley, weu*er*		1	0
Joh. Copsey		1	0
Hen. Clerk		2	0
Nic. Palmer		4	0
Joh. Baynton		1	0
Ric. Boyse		6	8
Ric. Jacombe		3	0
Will. Parkes		1	0
Will. Ive		1	0
Tho. Bradmedowe		3	0
Will. Donyngton		6	8
Joh. Crosse		1	0
[5]Tho. Suettenham		6	8
Tho. ffaremon		2	0
Rob. Barnesley		2	0
Will. Holme		3	0
Joh. Northewode		10	0
Ric. Bartram		3	0
Rog. Mason, glouer		2	0
Ric. Clerke, skynn*er*		1	0
Joh. Preston		1	0
Tho. Abell		1	0
Tho. Morgon		1	0
Will. Huyron		1	0
Joh. Palmer, hosier		1	0
Joh. Aderton		1	0
Rob. Styf, pynn*er*		1	0

S*um*ma £11. 17*s*. 3*d*.

S*um*ma total*is* £100. 0*s*. 0*d*.

[1] leaf 141, back.
[2] Collectors: Tho. Bayly, Tho. Bradmedowe, Ric. Spake, Joh. Gauge.
[3] Blank. [4] Eathorp, Warwick. [5] leaf 142.

MICHAELMAS LEET.

[1][V. f. p. held on Tuesday after Michaelmas, 28 Hen. VI.] Sept. 30.

Ric. Braytoft, Joh. Leder, Joh. Brystowe, Joh. Warant, Will. Kerver, Will. Swan, Joh. Essex, Tho. Wirley, Joh. Walg*r*aue, Ric. Boys, Hen. Sircok, Joh. Lee, Will. Braytoft, Ric. Dene, Will. Pere, Gerv. Cole, Will. Kemp, Ric. Austen, Ric. Botone*r*, Rob. Bradmedowe, Will. Warrewik, Will. Clerk, Joh. Wilgrys, Joh. Cole. Jury.

[Tho. Warmyngton, Ric. Wode.] Bailiffs.

[Orders of leet. Any weaver can receive woollen thread in skeins (?) if he wish, taking for the winding notwithstanding any weavers' ordinance to the contrary, or 20*s.* to the bailiffs.]

Item, volunt & ordinant q*uo*d quilib*et* Textor infra Ciuitate*m* ista*m* legiti*m*e recipe*r*e potest filu*m* laneu*m* in keynes si volue*r*it, capiendo inde p*ro* le wyndyng, aliqua ordinac*io*ne inte*r* lez textores in contrariu*m* fact*a* non obstante, s*u*b pena xxs. ad opus ball*ivo*r*um* leuand*orum*.

Also they woll þat no mane*r* p*er*sone within þis Cite delyue*r* to eny mane*r* Spynne*r* within the same of woll to spyn but ij li. & a q*u*arte*r*n for a weight [or 6*d.* fine to the bailiffs' use.] "Woll." Weight of spinners' wool.

THE FIFTEENTH.

[[2]Collectors of the half-fifteenth collected and paid in this mayor's time at Martinmas. For sums *v.* p. 218–9.] Nov. 11, 1449.

Gosford-stret*e*.

Baldw. Metley, Joh. Langton, Tho. Straunge, Will. Knyght, weue*r*.

Jurden-well.

Rob. Eme, Joh. Peche, Joh. Crampe, Hugo Polard.

Much-p*ar*k-strete.

Will. Aubrey, Tho. Paunton, Ric. Staffordshire, Tho. Waron.

Erl-stre*te*.

Tho. Dey, Ric. Spake, Will. Holme, Joh. Bentley.

[1] leaf 148, back. [2] leaf 142, back.

Bayli-lane.

Joh. Gryme, Tho. Burley, Rob. Gloucetur, Rob. Skille.

Brode-yate.

Joh. Hony, Joh. Eborall, Tho. Gardener, Tho. Spenser.

Smythford-strete.

Joh. Maynard, Nic. Kente, Ric. ffynte, Rog. Rouke.

Spon-strete.

Joh. Mershe, Hugo Barbur, Rob. ffalke, Will. White, Joh. Harres.

Crosse-chepeng.

Will. Byrynton, Hen. Aderton, groc*er*, Hen. Banbury, Hen. Aderton, drap*er*.

Bysshop-stre*te*.

Ric. Spyser, Joh. Wode, Rog. Oswestre, Will. Baxst*er*, boch*er*.

PROVISION OF ARMOUR.

Jan. 15, 1450. "Provision by the inhabitants of Armor and weapons."

[1]Hit is to haue in mynde that thes Wurthy menne & also Comeners here vndur-writon Ordeyned[2] that for the welfare & also for the p*re*seruacion of the pece withe-in the Cite of Couentre,[3] & also to strengethe the kynges lawes, haue ordeynede (*sic*) That eu*er*y manne that hathe ben meyre Withe-in the Cite of Couentre shall haue redy & dayly withe-in his place that he duellethe in iiij jakkes[4] or iiij haburions,[5] iiij salettes,[6] iiij sheff arowes & iiij bowes & also oder wepons to the same stuff longeng: And eu*er*y bayly that hathe ben withe-in the same Cite shall haue iij jakkes, or iij haburions, iij salettes, iij Bowes, iij sheff arowes & oder wepons to the same stuff longeng: and also eu*er*y manne[7] that hathe ben warden or Chamburlen withe-in the seyde [8]Cite[8] shall haue ij jakkes or ij haburions, [8]ii salettes,[8] ij Bowes, ij shef arowes

Ordained that late mayors, bailiffs, other officers,

[1] leaf 143. [2] MS. ordeyneyned.
[3] "forto be hadde" deleted.
[4] A sleeveless coat, usually quilted leather.
[5] Sleeveless coats of mail.
[6] Headpieces having fixed projections behind.
[7] "Chamburlen & euery warden" deleted. [8–8] repeated.

& oder wepons to the seyde stuff longeng; and euery oder Comener of the seyde Cite, that may bere the coste, shall haue a jakke or an haburion, a salette, a bowe & sheffe of arowes & also oder wepon to the seyde stuff longeng: Euery manne that hathe ben meyre apon the peyne to lose iiij li.: euery manne that hathe ben bayly to lose iij li.[1]: & euery manne that hathe bene Chamburlen & warden to lose xl s.: and euery oder comener to lose xx s.: and that euery manne make his stuff redy be-twene this day, that is to sey, the Thursday next after the feste of sent Hillary the xxviij yere of Kyng Herry the syxte & the fest of Ester thenne next foloweng, euery manne apon the payne as hit is aboue rehersede.

and commoners, under certain penalties shall provide armour for the city's defence.

Also hit is ordeynede be the seyde parsons that euery manne whanne he hathe ordeynede hym his stuffe, as hit is aboue rehersede, That he selle, lene, alen, ne do awey non of the seyde stuff, ne wepons out of this Cite, ne no parcell of hem, but that they kepe hem withe-in this Cite, ne that no manne of this Cite were non of this seide stuff ne wepons withe-in this Cite but when he is comaundude be the meyre that shal-be for the tyme, or elles when the comen belle is rongen, or in preseruacion of the pece & kepeng the kynges lawes, or for the goode rule of this Cite, or elles for some oder resonabull cause, the kynges lawes ne his pece therbie hurte ne empeyrede.

No one to lend or alienate his weapons, or wear them unless occasion demands.

Also that no taylour of this Cite make no jakke but hit be abull & of goode stuffe to kepe the mannes body that shall were hite, apon the peyne that who dothe the Contrary to lose xl s. at euery defaute.

Tailors to make good "jacks."

Tho. Wyrley, Joh. Leder, Ric. Sharp, Will. Swanne, Will. Kerver, Joh. Walgraue, Will. Braytoft, Ric. Boyse, Tho. Warmynton, Ric. Wode, Hen. Sircoke, Ric. Dene, Will. Piere, Geru. Cole, Joh. Stafford, Joh. Northewode, Will. Betley, Joh. ffremon, Will. Kempe, Ric. Clerke, Ric. Austen, Ric. Alen, Sim. Birches, Ric. Charite, Tho. Whighte, Joh. Goolde, Joh. Baker, deister, Reg. Bere, Will. Clerke, Rob. Bradmedowe, Will. Warrewyke, Joh. Garton, Ric. Dyvette, Joh. Byrome, Will. Saundres, [2]Joh.

78 names of those who assembled.

[1] "& euery manne that hathe bene Chamburlen, Bayly & warden to lose iij li." deleted. [2] leaf 143, back.

Hadley, Gui. Wyston, Joh. Boteler, Hen. Aderton, mercer, Tho. Haddon, Hen. Aderton, hosier, Ric. Penson, Will. Cobbes, Tho. Skotte, Joh. Draper, Ric. Spake, Rob. Eme, Tho. Bradmedowe, Rob. Nevell, Will. Aubrey, Will. Vale, Joh. Davy, draper, Dav. Edmunde, Joh. ffrankelen, Ric. Cokkes, baker, Joh. ffynche, Joh. Maynarde, Rob. Mason, Joh. Mersche, Joh. Pynchebeke, Will. Pynchebekke, Tho. Parbron, Wal. Norfolke, Hug. Barbur, Joh. Appalby, Will. Horsley, Moric. Bocher, Tho. Gylbarde, Rob. Gloucestre, Joh. Gryme, Rog. Oswestre, Tho. Bower, Joh. Perpoynte, Tho. Wolff, Joh. Kebull, Will. Mason, Tho. Grene, Tho. Cockes, weuer.

Crafts give names.

Wherapon the Craftes of the Cite of Couentre be comaundement of Edmonde Brogreue, then meyre, acordeng to the ordenaunse afore rehersede, han brought in to the seide meyre the names of euery parsone that is abull to make hym stuff & to aray hym after the seide ordenaunce. That is to sey:

38 "Mercers," 60 jacks. 4 jacks, mayors, 3 jacks, baillifs, 2 jacks, chamberlains and wardens, 1 jack, commoners.

The craft of mersers.

Ric. Braytoft iiij Jakkes etc.
Joh. Mychell iiij Jakkes etc.
Will. Braytoft iij Jakkes etc.
Ric. Wode iij Jakkes etc.
Ric. Dene iij Jakkes etc.
Joh. ffremon iij Jakkes etc.[1]
[2]Ric. Austen iij Jakkes etc.
Reg. Bere iij Jakkes etc.
Joh. Byrome, ij Jakkes etc.
Ric. Charite ij Jakkes etc.
Joh. Garton ij Jakkes etc.
Will. Clerk ij Jakkes etc.
Joh. Shadde j Jakke etc.
Hen. Aderton j Jakke etc.
Ric. Penson j Jake etc.
Ric. Dyvette ij Jakkes etc.
Will. Gylbard j Jakke etc.
Joh. Dey j Jakke etc.
Rog. Costantyne j Jakke etc.
Tho. Towh j Jakke etc.
Ric. Clerke j Jakke etc.
Joh. Clyffe j Jakke etc.
Joh. Dagette j Jakke etc.
Tho. Paunton j Jakke etc.
Joh. Charite j Jakke etc.
Tho. Manston j Jakke etc.
Will. White j Jakke etc.
Tho. Tate j Jakke etc.
Rad. Caldebek j Jakke etc.
Baldw. Smyth j Jakke etc.
Tho. Allesley j Jakke etc.
Rob. Leche j Jakke etc.
Will. Potter j Jakke etc.
Hugo Pollar j Jakke etc.
Tho. Hobbes j Jakke etc.
Tho. Hobbes j Jakke etc.
Joh. Suettenham j Jakke etc.
Tho. Illage j Jakke etc.

Drapers.

59 "Drapers," 93 jacks.

[Tho. Lytelton, Recorder, blank; Ed. Brogreue, Tho. Wyrley, Joh. Leder, Joh. Bristowe, Ric. Sharp, Will. Swanne four each; Ric. Boyse, Tho. Warmynton, Ric. Alen, Ric. Clerke, Hen. Sircokke, Joh. Wildegryse three;

[1] xx. *i. e.* 20 jacks stands at the foot of the page. [2] leaf 144.

Joh. Goolde, Joh. Catur, Rob. Bradmedowe, Tho. Swettenham, two; Tho. Bradmedowe, Joh. Smyth, draper, Joh. Gawge, Ric. Jacombe, Joh. Draper, Joh. Pynchebek, Tho. Parker, Tho. Dey, Joh. Myrifelde, Ric. Spake, Joh. Copesey, Jac. Grene, Will. Chauderell, Ric. Pultun, Joh. Adirton, Rob. Adurton, Ric. Mildenale, Joh. Warmynton, Joh. Davy, Humf. Swanne, Joh. Wyponbury, Joh. Preston, Joh. Palmer, Will. Ive, Joh. Couper, Tho. Grene,[1] [2]Tho. Ipstones, Tho. Swquyer, Tho. Kyrke, Joh. Wirley, Tho. Bristowe, Tho. Wodard, Ric. Pratte, Rob. Barnesley, Hen. Halows, Will. Corby, Tho. Wolff, Ph. Draper, Tho. Burley, Will of the Vale "j Jacke etc, & j Jacke outer," Tho. Colette, Will. Donynton, one each.]

Deysters.

[Joh. Esex four; Will. Piere, Gerv. Cole, three; Joh. Baker, Will. Warrewyke, Will. Saundres, Tho. Rastell two; Tho. Haddon, Eust. Golofur, Joh. Eston, Will. Smythe, Rob. ffalke, Will. Tuttebury, Rog. Burnes, Tho. [3], Tho. Ryngeley, Will. Bayly, Joh. Garnet, Tho. Colmer, Geruard Crampe, Will. Horsley, Joh. Smythe, Ph. Large, Ric. Spyser, Joh. Hoten, Will. Cobbes, Tho. Cawdrey, Tho. Swayne, Will. Swayne, Tho. Kelmstowe, Ad. Hulle, Will. Bochar, Will. Harries, Joh. Massyngham, Tho. fforget, Hen. Knotte, Will. Oxton, one each.] 37 dyers, 48 jacks.

Gurdelers.

[Will. Clerke, Ric. Dyvette two; Joh. Crosse, Hen. Watford, Joh. Wylde, Joh. Barton, Joh. Gryme, Joh. Syrcok, Nic. Russell, Joh. Power, Joh. Whitehede, Tho. Hobbes, Joh. Bayly, Joh. Orderiche, Tho. Sweteglade,[4] [5]Joh. Gylbard, Hen. Wright, Ric. Oderiche, Will. Crowe, Tho. Gryme, Joh. Castell, Joh. Sircok jun., one each.] 22 "Girdlers," 24 jacks.

Weuers.

[Joh. Grynder three; Ric. Osbarne two; Joh. Lote, Tho. Broun, Ric. ffreynes, Tho. Stone, Joh. Maydeford, 57 weavers, 60 jacks.

[1] clviij. *i. e.* 158 jacks. Really the number is 117 on this page.
[2] leaf 144, back.
[3] Blank. [4] iiij^{xx}. *i. e.* 80 jacks. Really 82. [5] leaf 145.

Tho. Broun, Ric. Molle, Joh. Egull, Ric. Cockes, Tho. Dykons, Ric. Clerke, Will. Jones, Tho. Maydeford, Joh. Wamburn, Ric. Glouer, Joh. Arowe, Tho. Irysshe, Joh. Bradley, Rog. Chapmon, Joh. Reynolde, Joh. Strete, Will. Knyght, Ric. Waterfall, Joh. Purs, Tho. Lyons, Will. Thom*as*, Will. Brvyngton, Rob. Harbard, Sampson Lyuerey, Nic. Bee, Ric. Couche, Hugo Harper, Will. Blakenale, Rob. Bulkeley, Tho. Shustoke, Tho. Stryngar, Joh. Thorpe, Will. Ronkorne, Tho. Spyser, Rob. Agar, Tho. Okeham, Ric. Smale, Joh. Draughton, Ric. Wode, Tho. Cockes, Ric. Somer. Joh. Rothewell, Will. Huyron, Will. Arnolde, Tho. Garnet, Joh. Wakefelde, Rob. Balle, Ric. Coucher, Will. Edward, Laur. Huyron one each.]

Taylours & Shermen.

64 "Taylors Shermen." [Joh. Bentley, Rog. Thornton, Dav. Edmu*n*de, Will. Dawe, Will. Abrey,[1] [2]Ric. Alde, Rob. Oswestre, Joh. Perpoynt, Tho. Bayly, Joh. Marshe, Tho. Joy, Joh. Bylston, Joh. fforest, Joh. Locok, Joh. Wurthynton, Tho. Cholley, Joh. Nele, Hen. Louthe, Will. Joneson, Joh. Clyfford, Joh. Neuton, Tho. Kekewyke, Alan Snape, Hen. Adurton, Ric. Bylston, Ric. Bylston, jun., Joh. Baker, Will. Ludlowe, Bened. Corkar, Ric. Gene, Will. fforde, Joh. Stanbury, Joh. Chybsey, Joh. Dauid, Joh. Dykar, Ph. Shermon, Joh. Shrouesbury, Tho. Stapulford, Tho. Newthorp, Tho. Wyndall, Tho. Strete,

[3]Legburn, Taylo*ur*, Thrustan*us* of the Lye, Ric. Preese, Joh. Radley, Rog. Milner, Rob. Kendale, Will. Corbette, Joh. Sharp, Tho. Wylotte, Tho. Michell, Rob. Melton, Tho. Holande, Olyuer Bordeman, Will. Clerke, Tho. Parkyns, Joh. Haukyns, Will. Molle, Joh. Nedame, Tho. Bathe, Will. Adbaster, Will. Russheton, Hen. Taylour, Will. Jones, one each.]

Walkers.

27 "ffullers." [Tho. Parbron, Rob. Walker, Will. Reynolde, Tho. Tokeby, Rob. Jones, Wal. Norfolke, Ric. Norfolke, Joh. Inner, Rob. Crofte, Joh. Langton, Will. Hardewyk, Rob.

[1] lxxij *i. e.* 72 jacks. [2] leaf 145, back.
[3] Blank.

Whitacur, Joh. Beynton,[1] [2]Joh. [3], Joh. Chambur, Rob. Blubery, Ad. Gawge, Tho. Horsley, Will. ffyppe, Joh. Bowdy, Tho. Ronton, Rad. Wright, Will. Flecher, Tho. ffuller, Ric. Tokeby, Ric. Olyuer, Tho. Rowby, one each.]

Wiredrawers.

[Joh. Stafford three; Joh. Recheford two; Tho. Elderbek, Ric. Recheford, Tho. Stafford, Will. Orsley, Will. Cleybroke, Tho. ffaukes, Joh. Sheldon, jun., Joh. Peche, Joh. Shurley, Nic. Taylour, Joh. Manton, Joh. Stafford, jun., Will. Stafford, Rad. ffolkeshull, Joh. Hasteng, Rob. Othewode, Will. Dowbryg, Ric. Wygens, Joh. ffolkeshull, sen., Will. Bolton, Tho. Smyth, card-wirdr*awer*, Tho. Hoten, Hen. Tredsyn,[4] Joh. Elderbek, Ric. Rage, Hen. Dalton, Rob. Garette, Tho. Bateman, Tho. ffolkeshull ext*ra* l*e* New-yate, Tho. Jones of Dede-lone, Joh. Onley, Joh. Symson, Ric. Bocher, Will. Rolff, Joh. Mathowe, Nic. Jones, Joh. Marshall, Rob. Rasshe one each.] 40 "wier-drawers," 48 jacks.

Journeymen eiusde*m* artis.

[Will. Gyam, Joh. Kebull, Tho. Prikonshawe, Will. ffawkonbruge, Tho. Smyth, card-wirdr*awer*, Tho. Smyth de Gosford-str*ete*, Tho. Mountfort, Ric. Persons, one each.] 8 journeymen of this craft.

Coruysers.

[Tho. Mason, Joh. Eborall, Ric. Staffordshire,[5] [6]Tho. Paunton, Will. Compton, Joh. Derby, Joh. Ardurn, Tho. Norwyc, Tho. Jakemon, Will. Mason, Hen. Barker, Hugo Manten, Joh. Maynard, Bened. Stockton, Joh. Crulle, Joh. Lorde, Will. Shipston, Tho. Cowcher, Joh. ffoster, Ric. Palmer, Will. Alansonne, Ric. Drought, Rob. Mason, Will. Rowlot, Joh. Nele, coruyser, Ed. Wylson, Joh. Colyns, Joh. Golofur, Hen. Mason, Tho. Alen, Will. Mason, Will. Marchall, Joh. Botte, Ric. Drought, sen., Will. Huett, Will. Hende, Joh. Sponne, Joh. Symondes, Tho. Walker, one each.] 39 "Coruisers."

[1] lxxij *i. e.* 72 jacks. [2] leaf 146. [3] Blank.
[4] or Tredfyn. [5] lxix jack*es*, *i. e.* 69, really 68.
[6] leaf 146, back.

Smythes.

49 "Smiths." Ric. Bedon, Will. Haddon, Rob. Burnell, Hen. Hobbes, Ric. Bromley, Will. Stedeman, Joh. Plumpton, Joh. Yong, Joh. Esex, forbur,[1] Joh. Sedyngwode, Will. Dyngley, Rob. Wodeward, Galf. Rose, Coteler, Will. Chaterton, Will. Malory, Tho. Morton, Tho. Gardener, Rob. Skille, Hugo Chadurton, coteler, Tho. ffalkes, gol . . . .[2] Will. Hothoos, bokilmaker, Will. Smyth, wolleman,[3] Ric. Lyng peut*er*ere, Ric. Burnell, goldsmyth, Will. Goodeyere, gold*smyth*, Reg. Bere, Ric. Lane, Joh. Kyrkeby, smyth, Will. Bedon, Cariour,[3] Joh. Malory, Joh. Bedwurthe, Joh. Walker, lorymere,[3] Will. Dillare, smyth, Will. Ive, smyth, Tho. Chapman, chaundeler,[3] Joh. Yale, peut*er*ere,[3] Joh. Hampton, Will. Mariot, Will. Melodye, Tho. Marshall, Joh. London, Hugo fforthe, barbur,[3] Will. Morton, brasier,[4] [5]Sim. Busteler, Nic. Balche, Will. Radclyf, Will. Dyvette, Joh. Orderiche, [6], coteler, one each.

ffysshemongers.

13 "fishmongers." Joh. Walle, Will. Sporiour, Guydo Wyston, Joh. Savage, Laur. Barton, Joh. Patter, Joh. Bette, Joh. Whittoft, Tho. Miller, Will. Benyfeld, Tho. Napton, Joh. Lychefeld, Joh. Reve, one each.

Whittawers.

20 Whittawers,[7] 25 jacks. [Will. Kerver, four; Joh. Deyster, three; Joh. Honyburn, Will. Pynchebek, Joh. Wyllyams, Hugo Neuton, Ric. Went, Will. Bayly, Rob. Rodes, Rog. Mason, Hen. Horsley, Tho. Clerk, Joh. Rycongey, Joh. Burdewes, Will. Chester, Hen. Rogers, Will. Bentley, Tho. Bukbrig, Tho. Grenewey, Hugo Par, one each.]

Bochers.

23 "Butchers." [Tho. Parker, boch*er*, Will. Baxst*er*, Joh. Bynley, Joh. Halle, Tho. Mores, Will. Deyster, Tho. White, Joh.

[1] =furbisher, one who polishes rust from the metal.
[2] rest deleted; it looks like goldgeler (?).
[3] Nondescript crafts seem classed under smiths.
[4] iiij^{xx} xviiij jack*es*, *i. e.* 98, really 79. [5] leaf 147.
[6] Blank. [7] "? Chandlers" MS. marginal note.

Northampton, Will. Spenser, Joh. Deyster, Will. Northampton, Gal. Wulpynne, Joh. White, Wal. Broun, Joh. Imayne, Ric. Bocher, John Newmon, Tho. White, Will. Bydell, Nic. Swalynton, Rob. Burne, Will. Norton, Rog. Lyllynton, one each.[1]]

[2] Sadelers.

[Will. Spenser, Tho. Spenser, Nic. Kent, Joh. Cooke, Ric. Clerke, Joh. Spenser, Joh. Bredon, one each.] 7 "Sadlers."

Cardmakers.

[Rob. Eme, Joh. Othe lee, Ric. Clerk, Rob. fforthe, Rob. Gydlowe, Will. Coton*er*, Joh. ffranklen, one each.] 7 "Cardmakers."

Masons.

[Hen. Clerk, Rob. Stretton, Will. Cardyf, Will. Storiour, Tho. Braymere, Tho. Yemons, Ric. Peyntour, one each.] 7 "Masons."

Skynners.

[Joh. Shemeng, Rob. Torsote [? Torfote], Tho. Tyler, Joh. Alderwas, Joh. Oldenhale, Ric. Knightley, Tho. Colchowe, Ric. Clerk, Ric. Peche, one each.] 9 "Skinners."

Pynners, tylers.

[Rob. Gloucetur two; Will. Swyft, Joh. Hoges, Joh. Bayly, Joh. Crosse, Joh. Smyth, Joh. Ravon, Tho. Bette, Ric. Cardyf, Joh. Langcastell, one each.] 10 "Tylers," 11 jacks.

Bakers.

[Ric. Rede, baker, Rob. Nevell, Ric. Cockes, Ric. Parbron, Will. Crampe, Ric. White, Joh. Hulle, Joh. Smyth, Will. Mylner, Tho. Shawe, Ric. Botell, Ph. Kaytewayte, Tho. Hulle, Hen. Stevenson, Joh. Oldebury, Mat. Curtes, Joh. Thomason,[3] [4] Tho. Hakette, Joh. Enggillon, one each.] 10 "Bakers."

Barburs.

[Joh. Hopton, barbur, Tho. fforthe, Godefrid Barbur, Ric. Barbur iux*t*a Bablake, Hugo fforthe, barbur, Rob. ffyge, barbur, Joh. Barbur atte Bulryng, Joh. Bylston, 15 "Barbers."

[1] lxvij jack*es*, *i. e.* 67.
[2] leaf 147, back.
[3] lviij jack*es*, *i. e.* 58.
[4] leaf 148.

Hen. Burbur, Tho. Grysley, Ronulph Barbur, Will. Barbur, Ric. Barbur atte Gosford stulpes,[1] Joh. Wode, barbur, Will. Bedford, one each.]

Wrightes.

20 "Wrights." [Tho. Cleybroke, Joh. Powes, Hen. Dalby, Joh. Clyfton, Joh. Halle, Will. Wyresdale, Tho. Gybons, Joh. Toppe, Rob. Toppe, Tho. Jabette, Joh. Davy, Hen. Warmynton, Joh. Cleybroke, Will. Kyng, Will. Bowman, Tho. Hamond, Tho. Grene, Joh. Whyte, Joh. Wodecote,[2] Alan. Wytham, one each.]

Barkers.

8 barkers. [Joh. Coupar, Ric. Pysford, Joh. Reynold, Joh. Harres, Ric. Stone, Will. Sponar, Tho. Gylbard, Joh. Pysford, one each.]

Cokus ete.

5 "Cookes." [Rob. Persale, Joh. Dalton, Rog. Stanley, Will. Togoode, Will. Taylour, one each.[3]]

RIC. SHARP, MAYOR, 1450.

Jan. 25. [4][Election of officers.]

24 electors. Tho. Wirley, Joh. Leder, Ric. Braytoft, Joh. Bristowe, Will. Swanne, Will. Kervar, Joh. Warant, Joh. Walgrave, Will. Braytoft, Joh. ffreman, Ric. Clerk, Joh. Wildegrise, Ric. Dene, Will. Peere, Ric. Botoner, Ric. Austen, Will. Kempe, Joh. Stafford, Rob. Bradmedowe, Joh. Byram, Will. Warrewyke, Joh. Baker, Joh. Goolde, Will. Clerke.

Officers. [m. Ric. Sharp; cor. Joh. ffynche; ch. Will. Saunders, Will. Gloucestre; w. Joh. Garton, Ric. Dyvet; mace, Will. Oxton.

J. Ps. [Ric. Sharp, m., Tho. Litulton, rec., Ric. Braytoft, Joh. Leder, Will. Swanne, Joh. Walgraue etc. Afterwards Joh. Leder died on (blank) day, and Ed. Brogreue was chosen (electus) in his place.

[1] v. *E. D. D.* stoop, a post. O.N. stólpi; stolpe, *Prompt. Parv.* 533 (Mr. Stevenson).
[2] Depopulated village near Warwick.
[3] l Jack*es*. *Summa* tot*alis* = vij^{c} xliiij Jack*es* (or 744), ? 685.
[4] leaf 149.

[The mayor, Tho. Wirley, Joh. Leder, Ric. Braytoft, Joh. Walgraue.

[The mayor, Tho. Wirley, M. G. S. T., Ric. Braytoft, Will. Braytoft, M. G. C. C., have one apiece; the wardens have another, and a key of the door of the tower where the chest is kept.]

Guardians of the keys of the chest where the common seal is, and of the chest where the standard measure is kept.

EASTER AND MICHAELMAS LEETS.

[1][V. f. p. held before Ric. Sharp, m., Tho. Warmyngton, Ric. Wode, b., on Saturday after the close of Easter, 28 H. VI.]

Couentre. Ap. 18, 1450.

Tho. Wyrley, Joh. Leder, Ric. Braytoft, Will. Swan, Will. Kerver, Joh. Walgraue, Ed. Brogreve, Will. Braytoft, Joh. Grynder, Ric. Boys, Hen. Sircok, Ric. Alen, Gerv. Cole, Joh. Catur, Will. Pere, Will. Warrewyk, Will. Kempe, Ric. Clerk, draper, Joh. Stafford, Joh. ffreman, Rob. Bradmedowe, Joh. Biram, Joh. Wilgris, Joh. Garton.

[Orders of leet.

[Forty decent men of good and honest behaviour and bodily strength, shall keep watch in the city from the ninth[2] hour until the ringing of the Daybell, within which time according to the accustomed oath they shall guard the city well and sufficiently. Which men every night shall be well and sufficiently arrayed in jacks, sallets, pole-axes or glaves and the like; and how further these men shall be ruled in watch hours the leet place in the mayor's and council's discretion.]

Qui ordinaverunt quod xl homines decentes, bone & honeste conuersacionis, ac fortes in corpore ad laborandum & ad vigilandum, noctanter custodient & vigilabunt villam a hora nouena,[2] vsque ad pulsacionem campane vocate Daybell; per quod tempus secundum Juramentum consuetum bene & sufficienter custodient villam istam etc. Qui homines quolibet (*sic*) nocte erunt bene & sufficienter apperalti (*sic*) in Jakkis, Salettis, polaxes vel Gleyues & aliis consimilibus etc. Et quomodo ipsi xl homines vlterius tempore vigilacionis erunt gubernati illud ponunt in discrecionem Maioris & consilii, si etc.[3]

[1] Scribe B. leaf 149, back.
[2] 9 p.m. The same time as the gates were shut.
[3] Evidently owing to the disturbed state of the country an attack was feared. The month of June in this year witnessed the rising of Jack Cade.

"A ground in Bishop-street graunted for 80 years, 12*d.* per ann."

Hit was graunte at þis [lete] to John Norwode at his request & desire a voyde grounde lying in the Bysshop-strete besides a house of his there-in, which Will. Buxston late helde, for the terme of iiij^{xx} ȝeres, paying þerfore yerely to the Chambre xij d., and the seid grounde conteyneth in lengh xij fote, & in brede x fote, & þe seid John duryng þe seid terme to kepe all maner reparacions.

The town-ditch.

Also they ordeyn that the Town diche without Gosford-ȝate lying & strecchyng towardes Harnall be clensed & þat euery man clense before his owne grounde & þat to be doon within viij daies next folowyng.

A spire at Gosford-gate.

Also they ordeyn that a spyre be made besides the Gosford-ȝate as hit hath be of olde tyme; & hit to be made at þe wardeyns coste.

No filth from the jail to be thrown on the highway.

Also they ordeyn that no person within þe Gayle of Couentre fro this tyme furth cast no pysse in-to the high weye, vppon þe peyn of þe Gayler to lese [1]at euery defalt[1] xl d.

Also hit was ordeyned at þis present lete, at the request & desire of þe Chamberleyns that there shuld be ordeyned & named in euery warde iiij persones which shuld haue the kepyng & guydyng of þe town yates, & they iiij in euery ward to chese on person, which shuld haue the kepyng of þe keyes of euery ȝate, & he to open þe ȝate euery mornyng & to lok hit at ix of þe Clok in þe night; and þey þat kept þe keyes of þe Newe-ȝate, Spon-strete-ȝate, Bishop-ȝate & Frere-ȝate & Gosford-ȝate to haue ȝerely for their labour iiij s. apece; and they þat kept þe keyes of all the other ȝates to haue ij s. apece & to be paide be þe Chamberleyns for þe tyme beying.

"Gates to be locked."

Keepers of keys appointed.

Sept. 30.

[[2]V. f. p. held on Wednesday after Michaelmas, 29 H. VI.]

Tho. Wyrley, Joh. Leder, Ric. Braytoft, Joh. Bristowe, Will. Swanne, Will. Kerver, Joh. Essex, Joh. Walgrave, Ed. Brogreve, Will. Braytoft, Ric. Boys, Hen. Sircok, Joh. Anabull, Ric. Botoner, Joh. Grynder, Ric. Dene, Will. Pere, Will. Kempe, Ric. Clerk, Ric. Austen, Joh. Stafford, Joh. ffreman, Joh. Wylgris, Will. Warrewyk etc.

[1] Repeated. [2] Scribe B. leaf 150, back.

[Rob. Bradmedowe, Joh. Biram.] Bailiffs.

At þis present lete & be auctorite of the same was graunted vnto John Shirwode for xxxvj li., wherof xxvj was paide then & there vnto the wardeyns of this Cite, a Mese[1] place lying before Bablak, which some tyme was Gyles Corbrond, to haue & hold to þe seid John, & to the heris of his body lawefully begoten, & for lak of such issue to reuerte vnto þe Towne aȝeyn etc. Orders of leet. "Graunted vnto John Sherwode a tenement *against* Bablake."

[Ordinance concerning spinners[2] (*v.* p. 243) confirmed.] "Spinners" to have their work weighed by sealed weights.

And they nowe ordeyn þat no man delyuer no werk but be weyghtes ensealed & that þe officers take no more for sealyng of a wyght & di*midium* wyght but ob. & no more, vppon peyn etc. ½*d.* for sealing a weight and half a weight.

[*v.* p. 232. Brewer only to use conduit water "for dressing of his mete."] "Maltsters and brewers not to fetch water out of Conduits."

THE FIFTEENTH.

[3][Collectors of the fourth part of a fifteenth paid at Martinmas, 29 H. VI. Nov. 11, 1450.

Sums as in p. 142 (1432). Total £12. 10*s.* 0*d.*

Names as in p. 243–4; except that in Bayly-lane Tho.[4] Gryme and Tho. Wirley stand for Joh. Gryme and Tho. Burley.]

RIC. BOYS, MAYOR, 1451.

[[5]Election of officers.] Jan. 25.

Joh. Walgrave, Ric. Braytoft, Will. Swanne, Will. Kervar, Joh. Esex, Joh. Warant, Tho. Wyrley, Edm. Brogreve, Will. Braytoft, Joh. ffreman, Tho. Warmynton, Joh. Wildegryse, Ric. Botoner, Will. Pere, Ric. Dene, Will. Kemp, Ric. Austen, Joh. Stafford, Joh. Goolde, Will. Clerke, Joh. Baker, Joh. Catur, Reg. Bere, Hen. Watford. 24 electors.

[m. Ric. Boys; cor. Joh. ffynche; ch. Ric. Spake, Will. Gylbard; w. Joh. Gryme, Joh. ffranklen; mace, Will. Oxton.

The names of the justices of the peace and both sets of keepers of the keys are blank.]

[1] = a messuage.
[2] The sweating of women workers in industrial life is ancient.
[3] leaf 150. [4] Joh. is written over the top.
[5] leaf 153. Scribe of type p. 102.

FORTIFICATIONS AND LEET PETITIONS.

Mar. 27, 1451.

[1]Hit is to haue in mynde that the Seturdy nest after the feste of the Purificacion of our Lady last past all thes wurthymen foloweng into seynt Mary halle called to-gidur afore the Meyre, Ric. Boys, a co*mm*un*i*cacion there to be hadde of & for dyuers maters for the wele & wellfare of[2] this Cite etc. That is to sey: Joh. Walg*r*aue, Ric. Sharp, Ric. Braytoft, Will. Swanne, Will. Kerver, Joh. Warant, Edm. Brogreue, Rob. Bradmedowe, Joh. Byram, Will. Braytoft, Hen. Syrcok, Joh. Grynder, Will. Pere, Geru. Cole, Will. Kempe, Ric. Boton*er*, Ric. Dene, Ric. Alen, Ric. Clerk, Joh. ffreman, Joh. Stafford, Tho. Warmynton, Joh. Whalley, Ric. Austen, Will. Gylbard, Ric. Spake, Joh. Baker, Will. Clerk, Reynold Bere, Tho. Whyte, Joh. Goolde, Tho. Rastell, Ric. Osbarne, Will. Saundres, Rob. Glouseter, Joh. Gryme, Joh. ffrankelen, Joh. Garton, Ric. Dyvette, Ric. Cockes, weu*er*, Eustas Golofur, Rob. Nevell, Rob. Eme, Joh. Alderwas, Will. Awbrey, Tho. Waren, Ric. Wymondeswold, Ric. Bromley, Hen. Watford, Ric. Alde, shermon, Joh. Bentley, Tho. Jakemon, Ric. Tokeby, Joh. Boteler, Gye Wyston, Edm. Dalby, Ric. Penson, Ric. Bedon, Joh. Mores, drou*er*, Ric. Clerk, weu*er*, Hen. Banbury, Tho. Haddon, Joh. Maynard, Galf. Bower, Joh. Wylde, Joh. Mershe, Wal. Norfolk, Joh. Honyburn, Tho. Broun, lynne-drap*er*, Tho. Bradmedowe, Rog. Burnes, Joh. Lote, weu*er*, Tho. Gylbard, Joh. Bentley, Will. Deyster, boch*er*, Joh. Savage, Will. Pynchebek, Raff Wright, Tho. Tokeby, Tho. Bredon, Hugo Barbur, Tho. Grene, hosier, Ric. fflynt, Nic. Kent, Tho. Skotte, Joh. Nele, taylour, ffylippe Gosnore, Rob. ffalkes.

An assembly of worthy men, 89 in number,

consult concerning the fortifications.

Town-ditches to be cleansed.

The wheche wurthymen, maters dyuers for the wele of this Cite meved & hard & comende etc., han ordeyned & prouyded that the Town dyches of this Cite shullon be clansed and that to do [3]euery howseholder of this Cite shall fynde a man, howse be howse, & warde-be-ward, in lyke wyse as the wache gothe, excepte that euery

[1] leaf 153, back. [2] "than necessari to be" deleted. [3] leaf 154.